Enterprise and history

CHARLES WILSON

[Photograph by Barry Supple]

Enterprise and history

Essays in honour of Charles Wilson

Edited by

D. C. COLEMAN

and

PETER MATHIAS

The right of the
University of Cambridge
to print and sell
all manner of books
was granted by
Henry VIII in 1534.
The University has printed
and published continuously
since 1584.

CAMBRIDGE UNIVERSITY PRESS

Cambridge
London   New York   New Rochelle
Melbourne   Sydney

Published by the Press Syndicate of the University of Cambridge
The Pitt Building, Trumpington Street, Cambridge CB2 1RP
32 East 57th Street, New York, NY 10022, USA
296 Beaconsfield Parade, Middle Park, Melbourne 3206, Australia

First published 1984

Printed in Great Britain at the University Press, Cambridge

Library of Congress catalogue card number: 83-26329

British Library Cataloguing in Publication Data

Enterprise and History.
I. Business – History
II. Coleman, D.C.C. II. Mathias, Peter
III. Wilson, Charles, *1914–*
338.6'09   HF5341

ISBN 0 521 24951 1

TM

Contents

v

Contents

Preface

The essays which comprise this book have been written to honour Charles Wilson, on the occasion of his seventieth birthday, by friends, colleagues and former students. Their range, both in period and in theme, reflects the breadth of the academic friendships (only a small proportion of which can find representation here) inspired by him, in the course of an active career, and they mirror the range of his own historical studies which has steadily expanded since he began research in 1936. Even by that time, however, his academic and intellectual horizons were wider than most in his position. Having come up to Jesus College, Cambridge, as an undergraduate with a scholarship from De Aston Grammar School – in Market Rasen, a small Lincolnshire market town – he had taken a First both in the Historical Tripos and in the English Tripos; he subsequently became a Fellow of the college in 1938. Jesus College had vigorous, independent intellectual roots, somewhat outside the mainstream of Cambridge history (as, indeed, was the location of the college, seemingly in ample rural isolation from the town), so that he owed more to Bernard Manning of his own college and to Edward Walbourne of Emmanuel (also, as it happened, from the same grammar school in an earlier generation) than to more acclaimed luminaries in colleges closer to the banks of the Cam.

Charles Wilson's first research project, which resulted in the publication in 1941 of *Anglo-Dutch Commerce and Finance in the Eighteenth Century*, had taken him to the Netherlands and Germany in 1937–8. From this beginning there started a connection with the Netherlands, Belgium and Denmark which has never been lost or become inactive. The Anglo-Dutch connection in particular became sustained as it provided the bridge to business history, the second pervading interest of his scholarship. He published the small and charming study *Holland and*

Britain in 1945 written (he claims) mainly on the London Underground on his way to and from the Admiralty during the war. He returned to Cambridge after the end of hostilities and was made University Lecturer in History in 1945. It was through the intermediation of G. N. – later Sir George – Clark, the instigator of his first research project, that he then became the historian of the great Anglo-Dutch business group, Unilever. The publication of the two initial volumes of *A History of Unilever* in 1954 set new levels of expectation for business histories and made Charles Wilson, in one stroke, the doyen of British business historians. Other works in the same area followed, including a third volume on Unilever in 1968, and we now await the publication of his most recent work in this field, the history of W. H. Smith.

Eminence as an historian of business did not mean that he abandoned his earlier interests. Indeed he had always made a point of not being confined to one specialism or one period of history. His work on business history centred, and still does centre, on the nineteenth and twentieth centuries; his work on Holland and England, though embracing the modern world of Unilever, was rooted in the seventeenth and eighteenth centuries. Despite making his name earlier as an economic historian – for seven years he co-edited the *Economic History Review*, and he became Reader in Modern Economic History at Cambridge in 1964 – his election to the Chair of Modern History in 1965, rather than to that of economic history which had been expected, confirmed these wider historical horizons. A succession of books demonstrated his commitment to the broader themes of Dutch and English history: *Profit and Power* (1957); *England's Apprenticeship, 1603–1763* (1965); *The Dutch Republic and the Civilization of the Seventeenth Century* (1968); *Queen Elizabeth and the Revolt of the Netherlands* (1970) – based on his Ford Lectures at Oxford University in 1968–9; and *The Transformation of Europe, 1558–1648* (1976).

Common to all these books, as well as to many of his learned articles, has been an enduring concern with enterprise, not simply in its common connotation of 'private enterprise' but rather with human endeavour, with individual achievement as the vital motivating element in history. The title and contents of the present volume attempt to bear witness to this concern as well as to reflect some of that variety of interest in historical periods and places which has been the hallmark of his scholarship. In Part I the first three essays provide varying views of business history and businessmen, and the fourth looks at certain interpretations of that notable set of happenings in the history of individual economic enterprise: the British Industrial Revolution. Those in Part II seek to pay tribute both to his involvement with the history of England and Holland before the Industrial Revolution and to his concern with enterprise in diverse forms, be it exhibited by Netherlands merchants or by an English parliamentarian. Likewise, the contributions which make up Part III reflect his international interests in modern economic history and also, as in Part II, some of the ways in which enterprise meshed or conflicted with the aims of the state.

It is appropriate that seven out of the fifteen contributors to this volume should be based outside Britain. This in itself offers a mirror to the international quality of Charles Wilson's historical interests. That quality was emphasized by his having devoted the last five years of his formal university career, 1976–81 (he retired from his Cambridge Chair in 1979) to the newly formed European University Institute at Florence. And it has received recognition in various other ways: in honorary degrees from the Universities of Groningen and Louvain; in his appointment as a Commander of the Order of Oranje-Nassau; in his Corresponding Fellowships of the learned Academies of Belgium and Denmark; in his continuing membership of the executive committee of the International Economic History Institute 'Francesco Datini' at Prato; and at home not only in his Cambridge Litt. D. and his Fellowship of the British Academy but also in his CBE which in 1981 honoured his services to international scholarship.

Those who have joined together in this volume wish him well and look forward to his continuing good health and to new scholarship. We salute him as the most congenial of companions; a man shrewd in the ways of the world (who acknowledged how much he had learned as an economic historian from his experience as estates bursar of Jesus College for a decade after 1945); and as one whose particular blend of intelligence and humanity has added an extra increment of understanding and pleasure to that pursuit of the past in which we are all engaged.

List of contributors

Henri Baudet, *Professor in the Faculty of Economics, University of Groningen*

Alfred D. Chandler, Jr, *George Straus Professor of Business History, Harvard University*

D. C. Coleman, *Emeritus Professor of Economic History and Fellow of Pembroke College, University of Cambridge*

Luigi de Rosa, *Professor in the Faculty of Maritime Economics, University Institute of Naples*

R. W. Ferrier, *Group Historian, British Petroleum*

Kristof Glamann, *President, The Carlsberg Foundation, Copenhagen*

R. M. Hartwell, *Emeritus Fellow, Nuffield College, University of Oxford*

Peter Klein, *Professor of Economics, Erasmus University, Rotterdam*

Peter Mathias, *Chichele Professor of Economic History and Fellow of All Souls College, University of Oxford*

David Ormrod, *Lecturer in Economic and Social History, University of Kent at Canterbury*

W. J. Reader

Henry Roseveare, *Reader in History, King's College, University of London*

Barry Supple, *Professor of Economic History and Master of St Catharine's College, University of Cambridge*

Herman van der Wee, *Professor of Social and Economic History, Catholic University of Leuven*

J. A. van Houtte, *Professor Emeritus in the University of Louvain*

PART I

Images and interpretations

1

Comparative business history[1]

ALFRED D. CHANDLER JR

The historian's challenge

The historian has at least two exacting and exciting challenges. One is that of relating specific human events and actions to the ever-changing broader economic, social, political and cultural environment. A second is the development of generalizations and concepts which, although derived from events and actions that occur at a specific time and place, are applicable to other times and places, and are, therefore, valuable as guideposts for or as tools of analysis by other historians as well as economists, sociologists, anthropologists and other scholars. They may even be of interest to the informed general public and of some use to actors in contemporary political, social or cultural dramas.

But before such challenges can be met, data are needed. The first step must be detailed description of the actors and their actions; and for business history that means, of course, of businessmen and business-women and the enterprises they managed. If descriptions are carefully related to the larger scene, then the second challenge can be taken up. Only after the accumulation of a multitude of case-studies can generalizations and concepts which are not tied to a specific time and place be induced. This paper attempts to describe for the non-specialist the process by which business history, that small sub-field of economic history, has moved from the writing of historically specific descriptive history to the writing of comparative institutional history that can generate non-historically specific generalizations and concepts.

[1] A different version of this piece was delivered as a Walker-Ames Lecture at the University of Washington and appeared in the *Journal of Contemporary Business*, vol. 10, no. 3.

Business history evolves

Business history appeared first as a distinguishable sub-field of economic history in the late 1920s and the 1930s. Its parent, economic history, became an identifiable discipline only a few years earlier. In the United States, and in Britain too, economic history was rooted more in the discipline of history than in that of economics. Economists interested in institutional change did write impressive historical studies. Consider Arthur H. Cole's two volumes on the history of the American woollen industry, Melvin T. Copeland's work on the cotton textile industry and John R. Commons's studies in labour and labour union history. Better known and more influential, however, were such historians as Frederick Jackson Turner, Ulrich B. Phillips and Charles A. Beard, who, as products of the first generation of graduate education in the United States, found their training in political, diplomatic and military history inadequate to evaluate a variety of economic issues raised by their investigations. Turner achieved fame through his essay on the impact of the frontier on American institutions. Phillips related the plantation and slavery to the broader history of the South. And Beard, after completing a case-study on the making of the Constitution, developed an economic interpretation of the history of the American republic – one in which he depicted a recurring conflict between country and city and between agriculture and business.[2]

By pushing history beyond past politics these three scholars helped to create the new sub-field of economic history for which they set the agenda for research and debate for more than a generation. They continued to use the historical methods they had learned in graduate school. Their generalizations were induced from correspondence, reports and statistical data taken from archives and other contemporary sources. Such generalizations, however, remained very much historically specific, that is rooted in a specific time and place. The concepts of the moving frontier, of the plantation as a way of life and even of the recurring conflict between farmer and businessman, were not easily applied by other historians to different times and different cultures. Nor were they used by their colleagues in the economics, sociology and social science departments of Harvard, Hopkins, Columbia, Chicago and other new graduate schools.

Thus, the giants of the first generation of professionals enlarged Clio's domain but retained her basic approach to research and analysis. Their

---

[2] Useful here is William Parker, 'The Historiography of American Economic History', in Glenn Porter (ed.), *Encyclopedia of American History* (New York, 1980), pp. 5–7.

students followed their example. And as was true for other new sub-fields of the historical discipline, such as social and intellectual history, economic history was quickly fragmented into still smaller sub-sub-disciplines – into labour history, agricultural history, business history and even narrower fields such as transportation and maritime history. This fragmentation, plus the continuing and absolutely essential commitment to careful archival work, intensified the professional historian's concentration on the case-study and turned him even further away from making generalizations. Few historians of the generation that followed Turner, Phillips and Beard produced even historically specific generalizations. Nearly all viewed still broader ones – those not rooted in time and place – with the deepest scepticism.

This was the situation when my generation came to graduate school in the years immediately following World War II. At that time the emphasis in course reading, in lectures and particularly in seminars was on the case-study – on how specific individuals and groups responded to and helped to shape very specific situations. At Harvard my own mentors, Frederick Merk, one of Turner's ablest students, and Samuel Eliot Morison, the leading historian of the colonial period, did generalize occasionally from their data but rarely in a sharp, precise way and nearly always in terms of historically specific situations. As was true of their predecessors, their generalizations were little used by economists, by sociologists or even by historians in other fields.

This was also the case across the Charles River where business history had first become identified as a separate sub-discipline when in 1928 N. S. B. Gras was appointed the first Straus Professor of Business History at the Harvard Business School. For Gras business history meant the writing of biographies of businessmen and business firms from their own personal or company records. His was, it should be stressed, a pioneering venture, for up to that time historians had made little use of the business records. Studies sponsored and encouraged by Gras revealed for the first time how businessmen and firms actually carried on their day-to-day activities. Gras directly encouraged and often sponsored the work of others, many of whose studies were published in Gras's *Harvard Studies in Business History* – a series that began with Kenneth W. Porter's two-volume biography of John Jacob Astor, published in 1931. Of the twenty volumes published during the next quarter of a century all but two (J. Owen Stalon's book on marketing life insurance and Henrietta Larson's encyclopaedic bibliography, *A Guide to Business History*) were biographies of men or enterprises. Gras's efforts culminated in the history of the Standard Oil Company (New Jersey), which consisted of three volumes on the history to 1950 of the parent company, Jersey Standard, and of one on a major subsidiary, Humble Oil. This was a massive project which took a team of scholars more than twenty years to complete.

The work at Harvard encouraged a continuing stream of comparable business history and biography. The several volumes by Richard C. Overton on railroads and Harold F. Williamson on industrial companies were particularly notable. In the years following World War II detailed and accurate histories appeared on other oil companies, including those on Standard Oil of Indiana, Standard Oil of California and Shell; on railroads such as the Burlington, the Illinois Central and the Southern; on commercial and investment banks like the First National Bank of Boston, and Kidder, Peabody; on manufacturing concerns like the Pabst Brewing Company, Waltham Watch and Winchester Arms; and on marketers like Macy's and Sears, Roebuck. At the same time leading political and social historians turned to writing business history. For example Allan Nevins at Columbia completed a most impressive two-volume study of John D. Rockefeller and then a three-volume biography of Henry Ford.

The work begun by Gras and his associates was carried abroad in the 1950s. In Britain Charles Wilson was the pioneer. His history of Unilever, the first two volumes of which appeared in 1954 (with a follow-up on the period after World War II in 1965), was something of a counterpart to the Gras-sponsored Standard Oil history. As the work of a single broadly trained, perceptive historian rather than a team of specialists, Wilson's volumes were more concise and far more readable, with the actors and events placed much more carefully in their larger historical setting. Wilson's study fostered others. One, Peter Mathias's *Retailing Revolution*, was a history of the forerunners of Allied Supplies, whose fortunes were intimately related to those of Lever and that company's associates and competitors. One of Wilson's students, William Reader, produced an impressive array of admirable histories including those of Imperial Chemical Industries, Metal Box, Bowater and the Weir Group. Another, Ronald Ferrier, has just completed the first volume of a history of British Petroleum. In the 1960s and early 1970s came other significant studies, including B. W. E. Alford's of Imperial Tobacco, T. C. Barker's of Pilkington, D. C. Coleman's of Courtaulds and S. .D Chapman's of Jesse Boot, to name only a few. At the same time studies were being produced on the Continent and in Japan on such major business enterprises as Siemens, Renault, the Chemin de

Fer du Nord, Swedish Match and the two great Zaibatsu, Mitsui and Mitsubishi.

Output continues. At this moment, for example, I am involved in helping to supervise the histories of John Deere, Du Pont, Alcoa, Norton Abrasives, National City Bank, and Kikkoman, the Japanese soy sauce maker. In other words, a major part of the writing of business history today continues along the traditional lines first embarked upon by N. S. B. Gras in the United States and by Charles Wilson in Britain. Such traditional case-studies must continue to provide the absolutely essential information on which any broad generalizations and concepts about the history of business and business institutions can be based.

Beyond the case-studies

Nevertheless descriptive case-studies were clearly not enough. In the late 1950s and early 1960s, in conferences at Harvard and elsewhere, the cry was raised for more synthesis and more analysis in the writing of business history.[3] This concern was not new. It had been voiced by many of my fellow graduate students during our training in the immediate post-war years. In all fields of history we were asked to read a great number of descriptive biographies and narratives but rarely asked to relate them precisely to the broader environment in which the events described took place or to indicate how they might help to explain deeper, underlying trends in Western history. In our search for broader meaning we had little help from our mentors. In the field of business history, for example, the paucity of analysis and conceptualization is suggested by the fact that the major issue at that time was whether businessmen were robber barons or industrial statesmen, that is whether they were bad guys or good guys. The debate generated much heat but little light. Indeed, what could be less likely to produce useful generalizations than a debate over vaguely defined moral issues based on unexamined ideological assumptions and presuppositions?

This unease with the descriptive case-study caused young historians to look to the social sciences for help. At the time the economists did not have much to offer. Earlier, at the time of World War I, economists and historians had been closer. The then-rising school of institutionalists – including Wesley Mitchell, F. W. Taussig and William Z. Ripley as well as Commons – had made careful studies about railroads, tariffs, labour

---

[3] See, for example, Arthur M. Johnson, 'Conference on the History of American Business: A Summary Report', *Business History Review*, 33 (Summer, 1959), 204–15.

unions, banks and monetary instruments, and other institutions and institutional arrangements. Our post-war generation could have learned much from observing how Commons's concepts of legal rights and of economic transactions permitted him to generalize about economic processes and how Mitchell and later Schumpeter used their massive data to generalize about the dynamics of business cycles. In the late 1940s, however, the institutionalists were out of favour among economists. The driving edge of their discipline was in the new Keynesian macroeconomic analyses and the new mathematical techniques of econometrics. Historians dealing with complex human actions found both the new approaches and the methods of the economists difficult to apply. Too often such quantitative techniques demanded the isolation of a relatively small number of quantifiable variables, an isolation which distorted the reality of the situation under analysis. In micro-economics, for example, the business enterprise continued to be defined primarily as a unit of production (that is, a factory), one that responded dutifully to the motive of profit maximization, rather than as a complex human organization that co-ordinated productions with distribution, finance and changing technology. The theory of the firm remained a theory of production. And in econometrics, individuals – their thought and action – simply disappeared from the scene.

On the other hand, in the late 1940s other social sciences, particularly sociology, had much to offer younger historians seeking to do something with their case-studies. In sociology the thought and action of individuals still remained at the centre of analysis. In observing men and women at work at play, sociologists had generated valuable ideas about the structure and process of human organizations and action. They had demonstrated that such generalizations, typologies and concepts need not be tied to a specific time, place or culture. For example, at Harvard in these post-war years Harry Murray was developing psychological concepts that related individual action to the family group and to the other institutions in which the individual operated. Talcott Parsons was working out similar generalizations relating groups and institutions to the larger polity, economy and society; while Clyde Kluckholm was analysing the role of the broader culture in integrating the individual groups and institutions to make possible the carrying out of the many functions required to keep a society going. Here then were brilliant examples of systematic, analytical integration of details of case-studies with broader societal activities. The work of these men and their colleagues in other universities offered a far greater challenge to younger historians than did the ideas and techings of their own mentors.

8

The problem was that of getting the time and the guidance to understand these new and challenging approaches. Most graduate history departments frowned on their students doing much work outside of history; and, once one began to teach, there was hardly time to read more than the current output in one's own specialized field of history. However, opportunities did appear. I was able, for example, to take sociology with Talcott Parsons as one of my five fields required for the general examination. Also during my last years of graduate school and my first years of teaching I participated in the workshops and discussions of Harvard's Research Center in Entrepreneurial History. Inspired by Joseph Schumpeter and guided by Arthur Cole, that centre brought together junior and senior economists, sociologists and historians around a topic that was of particular interest to a budding business historian. In our discussions about the entrepreneur, scholars young and old effectively struggled to tie the archival-based case-studies to the broader environment by using existing concepts and generalizations and by developing new ones.

While I was certainly fortunate in the ease of my exposure, clearly my experience was not unique. During the 1950s American historians were increasingly making use of the social sciences, particularly sociology. In 1965 John Higham concluded a review of the writing of history in the United States by noting that since World War II there had been two significant trends. One was psychological, dealing at the cultural level with myths, symbols and images and at the individual level with Freudian, Jungian and other motivational and developmental concepts. The other was institutional. In describing the second Higham wrote:

Fortunately, American historians have not yielded wholly to the psychologizing trend. Among those who still respect the force of overt principles, a strain of rationalism persists. It is also reappearing in a small but rising number of historians who take a fresh look at organizational patterns. The latter wish to know how groups and agencies – such as political parties, corporations, and communities – have molded the behavior and regulated the distribution of power. Deriving partly from studies in entrepreneurial and business history, and partly from contemporary American sociology this kind of history is less concerned with motives than with structure and process. It shows men managing and being managed through rational systems of control and communication. Perhaps we can call this the new institutionalism; for it is bringing back to life a morphological study of organizations now freed from the formalistic evolutionary emphasis of 19th century scholarship.[4]

[4]John Higham *et al.*, *History* (Englewood Cliffs, New Jersey, 1965), pp. 230–1.

ALFRED D. CHANDLER JR

Business history as institutional history

Since the 1950s business historians have become increasingly involved in the writing of institutional history. Some have dealt not with individuals or firms but with institutions – with the industrial and the transportation enterprise, the factory and other technological modes of production, the investment and commercial bank, the exchanges and other financial institutions, the advertising and other specialized agencies and the industrial research laboratory. Others have dealt with carefully defined groups of individuals – railroad presidents, top managers, or entrepreneurs in small businesses; while yet others have analysed the changing governmental framework by which business is regulated. Comparable studies have been done in allied sub-fields of technological, labour and legal history. The resulting concentration on institutional processes, structures and functions has permitted specific case-studies to be integrated into the broader history of the changing environment and has made possible the development of generalizations and concepts that are not historically specific.

The underlying method and approach of the new institutional historians remain those of the traditional ones. Like all historians, they are concerned with change over time. Their data remain contemporary correspondence, reports, periodicals and statistical compilations available in public and private archives and libraries. They embark on their research by asking the historian's traditional questions of when, where, how and why the institution or phenomenon studied began and continued to develop. Their generalizations are derived from their answers to these traditional questions.

What is new about institutional history is that, almost by definition, it is comparative. The histories of many different individual enterprises, factories, regulatory commissions, railroad leaders, legal cases and the like must be compared, contrasted and analysed. And it is precisely these comparisons that make possible the derivation of generalizations and concepts that are not tied to a specific time or place. Such generalizations, induced from a large mass of historical data, can be of value to historians working in other fields, to economists and social scientists, and to teachers and practitioners of the science and art of management.

The approaches and methods used in, and the types of findings and generalizations derived from, such comparative business history can best be illustrated by examining the historical development of one major business institution, the large industrial corporation. This examination involves three sets of comparisons: first, a comparison of the organizational structure of the largest American industrial enterprises; second, a comparison of the differing development of this type of business enterprise in different industries; and third, the growth of this institution in different national economies. In illustrating these comparisons I draw upon my own work, because so much of it has been informed by the teachings of Talcott Parsons, who maintained that careful comparative analysis could do for the social sciences what the controlled experiment has done for the physical and natural sciences.

Comparisons of companies

The first set of comparisons comes out of my initial venture into institutional history – a venture that was made easier by Charles Wilson. For I had the good fortune to have long talks about my project with Professor Wilson when he was in Cambridge, Massachusetts, in the fall of 1954 shortly after the publication of the first two volumes of his Unilever history. At that time many of the largest industrial companies in the United States, already among the most complex of human organizations, were undergoing massive administrative reorganization. They were shifting from a centralized organizational structure to what was, in the parlance of the day, called the 'decentralized structure'. Now to a historian this was a curious phenomenon. Powerful administrators rarely change their daily routine or relinquish their position of control except under the strongest of pressure. A study of the administrative histories of these and other large business enterprises, with a focus on these recent reorganizations, therefore, promised to reveal new information about and insights into the internal activities and operations of large American corporations and the changing environment in which they operated. The *approach* for such a collective administrative history was, then, one of organizational innovation. Who invented the new decentralized form, when, and why? And which companies adopted it, which did not, and why?

The method of research was straightforward. First, the different structures had to be clearly defined, and then the pioneers in the new form of management located. The preliminary investigation of the history of the nation's 80 largest industrial corporations revealed two important facts. One was that nearly all had reached their great size by integrating the high-volume production of relatively standardized products with mass distribution in national and world markets; the other was that nearly all had adopted a centralized, functionally departmentalized structure to manage their enterprise. In this type of structure each

11

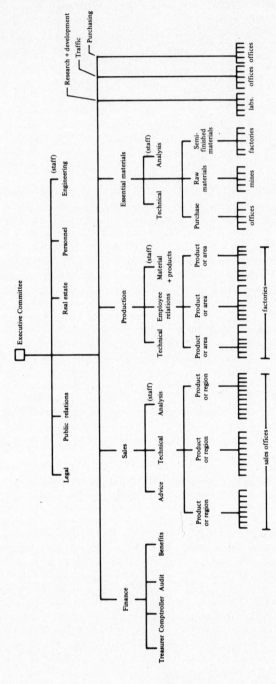

Fig. 1.1. Multi-unit, multi-functional manufacturing enterprise (used by integrated manufacturing companies from the 1890s on)

12

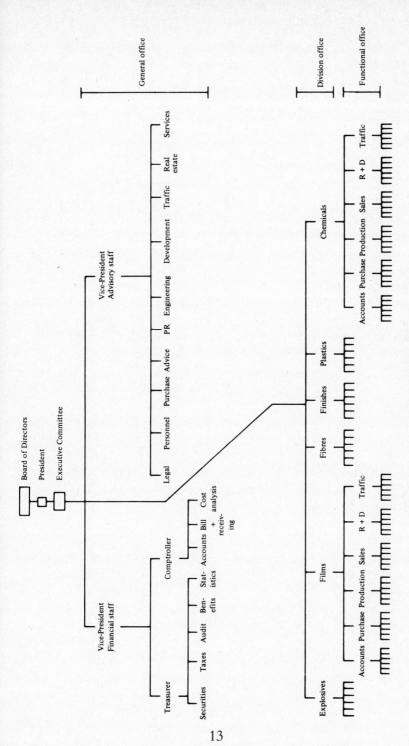

Fig. 1.2. The multidivisional structure

13

basic functional activity – manufacturing, raw material production, transportation, distribution, finance, and research and development – was administered by a separate department. This form, which economists now call the 'unitary' or 'U' form, is depicted in Fig. 1.1. On the other hand, the new organizational structure which so many companies were adopting in the 1950s, the so-called decentralized form, was made up of a number of autonomous divisions (each with its own centralized, functionally departmentalized structure) and a general or corporate office which co-ordinated, monitored and controlled the divisions. That form, christened by economists as the 'multidivisional' or 'M' form, is illustrated in Fig. 1.2.

Further investigation showed that the innovators of the new multidivisional form were Du Pont, General Motors, Jersey Standard (now Exxon), and Sears, Roebuck. The next step in the research, a diplomatic one, was to get access to the internal records of these firms in order to determine when, how and why the organizational innovation was carried out. When these case-studies were completed, I tracked down from annual and other corporate reports, articles in journals and interviews with senior executives which of the nation's largest corporations had adopted the new form and which had not.

The *findings* were clear-cut. Most of the firms that decided to reorganize did so because of crises which were quickly reflected in a drastic drop in profits. The managerial problems that created the crises and brought on reorganization resulted from growth, but from only a certain type of growth. They were not the result of growth in terms of greatly increased output, or the building of new factories, or the expansion of the work-force. Rather they were the result of administrative complexities that came when the enterprise entered new markets or diversified into new product lines. A 10 per cent increase in business resulting from diversification led to many more administrative problems than 100 per cent expansion of the existing line of business. For with diversification the heads of the functional departments in the centralized organizations had to co-ordinate the flow of several product lines rather than one. Overwhelmed by the growing day-to-day operating problems, these senior executives had neither the time nor the information necessary to carry out their most important managerial functions – those of allocating resources for future production and distribution. The solution to this administrative crisis was to create autonomous divisions whose managers became responsible for co-ordinating the flow of materials through their divisions, for the monitoring of the performance of the operating units under their command and for the resulting

14

divisional profit or loss. These autonomous divisions were, in turn, administered by a general or corporate office, consisting of general executives who were explicitly relieved from day-to-day operating responsibilities, and by an extensive staff specialized along functional lines which advised both the divisions and the corporate office. On the corporate level, the general executives assisted by the staff monitored the divisions and concentrated on strategic planning and on allocating resources to implement their long-term plans.

These findings about the nature of the structural transformation led to others. One was that, unless some form of the new structure was adopted, crisis continued. Thus, unless a change in strategy was followed by a change in structure, inefficiency resulted. Another was that the top management of these enterprises rarely diversified into new markets and products unless their existing personnel and facilities were not fully utilized and, of even more importance, unless their personnel and facilities were transferable to new products or markets. Firms in science-oriented industries such as chemicals, electrical machinery and electronics found that through systematic research they could develop new products that used more profitably many of their existing technological skills and facilities. Others in food and similar non-durable consumer products began to diversify by adding new lines that used their existing marketing plant and personnel. There were, however, enterprises in industries such as iron, steel and other metals, and metal fabricating, where skills and facilities were not easily transferable into other lines or activities. Such firms were slow to diversify and were, therefore, under little pressure to set up multidivisional structures. In other words, the potential of an enterprise to diversify depended on the transferability of existing facilities and, far more important, on the transferability of its particular set of specialized functional skills – those in production, marketing, research and the like – to other product lines. The fungibility of these facilities and skills, in turn, reflected the technology of production and nature of the market of the firm's original line.

The processes of organizational and institutional change described and analysed in the study were, of course, historically specific. But the comparison of the institutional response of many firms over an extended period of time revealed much, not only about the basic problems of corporate growth and their solutions, but also about the way in which the large American industrial enterprise operated and changed. Thus the information developed and the definitions, generalizations and concepts derived were not historically specific. The concept of strategy and that of

15

structure, and the complex relationship between the two, the concept of transferable resources, and the definition of the basic functions of general management – those of co-ordination, monitoring and resource allocation – have been of value both to social scientists and to teachers and practitioners of business management. Economists have used these generalizable concepts to help develop what Oliver Williamson has termed the field of 'new institutional economics', a field that picked up where John R. Commons left off 40 years earlier. So too, sociologists such as James Thompson employed them to develop new views of organizational behaviour based on analysis of inter- and intra-organizational strategies and structures for coping with uncertainties posed by external environments. The concepts of strategy and structure also became central in teaching and research in the fields of business policy and general management. Finally, industrial managers themselves began to look at the lessons of history. McKinsey and Company made a fortune reorganizing European companies in the 1960s into an M-form structure. One European manager even reported that he advised his colleagues to save the $100,000 fee McKinsey charged by reading the edition of *Strategy and Structure* which then sold for $2.95.

Comparison of industries

The second set of comparisons examines the differences in the development of the large firm in different industries. The information for this set of comparisons came out of the research I did when writing *The Visible Hand*, a history of the beginnings and initial growth of the modern business corporation in the United States. Research in a wide variety of contemporary documents revealed two basic facts of the history of this institution. First, the large business enterprise with its hierarchy of middle and top managers did not exist at all before the 1850s. It came first to operate the railroads and the telegraph. Then in the 1880s it appeared suddenly, but selectively, in American industry. The new giant firms clustered in a relatively small number of industries, and these they quickly dominated. In metals, machinery, oil, chemicals and some foods very often almost the first person to try succeeded in creating giant, usually multinational, business enterprises. Their names are well known today – Rockefeller, Carnegie, Du Pont, Duke, Armour, Swift, Procter and Gamble, Eastman, McCormick, and Deere, to list only a few. But in textiles, apparel, furniture, lumber, leather, and publishing and printing, entrepreneurs were not able then, nor have been able ever

16

Table 1.1. *Distribution by industry of the 200 largest manufacturing firms: United States (firms ranked by assets)*

Standard Industrial Classification	1917	1930	1948	1973
20 Food	30	32	26	22
21 Tobacco	6	5	5	3
22 Textiles	5	3	6	3
23 Apparel	3	0	0	0
24 Lumber	3	4	1	4
25 Furniture	0	1	1	0
26 Paper	5	7	6	9
27 Printing and publishing	2	3	2	1
28 Chemical	20	18	24	29
29 Petroleum	22	26	24	22
30 Rubber	5	5	5	5
31 Leather	4	2	2	0
32 Stone, clay and glass	5	18	5	7
33 Primary metal	29	24	24	19
34 Fabricated metal	8	10	7	5
35 Machinery	20	22	24	18
36 Electrical machinery	5	5	8	13
37 Transportation equipment	26	21	26	20
38 Measuring instruments	1	2	3	4
39 Miscellaneous	1	1	1	1
Diversified/conglomerate	0	0	0	15
Total	200	200	200	200

since, to build multinational business empires that dominate their trade. In other words, if one has wanted to be a robber baron or an industrial statesman, one has had to pick one's industry carefully. As Table 1.1 indicates, such firms have continued to cluster throughout the twentieth century in the same industries in which they first appeared in the last two decades of the nineteenth century. Over two-thirds of the 200 largest industrial companies have since then been in food, chemicals, petroleum, metals and machinery.

The sudden appearance of the large industrial firm in the 1880s is easy to explain. It was not the result of legislation, regulation, pressure tactics or manipulative manoeuvres. Rather it was the product of a rational economic response to the completion of the railroad and telegraph network and the perfection of their operational techniques, which made possible a totally unprecedented volume of flow of materials and goods in and out of factories. For the first time in history both mass production and mass distribution were possible, and in nearly every case the new industrial giants came into being by integrating the two.

The reason why hierarchical enterprise came in some industries and not in others is, however, more complicated. In all cases the new large firms integrated high-volume production with high-volume distribution by creating their own national, and usually international, marketing networks. This move was quickly followed by the creation of an extensive purchasing organization. In other words, the large industrial firm came into being by internalizing the wholesalers' function within the enterprise. Why, then, did enterprises integrate production with distribution (both marketing and purchasing) so quickly in some industries and not in others? The answer was that such integration came when and where the wholesalers had difficulty in co-ordinating the massive flow of mass-produced finished goods on schedule to thousands and even hundreds of thousands of customers or were unable to ensure a comparable flow of raw materials and semi-finished materials into production plants. By the late 1980s, for example, American Tobacco was already producing and distributing 6 billion cigarettes a year; Armour and Swift were butchering and distributing 6 to 7 million cattle a year; Singer Sewing Machine was making 10,000 machines a week in each of its two major plants, one in New Jersey and the other in Glasgow; and General Electric was producing annually over 100,000 complex machines for generating, transmitting and using electricity. The co-ordination of such flows into and out of the factory demanded intricate, controlled scheduling that existing wholesalers were unable to provide.

A second reason for forward integration was that the wholesalers were unwilling or unable to invest in specialized marketing and distributing facilities and personnel, which many of the new mass-produced products required if they were to be sold in the volume in which they could be produced. Such investment was costly; and it was product-specific—that is, it could be used to distribute only a small number of product lines produced by a small number of high-volume manufacturers. The wholesaler made his profits from handling related lines for many manufacturers. He had little incentive, therefore, for making the large investment in facilities the use of which depended wholly on the supplies he received from a small number of large producers. Thus the volume distributors of perishable products such as meat, beer and bananas required a massive investment in refrigerator ships, railroad cars, warehouses and branch offices in order to deliver their products daily in fresh condition to thousands of retailers. Volume distribution of petroleum and vegetable oil called for specialized tankers, tank cars and storage areas. The mass distribution of new volume-produced machinery such as sewing machines, office machines, agricultural machinery, electrical machinery, telephones, elevators, pumps, printing presses and the like required national and often world-wide networks of branch offices with trained salesmen to demonstrate the new machines (and in the case of producer goods to install them), to provide after-sales service and repair, and to extend extensive and expensive consumer credit. In all these cases the mass manufacturers had more incentive and more of the necessary resources to make this investment than did the wholesalers. Finally, in new technologically advanced industries such as chemicals and machinery, particularly electrical machinery, product design and then product improvement demanded close co-ordination between the sales force, the production managers, the product designers and the researchers in the laboratories, all of whom had to be specialized mechanical, chemical or electrical engineers. Wholesalers or manufacturers' agents rarely had the skills or facilities to provide such co-ordination. Enterprises in these science-oriented industries normally invested generously in research and development after they had completed their marketing network.

Thus, in those industries in which the large firms clustered, salaried managers were able to handle the scheduling and moving of the high-volume flows, to provide the necessary marketing facilities and services, and to ensure continuing research in product and process development far more efficiently than could independent wholesalers, manufacturers' agents or other middlemen. In these industries the 'visible hand' of management quickly replaced Adam Smith's invisible hand of the market in co-ordination, monitoring and resource allocation. On the other hand, in industries where the scheduling of flows was not complex, where marketing did not require specialized services and facilities, and where close co-ordination of production, marketing, design and research was not essential to improve product and process, large integrated enterprises and the resulting administrative co-ordination had few advantages. In such industries the small non-integrated firm continued to flourish in manufacturing and the wholesaler and other middlemen in distribution. In these circumstances the invisible hand of the market mechanism continued to play a part as the co-ordinator, monitor and even allocator of resources, although the new mass retailers – the department store, the mail-order house and the chain store – increasingly took over these functions.

As in the case of comparisons between companies, these comparisons between industries provided generalizations that are not tied to specific situations or events and so have value beyond just the study of business history. The concept of administrative co-ordination – that of the visible hand – has relevance to the growing field of transaction cost economics in which Oliver Williamson and Douglass North have pioneered. It is of use also to sociologists who in recent years have been differentiating between the core economy, where the large firm lives, and the peripheral economy, the home of the small competitive firm, but have been doing so largely in terms of the labour force. Business school professors and business executives need to keep in mind these characteristics of different industries in their teaching and in their strategic planning. An under-standing of such differences is, for example, particularly important when an enterprise in the core economy begins to diversify into industries in the periphery where size, vertical integration and administrative co-ordination provide little competitive advantage. Finally, the distinctions between industries need to be, and I think are already being, contem-plated by the policy-makers and regulators in Washington. Clearly the clustering of the large firm in some industries and not in others was a result not of anti-trust or regulatory laws or policies but of more deep-rooted economic imperatives. Surely different anti-trust policies need to be applied to concentrated industries where vertical integration has lowered production and transaction costs than to those industries where it has not.

National comparisons

The final set of comparisons looks at the large industrial enterprise in different nations. Table 1.2 indicates the location by country and industry of all industrial firms in the world that in 1973 employed more than 20,000 workers. Over 80 per cent of the 401 listed here are multinationals. One striking fact illustrated by this table is the dominant position of the American firms in international markets. Thus 52 per cent of the 401 are American, with the UK a distant second with 12.7 per cent, followed by Germany and Japan with about 7 per cent each. An even more striking point is that the large industrial firms cluster world-wide in precisely the same industries as they always have in the United States. The similarity in the numbers in columns 1 and 2 of Table 1.2 is impressive. These numbers emphasize that the modern industrial corporation has been concentrated in the same types of industry at all times and places since its beginnings in the 1880s. This point is further documented by Tables 1.3, 1.4 and 1.5, showing the location of large

20

Table 1.2. *Distribution by country and industry of the largest manufacturing firms (those with more than 20,000 employees), 1973*

SIC	US	Out-side of the US	UK	Ger.	Jap.	Fr.	Others	Total
20 Food	22	17	13	0	1	1	2	39
21 Tobacco	3	4	3	1	0	0	0	7
22 Textiles	7	6	3	0	2	1	0	13
23 Apparel	6	0	0	0	0	0	0	6
24 Lumber	4	2	0	0	0	0	2	6
25 Furniture	0	0	0	0	0	0	0	0
26 Paper	7	3	3	0	0	0	0	10
27 Printing and publishing	0	0	0	0	0	0	0	0
28 Chemical	24	28	4	5	3	6	10	52
29 Petroleum	14	12	2	0	0	2	8	26
30 Rubber	5	5	1	1	1	1	1	10
31 Leather	2	0	0	0	0	0	0	2
32 Stone, clay and glass	7	8	3	0	0	3	2	15
33 Primary metal	13	35	2	9	5	4	15	48
34 Fabricated metal	8	6	5	1	0	0	0	14
35 Machinery	22	12	2	3	2	0	5	34
36 Electrical machinery	20	25	4	5	7	2	7	45
37 Transportation equipment	22	23	3	3	7	4	6	45
38 Measuring instruments	4	1	0	0	0	0	1	5
39 Miscellaneous	2	0	0	0	0	0	0	2
Diversified/conglomerate	19	3	2	1	0	0	0	22
Total	211	190	50	29	28	24	59	401

Source: Fortune, May 1974 and August 1974.

firms in the United Kingdom, Germany and Japan during the twentieth century. In these three economies the one exception to the American pattern is the clustering in textiles, which in all countries was the first modern industry. But in all three countries the number of textile firms declines as the twentieth century moves on.

These tables suggest national differences as well as basic similarities. Britain has close to 40 per cent of its 200 largest firms in food, tobacco, textiles, printing and publishing, and other non-durable consumer goods and a smaller number in chemicals, machinery and metals. In Germany and Japan, on the other hand, there are many more companies in chemicals and machinery than in food. In Britain therefore the large firm

Table 1.3. *Distribution by industry of the 200 largest manufacturing firms: United Kingdom (firms ranked by sales for 1973 and by market value of quoted capital for other years)*

SIC	1919	1930	1948	1973
20 Food	63	64	52	33
21 Tobacco	3	4	8	4
22 Textiles	26	24	18	10
23 Apparel	1	3	3	0
24 Lumber	0	0	0	2
25 Furniture	0	0	0	0
26 Paper	4	5	6	7
27 Printing and publishing	5	10	7	7
28 Chemical	11	9	15	21
29 Petroleum	3	3	3	8
30 Rubber	3	3	2	6
31 Leather	0	0	0	3
32 Stone, clay and glass	2	6	5	16
33 Primary metal	35	18	28	14
34 Fabricated metal	2	7	8	7
35 Machinery	8	7	7	26
36 Electrical machinery	11	18	13	14
37 Transportation equipment	20	14	22	16
38 Measuring instruments	0	1	4	3
39 Miscellaneous	3	4	3	1
Diversified/conglomerate	0	0	0	2
Total	200	200	204	200

has been heavily involved in producing consumer goods, while Germany and Japan have until recent years concentrated on producer goods. In the United States the proportion between the two is more even, with those corporations making producer goods being somewhat more numerous than those making consumer goods.

A closer look at the activities carried on by the leading firms in these countries makes these national differences more striking. For even though the large industrial corporations are concentrated within a few major industrial groups, within these groups the firms of each nation produce quite different products. For example, before World War II only two or three of the 200 largest German companies produced packaged, branded, nationally advertised non-durable consumer goods. On the other hand, nearly all of the makers of non-durable consumer products on the American and British lists were mass producers of packaged,

Table 1.4. *Distribution by industry of the 200 largest manufacturing firms: Germany (firms ranked by sales for 1973 and by market value of quoted capital for other years)*

SIC	1913	1928	1953	1973
20 Food	23	28	23	24
21 Tobacco	1	0	0	6
22 Textiles	13	15	19	4
23 Apparel	0	0	0	0
24 Lumber	1	1	2	0
25 Furniture	0	0	0	0
26 Paper	1	2	3	2
27 Printing and publishing	0	1	0	6
28 Chemical	26	27	32	30
29 Petroleum	5	5	3	8
30 Rubber	1	1	3	3
31 Leather	2	3	2	1
32 Stone, clay and glass	10	9	9	15
33 Primary metal	49	47	45	19
34 Fabricated metal	8	7	8	14
35 Machinery	21	19	19	29
36 Electrical machinery	18	16	13	21
37 Transportation equipment	19	16	14	14
38 Measuring instruments	1	2	4	2
39 Miscellaneous	1	1	1	1
Diversified/conglomerate	0	0	0	1
Total	200	200	200	200

branded items. Nor did the Germans volume-produce highly standardized machines. In 1930, when Ford made 1.4 million cars and General Motors 1.6 million, only one German automobile manufacturer produced over 10,000 cars. That company, Adam Opel, with an output of 25,000, was a subsidiary of General Motors. As early as World War I, subsidiaries of American firms in Britain, Germany and France were the largest producers in each of these three countries of agricultural machinery (International Harvester, John Deere, J. I. Case and others), office machinery (Remington Typewriter, National Cash Register, Burroughs Adding Machine and others), sewing machines (Singer and United Shoe), telephones (Western Electric), elevators (Otis), printing presses (Mergenthaler), as well as radiators, air brakes, storage batteries and pumps. Manufacturers in Britain, Germany or France rarely

23

Table 1.5. *Distribution by industry of the 200 largest manufacturing firms: Japan (firms ranked by assets)*

SIC	1916	1930	1954	1973
20 Food	31	30	26	18
21 Tobacco	1	1	0	0
22 Textiles	54	62	23	11
23 Apparel	2	2	1	0
24 Lumber	3	1	0	1
25 Furniture	0	0	0	0
26 Paper	12	6	12	10
27 Printing and publishing	1	1	0	2
28 Chemical	23	22	38	34
29 Petroleum	6	5	11	13
30 Rubber	0	1	1	5
31 Leather	4	1	0	0
32 Stone, clay and glass	16	14	8	14
33 Primary metal	21	22	28	27
34 Fabricated metal	4	3	6	5
35 Machinery	4	4	10	16
36 Electrical machinery	7	12	15	18
37 Transportation equipment	9	11	18	20
38 Measuring instruments	1	1	3	5
39 Miscellaneous	1	1	0	1
Diversified/conglomerate	0	0	0	0
Total	200	200	200	200

attempted to compete with these American firms even in their own domestic markets. The Germans, on the other hand, made and distributed throughout the world high quality, more specialized industrial machinery, and their great integrated chemical firms dominated world markets until the 1930s.

As space does not permit further description, let me only suggest very briefly generalizations derived from data collected and collated about more than a thousand of the largest industrial enterprises in the world.

First, the growth of modern, large-scale industrial (i.e. manufacturing or processing) enterprises had been much more the result of investment in non-manufacturing personnel and facilities than in manufacturing plants and personnel. Non-manufacturing investment is that which is made in personnel and facilities used to market and distribute the firm's products and to obtain raw and semi-finished materials and that used for transportation, for research and development and, finally, for the administrative, legal and financial activities of the central or corporate office. It is investment not related directly to the production of goods.

Second, such non-manufacturing investment first came when manufacturing enterprises were able to carry out non-manufacturing functions more effectively at lower costs than they could by buying from, selling to or contracting with other firms or individuals handling such functions. That is, such investment came when the internalizing of such functions and of the transactions between them permitted the lowering of production, distribution and other transaction costs involved in the manufacturing and distribution of the enterprise's product line.

Third, such non-manufacturing investment initially appeared when new technologies permitted manufacturing establishments to produce in an unprecedented volume for distribution in national and international markets. Such opportunities first came into being on a significant scale in the 1880s, when the completion of modern transportation and communications systems – those of the railroad, steamship, telegraph and cable – and the perfection of techniques to operate them made possible such high-volume production and distribution.

Fourth, in the 1880s the new volume-producing enterprises in each of the leading industrial nations faced quite different situations as regards domestic and foreign markets, sources of materials and even available technologies. Therefore, although in each nation these enterprises invested in non-manufacturing personnel and facilities, in each they concentrated on the production of different types of goods which, in turn, brought differing types of and differing intensity in non-manufacturing investment. These differences in non-manufacturing and also manufacturing personnel and facilities, reinforced and replicated for over 100 years, have been as responsible for the variety in the performance of enterprises in national economies, and even for differences in the performance of the different economies as a whole, as have differences in the standard factors of production – natural resources, capital and labour. I do think that historians, economists, other social scientists and even government policy-makers and managers of multi-nationals should ponder these sets of generalizations.

Comparative business history

The limitations of space prevent a detailed analysis of these national differences. However, the purpose of presenting these comparisons of companies, industries and nations has not been to delineate in detail the history of the modern industrial corporation or even to raise questions about its continuing evolution. The purpose has been rather to illustrate the approaches and methods used and the types of findings and concepts that can be derived from comparative institutional business history.

I hope that these comparisons make clear that the institutional historian in business history, as in other sub-fields of economic history, remains an historian. He is not an economist, sociologist or management scientist, although he has learned a great deal from these social scientists. He does not, as they do, deduce hypotheses or theorems *a priori* from an existing body of theory which is then tested with empirical data. His generalizations are derived from his data–data which are collected and collated to answer the historian's questions of when, where, how, and, then, why. Such institutional business history may be less lively, less dramatic, less personal than the more traditional historical narratives of businessmen and enterprises. However, I am convinced that the comparative institutional approach enables the business historian to make unique contributions to broaden our knowledge and understanding of our industrial, urban, technologically driven, modern world – a world which had its beginnings only in the middle of the last century and which has created in so brief a period an environment far, far different from anything that man had hitherto encountered.

2

Historians and businessmen

D. C. COLEMAN

I

In May 1960, Harold Nicolson, biographer, journalist, novelist, Member of Parliament and ex-diplomat, recorded in his diary that he had told his son Nigel that 'I must get a job as a hack-writer who wrote the history of City companies and that I should ask for a fee of £5,000; otherwise I should have to give up living in the Albany.'[1] In fact he was spared this ultimate descent into literary degradation because his publisher son fixed up a contract for him to write a book for the same fee on the much more socially acceptable topic of monarchy. But the diary entry nicely encapsulated a prevalent British attitude towards the history of business and businessmen: it was not a suitable subject either for the historian or for the literary man. Although Nicolson would not have been aware of it, by 1960 the historian's attitude was beginning to change. That it was so doing owed not a little to the publication in 1954 of the first two volumes of Charles Wilson's *History of Unilever*. Since then there have appeared a growing number of scholarly books which provide a view of the historical British businessman. What do they say? In particular, what do they say about the character of the big businessman?

II

Perhaps the most obvious and frequently made comment is that such men were in various ways exceptionally energetic, vigorous, autocratic, dictatorial, dynamic figures who engendered awe, respect or fear rather

---

[1] Harold Nicolson, *Diaries and Letters*, ed. Nigel Nicolson, 3 vols. (London, 1966–8), III, 384.

27

than affection. William Lever (1852–1925), founder of Lever Brothers and the British end of Unilever, will serve as an initial exemplar. Wilson tells us that he 'radiated force and energy', gave out an 'unending stream of commands, prophecies and exhortations'; and 'by unremitting effort, boundless ambition and powerful imagination' he built up his business.[2] Anyone presumptuous enough to suggest a course of action was firmly put in his place – which place was to carry out Lever's orders. His business was his life. 'My happiness', he said, 'is my business ... the possibilities are boundless ... one can organize, organize, organize ... very big things indeed. But I don't work at business only for the sake of money. I am not a lover of money as money and never have been. I work at business because business is life. It enables me to do things.'[3] In later life this particular god of happiness could exact a toll even to the end. 'I ask myself', he wrote in 1923, two years before his death, 'what has caused me to begin work at 4.30 in the morning during the last two or three years ... and I am bound to confess that it has not been the attraction of dividends but "fear" ... fear ... that Lever Brothers would have to pass their dividend. We have', he wrote ominously, 'been combining out inefficient men ... and this has produced a state of "fear" in the minds of the remainder.'[4]

Such characteristics have echoes in other histories of other businessmen. 'A smart, lively, energetic little man; born for action and full of eagerness and enthusiasm to shine in his business': thus runs a contemporary comment in 1817 on the rising John Dickinson (1782–1869), the founder of the paper-making firm of that name. He was hot-tempered, dictatorial, autocratic and highly successful.[5] John Gladstone (1746–1851), Liverpool 'merchant prince', owner of West Indian sugar plantations and slaves, father of the famous statesman, was another 'man of driving energy' who sent out, according to his biographer, 'a continuous stream of orders'.[6] Samuel Courtauld (1793–1881), founder of the textile firm (*not* his twentieth-century great-nephew of the same name), was, in a quite different line of business, 'a man of prodigious energy', arrogant, domineering, autocratic, ambitious; like Lever his business was his life.[7] Some reflections which he made in the 1850s nicely

[2] Charles Wilson, *The History of Unilever*, 3 vols. (London, 1954 and 1968), I, 48, 49, 290.
[3] *Ibid.*, p. 187.
[4] *Ibid.*, pp. 291–2.
[5] John Evans, *The Endless Web: John Dickinson & Co. Ltd. 1804–1954* (London, 1955), pp. 17, 21, 59.
[6] S. G. Checkland, *The Gladstones: A Family Biography, 1764–1851* (Cambridge, 1971), p. 228.
[7] D. C. Coleman, *Courtaulds: An Economic and Social History*, 3 vols. (Oxford, 1969 and 1980), I, 120–6.

anticipate those of the soap-maker of the next century: 'it is not by any means to mere money gain so much as success in well-contrived and well-conducted action that our interest and satisfaction in our business is found; the money gain is a legitimate result ... but it is not the spirit and soul of it, infinitely less is it the measure of it'.[8]

Devotion to business and business achievement as the source of personal satisfaction rather than merely of money was more or less inevitably complemented by statements about the virtues of hard work, usually expressed retrospectively. Sam Courtauld worked very long hours and made sure that his partner knew it; in later life he preached a philosophy of the merits of work and energy and in 1880 accompanied a £1,000 birthday-gift to a nephew with a 2,500-word homily on the merits of work.[9] William Morris, Lord Nuffield (1877–1963), creator of the biggest and most successful business in the British motor industry, 'worked extremely long hours throughout his career' and maintained in later life that 'work is still the natural mission of every man'. Like Courtauld, he was driven by an urge to succeed, was individualistic, would tolerate neither interference from outside nor rivals inside, and clung to power too long.[10] If Morris was difficult to work with and Lever's immediate subordinates were told where to get off, Sam Courtauld's own brother and partner, George, was finally driven to protest about Sam's carrying on a discussion about the renewal of their partnership in 1849 'in the character of a lord with his vassal'.[11]

Such complaints were not confined to Britain. Here is another junior partner complaining about his senior counterpart: 'It is now two years that I am your partner, and I tell you, since then I have known not one joyful day, and furthermore know not even now how much I earn.' In fact, however, that partnership lasted for fifteen years and the senior partner was another man who attracted all those familiar descriptions: ambitious, shrewd, tenacious, possessed of great powers of organization, difficult, grasping, wilful, and, once again, having a formidable temper. This was Francesco Datini, merchant of Prato, who died in 1410.[12] Jump the centuries again and the picture is much the same. David Colville (1860–1916), 'the driving force behind the growth' of what was to become the dominant firm in the Scottish steel industry and one of the biggest in the UK before nationalization, was the second generation of

---

[8] *Ibid.*, p. 175.
[9] *Ibid.*, pp. 121, 122.
[10] R. J. Overy, *William Morris, Viscount Nuffield* (London, 1976), pp. 102–8.
[11] Coleman, *Courtaulds*, I, 125.
[12] Iris Origo, *The Merchant of Prato* (London, 1957), pp. 15–16, 21, 65, 112, 172, 341.

the family in the business. He 'possessed a magnetic personality'; he was '*the* master: everyone from the board to the office-boy knew it'. He had 'a violent temper', 'incredible energy', and it was his 'daemonic drive and energy' which built up the company.[13] Here is another man of the same generation in another business: 'more than one person described him as possessing boundless energy'; he was 'like a tornado who used to tear around the works and offices'. These were contemporary descriptions of Herbert Austin (1866–1941), founder of the Austin motor company and great rival to William Morris, Lord Nuffield.[14] And here is a tycoon of a similar generation: Harry McGowan, Lord McGowan (1874–1961), successor in 1931 to Alfred Mond, Lord Melchett, as Chairman and Managing Director of ICI. 'A natural autocrat', possessed of an excellent memory and a quick, probing mind, he dominated his Board, inspired respect rather than affection, bullied almost all his colleagues at one time or another, exercised such a complete dictatorship that ICI under McGowan was, it has been said, 'as near to being run by one man as any business of its size could be'.[15] And still later, in a different line of business, Sir Eric Bowater (1895–1962), creator of the modern paper-making giant, is said to have enjoyed unconcealed dominance over the firm and to have exercised 'naked autocracy'; to have possessed a temper which 'was very rarely lost, but terrifying if it was'; and whose behaviour towards the British and North American sides of the business was 'reminiscent of nothing so much as the style of government of earlier autocrats: the Norman and Angevin kings of England'.[16]

The majority of the samples so far considered have been nineteenth- and twentieth-century industrialists. Most of the big businessmen who date from before the Industrial Revolution and who have been caught in the historian's net were merchants and/or financiers. The seventeenth century offers some notable participants in the great business game. If a prize were to be given for unattractive historical businessmen, then two early-seventeenth-century operators would probably tie for first place. Sir Arthur Ingram and Lionel Cranfield, later Earl of Middlesex, were almost exact contemporaries, their lifespans both stretching from the 1560s and 1570s to the 1640s. Both were the sons of London merchants; both also started as merchants; both moved into the risky but lucrative half-world of government contracts and finance; and both finished up as

---

[13] Peter L. Payne, *Colvilles and the Scottish Steel Industry* (Oxford, 1979), pp. 117, 131.
[14] Roy Church, *Herbert Austin* (London, 1979), pp. 161–2.
[15] W. J. Reader, *Imperial Chemical Industries: A History*, 2 vols. (Oxford, 1975), I, 380; II, 135–6, 143, 235.
[16] W. J. Reader, *Bowater: A History* (Cambridge, 1981), pp. 89–90, 173.

landowners. Cranfield was a bigger merchant and made a fortune as such before entering politics and becoming Lord Treasurer in 1621–4; Ingram achieved his wealth and reputation as an intermediary between court and business, a 'fixer', a contact man, exploiter of court monopolies. Ingram's road to fortune has been described as 'littered with the wretched lives of those who had dealt with him as clients or partners'; and his character impressed his biographer as twisting, devious and unreliable, unreasonable and overbearing, excessively suspicious and always self-righteous.[17] His fortune is said to have represented 'the parasitical wealth of a brilliant speculator who seized all the opportunities of a corrupt political system'.[18] Cranfield presented almost a mirror image: he was, it seems, arrogant and grasping, mean and suspicious, tactless and self-righteous, hard, ambitious and exacting, energetic and unscrupulous. He differed from Ingram apparently only in earning the epithets 'inflexible and intransigent' whilst Ingram's flexibility was so near slipperiness as makes no matter.[19] Cranfield's urge to make money was powerful and soon remarked upon; an early business partner told him in 1601 that 'the worm covetousness gnaws you, by stretching it to the uttermost as all the world takes notice you do'.[20] Cranfield and Ingram were partners themselves in sundry ventures, and in a letter of 1607 the former offered to the latter a classic invitation for the joint exploitation of opportunities for gain: 'one rule I desire be observed between you and me, which is that neither of us seek to advance our estates by the other's loss, but that we may join together faithfully to raise our fortunes, by such casualties as this stirring age shall afford'.[21] Not even this worked, for, treacherous to the end, Ingram managed in the 1630s to double-cross Cranfield when the latter was in difficulties.[22]

In contrast to this early-seventeenth-century pair stands a later-seventeenth-century counterpart whose character sounds like the exception to prove the rule in the shape of a man who made a great deal of money in public finance (he was described in his own day as 'the richest commoner in three kingdoms') and yet who was apparently popular, respected and honest.[23] Sir Stephen Fox (1627–1716) seems, according to

[17] Anthony F. Upton, *Sir Arthur Ingram* (Oxford, 1961), pp. 259, 261.
[18] Menna Prestwich, *Cranfield: Politics and Profits under the Early Stuarts* (Oxford, 1966), pp. 64–5.
[19] *Ibid.*, pp. 54–5, 65, 92, 508, 523–4.
[20] *Ibid.*, p. 54.
[21] *Ibid.*, p. 72.
[22] *Ibid.*, p. 406.
[23] Christopher Clay, *Public Finance and Private Wealth: The Career of Sir Stephen Fox, 1627–1716* (Oxford, 1978), p. 302.

his biographer, to have been 'one of the most likeable parvenus of any age'. He had a reputation for honesty and competence, great personal charm and considerable presence; nobody ever seems to have levelled any charge of malpractice against him; and he sent the diarist John Evelyn into raptures of praise: 'generous ... of a sweet nature ... never was man more fortunate than Sir Stephen: he is a handsome person, virtuous and very religious'; and as for his wealth, it was 'honestly gotten and unenvied, which is next to a miracle'.[24] It is almost a relief to find him possessed of a few resemblances to the emerging prototype of the big businessman: he was sometimes overbearing to dependents; he liked to get his own way; beneath the charm lurked a sharp temper; he was intolerant of weakness or failure in others, and he became irritable in old age.[25] He begins to sound quite human.

Lest it should be supposed that I am suggesting that *all* leading businessmen have been seen by historians as bad-tempered, over-energetic, innovating dynamos let me at this point introduce an associated historical character to modify the picture. Along with the vigorous innovator there has often gone a business associate of a different temperament. For the sake of a convenient lable, he can be called the 'organization man', though that does not necessarily describe his function. He has characteristically appeared as the essential complement to the innovator. Sometimes he has been a finance expert, an accountant or a lawyer, a negotiator, a manipulator, a man concerned with structures of organization or tactics to be pursued, a man of careful judgement but not a visionary or a major innovator either in organization or in production techniques. He has been an important decision-taker in his own right, has sometimes been of crucial importance in a firm's development by preventing the daemon of innovation from taking decisions so radical and innovatory as to be crazy, and has sometimes succeeded him in command of the business, bringing in a necessary period of consolidation and stability. Francis D'Arcy Cooper, who succeeded Lever as Chairman of Lever Bros in 1925, provides a classic example of the man who had kept control over finance and who then ushered in a period of consolidation and rationalization.[26] In Colville's history, during the period of rapid growth under the aegis of the dynamic David, his brother Archibald was 'the only person who could withstand David's violent temper and harness his incredible energies to

---

[24] *Ibid.*, pp. 17, 232–3, 303; *The Dairy of John Evelyn*, ed. E. S. de Beer, 6 vols. (Oxford, 1955), IV, 217–19.
[25] Clay, *Public Finance*, pp. 314–15.
[26] Wilson, *Unilever*, I, 297–303; II, 309–14.

attain realistic objectives'. Archibald, in contrast to his flamboyant brother, was 'shrewd, calculating and cool'.[27] The history of Courtaulds provides more than one example of similar partnerships of different temperaments. The most striking was probably that of H. G. Tetley (1852–1921) and T. P. Latham (1855–1931) who between them, at the beginning of the twentieth century, transformed a family silk firm into a world leader in the first of the man-made fibres, rayon. Tetley seems to have had the standard ration of relentless energy, arrogant and domineering manner, furious temper, a single-minded devotion to business, and a ruthless impatience which sent out a stream of letters, plans, ideas, demands and orders. Latham, in contrast, was calm, close, calculating, shrewd, efficient, devoid of the imaginative vision of Tetley but possessed of a certain charm of manner and an ability to smooth the troubled waters left in Tetley's wake.[28] Similar examples of this duality could be provided from the modern leaders of some well-known big corporations as well as from the merchants and financiers of an earlier age.

To these character-sketches of the businessman roughed out on the historian's pages should be added some recurrent motifs or highlights provided by the subjects themselves. One such motif is the observation of the separateness of the business world from other worlds. The former was consistently seen as a world inhabited by peculiarly malevolent men; it was full of traps; and it called in turn for special qualities for survival. 'You are young', wrote Datini in 1397 to one of his factors, 'but when you have lived as long as I and have traded with many folk you will know that man is a dangerous thing and that danger lies in dealing with him.'[29] The worthy Fox three hundred years later had a wary eye for those with whom he dealt, and no doubt he needed it: 'as I am an honest man I don't know but I may want bread before I dye'.[30] John Gladstone warned his son Tom at Eton in 1820 about the hazards of the business life compared with public life. The latter was the 'road to honour and usefulness'. In the former, 'great respectability' was to be got by 'honourable, punctual, correct conduct', and the prime object of mercantile men was to accumulate or acquire property, but 'all their prudence and discretion is required to guard against measures that so often lead to ruin and loss of fortune'.[31] That the business world had its traps for the young is testified to in books of guidance and by the homilies

---

[27] Payne, *Colvilles*, p. 131.   [28] Coleman, *Courtaulds*, II, 205–7.
[29] Origo, *Merchant of Prato*, p. 81.   [30] Clay, *Public Finance*, p. 315.
[31] Checkland, *The Gladstones*, p. 410.

addressed by older men to young merchants. 'God is a god of order among men', Sir John Banks (1627–99), East India Company merchant and financier, told a young protégé and apprentice: 'Keep your accounts punctual, be honest to all men. Be careful of your company, converse not with ill company. Many evils do follow thereon.'[32] Closely related to this theme was the frequently made distinction between private morality and business morality. The private lives even of Cranfield and Ingram seem to have been notably more attractive than their business counterparts; and both were apparently religious men.[33] The notion seems long-enduring and to stretch out through the centuries. Here is a modern version of it, written in a letter in 1965 by a leading businessman, Frank Kearton, just as he was about to become Chairman of Courtaulds: 'a positive and indeed a very baleful personality is needed to make a success of the tough businesses. One can still remain – I hope – sweetly considerate in private life, business is quite different.'[34] Eleven years later, as Lord Kearton, he became the head of the state-owned British National Oil Corporation. Presumably the same sentiments were deemed equally appropriate for a nationalized industry in 1976 as they had been for a private one in 1965 – or 1397.

III

Hunting down character has not of course been the only form taken by the pursuit of the historical businessman. Interest in the subject has been stimulated amongst economic historians by their central obsession with the Industrial Revolution. The question has inevitably been asked whether it was perhaps due in some measure to particularly efficient and powerfully motivated businessmen. If so, what circumstances bred such beings? The search was on for the entrepreneur. That search – with all its exploration of psychology, social structure and religion – is not the subject of this essay. But a few features of motive and attitude are perhaps worthy of emphasis if only because, in this pursuit, they can be picked up in other contexts and at other times.

A feature which occurs in a number of accounts is the seeming importance of particular family circumstances in helping to provide the initial motivation which has set the future businessman *en route* for success. The young William Morris, the future Lord Nuffield, is said to

[32] D. C. Coleman, *Sir John Banks: Baronet and Businessman* (Oxford, 1963), pp. 66, 145–6. The remarks were made in 1658 and 1662.
[33] Upton, *Sir Arthur Ingram*, p. 262; Prestwich, *Cranfield*, p. 537.
[34] Quoted Coleman, *Courtaulds*, III, 319.

have been spurred on to his vigorous early efforts by awareness of his having to be main source of support for his mother, his father being in such poor health that by 1893, when Morris was only sixteen years of age, he could no longer work to support the family.[35] The ambitions of Sir Alfred Jones (1845–1909), future Liverpool shipping magnate and the only surviving son of an impoverished middle-class family in which the father's ill-health and early death left young Alfred's mother in a vulnerable position, were apparently much influenced by an urge to remedy this family decline.[36] Samuel Courtauld's driving energy was given impetus by his awareness – as the eldest son in a family of seven born of an idealistic father who was a singularly incompetent business-man – that he would sooner or later have to help to support the family and remedy its social position. He did.[37]

Whatever the initial motivation, it is clear that throughout Western history the businessman has very rarely come from high social strata; and if he has climbed the social ladder, the regard paid to him by the hierarchy in which he lived has often been both ambivalent and variable. Though Britain never had the formal penalty of derogation as in France during the *ancien régime*, sundry changing and far from logically consistent practices and prejudices combined to ensure a social pecking order of business activities. At the nether end were those involving manual labour and retail trade; at the top were overseas trade and international finance. Social attitudes to business and businessmen were long affected by two potent influences which had deep roots in Christian society: the moral suspicion of profits, embracing in particular the condemnation of usury; and the notion of social hierarchy. The former was commonly ill-enforced, the latter remarkably adaptable. In both, ambiguity in practice ensured a long-enduring detestation of the local money-lender, a continuing use of the term 'usurer' as a smear word; and first a tacit acceptance and then an honoured place for those who, in England at least, practised what came to be called 'merchant banking' and meant, mainly, arranging loans for foreign governments. So in twentieth-century Britain before the Second World War, to be a pawnbroker was mildly disreputable; to be a bank-clerk was respectable but petty bourgeois; to be a merchant banker was so prestigious as to require an acquaintanceship with (or better still membership of) one of a small group of dominant families who between them had a goodly sprinkling of peerages. When Datini went into banking at the end of the fourteenth

---

[35] Overy, *William Morris*, p. 102.
[36] P. N. Davies, *Sir Alfred Jones* (London, 1978), pp. 16–18, 25, 101.
[37] Coleman, *Courtaulds*, I, Chap. 4, *passim*, and 125–6.

century, however, some people commented that he would 'lose his repute' as a great merchant by becoming a money-changer, adding that 'there is not one of them who practices no usury in his contracts'.[38] And nearly three hundred years later, in late-seventeenth-century London, Evelyn wrote in his diary in August 1678 after dining with Sir John Banks that the latter was 'a merchant of small beginnings' who had amassed a large estate 'by usurie, etc.';[39] and a half-century after that, Defoe, seen by some historians as a veritable spokesman for bourgeois mercantile ideology, was warning readers of his *Complete English Tradesman* against the wiles of 'usurers ... [and] ... money-lenders'.[40] What Evelyn did not note in his little smear about Banks's 'usurie' was that most of the money-lending had been made to Charles II's government. How, then, did Fox, who provided similar services, only on a larger scale, acquire such a splendid reputation for virtue, honesty, popularity and charm, in complete contrast to most of those who came to represent what eighteenth-century Tories so detested as 'the monied interest'?

The answer to this question provided by Sir Stephen Fox's biographer is interesting for the light which it sheds not simply on Fox, but on what impresses an English historian as having been important in determining attitudes to a businessman at that time. Fox, writes his biographer, 'made an immense fortune as a financier but he was a courtier who had learnt the ways of finance, *not a business man who was trying to pick up the rudiments of gentility*' (my italics).[41] He had indeed had a most unusual upbringing for a businessman. Coming from humble circumstances, he had secured employment as a boy in a more or less menial capacity in the royal household. As the latter went a-wandering during the Interregnum, he rose from page-boy to Clerk of the Stables and so on up the ladder of court appointments, eventually, on the restoration of Charles II, reaching those dangerous heights where money was borrowed, handled and disbursed on a large scale. By the time he had become both a royal financier and a financier in his own right he had 'no past of "trade" or petty moneylending to live down'.[42] So whilst Evelyn delivered his disapprobation of Banks or condemned Banks's fellow East India Company magnate Sir Josiah Child (1630–99) as 'this merchant most sordidly avaricious',[43] he could yet be enraptured of Fox and write a

---

[38] Origo, *Merchant of Prato*, p. 149.
[39] Evelyn, *Diary*, iv, 96.
[40] D. Defoe, *The Complete English Tradesman* (London, 1727), suppl., p. 15.
[41] Clay, *Public Finance*, p. 304.
[42] *Ibid.*   [43] Evelyn, *Diary*, iv, 305–6.

fulsome encomium on merchants in general as 'that most honourable and useful race of men (the pillars of all magnificence)'.[44] And when Pepys referred to Fox as a 'very fine gentleman'[45] he meant it in that literal sense which so appeals to the peculiarly English feeling for social order.

Money-lending and the regard for social hierarchy could thus be reconciled by the magic of gentility – which had ultimately to be in the eye of the beholder and might have to wait a generation. And 'trade' became respectable, though not proof against charges of avarice, the more it was concerned with exports and imports and could thus be seen, as to some extent it was at that time, as almost a series of acts of state. Indeed, the very age of Evelyn and Fox was one which, briefly, saw a remarkable enthusiasm for the alleged glories of commerce. The merchant, in the abstract, was lauded by writers of varying political hue. Without the merchant, asserted one writer in 1686, 'the world would still be a kind of wilderness'.[46] In 1711 Addison can be heard eulogizing merchants as the most useful members of the commonwealth because they 'knit mankind together in a mutual intercourse of good offices, distribute the gifts of nature, find work for the poor, add wealth to the rich and magnificence to the great'.[47] And in George Lillo's play *The London Merchant*, a moral tale which ran to packed houses in Drury Lane after its first performance in 1731, the very virtuous and very boring merchant Thorowgood tells his apprentice Trueman that 'the method of merchandize' has promoted 'arts, industry, peace and plenty; by mutual benefits diffusing mutual love from pole to pole'.[48] Such attitudes towards business stood in total contrast to the anti-merchant sentiments typical of a group of mid-sixteenth-century writers to whom most traders were rogues: 'next to sham priests, no class of men is more pestilential to the commonwealth'.[49] Or, more explicitly:

All merchants, buyers and sellers in London or elsewhere are commonly poor men's sons natural born to labour for their living, which after they be bound apprentices to be merchants, all their labour, study and policy is by buying and selling to get singular riches from the communalty, and never worketh to get

---

[44] Evelyn, *Navigation and Commerce* (London, 1674).
[45] Quoted Clay, *Public Finance*, p. 17.
[46] *The Character and Qualifications of an Honest Loyal Merchant* (London, 1686).
[47] Joseph Addison, *The Spectator*, no. 69 (19 May 1711), quoted H. R. Fox Bourne, *English Merchants* (London, 1886), pp. 205–6.
[48] George Lillo, *The London Merchant* (London, 1731; ed. and with introd. by Bonamy Dobrée, London, 1948), p. 41.
[49] Martin Bucer, quoted R. H. Tawney, *Religion and the Rise of Capitalism* (London, 1929), p. 142.

their living neither by works of husbandry nor artificiality, but liveth by other men's works, and of naught riseth to great riches, intending nothing else but only to get riches, which knoweth no common weal.[50]

By the second half of the eighteenth century not dissimilar sentiments had reasserted themselves. Writers as diverse as Samuel Johnson, Oliver Goldsmith and, in a quite different way, Adam Smith, were all showing notably less ardour for the abstract merchant than that of their immediate predecessors. Smith's indictment of the 'mean rapacity' of merchants and manufacturers which had caused commerce, 'which ought naturally to be ... a bond of union and friendship', to become 'the most fertile source of discord and animosity'[51] provided at least a partial echo of the anti-merchant attitude of the sixteenth century.

The coming of industrialization did not bring radical change to contemporary comments on the businessman. They retained their variable and ambivalent nature. Their targets came inevitably to include more manufacturers than merchants. In so far as the businessman figured in contemporary novels or drama the balance of comment shifted decisively towards hostility. Romantic admiration in the manner of Samuel Smiles proved less potent than that 'literary Luddism' of English fiction in the nineteenth and twentieth centuries which has been examined in detail by Neil McKendrick.[52] My concern with it here is simply to emphasize that ambivalent attitudes preceded as well as followed the Industrial Revolution. Sympathetic portraits of the businessman do exist in English fiction, but when he does appear – and there are large areas of the literary scene from which he is entirely absent – his character tends to range from the unpleasant to the comic, from the sinister to the absurd. A suitable butt for satire in Jacobean and Restoration drama, he pops up in sundry places and guises to illustrate the long-running English fascination with class and with social climbing by the self-made; from Dickens to Lawrence he struts and snarls as an unloved figure in an unloved industrial landscape; and in more modern manifestations he is sometimes presented as embodying ambiguous fantasies of sex and power, as in Anthony Powell's creation, Sir Magnus

---

[50] 'How to reform the realm in setting them to work and to restore tillage', *circa* 1535–6, quoted in R. H. Tawney and E. Power (eds.), *Tudor Economic Documents*, 3 vols. (London, 1924), III, 126 (spelling modernized).

[51] Adam Smith, *The Wealth of Nations*, Modern Library edition (New York, 1937), p. 460.

[52] See his valuable editorial introductions to four volumes (and especially the last two) in the Europa Library of Business Biography series (now seemingly terminated), viz: Overy, *William Morris*, pp. vii-xliv; Clive Trebilcock, *The Vickers Brothers* (London 1977), pp. ix-xxxiv; P. N. Davies, *Sir Alfred Jones* (London, 1978), pp. ix-lvi; Church, *Herbert Austin*, pp. ix-l.

Donners. And for an updated version of the sixteenth-century anti-merchant sentiments one could hardly better those expressed by Canon L. J. C. Collins in 1962 concerning the 'economic gangsterism of capitalism'.[53]

IV

So when modern professional historians have looked at the historical big businessman and sketched not wholly endearing personalities, they have doubly reflected long-enduring attitudes in British society. In one sense they may well have themselves been influenced consciously or unconsciously by the ambivalence or hostility of the literary tradition. Many will have been through educational processes similar to those which have helped to sustain that tradition. Yet the very fact that they have tackled so unpopular, indeed unfashionable, a topic suggests a substantial commitment to objectivity, even to sympathy, which should have minimized this influence. More important is the refraction of these social attitudes though the historical businessmen themselves as they made their way to power and wealth, leaving their marks as evidence for the historian to use. If the latter has seemed to create stereotypes – the impatient entrepreneurial dynamo or the patient organization man – it is largely because these are the immediate equivalents in business history of the ambitious politicians, the scheming prelates, the astute lawyers, and all the other more familiar climbing plants in the historical garden. In time, more varieties will doubtless be discovered. Nature may come to imitate art. So far, the likely extent of this must be small. When Lever said 'my happiness is my business' he is unlikely to have known that he was almost precisely echoing the words which, some 250 years earlier, William Wycherley had put into the mouth of his pompous, fictional businessman, Sir Jaspar Fidget, when the latter told his wife and her companions to go to their 'business, I say, pleasure' whilst he went to his 'pleasure, business'.[54]

The longevity of ambivalent attitudes towards the businessman is worthy of emphasis. They are much older than is popularly supposed by those who look only at modern industrialization and its problems. A recent (and grossly overpraised) book has, for example, declared that something called 'the decline of the industrial spirit' in England is attributable to anti-business sentiments in English culture *since 1850.*[55]

[53] *Guardian*, 19 March 1962, quoted Coleman, *Courtaulds*, III, 230 and n.
[54] William Wycherley, *The Country Wife* (1675).
[55] Martin J. Wiener, *English Culture and the Decline of the Industrial Spirit, 1850–1980* (Cambridge, 1981).

By starting only in 1850 the author neatly evades the task of having to explain why that 'industrial spirit' presumably succeeded earlier in rising so vigorously despite the prior existence of similar anti-business sentiments. The attitudes are old but they still survive; they continue to coexist with the enjoyment of the fruits of business. The very facilities which permit our historical studies are amongst those fruits. Yet our society has retained the suspicion of profits, looked disapprovingly at acquisitiveness, found the businessmen unappealing, and gazed unenthusiastically at the self-made unless or until they have conformed to our notions of social ordering. Until very recently, we have even looked upon the very study of business history as a sort of intellectual derogation.

Those who have attracted this opprobrium, and indeed those who have been examined by the historian, have in the main been untypical businessmen in the sense that they were tycoons, made large fortunes, rose to the top of the tree, created big new enterprises or the like. The average businessman, whether a provincial trader of the fifteenth century or a garage proprietor of the twentieth, has performed at a less spectacular level of achievement. He has not been a major innovator in any sense; he has typically run a small to middle-sized firm and made moderate profits, or, in recent times, has been a salaried director. If he has moved up the scale of prosperity and the social hierarchy he has become a solid citizen of the middle class. Unlike the tycoon, he has not sought to live in some remote baronial fantasy, like Citizen Kane or, as John Evelyn said of Josiah Child's new seat, 'in a cursed and barren spot, as commonly these overgrown and suddenly monied men do for the most part seat themselves'.[56] He is more likely to have lived in an Elizabethan house in the middle of a sixteenth-century town or a mock-Elizabethan house in the suburbs of a twentieth-century town. Unfortunately the average businessman rarely figures individually on the professional historian's pages. He remains hidden as a number in a total, an anonymous bit of an aggregate, subsumed within calculations of output or of firms within industries. Of course, in this he is no different

[56] Evelyn, *Diary*, IV, 305–6. He had commented similarly on the habits of the new rich when, in 1677, he had visited Sir Robert Clayton, scrivener and banker, whose house in Surrey, from being a mere farm, had been 'erected into a seat with extraordinary expence. 'Tis in such solitude among hills as, being not above 16 miles from London, seems incredible, the ways up to it are so winding and intricate.' (*Ibid.*, II, 331.) His ambivalence is also evident in his comments in 1679 on the 'excessively rich' Clayton: 'some believe him guilty of hard dealing, especially with the Duke of Buckingham whose estate he had swallowed, but I never saw any ill by him, *considering the trade he was of*' (my italics; *ibid.*, II, 357).

from average historical lawyers or average historical politicians. When history was assumed to be 'past politics', it was the political leaders who figured in it, not back-bench Members of Parliament. So it is not inherently unreasonable that business history as it progresses should want to know about business leaders: their functions within the firm or industry, their origins, achievements, motivation, methods, personalities and relations with the wider world. But the historian of business, like other sorts of historian, will have to be prepared also to look more closely at a wider range of businessmen at varying levels of society. The creation of employment, the building of wealth, the use of resources: all have depended and still depend upon the decisions of businessmen, whether they are private capitalists, salaried directors, or the bosses of nationalized industry. Their historical doings are part of the totality of history. And until historians are willing and, indeed, actively encouraged to look at the businessman in history in much the same way as we try to look at other actors in the historical drama we shall be missing a good part of the play.

3

Businessmen and their motives

W. J. READER

Writing in 1954, and on this subject I have no reason to think he has since changed his mind, Charles Wilson said: 'In economic history as elsewhere a man is limited by circumstances: yet at the heart of the economic process there is human intelligence, human character, ingenuity and enterprise.' Then, discussing the nature of business history, he said: 'it brings the historian to close grips with a problem fundamental to the philosophy of history–the essential relationship of the individual and society. Thus, the business historian must sometimes feel that he is a biographer writing primarily biography conceived in terms of a particular kind of concrete achievement–the business itself.'[1]

The circumstances which govern a businessman's activities are economic, political, technical, social. Does he live through times of boom or slump? Is the general framework of the state, in such matters as taxation, monetary policy, social services, planning controls, anti-monopoly legislation, restrictive or liberating to private enterprise? Are technical innovations coming forward freely? If they are, do the necessary skill and plant exist for developing them or can they readily be assembled? Can the money be found to carry innovations through the phase of development? Can the resulting products be effectively marketed? Above all, what is the general attitude of society towards business, as reflected in the educational system, in labour relations, in the media, in the esteem or otherwise in which businessmen and business are held?

In relation to matters like this the businessman is a fish in the economic and social sea. The tides, the currents, the temperature of the ocean are not for him to control, but he can use them to shape his course. In doing

[1] Charles Wilson, *The History of Unilever*, 3 vols. (London, 1954 and 1968), I, vi, ix.

so he may exert considerable and sometimes unexpected influence not only on the development of his own firm but also on the business environment at large, leaving the mark of his personality on each.

Consider the example of the modern can-making and canning industry in Great Britain. Up to 1929 no such industry existed in Britain, only tin-box making, which is quite different. Then the American Can Company made a determined attempt to establish itself in the British market, offering terms to the alliance of British firms which in August 1930 became the Metal Box Company. Among the Directors of the allied firms the strongest character, Robert Barlow (1891–1976), had ambitions of his own. He persuaded his colleagues to repulse American Can and to seek, instead, an agreement with American Can's slightly smaller competitor Continental Can.

By negotiating an agreement with Continental, Barlow gained for Metal Box access on favourable terms to American can-making and food-canning technology. Then, in ruthless commercial warfare directed by Barlow, Metal Box drove American Can out of the British market for twenty-one years, leaving a clear field for Metal Box to build up a British-owned can-making industry which in turn became the base for the multinational packaging business which Metal Box runs today.[2]

That a can-making industry would have been founded in Great Britain round about 1930 seems beyond doubt. The conditions were right and American Can was preparing to take advantage of them. Then Robert Barlow stepped in and ensured that the industry developed under British ownership.

It was this kind of episode, probably, that Wilson had in mind in saying that the business historian 'must sometimes feel that he is a biographer', for immediately the question arises: What kind of man was Robert Barlow, that he could turn such unpromising circumstances to his own advantage, taking on and defeating an opponent disposing of far greater resources than any available to him? Putting the question in general terms: What kind of person is the successful businessman? (For present purposes, and without prejudice, the male includes the female.) What are his motives and his aims? What makes him go, usually long after he could have stopped: too often, long after he should have stopped?

In this essay I intend to apply these questions to a small group of businessmen, all but one British and all active during the late nineteenth and twentieth centuries, who have come to my notice in the writing of

[2] W. J. Reader, *Metal Box: A History* (London, 1976), Chapter 5.

various company histories. As a sample the group has no statistical validity and observations based on it must be speculative. They seem to me suggestive, nevertheless, of what might emerge from a more systematic treatment of the topic, and I am convinced the topic is an important one.

In looking at motives, let us first of all get the question of money out of the way. 'No man but a blockhead', Dr Johnson is reported to have said, 'ever wrote, except for money.' No man but a blockhead, it is to be hoped, ever went into business without intending to make money, and certainly no man ever succeeded without making it, usually for a good many people as well as himself. But money is raw material: a means to an end. It is not usually, to the creative businessman, an end in itself.

It comes closest to being an end in itself when the end to which it is a means is security, and this may be particularly the case with persecuted minorities such as the Jews and, in time gone by, the Quakers. Many who left Germany and Central Europe to escape Hitler possessed a steely determination to survive and the ability to do much more: indeed, to put their future material security far beyond doubt. In one case known to me, a Czech Jew of Austrian origin, who lost both his parents in Auschwitz, has made himself a millionaire many times over by property development, chiefly the building of factories to let, since the end of the Second World War. His motive is to put himself and his family in a position of impregnable security founded on the solidest of all assets: landed property. Taking account of his life-history, there is nothing to wonder at in his motive, only in the strength of purpose which has enabled him to succeed. His case cannot be unique. The drive for security must have been very strong behind many of those who came to Great Britain in the thirties and have prospered since.

For businessmen who succeed on the grand scale, in the founding or managing of large enterprises, wealth opens the door not only to security but also to power: power to develop the business along any line that may seem attractive; power to go off in other directions altogether. W. H. Lever, first Viscount Leverhulme of the Western Isles (1851–1925), whose title indicates how widely his activities ranged beyond Sunlight Soap, went to the heart of the matter with clarity and force. 'My happiness', he is reported as saying, 'is my business. I can see finality for myself, an end, an absolute end, but none for my business. There one has room to breathe, to grow, to expand, and the possibilities are boundless ... But I don't work at business only for the sake of money. I am not a lover of money as money and never have been. I work at business because business is life. It enables me to do things.'[3]

'To do things': in other words, to take off, to cruise in higher and wider orbits, sometimes, it seems to the earth-bound observer, in wilder and wilder flights of creative imagination – of self-indulgence.

'To do things': what things?

Lever, as soon as he had the means, founded Port Sunlight as a kind of feudal estate beneath the walls of the soap factory which was his castle. A quarter of a century later he began to carve oil-palm plantations from the rain-forests of the Belgian Congo and to establish settlements there which would confer some of the benefits of Port Sunlight on some of the inhabitants of the Congo. Later again in his life, he bought estates in Lewis and Harris and set out to transform the depressed economy of the Western Isles. He always denied being a philanthropist, but always he was striving to see that people had good done to them on the banks of the Mersey, in the Congo, in the Hebrides, strictly on the basis 'Lord Leverhulme knows best.'

Julius Drewe (1856–1931), one of the founders of Home & Colonial Stores, made enough money between 1885 and 1893 to enable him to embark on realizing quite ungrocerly ambitions. He equipped himself with a Norman ancestor, Drogo. He added the final 'e' to his name. He employed Sir Edwin Lutyens for twenty years (1910–30) in designing Castle Drogo above Drewsteignton on the edge of Dartmoor: a castle such as never was by sea or land, certainly such as Drogo himself never beheld. It has granite walls six feet thick and a working portcullis.[4]

Sir Alfred Mond (1868–1930), first Lord Melchett and first Chairman of ICI, was a politician by choice but a businessman by force of circumstances, and in business he strove to satisfy ambitions which in politics had been frustrated. In the two great interrelated projects of ICI's early days, synthetic ammonia and oil-from-coal, he saw not only large profits for ICI but also wide-ranging political benefits. Synthetic ammonia, backed by an advisory service which ICI would set up, would serve the cause of the British empire by providing fertilizers for the empire's farmers. Home-produced oil products had obvious applications in imperial defence (though the Board of Admiralty was sceptical) and it

---

[3] Wilson, *Unilever*, I, 187.
[4] Michael Trinick, *Guide to Castle Drogo* (National Trust, 1982); Peter Mathias, *Retailing Revolution* (London, 1967), pp. 125–8.

would do something (not very much) to relieve unemployment in the coal-mines.

Alfred Mond's colleague and successor in ICI, Sir Harry McGowan, later Lord McGowan (1874–1961), concentrated on commercial rather than political objectives, but his policies were scarcely less wide-ranging. He greatly admired the Du Pont business and its founding family, and in 1920, as Chairman and Managing Director of Nobel Industries Limited, he caused NIL to follow Du Pont into investing in the shares of General Motors. As a result, for fifteen years after the formation of ICI by the merger between NIL, Brunner Mond, United Alkali and British Dye-stuffs, ICI had a considerable portion of its reserves tied up in General Motors, a business unrelated to the chemical industry over which ICI exercised no control whatever.[5]

Politics perhaps came more readily to the mind of McGowan's close contemporary William Weir, first Viscount Weir of Eastwood (1877–1959). From 1928 to 1953 he was on the ICI Board, but the strength of his position was drawn from the engineering business founded in Glasgow by his father and uncle, George and James Weir, to make pumps and other ancillary machinery for ships in the great days of Clyde shipbuilding. From 1915 until the Second World War he was close to the centre of public affairs (he was Secretary of State for Air, presiding over the early days of the RAF, in 1918) and in his personality a keen political instinct coexisted with enthusiasm for technological development. Command of his firm's resources and his personal wealth enabled him to give practical expression to both. In 1924 he launched a scheme for producing houses, in a factory owned by Weirs, which could be put up by unemployed engineers, paid at their trade rates, instead of by builders' craftsmen. Publicly, the scheme was directed towards relieving the contemporary housing shortage. Very privately, but explicitly, it was aimed at shattering the restrictive practices of the National Federation of Building Operatives and other craft unions, including the unions in his own industry, whose activities he deeply resented, and to whom he was known as 'bluidy Wullie Weir'. The scheme was defeated by the combined opposition of unions and employers in the building industry. The unions remained entrenched and the housing shortage unrelieved.[6]

Very early, his eagerness to put his firm's resources behind his technological hobbies showed itself when he caused three racing cars to be built, in three months, for the 1904 Gordon Bennet Trophy race.

[5] W. J. Reader, *Imperial Chemical Industries: A History*, 2 vols. (Oxford, 1970 and 1975) II, 14–15.
[6] *Idem*, *Architect of Air Power* (London, 1968), Chapter 6 (II).

They were a disaster. Almost thirty years later, in 1932, in the pit of the depression, Weir and his partners, especially his younger brother James, a fanatical airman, put their firm's resources behind the development of the Cierva autogiro, later overtaken by Sikorsky's helicopter. Weir no doubt hoped to see a profit in the end, but profit was not the object of the enterprise. It was taken in hand by a group of enthusiasts who commanded the resources to give practical shape to their enthusiasm, and it is scarcely credible that it could have been launched except by a firm in which ownership was concentrated in very few hands.[7]

Little effort was made to dress up the Cierva project as an orthodox commercial proposition, but this is unusual. However soaring a businessman's flights of fancy, he will normally feel obliged to justify them commercially. Lever argued that his Congo adventure was undertaken to protect his supplies of palm-oil from blackmail by monopolists, overlooking the fact that, as Lever himself said, twenty-five years would be needed to get the plantations fully into production. Years before he went to the Congo, his raw materials buyer warned him that no plantation scheme he could conceivably undertake would be large enough to affect world prices for oils and fats, and that when they ruled high he would do better to sell his produce on the open market and take his profit than to pass it at unrealistic transfer prices to his soap companies. Moreover, in return for the concessions granted by the Belgian government, Lever had to pledge himself to provide schools, hospitals, roads and public services in districts covered with uninhabited rain-forest impenetrable except by river.

Lever's Congo enterprise endured and eventually succeeded, but in its conception it was not in any ordinary sense a commercial proposition, any more than was Port Sunlight or his plan for the Hebrides. If Lever had been mainly concerned either with protecting Lever Brothers' supplies or with making money in Africa, there would have been easier, quicker ways of doing it. He recognized that, *before* he committed himself to the Congo, by going into the Coast trade based on Liverpool. The Congo meant far more to Lever than commerce. It meant power, as he once put it, to 'organize, organize, organize, well, very big things indeed',[8] and the last long journey of his life, the last grand gesture of a romantic, was a semi-regal progress, undertaken in 1925 at the age of seventy-four, through his Congo domains. Within six weeks of getting back to England, Lord Leverhulme was dead.

[7] *Idem, The Weir Group: A Centenary History* (London, 1971), pp. 55–7, 58–60, 111–17.
[8] Wilson, *Unilever*, I, 187.

There is a parallel to Lever's Congo story. Sir Eric Bowater (1895–1962) was as nervous about supplies of the raw materials for newsprint as Lever was about supplies of the raw materials for soap, and just as much inclined to go to extremes in controlling his own sources of supply. In the early 1950s he went further. He decided that it ought to be the settled policy of the Bowater Group not only to control supplies of raw materials but also to control its own means of ocean transport: that is, to own a shipping line. Moreover, he decided that the line, rather than being managed by experts, should be run by the Bowater Group directly.[9]

How far was this a rational commercial decision? How far was it, like Lever's Congo enterprise, simply something that Sir Eric was determined to do? 'Every great man', said one of Sir Eric's successors, 'wants to own either a newspaper or a shipping line', and it may be noted in passing that Lever also, in 1915, became a shipowner. There is no doubt that once Bowater had his ships he thoroughly enjoyed them. They suited his style of life, so much so that he once took one on a Caribbean cruise, to the consternation of Bowater's insurance department because the ship wasn't covered for that sort of thing. There is no doubt, also, that he underestimated the difficulties of running a fleet. The effect on Bowater's transport costs was disastrous. Sir Eric died in 1962 ('Eric's sense of timing', his immediate successor observed to me, 'was always perfect'), and over the following fifteen years the fleet was handed over to the British & Commonwealth Group for management and gradually dispersed.

It would be monstrously unfair to dismiss Eric Bowater with no more than a glance at one of the more spectacular mistakes of his later years, when his judgement was beginning to fail. For the greater part of his career – from the early 1920s until the early 1950s – he was outstandingly successful, and during those years he was in many ways a model businessman: far-sighted, strong-minded, quick to recognize and seize an opportunity: above all, daring. If risk-taking is the mainspring of free enterprise, then Eric Bowater wound it as far as it would go.

Between 1926 and 1939 he transformed a smallish, family-owned firm of paper merchants, manufacturing nothing and selling other people's products, into a group of companies manufacturing about 800,000 tons of newsprint a year – 'the largest newsprint manufacturers in the world', he claimed in 1938.[10] To find the capital needed for this remarkable rate of growth, he resorted chiefly to issuing debenture stock and Preference

[9] W. J. Reader, *Bowater: A History* (Cambridge, 1981), Chapter 12.
[10] *Ibid.*, p. 154.

shares, so that in 1936, when the early growth of the Bowater Group was at its height, the ratio of fixed-interest capital to Ordinary capital was $8\frac{1}{2}$:1. Throughout his career, on both sides of the Atlantic, he pursued the same path, and in the 1950s he persuaded American financial institutions to find a great deal – on occasion, as much as 72 per cent – of the capital required for expansion in the United States, but on stiff terms.

The attractions of high gearing are evident, so long as a business goes well, since after interest has been paid, whatever is left is available for the Ordinary shareholders, and in recent years inflation has magnified the charms of loan capital. When earning power falters, however, as it did in Bowater during the Second World War and in the later fifties, and as it did in Lever Brothers, another highly geared business, in the early twenties, difficulties may become severe.

Why take risks like these? Why press ahead so recklessly as to incur them? Money-making is not a sufficient explanation. Risks are often taken long after the risk-taker is wealthy, and if wealth were the only end in view, far more businessmen would retire early to enjoy it, as James Nasmyth, Cromwell Varley and Julius Drewe did in the nineteenth century. Asking the question 'Why?' of great businessmen is like asking why people climb mountains. No purely rational explanation will do, and the emotional springs of action run deep: so deep as to be untraceable except along dark and precarious paths of psychology.

In Eric Bowater's case it may be that the Bowater Group had its origins when a shell hit a dug-out where he was resting on 4 September 1915. It not only stopped him from making a career in the army but also precipitated a prolonged psychological illness of which, it is said, he was so ashamed ('shell-shock' was not respectable) that he felt a perpetual need to prove himself – just like some mountaineers. In the case of Sir Robert Barlow, a good deal is probably attributable to the influence of his father, whom he both respected and feared. Old Edward Barlow (1846–1937), almost illiterate, fond of women, violent if crossed, an autocrat in his business, stood for years in Robert's way: so much so that in the early twenties Robert was seen to come on to the staircase in his father's house, dash his glasses to pieces, and exclaim 'I'm sick of this life!' [11] When Robert finally escaped, he proceeded to display many of his father's characteristics, notably in his autocracy and his occasional outbursts of anger, in which he might hurl a telephone across a room, though his behaviour generally was refined by an education superior to his father's, directed by high intelligence and clothed, when he chose, in

[11] Reader, *Metal Box*, p. 39.

overwhelming charm. Charm, allied with force of personality, is a quality which many great businessmen seem to share. Lever, small in stature but with a ready gift of speech, could quell a hostile Gaelic-speaking crowd and bring them – very nearly – on to his side. Barlow, ruthless, cunning and devious, sometimes cruel, left affection rather than resentment behind him, even among his victims, though an accountant who knew him well and quarrelled with him described him as 'an evil man'. Bowater, austere in manner and sometimes deliberately terrifying – a psychological bully – nevertheless inspired devotion among those who worked closely with him.

Men of the type of Lever, Barlow and Bowater – founders of great businesses rather than professional managers, who are a different species – are all autocrats. They usually choose advisers well and listen to what they have to say, but they will not tolerate opposition, power they will share with nobody, and rivals are not allowed. They surround themselves with dependants, recruited and promoted as they please, not according to set rules, and although these dependants may be able enough as departmental managers or specialists, they have not the commanding general grasp of the founder himself: that is not in the nature of the case.

Few of us care to contemplate our own demise, and the founders of great businesses, it seems, less than most. They behave, all too often, as if they were immortal. Like medieval monarchs, and for very similar reasons, they are reluctant to provide for the succession, and for the reasons outlined above a successor is unlikely to emerge naturally. Nor, as a rule, are they much interested in organization, and as the time approaches when the founder must depart, there is apt to be too little in the way of infrastructure to support his successor, whoever he may be.

The time of departure may be approaching, but will the founder recognize it? Power is like an addictive drug. Few who gain it willingly give it up, even if they find it burdensome, and this is as true for businessmen as for monarchs and politicians. Professional managers, nowadays, are usually carried off inexorably by the working of fixed rules of retirement. Founders are less fortunate. Almost without exception, they stay on too long. Their judgement deteriorates, perhaps megalomania sets in, and there is unlikely to be anyone in their immediate circle who can control them. Power is not only an addictive drug. If indulged in for too long, it is also destructive.

From what has been said, it follows that in the history of almost every successful business there is a period of deepening crisis as it becomes

50

obvious, perhaps to everyone except the founder, that the founder is reaching the end of his career. The crisis is likely to become acute when the founder finally goes and a successor must be found. The successor is unlikely to be out of the same mould as the founder, for his task is to carry on, rather than to create. He is likely to be a professional manager, and with a professional manager at the head of the company's affairs its history passes into a new and different phase.

Business history is a study of human behaviour against an economic background. Like other branches of history, particularly political history, it examines the way people react to the circumstances in which they find themselves, and especially–again like political history–the way in which exceptional individuals–dare one say, 'great men'?–seek to impose their purposes upon their times. It is for that reason, as Charles Wilson pointed out thirty years ago, that the business historian must try to understand the personalities of businessmen, which are no less varied, subtle and mysterious than the personalities of men in other occupations. That is what gives the business historian's craft both its difficulty and its fascination.

4

'La révolution manquée'

R. M. HARTWELL

I

The most famous scenario of *la révolution manquée* in England was written by F. Engels in *The Condition of the Working Class in England*, published in German in 1845 and in English in 1887 (in USA) and 1892 (in England).[1] This famous text, so influential with so many historians, demonstrated not Engels's powers of social analysis but rather his lack of understanding of the English working classes. He was convinced that the workers of England were so desperate that they needed only a crisis to precipitate bloody revolution. It is with this legend that this essay is concerned. Engels predicted that:

The fate of the middle classes will be sealed sooner than we have suggested. Commercial crises of ever-increasing severity (the most powerful stimulus to independent action on the part of the workers), coupled with the effects of foreign competition and the progressive ruin of the middle classes, will bring matters to a head before long. I do not think that the workers will put up with another commercial crisis. The next one – it is due in 1846 or 1847 – will probably lead to the repeal of the Corn Laws and the acceptance of the People's Charter. It remains to be seen how far the acceptance of the Charter will encourage the movement towards revolution. After the crisis of 1846 or 1847 the next crisis should (on the analogy of previous crises) occur in 1852 or 1853. It may be delayed by the repeal of the Corn Laws or it may be hastened by foreign competition or other circumstances. But before that crisis arrives the English workers will surely have reached the limits of their endurance. They will no longer be prepared to allow themselves to be exploited by the capitalists only to be thrown on the scrap heap when their services are no longer needed. If the English middle classes have not come to their senses by that time – and there is no reason to anticipate any change of heart in that quarter – then a revolution is to be expected. And it will be more violent than any previous revolution ... Popular

---

[1] Unless otherwise stated, the edition used in this essay is the Basil Blackwell edition, translated and edited by W. O. Henderson and W. H. Chaloner (Oxford, 1971).

52

fury will reach in intensity far greater than that which animated the French workers in 1793. The war of the poor against the rich will be the most bloodthirsty the world has ever seen.

Engels, moreover, by claiming that his history was scientific, took on the mantle of infallibility:

These are all conclusions that can be drawn with absolute certainty. They are based upon facts which cannot be disputed – facts of historical development and facts of human nature. It is particularly easy to forecast future events in England because in that country every aspect of social development is so plain and clear-cut. The revolution *must* come. It is now too late for a peaceful outcome of the affair to be possible.

The hints at qualification – a change of heart by the bourgeoisie – were dismissed.

I think that it is inevitable that open war will break out between the rich and the poor in England ... It is too late for the parties concerned to reach a peaceful solution. The gulf between the two classes is becoming wider and wider. The workers are becoming more and more imbued with the spirit of resistance. The feelings of the proletariat against their oppressors are becoming more and more bitter. The workers are moving from minor guerrilla skirmishes to demonstrations and armed conflicts of a more serious nature. Soon it will only be necessary to dislodge a stone and the whole avalanche will be set in motion.[2]

These passages have been quoted at some length, because they so clearly outline the *révolution manquée* thesis, and because Engels's admirers seldom mention the precision and confidence of his predictions. Unfortunately for Engels, and for those historians who applaud him and follow him, the revolution did not come – not in 1846 or 1847; not in 1852 or 1855; indeed, not ever. ('Revolution' is used here to denote either successful forcible change, aimed at overthrowing the existing government and implementing a fundamental reconstruction of society, or an attempt at such change that is successful enough to threaten seriously the existing government and its institutions.) Engels lived into the 1890s and realized not only that he had been wrong in his original predictions but also that he had to explain why he had been wrong. He had two excuses: embourgeoisement and prosperity. In a letter to Marx, dated 7 October 1858, Engels complained that 'the English proletariat is becoming more and more bourgeois, so that this most bourgeois of all nations is apparently aiming ultimately at the possession of a bourgeois aristocracy and a bourgeois proletariat as well as a bourgeoisie'.[3] The second excuse

---

[2] *Ibid.*, pp. 334–6.
[3] Engels to Marx, Manchester, 7 October 1858: *Selected Correspondences, 1846–1895, with Commentary and Notes: Karl Marx and Friedrich Engels*, The Marxist–Leninist Library (London, 1936), pp. 115–16. See also Engels to Marx, London, 9 April 1863: *ibid.*, p. 147.

can be found in the Preface to the 1892 English edition of *The Condition of the Working Class in England*, in which Engels argued that the economic crisis which would have precipitated the inevitable revolution had been circumvented by a remarkable commercial expansion in which the working classes had shared. 'The truth is this', Engels wrote:

During the period of England's industrial monopoly the English working class have, to a certain extent, shared in the benefits of the monopoly. These benefits were very unequally parcelled out amongst them; the privileged minority pocketed most, but even the great mass had at least a temporary share now and then. And that is the reason why, since the dying-out of Owenism, there has been no Socialism in England.

But the prophet in Engels could not be stifled: 'Even now the mere reduction of England's lion's share in the supply of the world's markets means stagnation, distress, excess of capital here, excess of unemployed workers there. What will it be when the increase of yearly production is brought to a complete stop?' And, ever hopeful, Engels could see already both the beginnings of international competition and economic decline and the consequent stirrings of revolt in the East End of London. 'The revival of the East End of London', he concluded, 'remains one of the greatest and most fruitful facts of this *fin de siècle*, and glad and proud I am to have lived to see it.'[4]

This is the classic version of the *révolution manquée* thesis, the thesis that England had a revolutionary situation in the early nineteenth century, but no revolution.[5] There were revolutions elsewhere in Europe, but although England had much social protest and some violence – riots and conflicts, mass meetings and monster petitions, strikes and lock-outs, machine-breaking and arson, agricultural unrest and ineffective revolutionary conspiracies[6] – there was no revolution. Nevertheless the evi-

---

[4] *The Condition of the Working Class in England in 1844: With a Preface Written in 1892*, by F. Engels, translated by F. K. Wischnewetzky (London, 1920), pp. xxvii–xxix. In the same Preface (p. xv), Engels referred to 'an aristocracy among the working-class' and the economic division of the working class which made it more bourgeois and less revolutionary. Here are the beginnings of another legend.

[5] There were many other writers in the period before 1850 who also predicted, or warned about, violence, but none were so influential in the long run as Engels. See, for example, J. P. Kay, *The Moral and Physical Condition of the Working Classes* (London, 1832), p. 112: 'If the higher classes ... will not endeavour to promote domestic comfort, virtue, and knowledge among them [the working classes], their misery, vice, and prejudice will prove volcanic elements, by whose explosive violence the structure of society may be destroyed.' See also J. F. Bray, *Labour's Wrongs and Labour's Remedy: or, The Age of Might and the Age of Right* (Leeds, 1839), p. 13.

[6] For details of civil disorders in the period of the Industrial Revolution, see, for example, J. Stevenson, *Popular Disturbances in England, 1700–1870* (London, 1979); J. Stevenson and R. Quinault, *Popular Protest and Public Order* (London, 1974); F. O. Darvall, *Popular Disturbances and Public Order in Regency England*, 2nd edn (Oxford University Press, 1969);

dence of discontent in England, and the existence of real revolutions in Europe,[7] have made some historians believe that there was a revolutionary threat in England before 1850, and the acceptance of a European-type revolution as the norm of working-class response to industrialization has biased many historians to ask the question, 'Why was there no revolution in England?', rather than the question, 'Why was there revolution in Europe?'.[8] The majority of historians, however, have argued that while industrialization created new, or enlarged old, social problems, it also provided, or was accompanied by, solutions: increasing wealth, humanitarianism, trade unions, co-operatives, religious revival and, above all, reform. The Hammonds, for example, stern critics of the Industrial Revolution, carefully documented the adverse effects of industrialization on rural, urban and skilled workers, and even hinted at revolution, but then traced 'the beginnings of a new society' in which 'the impulse to pursue wealth and the desire to create a civilization were matched against each other' so that England was able to 'turn the sharpest corner without revolution or violence'. In this transformation of society, the main contribution, according to the Hammonds, came from the governing classes, who passed legislation like the Factory Acts to remedy the evils of industrialization and then created an efficient civil service to see that the legislation was enforced.[9] To other historians, the working classes themselves were the instruments of reform (through trade unions and other working-class institutions) and of peaceful co-operation with the employing classes (through the influence of education and religion). 'Why was it', asks E. Halévy:

that of all countries in Europe England has been the most free from revolutions, violent crises and sudden changes? We have sought in vain to find the explanation by an analysis of her political institutions and economic organization. Her political institutions were such that society might easily have lapsed into anarchy had there existed in England a bourgeoisie animated by the spirit of revolution. And a system of economic production that was in fact totally without

---

M. I. Thomis, *The Luddites* (London, 1970); M. I. Thomis and P. Holt, *Threats of Revolution in Britain, 1789–1848* (London, 1977); J. P. Dunbabin, *Rural Discontent in Nineteenth Century Britain* (London, 1974); F. C. Mather, *Public Order in the Age of the Chartists* (Manchester, 1959).

[7] The word 'Europe' is here used in the pre-EEC sense, i.e. to refer to mainland Europe as distinct from the Atlantic islands which constitute 'the British Isles'.

[8] The assumption of a European revolutionary norm is widely accepted. See, for example, E. J. Hobsbawm, *The Age of Revolution, 1789–1848* (London, 1962) and C., L. and R. Tilly, *The Rebellious Century, 1830–1930* (Cambridge, Mass., 1975).

[9] See J. L. and B. Hammond, *The Village Labourer, The Town Labourer* and *The Skilled Labourer* (London, 1911, 1917 and 1919) and *The Rise of Modern Industry* (London, 1925), Ch. XV. Two chapters in *The Village Labourer* are entitled 'The Last Labourers' Revolt', and the Hammonds use freely terms like 'riot', 'rising' and 'rebellion'.

organization of any kind would have plunged the kingdom into violent revolution had the working classes found in the middle class leaders to provide it with a definite ideal, a creed, a practical programme. But the elite of the working class, the hard-working and capable bourgeois, had been imbued by the Evangelical movement with a spirit from which the established order had nothing to fear.[10]

Religion, and especially Methodism, according to Halévy, siphoned off both political passion and potential leadership into the chapels, where they were converted into class collaboration and the gospel of work.

But some of the most notable scholars of the Industrial Revolution either saw no revolutionary situation or threat, or, implausibly, saw a threat and failed to mention it in their writings. A. Toynbee, pioneer of Industrial Revolution studies, while arguing that industrialization led to 'a rapid alienation of classes and to the degradation of a large body of producers', was, nevertheless, scornful of those who believed that only revolution could solve the problems of the working classes.

We in England smile at all this as a mere dream, 'so remote does revolution seem from our slow course of even progress. But if it is remote, it is because we in England have taken steps to modify the conditions which make revolutions imminent... There are two great agencies which have been at work in England to produce that result: First, those voluntary agencies, the result of... self-help... and secondly, the action of the State.[11]

J. H. Clapham, arguing against those who 'cast a shadow over the constructive energies of the industrial revolution', saw the period of the Industrial Revolution as one of the peaceful advance of the working classes, both economically and politically.[12] H. L. Beales, in considering 'the response of labour' to the Industrial Revolution, argued that 'violence left no permanent influence on the English labour movement, however large it loomed in the eyes of contemporaries. Nor was it typical of it.' 'Far more significant than machine-breaking', he continued, 'was the rise of labour organizations.'[13] G. M. Young reckoned that: 'It is impossible to gauge the danger of a revolution which refused to happen.' And he warned that 'in estimating the alarm we must allow for the melodramatic streak in the early Victorian temperament', and that the 'generation [of the 1830s and 1840s] was still overshadowed by the revolutionary years and read itself in their volcanic light'. In any case,

---

[10] E. Halévy, *A History of the English People in 1815*, 4 vols. (London, 1938), III, 47. This thesis has been adopted enthusiastically by E. P. Thompson; see below.

[11] A. Toynbee, *Lectures on the Industrial Revolution in England* (London, 1884), p. 213.

[12] J. H. Clapham, *An Economic History of Modern Britain: The Early Railway Age, 1820–1850* (Cambridge, 1926), Chs. V and XIV.

[13] H. L. Beales, *The Industrial Revolution, 1750–1850* (London, 1958).

Young concluded, 'England had hardly the elements of a civil force capable of stopping disorder before it reaches the point where factories are burnt and the troops must shoot.'[14] T. S. Ashton's classic *The Industrial Revolution*, which contains the summing-up of a lifetime's study of England's industrialization, contains no discussion of revolution and only one mention of riots. Ashton admitted 'a growth of class feeling and bitterness', that 'under-employed and under-fed men were not over-nice in theorizing as to the cause of their distress' and hence resorted to machine-breaking, but he nowhere speculated on the threat or possibility of revolution.[15]

Since 1945, however, the *révolution manquée* thesis has thrived, and there is now a small group of influential historians who argue that the Industrial Revolution in England produced social conflict of an explicitly revolutionary character which, nevertheless, was resolved without real revolution. To these historians, of whom the best known are E. J. Hobsbawm and E. P. Thompson, class confict was the essential characteristic of English industrialization, and the absence of revolution was proof not of peaceful social evolution but of successful counter-revolution. The class struggle is the essence of history, they argue, and it cannot be eliminated by suppression or reform or prosperity. It is with these historians that this essay deals and, implicitly, with a larger group who, while not accepting *la révolution manquée* as a reality, nevertheless write as though revolution were a real possibility in England during the first half of the nineteenth century. Thus, for example, H. Perkin writes of 'the violent class struggles of the generation after Waterloo' as a preface to 'the rise of a viable class society'. 'The rise of a viable class society in Britain', he reasons, 'was in round terms an evolution of class conflict from the pursuit of civil war by other means to a process of mutual bargaining.'[16] As a result of this general acceptance of the possibility of revolution, and of an equally widespread interest in all forms of civil disorder,[17] it has been possible recently for two books, more or less explicitly on the theme of *la révolution manquée*, to appear: M. I. Thomis and P. Holt, *Threats of Revolution in Britain, 1789–1848* (London, 1977), and J. Stevenson, *Popular Disturbances in England, 1700–1870* (London, 1979). Even revolutions which never occurred look

[14] G. M. Young, *Victorian England: Portrait of an Age* (Oxford, 1936), p. 37.
[15] T. S. Ashton, *The Industrial Revolution, 1760–1830* (Oxford, 1948), pp. 153–4.
[16] H. Perkin, *The Origins of Modern English Society, 1780–1880* (London, 1969), pp. 340–1. Perkin sees violence (p. 342) as 'the mark of an immature class society in which the classes had not yet learned to live in peaceful co-existence with each other'.
[17] Here the literature is now extensive; but see in particular the work of G. Rudé, A. Soboul, E. Hobsbawm and C. Tilly.

more like the real thing when they command the research attention of scholars and the financial support of publishers. As a subject of continuing scholarship, *la révolution manquée* has definitely arrived.

II

To make clear just what the modern version of *la révolution manquée* is, there follows in this section a résumé of the writings on this subject by some of its leading exponents.

(a) E. J. Hobsbawm

We, who see the period from the 1780s to the 1840s in the light of later developments, see it simply as the initial phase of industrial capitalism. But might not [it] also be in its final phase? The question seems absurd, because it so obviously was not. This is to underestimate the instability and tension of this initial phase – particularly of the three decades after Waterloo – and the malaise of both the economy and those who thought seriously about its prospects.

Thus writes Hobsbawm in *Industry and Empire,* adding:

At no other period in modern British history have the common people been so persistently, profoundly, and often desperately dissatisfied. At no other period since the seventeenth century can we speak of large masses of them as revolutionary, or discern at least one moment of political crisis (between 1830 and the Reform Act of 1832) when something like a revolutionary situation might have developed.[18]

In *Labouring Men*, also Hobsbawm argues that:

It is conceivable that something like a 'revolutionary situation' might have developed, had the Unreformed Parliament not been wise enough to yield peacefully to the pressure of middle-class reformers ... Though there was no revolution in Britain in the eighteenth and nineteenth centuries, there was, nevertheless, a good deal of revolutionary feeling in large parts of the country, particularly during the bleak half-century from the middle 1790s to the late 1840s.[19]

Of the agricultural labourer, Hobsbawm and Rudé write that, in 1830: 'His situation was such as to make some sort of rebellion inevitable.' The Captain Swing movement 'was as near to a national movement as so spontaneous and unorganized an upsurge could be'. 'Perhaps its greatest tragedy was that it never succeeded in linking up with the rebellion of mine, mill and city.'[20] Elsewhere, in *The Age of Revolution, 1789–1848,*

[18] E. J. Hobsbawm, *Industry and Empire* (London, 1968), pp. 54–5.
[19] *Idem, Labouring Men: Studies in the History of Labour* (London, 1964), p. 24.
[20] E. J. Hobsbawm and G. Rudé, *Captain Swing* (London, 1968), pp. 16, 17, 19. Ironically, the authors add, 'But it is not the historian's task to speculate on what might have been. His duty is to show what happened and why.'

Hobsbawm argues more generally for the inevitability of revolution: 'the world of the 1840s was out of balance... Given the remarkable acceleration of social change after 1830, and the revival of the world revolutionary movement, it was clearly inevitable that changes – whatever their precise institutional nature – could not long be delayed.' 'Never in European history and rarely anywhere else has revolutionism been so endemic, so general, so likely to spread by spontaneous contagion as well as by deliberate propaganda.'[21] Here, clearly, is the *révolution manquée* thesis. Hobsbawm explains the absence of revolution in several ways: 'the restraint of both Whig and Tory parties', [22] and the wisdom of 'the Unreformed Parliament... to yield peacefully to the pressure of the middle-class reformers (or to be exact, to the pressure of the masses under the leadership of the middle-class reformers)';[23] 'the political incapacity of its [revolutionary] leaders, local and sectional differences, and an inability for concerted national action other than the preparation of monster petitions';[24] and the absence of a crisis of sufficient magnitude to precipitate revolution. Hobsbawm notes that, 'as Lenin argued – a specialist on the subject – a deterioration of the condition of life for the masses, and an increase in their political activity, is not enough to bring about a revolution. There must also be a crisis in the affairs of the ruling order, and a body of revolutionaries capable of directing and leading the movement. Both these were absent.'[25] The classic recipe for revolution – an alliance between the middle and working classes – had only temporary success in England. 'From 1829 and 1832 their discontents fused in the demand for Parliamentary Reform, behind which the masses threw their riots and demonstrations, the businessmen the power of economic boycott. After 1832, when several of the demands of the middle-class radicals were met, the workers' movements fought and failed alone.' So, in spite of 'that worst of nineteenth-century depressions, 1841–2', 'pervasive social and political unrest [which] reflected not merely material poverty but social pauperization', 'waves of desperation [which] broke time and again over the country: in 1811–13, in 1815–17, in 1819, in 1826, in 1829–35, in 1838–42, in 1843–4, in 1846–8', and mass movements in the forms of the 'general trades union' (and the 'general strike') and Chartism, there was no revolution.[26]

---

[21] Hobsbawm, *Age of Revolution*, pp. 356–7, 136.
[22] *Ibid.*, p. 139.
[23] Hobsbawm, *Labouring Men*, p. 24.
[24] *Idem, Age of Revolution*, p. 152.
[25] *Idem, Labouring Men*, p. 24.
[26] *Idem, Industry and Empire*, pp. 58, 59, 74, 75.

(b) E. P. Thompson

Thompson is perhaps the historian most disappointed about the absence of revolution in England between 1790 and 1830. He is convinced that a revolutionary situation existed, that near-revolutions occurred and that, given a slightly different course of history, a revolution would have occurred. 'In the 1790s', Thompson writes, 'something like an "English revolution" took place, of profound importance in shaping the consciousness of the post-war working class', the result of the 'conjunction between the grievances of the majority and the aspirations articulated by the politically conscious minority'. In 1831 and 1832, again, 'the country was *in fact* in a state of revolutionary crisis'. In both 1819 and 1832, 'a revolution was possible (and in the second year it was very close)'. Throughout the period there were, according to Thompson, both 'the great political risings of the "mob"' (like the Gordon Riots and the Bristol Riots) and the 'organized forms of sustained illegal action or quasi-insurrection' (like Luddism and the Rebecca Riots). There were, in consequence, 'insurrectionary climaxes', 'the preliminaries to civil war' and near-misses ('If at any of these crises the "news" *had* come, if a major centre had been "captured" by the revolutionaries, then insurrection might have spread rapidly to other districts'). However, when, for example, the 'revolt' of the agricultural labourers came in 1830, it was ineffective 'with its curiously indecisive and unbloodthirsty mobs'. The failure of the revolution in England, Thompson argues, was mainly because of counter-revolution, Methodism and constitutionalism, but also because 'the "natural" alliance between an impatient radically-minded industrial bourgeoisie and a formative proletariat' was either broken or never developed. The counter-revolution began in the 1790s when 'the revolutionary impulse was strangled in its infancy'. 'The counter-revolutionary panic of the ruling classes expressed itself in every part of social life; in attitudes to trade-unionism, to the education of the people, to their sports and manners, to their publications and societies, and their political rights.' Methodism was important because 'its gains were greatest among the new industrial working class' and because its ministers 'regarded it as their duty to manipulate the submissiveness of their followers and to discipline all deviant growth within the Church which could give offence to authority'. Methodism, according to Thompson, was a 'component of the psychic process of counter-revolution', 'a ritualized form of psychic masturbation', whose 'box-like, blackening chapels stood in the industrial districts like great traps for the human psyche'. Finally, 'The fact that revolution did not occur was due, in part, to the deep constitutionalism of that part of the Radical tradition of which Cobbett . . . was the spokesman; and in part to the skill of the middle-class Radicals in offering exactly that compromise which might not weaken but strengthen both the State and property-rights against the working-class threat.' And so there was no revolution, although, according to Thompson, there could and should have been one, had it not been for 'the flood-tide of counter-revolutionary feeling'.[27] After the failure of Chartism to overthrow the capitalist system, however, the working class proceeded in the following decades 'to warren it from end to end'. Success was only delayed?

(c) J. Saville and J. Foster

Hobsbawm and Thompson are certainly the leading exponents of the *révolution manquée* thesis, but there are other, if less influential, historians who argue the revolutionary thesis vigorously and explain the absence of revolution differently. J. Saville, for example, argues that a radical-revolutionary tradition in the first half of the nineteenth century gave way after 1850 to 'the theory and practice of class collaboration'. 'Labourism, as it developed through the third quarter of the nineteenth century, was a theory and practice which accepted the possibility of social change within the existing framework of society; which rejected the revolutionary violence and action implicit in Chartist ideas of physical force; and which increasingly recognised the working of political democracy of the parliamentary variety as the practicable means of achieving its own aims and objectives.' The working classes accepted 'labourism', as Saville calls it, because they were unable to recognize the realities of their situation ('false consciousness'?), and this because of the lack of a revolutionary intellectual elite to inform them. There was, according to Saville, a 'general parochial quality of intellectual life in Britain', a 'general mediocrity', an 'intellectual greyness' and a 'complacent acceptance of the fundamentals of bourgeois society'. Thus, 'while the philosophy and doctrines of labourism are deeply rooted in the historical evolution of industrial society, it does not follow that it was "inevitable"... What helped to make it "inevitable" was the absence of any sustained critique of bourgeois society by its traditional intellectuals'.[28]

J. Foster is concerned with 'the development and decline of a

---

[27] E. P. Thompson, *The Making of the English Working Class* (London, 1963), pp. 177, 168, 671, 62, 74, 691, 652, 226, 177, 351, 381, 368, 817 and 177 (page references in the order of the quotations in the text).

[28] J. Saville, 'The Ideology of Labourism', in R. Benewick *et al.* (eds.), *Knowledge and Belief in Politics* (London, 1973), pp. 215, 222, 224, 225. Saville believes strongly that the intellectuals of Britain were mediocre and that the working classes were stupid.

revolutionary class consciousness in the second quarter of the [nineteenth] century'. According to Foster, there was 'a critical change ... in the structure of English society in the middle years of the century'. Foster sees the period as one of a series of crises, 'when the whole objective basis of the social system seemed to be visibly breaking up'. In 1812 there was 'the use of industrial violence for mass mobilization'; in 1816, 'local insurrections' combined with 'an attempt to overcome the weakness of London by marching south a mass of northern industrial workers'; in 1819, 'a fairly sophisticated (and naturally concerted) plan of mass mobilization'; in 1820, 'an old-style insurrection'; in 1834, at attempt 'to harness the rising momentum of extra-legal unionism to a more syndicalist challenge to state power'; in 1842, 'the strategy involved the use of masses of armed, highly organized but ambivalently peaceful strikers to engulf and isolate troops'; in 1848 there was 'an almost straight repeat of the insurrectionist plans of 1817 and 1818'. In these events Foster sees an 'unchallengeable' continuity of revolutionary violence, but no successful revolution. 'Why', asks Foster, 'if the movement was so effective in mobilizing mass support, did it ultimately collapse so completely?' Foster's answer to this question is 'liberalization' ('a collective *ruling-class* response to a social system in crisis'), 'a critical change ... in the structure of English society in the middle years of the century' ('an altogether new pattern of social subdivision within the labour force'), and the absence of an external stimulus ('it should be remembered that even Lenin's revolutions required the external stimulus of war'). What destroyed the revolutionary movement was 'its inability to maintain its offensive' and 'the fundamental modification of the socio-economic system here called liberalization'.[29]

(d)

Common to those writers is the conviction that, even if there was no revolution in England, *there might have been*; indeed, *there should have been*. This is the thesis of *la révolution manquée*. *Manqué*, according to the *Oxford English Dictionary*, is 'that might have been but is not, that has missed being'. The historical problem for these writers is that of explaining *why* what might have been but was not, was not. Their reasoning, therefore, has common pattern which combines proposition with theory, fact and problem in logical order, as follows:

[29] J. Foster, *Class Struggle and the Industrial Revolution* (London, 1974), pp. 1, 3, 7, 144, 145.

La révolution manquée

Scene I: to 1850

I, Proposition: there was a revolutionary situation in England, 1790–1850.

    Ia, Proof: (i) Theory: the theory of capitalist development.

                  (ii) History: the evidence of riots, machine-breaking etc.

II, Fact: there was no revolution.

III, Reconciliation of proposition and fact: if there was a revolutionry situation and no revolution, there was a counter-revolution.

IV, The historian's task: to identify the counter-revolution in its direct forms (such as political suppression) and/or its indirect forms (religion, education, constitutionalism, etc.).

Scene II: after 1850

I, Proposition: there was no revolutionary situation in England after 1850.

    Ia, Proof: (i) Theory: the theories of imperialism and embourgeoisement

                  (ii) History: the evidence of declining violence and increasing class collaboration.

II, Fact: there was no revolution.

III, Reconciliation of Scenes I and II: there was a turning-point in 1850, before which there was a revolutionary situation, after which there was not, so that there was in 1850 a conversion of the working classes from class conflict to class collaboration.

IV, The historian's task: to identify the process of conversion (embourgeoisement and false consciousness; imperialism and the aristocracy of labour; democratization and labourism, etc.).

III

What historical and methodological issues are raised by this survey of the literature of *la révolution manquée*? The most obvious problem is that of explaining and reconciling the different interpretations of the course of events in early-nineteenth-century England. What actually happened? Why is there so much speculation about what might have happened? Why is Thompson full of revolution, while Ashton does not mention it? If there had been a revolution, what would have been its achievements? If there was no revolution, could there have been one?

Would there have been a revolution, for example, if there had been a more severe economic crisis and an external stimulus (as Hobsbawm and Foster suggest), or less religion and less intelligent government (as Thompson and Hobsbawm suggest), or more effective leadership and an alliance between the proletariat and the bourgeoisie (as Hobsbawm, Thompson, Saville and Foster all suggest), or a revolutionary intellectual elite (as Saville suggests)? Is Thompson correct when he writes: 'If at any of these crises the "news" *had* come, if a major centre had been "captured" by the revolutionaries, then insurrection might have spread rapidly to other districts'?[30] Is Saville correct when he writes: 'Had their [Carlyle's and Ruskin's] arguments gone beyond a critique of industrialization to a consideration of the possibilities of a new social order their contribution to the intellectual enlightenment of working men would have been much more far-reaching'?[31] Would the Swing Riots have been successful, as Hobsbawm and Rudé argue, had they 'succeeded in linking up with the rebellion of mine, mill and city'?[32] Would an alliance between 'an impatient radically-minded industrial bourgeoisie and a formative proletariat', had it not been broken, have been successful in revolutionary endeavour, as Thompson implies?[33]

It is impossible here to answer all these questions, but three points can be made. First, there is carelessness in the use of words, especially the word 'revolution'; there is implied approval of revolution, without consideration of means or ends or of the likely outcome of any revolution; and, third, there is a remarkable reluctance, against the evidence, to abandon the idea of a revolution that should have been the inevitable result of industrialization. As regards terms, the revolutionary-minded historians use a number of words more or less interchangeably as though they all have the same meaning, thus making it difficult to find out exactly what 'revolution' means. The words fall into two groups, on the one hand strong words like 'revolution', 'revolt', 'rebellion', 'insurrection', 'rising', 'crisis', and 'riot', and on the other, weaker words like 'tension', 'protest', 'resistance', 'desperation', 'unrest' and even 'radicalism'. When such words are used interchangeably, degrees of revolutionary action are lumped together and confused, and widely varying intentions and achievements are conflated. This blurring of distinctions allows these historians to argue that any form of protest, or any degree of violence, is revolutionary and hence a threat to

---

[30] Thompson, *Making of the English Working Class*, p. 652.
[31] Saville, 'Ideology of Labourism', p. 223.
[32] Hobsbawm and Rudé, *Captain Swing*, p. 19.
[33] Thompson, *Making of the English Working Class*, pp. 177–8.

government. The general effect of such rhetoric, therefore, is to inflate levels of protest and violence and to give spurious reality to the idea of a revolutionary threat.

This is not the place to trace the history of the idea of revolution, but there is in the minds of these historians both an eighteenth-century view of revolution (a romantic view of revolutionaries overthrowing monarchs and autocratic governments in the name of freedom and justice) and a Marxist view (in which revolution plays a crucial role in the predetermined evolution of society). There is no doubt that these historians assume that revolution was, or would have been, a good thing, and that, in the nature of industrial capitalism, it was necessary and inevitable, or should have been necessary and inevitable. The fact that there was no revolution makes it imperative for them to explain why the inevitable did not happen. Hence the preoccupation with 'what might have happened'. Because revolution was, or would have been, a good thing, the ends obviously justified, or would have justified, the means – although none of these historians gives any clear analysis of what the long-term consequences of revolution would have been. Not only do they not look beyond the revolution; they do not even look at the short-term implications of making revolutions in terms of violence and bloodshed. Only Hobsbawm explicitly considers bloodshed, and he dismisses it as unimportant and irrelevant. Of the French Revolution, for example, Hobsbawm writes that the year of the Terror was 'terrible and glorious', 'its mass killings were relatively modest: 17,000 official executions in fourteen months', 'it was an era not to be measured by everyday criteria', 'it was neither pathological nor apocalyptic', 'its achievement was superhuman'.[34]

It would seem reasonable, since there was no revolution, to forget about revolution and to concentrate on what actually happened. But there has been a reluctance, indeed a refusal, to let the idea of an English revolution die. This commitment of some historians to revolution can be attributed, charitably, to a mistaken interpretation of the historical evidence, or, less charitably, to a doctrinaire belief in the Marxist theory of capitalist development. Since mistaken interpretations can be corrected, and the Marxist theories here outlined can be tested, both against the facts, it is necessary to look at the history of the period to see what evidence there is which could give plausibility to the ideas of revolution, threatened revolution, attempted revolution and potential revolution.

No historian has yet comprehensively analysed, charted and mapped

[34] Hobsbawm, *Age of Revolution*, pp. 91, 94.

65

the history of civil disorder in England during the Industrial Revolution. There is plenty of contemporary evidence, however, to demonstrate that there was a problem of 'law and order', of 'popular disturbances' and of 'public order'.[35] And there is, now, a large modern literature on particular events and aspects of the history of public disturbances.[36] There were, for example, nation-wide food-riots in 1795–6, 1799–1801, 1810–13 and 1816–18; extensive machine-breaking in 1811–12, 1816, 1822, 1826, 1830 and 1842; widespread rural disturbances after 1816, culminating in the disorders of 1830–2;[37] and, included in these, some events that have been made famous by the historians–Luddism, the Peterloo Massacre, the Swing Riots, the Bristol Riots and the Chartist Movement. There was also a contemporary debate on law and order, on crime and crime prevention, on the 'labouring classes and the dangerous classes'.[38] The evidence is such that it could be interpreted as proof of revolution induced by industrialization, but only with damaging qualifications.

First, popular disturbance was not a new phenomenon and was as characteristic of the seventeenth and eighteenth centuries as of the nineteenth.[39] Indeed, the conclusion to be drawn from the historical evidence of popular disturbance is that revolution had been threatening long before the Industrial Revolution. This does not disprove the existence of a revolutionary threat during the Industrial Revolution; but it does suggest that, if such a threat did exist, it was not uniquely associated with industrial capitalism. Second, there were during the Industrial Revolution people who dreamed about revolution (and planned it), and people who feared revolution (and planned against it). There were also people who talked about revolution, like the 'physical force' wing of the Chartists, and people who wrote about revolution, like J. F. Bray.[40] But dreaming, talking, writing and even planning revolution do not in themselves constitute a revolutionary movement or

---

[35] These terms were used in one of the first books on this subject, M. Beloff, *Public Order and Popular Disturbances, 1660–1714* (Oxford, 1938), and subsequently by Stevenson, *Popular Disturbances* and Mather, *Public Order in the Age of the Chartists*.

[36] For example, Thomis, *The Luddites*; J. P. de Castro, *The Gordon Riots* (Oxford, 1926); W. J. Shelton, *English Hunger and Industrial Disorders* (Toronto, 1973); D. Read, *Peterloo: The 'Massacre' and its Background* (Manchester, 1973); A. Briggs (ed.), *Chartist Studies* (London, 1959).

[37] Stevenson, *Popular Disturbances*, pp. 91, 237, 244; Thomis and Holt, *Threats of Revolution in Britain*, pp. 24–9, 32–7.

[38] See, for example, D. Hay *et al.*, *Albion's Fatal Tree: Crime and Society in Eighteenth Century England* (London, 1975) and D. Philips, *Crime and Authority in Victorian England: The Black Country, 1835–1860* (London, 1978).

[39] See Beloff, *Public Order and Popular Disturbances* and Stevenson, *Popular Disturbances*.

[40] Bray, *Labour's Wrongs and Labour's Remedy*, p. 13.

a revolutionary threat unless they are translated into effective action, and there is no evidence of effective revolutionary action. Third, the existing institutions for the maintenance of law and order – the police, the magistrates and other civil authorities, the army and the militia – were inadequate both in size and in efficiency, and were certainly incapable of handling large-scale problems of public disorder.[41] Had the working classes really revolted, nothing could have stopped them; certainly not the police, and only doubtfully the army.[42] And so the absence of dangerous disorder is, in itself, a proof of the absence of any serious attempt at revolution. Fourth, at no time, however, did civil disturbance seriously threaten law and order on any large scale; at no time was government seriously challenged; at no time was there bloody confrontation of any magnitude between the populace and the authorities. In the early 1830s, and again in the 1840s, the popular movement for parliamentary reform united large numbers of people behind reform programmes with a great deal of noisy enthusiasm but with very little violence.[43] And even when violence threatened or occurred, the government in London was reluctant to intervene, preferring to leave 'law and order' to the local authorities. There was a particular reluctance to commit the army to any peace-keeping role. 'The behaviour of the Government' to Chartism, Mather writes, 'was ... characterised by forbearance and restraint'.[44]

The basic misunderstanding of the *révolution manquée* school lies in its interpretation of the working-class response to industrialization. The Industrial Revolution produced both social strains and opportunities, and the working classes responded creatively and responsibly to both. The creation of working-class organizations was more significant in this response than any working-class violence; and, in any case, the level of violence has been exaggerated.[45] What is surprising, in retrospect, is not that there was so much violence, but that there was so little! Chartism, for example, the first mass political movement of the working classes of

[41] See Mather, *Public Order in the Age of the Chartists*, for an account of the administration of law and order.

[42] Paradoxically, this proposition supports Thompson and Hobsbawm when they claim that 'if' the 'revolutions' had spread, they would have been successful.

[43] See M. Brock, *The Great Reform Act* (London, 1973).

[44] F. C. Mather, 'The Government and the Chartists', in Briggs (ed.), *Chartist Studies*, p. 395.

[45] On the magnitude of violence, even the *révolution manquée* school emphasizes its low level: 'curiously indecisive and unbloodthirsty mobs' (Thompson, *Making of the English Working Class*, p. 226); 'highly organized but ambivalently peaceful strikes' (Foster, *Class Struggle*, p. 143); 'inert and passive' rural workers (Hobsbawm and Rudé, *Captain Swing* p. 17). Other historians are less surprised: Stevenson, Thomis, Ashton, Clapham, and Beales, for example.

England, was an almost bloodless phenomenon. The two most famous riots in the first half of the nineteenth century, Peterloo and Bristol, resulted in a total of twenty-three deaths; and the most serious disturbance of the century of the Industrial Revolution, the Gordon Riots, in which 210 people died, was unique in the magnitude of its violence and bloodshed. To understand the working classes of England it is necessary not to concentrate on spasmodic outbursts of protest and violence but to examine their economic, social and political progress, in terms of living standards, status, representation and organizations. Except for a small minority, the workers of England were too sensible to wish for revolution and too prudent to plan for it. They recognized the realities of economic and political life and sought success within those realities. It is their lack of desire for violence which is so obvious to the objective observer, and it is this lack which so annoys the *révolution manquée* school. They claim, therefore, that the working classes must have been stupid, or timid, or suppressed, or bribed, or leaderless; it could not have been that they knew what they were doing and recognized that they were gaining from industrialization both in real income and in status without resort to violence.

IV

To cling to *la révolution manquée* is to perpetuate false problems and to concentrate historical effort in the wrong direction – to identify counter-revolutions, turning-points, conversions and structural transformations, none of which existed. This only leads to the history of possibilities. If there is to be more controversy about the Industrial Revolution, let it not be on non-problems. Not that this plea is likely to change the views of the historians who write about *la révolution manquée* who have political as well as historical purposes in mind. They use the theory of the revolution that failed to support the following propositions, all of which have contemporary political implications. First, industrial capitalism, by exploiting the workers, produced and produces a class conflict and the threat of revolution. Second, revolution was and is frustrated by the reactionary forces in society – government, army, police, schools and churches – either by force or by persuasion. Third, the working classes were and are still converted to bourgeois values and were and are diverted from their historic role of revolution and the destruction of capitalism. The fact that none of these propositions is historically accurate does not inhibit the historians who propagate them; nor does it prevent them from using the myth of *la révolution manquée* to condemn capitalism and to blame it for the ills of the modern world.

PART II

England and the Low Countries in pre-industrial times

5

Bruges as a trading centre in the early modern period

J. A. VAN HOUTTE

For educational purposes, historical findings are often presented in black and white terms and come to maintain themselves thus in the memory of the general public. One striking example of this is provided by the sequence of the chief trading centres of the Low Countries. In the common view, Bruges, the great market of the later Middle Ages, collapsed by the end of the fifteenth century, to be replaced in the sixteenth by the almost sudden, glorious emergence of Antwerp. A generation of historical research has revised this image. It appears now that the transfer of the market function from Bruges to Antwerp was a process of longer duration, extending over more than a century before the evidence of Bruges's complete decline was decisive.[1] Less attention has been paid so far to the fortune of Bruges after this downfall. The present essay will argue that the Flemish town, instead of sinking outright into the oblivion of a dead city, maintained itself as a trading centre of some importance during the years of Antwerp's dominance, and also after the latter town had yielded to the supremacy of Amsterdam in the course of the Low Countries' War of Religion at the end of the sixteenth century.

I

Bruges played this part despite its difficult access to the high seas. Indeed, this was no novelty. Even before the time of its commercial flowering,

[1] J. A. van Houtte, 'La Genèse du grand marché international d'Anvers à la fin du Moyen Âge', *Revue Belge de Philologie et d'Histoire*, 19 (1940), 87–126; *idem*, 'The Rise and Decline of the Market of Bruges', *Economic History Review*, 2nd Series, 19 (1966), 29–47; *idem*, *De geschiedenis van Brugge* (Tielt and Bussum, 1982); H. van der Wee, *The Growth of the Antwerp Market and the European Economy: Fourteenth–Sixteenth Centuries*, 3 vols. (The Hague, 1963).

when it inherited, from the end of the thirteenth century on, the central market function of the Champagne fairs, it had to cope with the unsatisfactory conditions of navigation resulting from the gradual silting-up of the Zwin River, which connected it with the coast. Despite constant efforts and considerable expense, the hydrographic state of the Zwin had become simply hopeless by the end of the fifteenth century. The outport of Sluis, at the river's mouth, dried up at every low tide, and the ships at anchor lay aground for about six hours. Nevertheless, it was not deserted. Under the guidance of pilots, ships of up to 200 tons burden, exceptionally even more, continued to visit it during the first half of the sixteenth century. The last two Venetian galleys, of 500 and 700 tons respectively, moored at Sluis in 1520. However, many ships did suffer damage by stranding, and the Zwin roads were increasingly abandoned in favour of safer moorings, either a couple of miles off the Flemish coast or, more often, off Arnemuiden, the outport of Middleburgh, on the east coast of the isle of Walcheren.[2]

After various vain attempts to restore the navigability of the river, for which the town tried without success to obtain financial support from the whole province of Flanders, it was decided to dig an entirely new waterway, to a depth of twelve feet. This was opened to shipping in 1566, and proved navigable for smaller sea-going vessels. In 1568, seven Spanish ships, one of them of 114 tons burden, reached Bruges along it. Unfortunately, this was precisely the time when the Revolt of the Netherlands broke out. During the revolt, Sluis, at the mouth of the canal, was occupied by the insurgents, who did their best to blockade the trade of the territory under Spanish domination. Thus, Bruges's access to the sea was cut off, first from 1586 until the ephemeral Spanish reconquest of Sluis in 1597, then for good after 1604. The construction of a Spanish fort opposite Sluis in 1605, over the very bed of the canal, put the latter effectively out of use. This necessitated henceforth a costly transshipment, apart from the danger of political interference, and the canal was almost entirely abandoned.[3]

It was not long, however, before it was replaced. As early as 1584,

---

[2] R. Degryse, 'Brugge en de pilotage van de Spaanse vloot in het Zwin in de XVIe eeuw', *Handelingen van het Genootschap voor Geschiedenis, gesticht onder de benaming Société d'Emulation, te Brugge*, 117 (1980), 105 and 136–66.

[3] L. Gilliodts-van Severen, 'Bruges port de mer: étude historique sur l'état de cette question principalement dans le cours du seizième siècle d'après des documents inédits reposant aux archives de la ville de Bruges', *Annales de la Société d'Emulation pour l'Etude de l'Histoire et des Antiquités de la Flandre*, 44 (1894), 1–540; A. de Smet, *Histoire du Zwin* (Antwerp, n.d.), reprinted in *Album A. de Smet* (Brussels, 1974), pp. 64–9; M. K. E. Gottschalk, 'Het verval van Brugge als wereldmarkt', *Tijdschrift voor Geschiedenis*, 66 (1953), 1–26; Degryse, 'Brugge en de pilotage', pp. 105–32.

Bruges had obtained grants from the government for digging two canals towards Ghent and Ostend, mainly with a view to inland transport. The War of Religion delayed the completion of this work until the 1620s. The Archdukes Albert and Isabella, sovereigns of the Southern Netherlands between 1598 and 1621, had urged it strongly during the Twelve Years' Truce (1609–21). They hoped that it would ensure their possessions a free outlet to the sea, now that the Dutch Republic was closing the Lower Scheldt to direct navigation between Antwerp and the outer world. Furthermore, another canal was branched off the one from Bruges to Ostend, to connect Nieuport in 1638 and Dunkirk in 1640 with this network of waterways. The loss of the latter town in 1658, however, ruined the expectations fostered in the Spanish Netherlands with regard to the part which it was to play in their trading arrangements.

In Bruges itself, port facilities were considerably improved by the digging of a spacious dock and the construction in 1665 of a warehouse on the northern outskirts of the town, where the Ostend canal began. These were repeatedly enlarged, and the canals excavated. The dock was undoubtedly the limit of navigation for by far the majority of ships coming from or bound for Ostend and the sea. The connection between the Ghent and Ostend canals was utterly inefficient. It had to make use of the shallow and narrow waterways, mostly natural, flowing across the town, which allowed passage only to very small craft. It was not until 1751 that it was decided to cut through the town the Coupure, a broad and deep junction, able to take sea-going vessels of a tonnage common at the time. It was opened in the direction of Ostend in 1758 and in that of Ghent in 1774.[4]

In addition to unsatisfactory hydrographic conditions, shipping in Flanders was also hampered by the claims made by the boatmen's guilds at Bruges, as well as in Ghent and in Ostend, on the transshipment on local boats of cargoes passing through their towns on board ships registered elsewhere. This resulted in a bitter contest between the three towns concerned, which was protracted despite repeated government intervention until the French conquest abolished all local privileges. As early as 1623, the Supreme Court at Mechlin enjoined the boatmen of

---

[4] Y. Urbain, 'La Formation du réseau des voies navigables en Belgique: développements du système des voies d'eau et politique des transports sous l'Ancien Régime', *Bulletin de l'Institut de Recherches Economiques de l'Université de Louvain*, 10 (1938–9), 278–9, 281, 284–5, 295–9; L. Gilliodts-van Severen, *Cartulaire de l'ancienne Estaple de Bruges: recueil de documents concernant le commerce intérieur et maritime, les relations internationales et l'histoire économique de cette ville*, 4 vols. (Bruges, 1904–6), III, 424–31, IV, 184; M. Ryckaert, 'De Coupure en het "Ijzeren Hekken" te Brugge', *Het Brugs Ommeland*, 19 (1979), 362–76.

Bruges and Ostend to allow each other free passage, but both sides seem to have disregarded the judgement. In 1664, free passage was granted to all foreigners or inhabitants of the Spanish Netherlands on their way to and from the sea. This decree fitted into the mercantilist efforts of the government to develop the country's trade, as did also the digging of the new dock, but it did not infringe the boatmen's claim on breaking bulk. Indeed, it was not observed for long: Ostend had to be called to order as early as 1669 and 1676, and the regulation had certainly fallen into disuse at Bruges by the eighteenth century. The Council of State, governing the Southern Netherlands under the control of the Anglo-Dutch coalition, even acknowledged in 1705 the prohibition by Bruges on ships from Dunkirk and Dieppe moving on inland; in 1725, Brussels skippers were its victims.

No wonder that freights for the country's shipments overseas via Bruges and Ostend were notably more expensive than those for export via the 'closed' Scheldt, making use of the Dutch intermediary. Thus the purpose of the Flemish canals, as it had been conceived by the archdukes, was achieved only very partially. Still less was it achieved for ships from Bruges, as there were too many boatmen, sixty-three in 1737, working by roster. Protected by their corporation monopoly, they charged high prices in order to draw a sufficient income from their few journeys and moreover gave their customers only poor service. It was senseless to have dug the Coupure without rescinding the boatmen's privileges. The cutting had been commissioned by the Austrian authorities, according to the maxims of mercantilism which inspired them, in order to promote a closer economic unity of the Belgian territories which they had governed since 1713. In reality the 'cuttings' plan originated from Ghent's wish to be accessible to sea-going ships. This was reason enough for the Bruges skippers, supported by the civic authorities, to oppose it fiercely, for fear of losing part of Bruges's port traffic to Ghent. Despite a government decree of 1753, again granting free passage to all sea-going craft, Bruges attempted, in December of that year, to stop a vessel from Nantes, bound for Ghent, and succeeded in 1755 in having the decree repealed as a matter of principle. As for inland lighters, free passage, instead of being granted to lighters registered anywhere in the Southern Netherlands, as had been intended in 1664, was limited in 1753 to those registered in the province of Flanders.

After 1755, exemptions from the prohibition on free passage were granted now and then by the government in favour of Ghent, despite the ill-feelings of Bruges. They were especially numerous during the American War of Independence, when Bruges and Ostend were used as sanctuaries, in order to maintain Anglo-Dutch trade after the Dutch Republic had become a belligerent on the American side in 1780. Of course, the end of hostilities was followed by a decline in the traffic of the Flemish ports. This made Bruges particularly sensitive again to infringements of the 1755 regulation. By way of compromise, dispensation from breaking bulk was restricted to ships flying the imperial flag, in effect those owned by Habsburg subjects in the Southern Netherlands. The political unrest which heralded the revolt against the emperor Joseph II allowed Ghent to retort by restoring on its own authority the general compulsion to break bulk within its walls. Apparently, a compromise was reached after some months between Ghent and Bruges, probably on the understanding that the latter would henceforth be accommodating in point of exemptions from the 1755 decree.[5]

Besides shipping, inland transport was a matter of concern to the authorities, at least in the eighteenth century. For the first time since the Roman era, efficient metalled turnpike roads were built in order to improve overland traffic with Bruges. The first one, towards Blankenberge, then primarily a fishing port, aimed at facilitating the town's fish supply. Likewise the construction of roads to a couple of villages in the marshlands to the north of Bruges served to improve the town's supply of agricultural produce. Other roads, to Courtrai and Menin, aimed to connect with interregional and international trade routes, and especially to attract part of the commerce with France. The attention thus paid to the communications system on land and water is proof in itself of the persistence of the movement of trade in town, and of the efforts made to maintain and develop it, after Bruges had passed its medieval heyday.

II

By the end of the Middle Ages the market of Bruges had fallen to a mere shadow of the hegemony which it exercised at the apex of its power. Business was mostly transacted at the Brabantine marts of Antwerp and Bergen. Ever more merchants moved their residence to Antwerp, where traffic gradually broke through the intermittent framework of the fairs and tended to spread over the whole year. Bruges, supported by other Flemish towns, lodged repeated complaints against what it considered to

[5] Gilliodts, *Estaple*, III, 390–4, 398–408, 480–2, 489–2, 554–5, 651–3, IV, 17–18, 106–8, 128–42, 184–8, 220–35, 340–3, 397–401; H. van Houtte, *Histoire économique de la Belgique à la fin de l'ancien régime* (Ghent, 1920), pp. 219–30; J. de Smet, 'De doorvaart voor de binnenscheepvaart te Brugge in de XVIIe eeuw', *Annales de la Société d'Emulation de Bruges*, 108 (1971), 192–208.

be a breach of law. Several times, on the last occasion in 1532, the protraction of the fairs was prohibited by government decree or by judgement of the Supreme Court, but to no avail.[6] Antwerp's victory over its Flemish precursor was the more evident as the years passed.

It seems that the political disturbances during the minority of Philip the Fair (1477–93) accelerated the exodus from Bruges of the alien merchants. They had the effect of interrupting the communications between the town and the sea almost continuously from 1487 until 1492 and of making the decision of the traders to leave for Antwerp irreversible. The same cannot be said of the 'nations' or 'consulates', the national corporations in which the foreign residents were grouped. Like every institution, they behaved in a more conservative way. The regent Maximilian of Austria had invited them twice to abandon their seats, in 1484 and in 1488, the second time specifically in order to repair to Antwerp. Yet within a year of the restoration of peace in 1492 the 'nations' had returned. Indeed, the town encouraged them to do so by making lavish presents to their authorities and by extending liberally the privileges of some of them, notably the Italians and the Spanish. A Sicilian 'nation', no doubt made up of a few silk-merchants of Messina, was even given corporate status for the first time, though apparently with little result for it was never heard of again. Moreover, the town promised to give the Aragonese, Biscayans, Castilians and Portuguese houses for their 'nations', just as it had built one already in 1478–81 for the German Hanse. This time, however, the promise seems to have been fulfilled only so far as the Castilians were concerned.[7]

Many individual members of the 'nations' certainly stayed in Antwerp, and their absence from Bruges made it very easy for them to evade the taxes which they owed to their corporate leaders. Inevitably, the latter were generally compelled to follow their nationals, mainly to Antwerp. The Portuguese 'consulate' was transferred thither in 1510 or 1511, those of Genoa, Florence and Lucca around 1516. Just as they had attempted, while still at Bruges, to exert their authority on their nationals at Antwerp, so there is some evidence of the reverse process once they had settled in the Scheldt town, the last on the part of the Genoese consul in 1522.[8] Some minor groups moved not to Antwerp but

[6] Gilliodts, *Estaple*, II, 317, 459, 510, 527–30, 632; idem, *Inventatire des archives de la ville de Bruges*, 9 vols. (Bruges, 1871–85), VI, 431–4.
[7] Idem, *Estaple*, II, 281–91; idem, *Cartulaire de l'ancien consulat d'Espagne à Bruges: recueil de documents concernant le commerce maritime et intérieur, le droit des gens public et privé et l'histoire économique de la Flandre*, 2 vols. (Bruges, 1901–2), I, 149–84.
[8] J. Maréchal 'Le Départ de Bruges des merchands étrangers (XV et XVIe siècles)', *Annales de la Société D'Emulation de Bruges*, 88 (1951), 30–44.

to one of the Zeeland towns which acted essentially as its outports. The Scots, under embargo for their privateering activities, had left the Low Countries altogether in 1498. When they returned in 1501, they did not come back to Bruges but took their abode first in Middelburg and then, from 1508 onwards, in Veere. The influential lords of this town, belonging to an illegitimate branch of the Burgundian dynasty, had become kin to the House of Stuart. Consuls of an Andalusian 'nation', clearly formed after the conquest of the kingdom of Granada by Ferdinand and Isabella in 1492, are mentioned, also for the first time, at Bruges in 1500, but their corporation was also transferred to Middelburg in 1505.[9] In 1501, while they were negotiating the engagement of the one-year-old Archduke Charles, the future Emperor, to Claude of France, Louis XII's daughter, the Burgundian diplomats proposed that Bruges should be made the sole staple of French trade in the Low Countries, evidently at the instigation of that town. Nothing came of it, after experts from Rouen and La Rochelle had been consulted by their king and had strongly opposed it, appealing to the freedom of commerce.[10]

Finally, a couple of 'nations' remained faithful to their residence of old. As the only medieval commercial power, the Hanse had displayed solidarity with the hopeless struggle of Bruges against its competitors, mainly in order to defend the German hegemony against the progress of Dutch trade in the Baltic and the Atlantic. It tried to bind its adherents to Bruges as a compulsory staple town, but the rules imposed on them were transgressed on a large scale. Only the hard core of Lübeck and its retinue of the so-called Wendish towns had obeyed them appreciably, at the risk of ruining their own trade.[11] Indeed, the waning of the *Kontor* appeared dramatically in the contraction of its governing body. While this consisted until 1472 of six aldermen and eighteen councillors, it had to be reduced gradually, for lack of eligible candidates, to four members in all by 1536. Moreover, these could no longer be found with certainty at Bruges, but were chosen from everywhere in the Low Countries. In fact, the decline of the Hanse in the European economy was apparent not only in their desertion of Bruges. In 1511, only a dozen cloth- and fur-

[9] W. S. Unger, 'Middelburg als handelsstad (XIIIe–XVIe eeuw)', *Archief uitgegeven door het Zeeuwsch Genootschap der Wetenschappen* (1935), p. 191.

[10] M. Mollat, 'Bruges ou Anvers? La notion de liberté commerciale au début du XVLe siècle,' *Revue du Nord*, 36 (1954), 165–70, reprinted in *idem, Etudes d'histoire maritime* (Turin, 1977), pp. 101–6.

[11] H. Rogge, 'Der Stapelzwang des hansischen Kontors zu Brügge im XV. Jahrhundert', unpublished doctoral thesis, University of Kiel, 1903; E. Remux, 'Die Hanse und das Kontor zu Brügge am Ende des XV. Jahrhunderts', *Zeitschrift des westpreussischen Geschichtsvereins*, 30 (1892), 1–51.

merchants, mainly from Lübeck, were still living in that town.[12] It had become rather exceptional for Hansards to reside permanently in the Netherlands, though in 1540 a hundred of them attended the funeral of one of their fellow-countrymen in Antwerp.The paradoxical designation 'Kontor of Bruges in Antwerp', which was used now and then, matched reality, the more so in that the Kontor's secretary resided in the Scheldt town from the 1530s onwards. As early as 1516 its transfer to Antwerp had been considered. The hostilities between the Hanse and Denmark, where Charles V supported his brother-in-law Christian II, had caused the plan to be dropped. The Hansards' belief in the virtues of legal privileges had made them stick to Bruges, where they amply enjoyed such protection, while having nothing of the sort in Antwerp. Finally, the Kontor's governors were no longer replaced after their death or their departure. The last one died in 1554. The following year, a completely new Kontor was set up in Antwerp. This was a belated tolling of the passing-bell for an institution which had survived the economic reality for a couple of generations.[13]

If the Hanse merchants, contrary to their Kontor, deserted Bruges, the Spanish 'nation' continued to represent a real economic asset for the town. Strictly speaking, only natives of Castile were grouped within it. In 1519, ten Castilian firms were extant at Bruges, with a personnel of at least thirty, among owners and employees. Later meetings of the 'consulate', dating from 1525 to 1576, assembled between forty-one and sixty-one members. Next to them came the Biscayans, who were by no means negligible; in about 1540 they were able to build a stately consular building. Moreover, the municipality recognized in 1530 a new 'nation' of Navarre, probably as a result of the conquest by Ferdinand the Catholic of the part of this kingdom south of the Pyrenees.[14] Furthermore, Bruges and its outport of Sluis remained the main gateways through which Spanish wool was imported into the Low Countries. One should bear in mind that the towns of southern Flanders, especially those along the Lys River, were then the most thriving centres of the cloth industry, which mainly used Iberian wool since the growth of the English textile industry had made English wool difficult to obtain.

The Spanish wool was carried from Bruges to the industrial districts inland either overland or by lighters via Ghent or Ypres. Between 14

---

[12] K. Friedland, 'Die "Verlegung" des Brüggeschen Kontors nach Antwerpen', *Hansische Geschichtsblätter*, 81 (1963), 9, n. 38.
[13] *Ibid.*, pp. 1–19.
[14] Gilliodts, *Consulat*, II, 282–4; A. Viaene, 'Het natiehuis van Biskaaie te Brugge', *Biekorf*, 39 (1933), 1–8.

November 1503 and 20 January 1509, a yearly average of 2,070 tons was imported by the Castilian 'nation' alone; between 1550 and 1572 it reached 2,200 tons.[15] The overall turnover had been estimated at 5,830 tons of wool in 1546; a recession in the Flemish woollen industry caused it to fall to *c.* 4,100 tons by 1560. These were certainly high figures relative to the productivity of domestic manufacture. The merchants could store the goods, which were unshipped at a short distance from the heart of the town, in warehouses of which there were some six or seven or, from shortly before 1580, as many as eleven.[16] The consulates of Castile, Biscay and Navarre codified in 1569 the customary law on maritime insurance and established model policies. Their *hordenanzas* clearly influenced in this respect the regulations promulgated in 1571 by the Duke of Alba, which remained the substance of the insurance law in the Southern Netherlands until the French occupation in 1795.[17]

The part played by Bruges in the wool trade became still more important in 1558, when Calais, for two centuries the English bridgehead on the continent, was taken by the French. A new location had to be chosen for the English wool staple. Several towns in the Low Countries applied for it, among others Middelburg and Bergen: being relatively near to the cloth industry of Leiden and Holland, where most of the English wool imported into the Low Countries was worked, they seemed to have the most favourable situation. Nevertheless, despite the fact that little of the material was still used in Flanders, Bruges was given the preference, on the recommendation of Philip II to his queen, Mary Tudor. This was probably a political calculation, with a view to gaining Bruges's consent to taxes to be voted by the reluctant Estates of Flanders in order to sustain the costly war with France. Curiously enough, Antwerp was not among the applicants. Apparently, it valued more highly its flourishing trade in English cloth, and was afraid of being involved in the recurrent quarrels between the Merchant Adventurers and the Merchants of the Staple.[18]

The import of English wool remained steadily below the level of the Spanish. In July 1558, the first wool fleet which moored at Sluis

---

[15] Maréchal, 'Départ', pp. 49–51.
[16] *Idem*, 'La Casa Negra: het Zwarthuis in de Spanjaardstraat te Brugge', *Biekorf*, 63 (1962), 359–65.
[17] C. Verlinden, 'Código de seguros marítimos según la costumbre de Amberes, promulgado por el Consulado español de Brujas en 1569', *Cuadernos de Historia de España*, 7 (1947), 146–91, 8 (1947), 15–193; *idem.*, 'Code d'assurances maritimes selon la coutume d'Anvers, promulgué par le consulat espagnol de Bruges', *Bulletin de la Commission Royale des Anciennes Lois et Ordonnances de la Belgique*, 16 (1949), 38–142.
[18] O. de Smedt, *De Engelse natie te Antwerpen in de 16e eeuw, 1496–1582*, 2 vols. (Antwerp, 1950–4), i, 208–11.

contained thrity-seven ships of small tonnage, seldom over 100 tons. Bruges paid the freight charges of the lighters which brought the wool from the roadsteads to the town. During the accounting year September 1558 to September 1559, fifty-four ships carried 3,221 pockets of wool, along with 165,450 sheepskins. This figure was probably not equalled again. In 1563, forty-three ships were counted, and in 1567–8, only twenty-five. Indeed, it was from this time on that the Dutch cloth industry, in its turn gave up using English wool and resorted more and more to Spanish wool. The Bruges wool staple was also increasingly drawn into the developments arising from the outbreak of the War of Religion.[19].

The Merchant Adventurers' attempts to curtail the English trade of the Low Countries merchants brought about in 1563–4 a reciprocal embargo and the departure of the English from Antwerp. To the Bruges administration this seemed an opportunity to persuade them to reside in their town after the quarrel was settled. The attempt did not succeed, however, though protracted negotiations about the settlement went on for months at Bruges. The seizure of the Duke of Alba's pay-ships at Plymouth in 1568 gave rise to a new embargo, which lasted this time for five years. Nevertheless, despite relations with Antwerp having become strained since 1572 because of the interference of the insurgents with navigation on the Scheldt, renewed efforts of Bruges to harbour the Merchant Adventurers in 1574 also failed, for the time being at least. Finally, the Spanish Fury, which struck Antwerp with bloodshed and looting in October 1576, enabled Bruges's expectations to be fulfilled for a short while, though by the Whitsun mart of 1577 the Adventurers were back in Antwerp.[20]

The Spanish and English wool trades were responsible for by far the greater part of the port traffic of Sluis in the sixteenth century. This appears to have fluctuated heavily, partly by reason of the trend of business, partly because the repeated Franco-Spanish wars exposed the long sea-route from Spain to Flanders to pirates and privateers. English hostility had the same effect in the North Sea. In 1506, a peak of ninety-five ships entered the harbour, but during other years only a couple of sea-going vessels moored, and in 1553 and 1554 none at all. In the longer run, five-yearly averages of the annual numbers of ships show a falling trend even in periods of peace, i.e. 68 in 1505–9, 37 in 1520–4,

---

[19] Gilliodts, *Estaple*, III, 109–23, 138–56; Degryse, 'Brugge en de pilotage', pp. 131, 133, n. 59, 163, n. 114; N. W. Posthumus, *De geschiedenis van de Leidsche lakenindustrie*, 3 vols. (The Hague, 1908–39), I, *De Middeleeuwen, veertiende tot zestiende eeuw*, 213–14.

[20] Gilliodts, *Estaple*, III, 233–4; de Smedt, *Engelse natie*, I, 179–416.

31.2. in 1535–9 and 25.6 in 1545–9. The corresponding figures of total tonnage in the same four periods were 39,761, 25,573, 29,674 and 26,876. So although there was an increase in the average tonnage of the ships, this was not enough fully to compensate for the downward trend in numbers. Anyway, despite the English wool cargoes, the figures fell further after 1550. The moorings on the coast of Walcheren became still more popular. At least the lighterage at Bruges made a nice profit by carrying the wool from Sluis or from the Walcheren roads to Bruges, albeit that Zeeland skippers were competing sharply with it.[21]

Of course, even after it had been superseded by Antwerp, Bruges was visited on and off by other merchants than the Spanish or English wool dealers. It remained for a large area the distribution centre for the goods of international trade, with which it provided itself from its lucky rival. Its traders, moreover, continued to play their part at high levels of business life, for instance at Seville or Lisbon, the thresholds of the Iberian colonial world, or in the sugar plantations of the Atlantic archipelagos. Louis van de Walle (d. 1584) settled in the Canaries, where he married and where his descendants remained, their family name distorted to Vendoval.[22] No less noteworthy is the persistence of the money market of Bruges. In a southern German merchants' manual dating from 1514–15, this town was still quoted as the main money market of the Low Countries. Yet this situation probably soon changed when the big Italian banking firms left Bruges about 1516, and in 1559 the Antwerp rates of exchange were posted up in the meeting-room of the Spanish 'consulate' at Bruges.[23]

III

So one should beware of drawing too dark a picture of Bruges's decline in the transition from the Middle Ages to the early modern period and, moreover, it should be remembered that this decline had set in before the end of the fifteenth century. It was altogether less sudden and less absolute than accepted beliefs represent it. No doubt, Antwerp had gained the victory, but Bruges was able to sustain a very honourable comparison with it and other towns. In 1569, when Alba levied a 1 per cent tax on property, both real and personal, Antwerp gave a return of

---

[21] Degryse, 'Brugge en de pilotage', pp. 227–63.
[22] J. A. van Houtte and E. Stols, 'Les Pays-Bas et la Méditerranée atlantique au XVIe siècle', *Mélanges en l'honneur de F. Braudel*, 2 vols. (Toulouse, 1973), i, 645–59.
[23] K. O. Müller, *Welthandelsbräuche, 1480–1540* (Wiesbaden, 1962), pp. 39, 41, 69–71, etc.; J. Maréchal, 'La Colonie espagnole de Bruges du XIVe au XVIe siècle', *Revue du Nord*, 35 (1953), 34.

160,500 florins and Bruges one of 36,400, this being 22.75 per cent of the Antwerp figure, with only Brussels and Ghent in between. More striking still, and indeed very surprising, is the comparison revealed by taking into account only the share of merchandise in the assessment. This accounted in Antwerp for 37,800 florins, equal to 23.54 per cent of the aggregate, as against 11,800 florins, 32.33 per cent of the total, at Bruges. The absence from Antwerp of the Merchant Adventurers as a result of the embargo could hardly account for the whole difference. Thus, with due regard to its inferiority in absolute terms, the commercial element appears to have been comparatively more important in the activity of Bruges than in that of Antwerp. In 1569, a duty was imposed on the Low Countries' trade with Spain. Antwerp was far ahead of Bruges as far as exports were concerned, with 78 per cent against 12 per cent. The latter figure still exceeded the total of all other collecting offices in the country. As for imports, the wool trade brought the share of Bruges up to 25 per cent against 68 per cent for Antwerp.[24]

The Spanish reconquest of Flanders during the War of Religion, and the final loss of Sluis, saw Bruges lose most of its remaining faithful. Unable to import through Sluis, the Merchants of the Staple had discharged at Nieuport early in 1585. Complaints about the tolls were hardly the only reason why they left Bruges in October. There is no further trace either of the Biscayans after 1585 or of the Navarrese after 1586. The latter transferred their 'consulate' to Lille. Only the Spanish 'nation' maintained its seat at Bruges. It had resisted with determination attempts by the Castilians in Antwerp, where they were more numerous than at Bruges, to move the 'consulate' to the Scheldt metropolis. In 1596, the 'nation' had fourteen, in 1606 twenty-four members at Bruges. In 1705, when there were only two, they dissolved their corporation.[25]

Military operations had scarcely subsided around the town before trade revived on a modest scale, as indeed it did in the Southern Netherlands as a whole, now that Antwerp had passed its zenith. Trade with Spain was more than ever vital to Bruges, at least until the accession of the Bourbon King Philip V to the Spanish throne in 1700 put France in a commercially advantageous position. Bruges continued to claim the staple for Spanish wool, albeit with increasing difficulty. The town had had to allow in 1578 the transport of 500 pockets directly from Calais to

---

[24] W. Brulez, 'Brugge en Antwerpen in de 15e en 16e eeuw: een tegenstelling?' *Tijdschrift voor Geschiedenis*, 83 (1970), 15–37.

[25] Gilliodts, *Consulat*, II, 381–6, 407–8, 519, 590–1; J. A. Goris, *Etude sur les colonies marchandes méridionales (portugais, espagnols, italiens) à Anvers de 1488 à 1567: contribution à l'histoire des débuts du capitalisme moderne* (Louvain, 1925), pp. 58–66; Maréchal, *Départ*, p. 54.

Armentières.[26] Together with Dunkirk and Nieuport, the French port had handled practically the whole import while Bruges joined the revolt against Philip II (1577–84). The king had even transferred the staple to Saint-Omer in 1580. It was returned to Bruges after the temporary reconquest of Sluis in 1589.[27] Later Bruges tried hard to oppose imports via Calais. Half a dozen men-of-war were even sent out *c.* 1592 to bring into Bruges by force a Spanish convoy bound for Calais.[28]

The competition of Lille gradually became a still greater threat. Because of the perils of Dutch privateering in the Channel, ships often discharged at Rouen, whence the wool was carried overland to Lille, near the cloth-manufacturing area. After the wool staple had been restored to Bruges in 1589, this continued to be allowed, until in 1602 Bruges succeeded in regaining recognition of its monopoly, although exemptions had to be granted from time to time because of the insecurity of transport. Thus, even wool brought from Rouen to Lille had first to pass the staple at Bruges and to receive its mark. This costly detour could not but encourage interlopers on a large scale. The loss of Lille to France in 1667 ended the dispute automatically by rendering this town immune to any action taken by the authorities in the Spanish Netherlands.[29]

There were still other ways to elude the staple. The prohibition of trade with the enemy, in force in principle on both sides during the Eighty Years' War, was obeyed only seldom because of the necessity or the advantage of maintaining the intercourse between the Dutch Republic and Spain.[30] Dutch ships unloaded large quantities of Spanish wool at Sas-van-Gent, at the mouth of the canal joining Ghent with the Lower Scheldt, or in Antwerp; the latter town handled, among other things, the wool worked by the fast-developing industry of Verviers or by Brabantine manufacturers. Bruges opposed this in 1649 and was declared in 1664 to be within its rights, but this favourable judgement did not by any means end the use of the alternative route. Much wool was also imported by Ostend without passing through Bruges's staple. Finally, the government became conscious in 1688 that maintaining the staple obligation was impossible and allowed free passage of the wool through Ostend, in order to promote at least this town's port. After some protest, Bruges had to submit to the ruin of this last vestige of its medieval privileges. Yet the decline of the Spanish wool trade was not

[26] Gilliodts, *Estaple*, III, 212, 236, 263, 265–6, 322; *idem*, *Consulat*, II, 467–8, 503.
[27] *Idem*, *Estaple*, III, 274–80, 312; *idem*, *Consulat*, II, 528–9.
[28] *Idem*, *Estaple*, III, 335, 354–5.
[29] *Ibid.*, pp. 312, 321–5, 335, 362, 366–70, 375, 396; *idem*, *Consulat*, II, 528–9, 563–5, 569–72, 577.
[30] J. H. Kernkamp, *De handel op den vijand, 1572–1609*, 2 vols. (Utrecht, 1931–4).

caused only by infringements of the staple. The gradual decay of the Flemish rural industry, under the competition of other manufacturing centres, was certainly not less instrumental.[31]

Return freights for wool and for other goods consisted mainly of manufactured textiles, which found a large outlet in the New World, via Spanish and Portuguese traders.[32] As has already been hinted, navigation to Spain was considered very perilous because of the privateering which the many European wars kept in being. Moreover, piracy was not much less that a normal means of subsistence in Barbary: it was practised not only in southern European waters but also as far north as the Channel. It was so greatly feared there that frequently the huge detour around the British Isles was made, or that part of the passage was made overland as far as Rouen, Brittany, La Rochelle or even Bordeaux. In so far as the journey went by sea, it normally made use of convoys under escort of naval vessels, such as Charles V had ordered as early as the mid sixteenth century. The 'Flemish convoy' left from Dunkirk annually until this town was lost in 1658, and from 1665 from Ostend. Ships leaving Spain also sailed in convoy. In wartime, neutral ships were often chartered in order to maintain a continuous trade. They were mostly Hansards or English, provided they were not involved in the conflict: the short crossing from the Flemish coast to Dover or the Downs, where transshipment took place, was not risky.[33]

Despite the Dutch hegemony in supplying Spain with all kinds of necessities during the seventeenth century, merchants from Bruges succeeded in maintaining their part in this current of trade. Some were of Spanish descent, like Diego de Aranda, whose turnover – mainly imports of wool and export of textiles – between 1602 and 1613 amounted to £56,000 groat, 36,500 of which was on his own account, and the remainder on commission for others. About 1620, one Thomas Criols was active in Cadiz; he emigrated twenty years later to America.

---

[31] Gilliodts, *Estaple*, III, 440–4, 491, 536–7, 572–95; *idem, Consulat*, II, 588–9; *idem, Cartulaire de l'ancien Grand Tonlieu de Bruges, faisant suite au Cartulaire de l'ancienne Estaple: recueil de documents concernant le commerce intérieur et maritime, les relations internationales et l'histoire économique de cette ville* (Bruges, 1908–9), VI, 312–57; van Houtte, *Histoire économique*, pp. 197–204.

[32] E. Stols, *De Spaanse Brabanders of de handelsbetrekkingen der Zuidelijke Nerderlanden met de Iberische wereld (1598–1648)*, 2 vols. (Brussels, 1971), I, 278; J. Everaert, *De internationale en koloniale handel der Vlaamse firma's te Cadiz, 1600–1700* (Bruges, 1973).

[33] J. Craeybeckx, 'De organisatie van de konvooiering van de koopvaardijvloot op het einde van de regering van Karel V; bijdrage tot de geschiedenis van de scheepvaart en de admiraliteit', *Bijdragen voor de Geschiedenis der Nederlanden*, 3 (1949), 179–208; Stols, *Spaanse Brabanders*, I, 292–308; Everaert, *Handel*, p. 89–109, 152–3, 663–6.

Guillermo Lootyns, who lived after 1630 in Seville or Cadiz, crossed the Atlantic three times between 1636 and 1645, sometimes with goods consigned to him from Flanders. Castilian naturalization was needed for such trade with the New World. In 1643, five holders of naturalization patents living at Seville originated from Bruges, the highest number from any single town except for the twenty-six who came from Antwerp. In 1632–3, at a moment when the advocates of an embargo on the Dutch got the upper hand during the Eighty Years' War, no less that 493 certificates of origin for imports into Spain were issued at Bruges. Only Lille and Antwerp accounted for more, 501 and 648 respectively. The Portuguese empire also attracted traders from Bruges: between 1592 and 1609 the two brothers De Coutere dealt in diamonds in Goa.[34]

In Bruges itself, the brokers had become commission agents on account of foreign merchants after these had, for the most part, left the town. In 1665, their guild was extended by the admission of some of the town's merchants and was converted by the magistrate into a Chamber of Commerce, with judicial powers in matters of trade. Two years later, the government also instituted a similar Chamber in the town. This, however, was conceived as having a wider scope, for not only was it given control over the maritime trade of the Spanish Netherlands as a whole, including the organization of convoys and the delivery of passports, but representatives of the other main centres of trade were called to sit on it. Yet the new institution seems soon to have been forgotten by those who had called it to life, thereby leaving room for the municipal Chamber to develop. In 1727, when Ghent put forward a claim on the seat allotted by the government sixty years before, the Chamber rejected it resolutely. During the eighteenth century it displayed much initiative in the interest of trade, for example in conducting the excavation of the Ostend canal and in fitting out the local docks with wharfs, cranes and warehouses.[35]

In medieval Bruges the money market had first taken the name of *Bourse*, which became thereafter, and still is, a generic term for Exchanges everywhere on the continent.[36] The town authorities revived

[34] Stols, *Spaanse Brabanders*, I, 41, n. 245, 58, 123, 243–7, II, 15, 21, 23, 191–2.
[35] Gilliodts, *Estaple*, III, 496–7, 502–9, 514–29, 538, IV, 27–8, 237–40, 300–14, 322–3; A. Vandewalle, *Beknopte inventaris van het Stadsarchief van Brugge*, I (Bruges, 1979), 122–4; Y. vanden Berghe, *Jacobijnen en Traditionalisten: de reacties van de Bruggelingen in de revolutietijd, 1780–1794*, 2 vols. (Brussels, 1972), I, 32–4.
[36] J. A. van Houtte, 'Von der Brügger Herberge "Zur Börse" zur Brügger Börse', in J. Schneider (ed.), *Wirtschaftskräfte und Wirtschaftswege: Festschrift für H. Kellenbenz*, 5 vols. (Stuttgart, 1978–81), V, 237–50.

it several times, whenever new expectations arose with regard to the growth of trade, as in 1665, 1699 and 1721.[37] In that respect, hope and disappointment succeeded each other. The traffic of the port amounted to c. 26,500 tons in 1675, 17,500 in 1685 and only 8,700 in 1691, including a number of sea-going vessels.[38] The setback appearing in the last figure was probably caused only in part by the Nine Years' War of 1688–97 and by the recession which had broken out in its wake but also, as stated above, by the suppression of the last remnants of the staple privileges.

IV

Barely were hostilities over when sundry bold plans for restoration took shape. The Governor-General of the Spanish Netherlands, Elector Maximilian Emmanuel of Bavaria, took a keen personal interest in them; his infant son being then the presumptive heir to the Spanish throne, he wanted to make the Spanish Netherlands as prosperous as possible. Part of these plans was the institution of a colonial company, which he chartered in 1698. Colonial trade was reputed to be very lucrative, and merchants of the Southern Netherlands had long sought direct access to the overseas world. Some had even risked encroaching on the monopolies claimed by other European countries over their possessions: in 1688 a frigate from Bruges had been captured off the coast of Guinea by the Brandenburgians. When the new company was instituted, the town applied immediately for the staple of Indian goods to be imported by it. But the charter had no effect at all. Not only was the government of Madrid highly indignant at the independent behaviour of its representative in Brussels, but the Dutch Republic feared the competition of the new company, and the elector could not face the possibility of losing its support for his ambitions with respect to the Spanish succession.[39] Shortly afterwards, the miseries of the War of the Spanish Succession broke over Europe. Until the Anglo-Dutch occupation of Flanders in 1706, the port of Bruges drew some advantage from the interlopers'

---

[37] Gilliodts, Estaple, III, 498–501; J. Maréchal, Geschiedenis van de Brugse Beurs (Bruges, 1949), p. 42.

[38] J. de Smet, 'Tables du commerce et de la navigation du port de Bruges, 1675–1698', Bulletin de la Commission Royale d'Histoire, 94 (1930), 103–244.

[39] M. Huisman, La Belgique commerciale sous l'empereur Charles VI: la Compagnie d'Ostende: étude historique de politique commerciale et coloniale (Brussels and Paris, 1902), pp. 29–33; R. de Schryver, 'Uit de voorgeschiedenis van de Oostendse Kompagnie: Bergeycks verklaringen van 1720 over het oktrooi van 1698 voor een Oostindische Kompagnie', Bulletin de la Commission Royale d'Histoire, 132 (1966), 143–59; Gilliodts, Estaple, III, 597–602 and 628–32 (misdated).

trade between the Dutch and the English on one side, and the French and Spanish on the other, despite the reciprocal blockade.

The end of the war brought about over the whole of Europe, a fever of enterprise, of which the speculative excesses, such as John Law's *Système* or the South Sea Bubble, have remained the most notorious examples. In what had now become the Austrian Netherlands, and especially in Bruges, many trading schemes were formed, before the new administration took the matter in hand and decided upon the constitution of a new colonial company, which was granted its charter in 1722. The Ostend Company, as it was called on account of the home port of its ships, had its seat in Antwerp, but its goods were to be auctioned either in Ostend or in Bruges, though the latter had petitioned to be selected as the sole place for auctions.[40] The company had only an ephemeral existence. Emperor Charles VI had to suspend its charter as early as 1727, and finally to repeal it in 1731 in order to gain the support of the sea powers, jealous as they were of the unwelcome competitor, for the succession of his daughter Maria Theresa. Yet the episode had lasting results: Bruges was now involved for good in the colonial trade. It continued to receive consignments of colonial goods, the more so as their turnover in the Western world was rising fast.[41]

Trade in Bruges reached a new peak, as has been intimated above, during the Anglo-Dutch War of 1780–4. Together with Ostend, the town was used as a sanctuary by the belligerents in order to pursue their mutual trade despite the official prohibition. Several foreign merchants, mostly English, applied to the magistrate for sea-letters, and dozens of ships based in Bruges traded with the American insurgents and with India. Slave-dealers carried textiles, arms and spirits to Guinea, whence they shipped negroes to America, and then, with the proceeds of their sales, bought colonial goods for import into Europe. Another warehouse was built near the harbour. The concourse of ships in the dock was so heavy that finding moorings in it became difficult, and a waterway inside the town had to be dredged in order to provide for more quays.

Native merchants also took a share in this activity. They developed an interest in destinations hitherto unusual for them. The local Chamber of Commerce printed the customs tariff of Russia, which, under Catherine II, was opening itself up more widely to the West; and, with the Austrian government, it insisted on opening negotiations with the Ottoman empire in order to get safe-conducts for navigation in the Mediterranean.

---

[40] Huisman, *Belgique commerciale*, pp. 41, 139, 235; Gilliodts, *Estaple*, III, 714–17, IV, 5, 9–15, 25–6, 40–4.
[41] Gilliodts, *Estaple*, IV, 114–18, 178.

Information was asked for from Brittany about Bruges's communications with the hinterland and whether there were personnel available and competent to translate from the Dutch or English. Merchants in the town not only acted as men of straw for subjects of the belligerent powers but also engaged in enterprise on their own account. One of them had up to eighteen ships at sea and traded to France, Spain, the Dutch Republic, Russia, the West Indies and the United States. Others took a keen interest in the slave trade to the New World. Between 1769 and 1779, the yearly average of ships mooring at Bruges had been about 200. In 1782 there were 368. From 1778 to 1783 a total of 307 sea-letters were delivered at Bruges. One-third of these referred to ships actually owned by subjects of the Austrian Netherlands; the remainder belonged to them only as figure-heads. A sequel to these ventures was the foundation in 1782 of the Société d'Assurances Maritimes Établie à Bruges. Citizens of the town applied for 1,430 out of the 2,000 shares, each of 1,000 florins, of the stock. The capital had to be paid up only to the extent of 1 per cent, and the dividend of the first year sufficed to refund this stake.[42]

The end of hostilities and the restoration of normal international intercourse put an end to this boom. The insurance company ceased operations. In the inevitable sobering down which followed, the old claims on breaking bulk were revived and, as already mentioned, were met in part at least. The return to normality seemed like a slump. Worse was to come with the French conquest of 1794 and the annexation to France. The Revolutionary and Napoleonic Wars nearly stopped all traffic in Bruges. Conversely, the restored freedom of the Scheldt again allowed direct navigation between Antwerp and the high seas. This created the conditions for the resurgence of Antwerp after Waterloo. It could not but develop at the expense of other commercial centres. Bruges was numbered among its victims. If it had not legitimized the title of Georges Rodenbach's famous novel *Bruges la morte* during the early modern period, it was certainly to do so during the nineteenth century.

---

[42] *Ibid.*, pp. 320–35, 340–3; vanden Berghe, *Jacobijnen*, I, 19–31; L. Couvreur, 'De zeeverzekeringsmarkt der Oostenrijksche Nederlanden op het einde van de achttiende eeuw', *Annales de la Société d'Emulation de Bruges*, 80 (1937), 58–86; L. van Acker, 'De Westvlaamse zeeverzekeringsmaatschappijen latsste jaren en liquidatie, 1807–1812', *Biekorf*, 67 (1965), 257–65.

6

English re-exports and the Dutch staplemarket in the eighteenth century

DAVID ORMROD

It was Professor Wilson's *Anglo-Dutch Commerce and Finance in the Eighteenth Century* which first drew the attention of English readers to the structure of the Dutch staplemarket and the workings of the closely integrated English and Dutch re-export trades driven to and from that market.[1] Little published work has subsequently appeared on the early history of English re-exports,[2] although a growing literature on the Dutch staplemarket has greatly modified our view of entrepreneurial behaviour in the seventeenth and eighteenth centuries, since Professor Wilson added his own researches to those of van der Kooy, de Jong-Keesing and others.[3]

Following the appearance in 1965 of Klein's massive study of the commercial and financial activities of the Trip family in the seventeenth century, there has been a tendency to play down the significance of the Republic's external free trade policies which according to Adam Smith had largely eliminated 'the mean rapacity, the monopolizing spirit of merchants and manufacturers'.[4] Klein has shown, however, that Dutch entrepreneurs, 'far from being partisans of free competition, reduced risks by applying an astonishingly wide range of monopolistic practices'

---

[1] Charles Wilson, *Anglo-Dutch Commerce and Finance in the Eighteenth Century* (Cambridge, 1941).

[2] See especially R. Davis, 'English Foreign Trade, 1660–1700', *Economic History Review*, 2nd series, 6 (1954), reprinted in W. E. Minchinton (ed.), *The Growth of English Overseas Trade in the Seventeenth and Eighteenth Centuries* (London, 1969), and *idem*, 'English Foreign Trade, 1700–1774', *Economic History Review*, 2nd series, 15 (1962), reprinted in Minchinton (ed.), *Growth Revisited'*, *Explorations in Entrepreneurial History*, 10 (1973).

[3] T. P. van der Kooy, *Hollands stapelmarkt en haar verval* (Amsterdam, 1931); E. E. de Jong-Keesing, *De economische crisis van 1763 te Amsterdam* (Amsterdam, 1939).

[4] P. W. Klein, *De Trippen in de 17ᵉ eeuw: een studie over het ondernemersgedrag op de Hollandse stapelmarkt* (Assen, 1965); A. Smith, *Inquiry into the Nature and Causes of the Wealth of Nations*, ed. J. R. McCulloch (London, 1838), pp. 218, 220.

within the staplemarket and the staple trades.[5] It is an optimistic, Schumpeterian view of monopoly which Klein applies to the staple-market, emphasizing the 'creative character of Dutch commercial capitalism, strongly based upon monopolistic entrepreneurial behaviour', which protected investment and promoted innovation and growth.[6] Of the range and persistence of restrictive practices there can be little doubt. M. G. Buist's study of Hope & Company, in many respects the eighteenth-century counterparts to the Trips, shows how monopoly arrangements continued through the eighteenth century and into the early nineteenth, especially the granting of state loans secured on the basis of a monopoly of the sale of certain commodities – for example, the West Indian plantation loans of the 1760s, the Portuguese diamond loan of 1801, and the company's attempt to monopolize the entire European market for Brazil-wood (an important dyestuff) in 1804, which seems to have originated as a Portuguese loan. The last of these adventures had been anticipated by the firm's attempt to monopolize European stocks of cochineal in the late 1780s, which ended in financial disaster.[7] It is difficult to see how such arrangements were uniformly and necessarily productive of growth and innovation, and J. W. Veluwenkamp has recently suggested that truly monopolistic practices could only be realized in very special circumstances where staple products came from a single production area. The more usual situation, according to Veluwenkamp, was one of *monopolistically competitive* practice, whereby merchants attempted by product differentiation, specialization and the development of customer loyalty to evade conditions of perfect competition, each controlling his 'own market'. Hence 'the staplemarket was not one big integrated market but was composed rather of a large number of "partial markets", the "private markets" of the separate merchants'.[8]

The history of the English re-export trade to Amsterdam tends to confirm Veluwenkamp's view. English merchants viewed with dismay the intervention of Dutch specialist bidders, frequently organized in 'rings' and stigmatized as *Liefhebbers*, at the East India Company's sales.

---

[5] P. W. Klein, 'Dutch Capitalism and the European World-Economy', in M. Aymard (ed.), *Dutch Capitalism and World Capitalism* (Cambridge, 1982), p. 90.

[6] Klein, *De Trippen*, 478–9.

[7] M. G. Buist, *At Spes Non Fracta: Hope & Co. 1775–1815* (The Hague, 1974), pp. 19–20, 407–8, 431–51.

[8] J. W. Veluwenkamp, *Ondernemersgedrag op de Hollandse stapelmarkt in de tijd van de Republiek: de Amsterdamse handelsfirma Jan Isaak de Neufville & Comp, 1730–1764* (Leiden, 1981), pp. 129–31, 137.

And the offence was compounded when, it was believed, these same merchants and their principals were able to fix the European price for different categories of Indian goods on resale in Amsterdam.[9] Such anxieties may have been exaggerated, but it is clear that quasi-monopolistic practices in this branch of trade came under attack and substantially disintegrated during the 1720s and 1730s, in ways which will be described below.

Apart from the question of entrepreneurial behaviour, recent work by Dutch historians has altered our view of the staplemarket in another important respect – that of the chronology of the Republic's general economic decline. The writings of van der Woude and Schoffer suggest that this set in during the 1670s and 1680s, and not the 1730s as was previously thought – a view which is clearly in line with that of contemporaries, especially the much-quoted *Observations* of Sir William Temple.[10] And it seems that Dutch trade as well as industry declined. Johan de Vries, in his classic study of Dutch economic decline, exaggerated the buoyancy of the commercial sector by failing to take account of the artificially inflated trade figures during wartime (the 1740s and 1750s).[11] It is true that M. Morineau has expressed certain reservations against the image of a Dutch golden age confined to the first half of the seventeenth century, or a little beyond; but his interventions have directed attention towards the earlier rather than the later period of Amsterdam's remarkable history, the late sixteenth century, when that port not merely replaced or 'reproduced' the Antwerp mart, but was actively built up through a process of extraordinary diversification.[12] In spite of several ingenious attempts to manipulate the available data, views about long-term trends in the English economy during the century after 1660 are less clearly defined and there is still no modern account of the commercial crises and fluctuations of this period. But there is some agreement that the 1660s, 1670s and early 1680s saw fairly vigorous

[9] PRO C103/131, Correspondence of Thomas Hall, London; e.g. Hall to D. Smith, Amsterdam, 2 May 1732; C. Davenant, Memorial to the Lord Treasurer concerning the Free Trade now carried on between France and Holland, 17 December 1705, PRO CO 389/13, f. 523.

[10] A. M. van der Woude, 'Het Noorderkwartier', in *A.A.G. Bijdragen*, 16 (1972), 3 vols; I. Schoffer, 'Did Holland's Golden Age Coincide with a Period of Crisis', *Bijdragen en Mededelingen van het Historisch Genootschap*, 78 (1964) and *Acta Historiae Neerlandica*, 1 (1966); W. Temple, *Observations on the United Provinces of the Netherlands* (London, 1673).

[11] J. de Vries, *De economische achteruitgang der Republiek in de achttiende eeuw* (Amsterdam, 1959), pp. 19–29.

[12] M. Morineau, 'Hommage aux historiens hollandais et contribution à l'histoire économique des Provinces-Unies', in Aymard (ed.), *Dutch Capitalism and World Capitalism*, pp. 302–3.

growth connected with the establishment of the re-export trades, with a serious crisis developing in the later 1690s.[13] Complaints of contraction in the markets for English textiles became common following the War of the Spanish Succession, and trade in general remained stagnant until the later 1740s, when colonial demand quickened.[14] It was in 1728 that Defoe conducted his 'Inquiry into that important question, whether our trade in general, and our woollen manufactures in particular, are sunk and declined'.[15] As far as internal demand is concerned, there are good reasons for doubting the alleged buoyancy of the home market during the years 1730–50, which were marked by agricultural depression, a slow increase in population and what appears to be a pause in metropolitan growth.[16]

In terms of cyclical rhythms and secular trends, the late seventeenth and early eighteenth centuries can be seen as the tail-end of a long period of stagnation or contraction of the European economy, and whilst Holland and Britain were firmly established at its core, Dutch commercial hegemony was disappearing.[17] It is significant, therefore, that during this period of stagnation, the relationship between these two economies and the peripheral areas of the world economy followed similar paths, especially in the Baltic regions and the Far East. Chaudhuri suggests that 'the development of European trade with Asia cannot be treated as an isolated historical event. It was an integral part of a much larger movement of expansion which in time was responsible for forging entirely new forms of economic ties between Europe and the peripheral areas'.[18] Although there was no direct connection, English and Dutch penetration in the Far East coincided with a much-reduced dependence upon Baltic grain imports from the late seventeenth century, which in the case of the Dutch had been substantial. English farmers generated larger surpluses which compensated for the shortfall, and the commercial resources of both countries flowed into the developing re-export and

---

[13] R. Davis, *English Overseas Trade, 1500–1700* (London, 1973), pp. 32–7; *idem*, 'English Foreign Trade, 1660–1700'; J. K. Horsefield, *British Monetary Experiments, 1650–1710* (London, 1960), pp. 3–6.

[14] Davis, 'English Foreign Trade, 1700–1774'.

[15] D. Defoe, *A Plan of the English Commerce* (London, 1728), Part II, Chapter 1, pp. 245–85.

[16] For a summary of the case for a slowing-down in the early-eighteenth-century economy, see A. J. Little, *Deceleration in the Eighteenth Century British Economy* (London, 1976); and for evidence suggestive of a pause in London's population, see E. A. Wrigley and R. S. Schofield, *The Population History of England, 1541–1871* (London, 1981), pp. 166–70.

[17] See I. Wallerstein, *The Modern World-System, II: Mercantilism and the Consolidation of the European World-Economy, 1600–1750* (New York, 1980), pp. 3–9; Aymard (ed.), *Dutch Capitalism and World Capitalism*, especially, pp. 1–10.

[18] K. N. Chaudhuri, *The Trading World of Asia and the English East India Company, 1660–1760* (Cambridge, 1978), p. 10.

colonial trades.[19] But the European demand for re-exported products was, if not sluggish, at least limited, and extra-European expansion produced commercial rivalry and a struggle for markets. It is worth asking, therefore, whether the neglected history of re-exports throws any light on the *relative* progress of these two commercial economies, Holland and Britain, during a period of stagnation or slow growth.

To locate the rise of the English re-export trade in the later seventeenth century is to recognize that English merchants, under the protection of the Navigation Acts, had learnt to apply the long-established methods of their Dutch counterparts. It became a major policy objective to make Britain, in Tucker's words, 'the common depositum, magazine, or storehouse for Europe and America, so that the medium profit might be made to centre here'.[20] It is true that there are certain parallels between English and Dutch re-export activity, but the differences are more marked than the similarities. Professor Minchinton was correct when he argued that the development of the English entrepôt involved a large investment in commerce which was not accompanied by industrial investment.[21] One of the few exceptions to this state of affairs was the establishment of an English calico-printing industy, which by the mid eighteenth century had reached a high degree of technical excellence. In 1751, a firm of London linen drapers, Nash & Eddowes, wrote to an Amsterdam correspondent:

[we] desire the favour of you to get some drawer to copy that curious fine pattern of India Chints which you were pleased to show Mr. & Mrs. Nash when they were at your house, & to ask your opinion, whether if it was well cut here & printed on a fine cotton or calico, it would not be saleable; because your printers cannot possibly execute those fine patterns like ours.[22]

But apart from this new industry, the extent of processing prior to re-export was relatively small before 1750, if we exclude the enterprise of Glasgow merchants. Most of the tobacco leaving England in the early eighteenth century was leaf tobacco which was exported to Holland where it was cut and mixed with the Dutch-grown (inland) product. A witness before the 1733 Commons Committee on the Frauds and Abuses

---

[19] D. J. Ormrod, 'Dutch Commercial-Industrial Decline and British Growth in the Late Seventeenth and Early Eighteenth Centuries', in F. Krantz and P. Hohenberg (eds.), *Failed Transitions to Modern Industrial Society: Renaissance Italy and Seventeenth Century Holland* (Montreal, 1975), pp. 36–43.

[20] J. Tucker, *A Brief Essay on the Advantages and Disadvantages which Respectively Attend France and Great Britain with Regard to Trade* (London, 1750), p. 72.

[21] Minchinton (ed.), *Growth of English Overseas Trade*, p. 44 (editors introduction).

[22] Gemeente Archief, Amsterdam (hereafter GAA), Archief Brants 1344, Nash & Eddowes, London, to J. I. de Neufville, Amsterdam, 31 July 1751.

in the Customs claimed: 'It is very seldom the Merchants re-pack any Hogsheads of Tobacco for Exportation (and when they do, it is such on which are very large damages).'[23] The same was true of printed East Indian cottons and silks, which were the first commodities to fall within the scope of the bonded warehousing system–which, together with the tariff structure itself, greatly inhibited the development of processing industry. This requires further explanation.

It is of course well known that the English tariff structure was transformed in the 1690s so as to become a highly protective system, and that this stands in marked contrast to the corresponding situation in the United Provinces, where duties on imports were low and remained so throughout the eighteenth century, even after the Dutch tariff reform of 1725.[24] The contrast between Dutch free trade and English protectionism is so obvious that we tend to ignore it, and few contemporary Englishmen before Adam Smith questioned the wisdom of English commercial policy. Matthew Decker, writing in the 1740s, was one of the few exceptions, and he was in any case a Dutchman by origin.[25] Yet the two commercial and fiscal systems continued to diverge during the eighteenth century, with English duties becoming increasingly protective, increasingly complex. Although this contrast was not accidental, as the product of a different commercial–industrial balance underlying each of the two economies, it nevertheless explains much about the subsequent development of the entrepôts of London and Amsterdam. It would be impossible to summarize the endless modifications and adjustments which were made to the increasing level of duties across the large range of imports which formed the basis of the re-export trade, although these increases were collectively substantial. It would be even more difficult to describe the adjustments made to the drawback system (namely the repayment of all or a part of the import duties when the goods were re-exported, provided that they were re-exported within a

---

[23] *House of Commons Reports and Papers*, XVII, Report on the Committee appointed to inquire into the Frauds and Abuses in the Customs, 7 June 1733, p. 618 (no. v, Mr Gilbert Higginson's Examination, 8 May 1733).

[24] R. Davis, 'The Rise of Protection in England, 1689–1768', *Economic History Review*, 2nd series, 19 (1966); J. Hovy, *Het voorstel van 1751 tot instelling van een beperkt vrijhavenstelsel in de Republiek* (Groningen, 1966), Chapter III; D. J. Ormrod, 'Anglo-Dutch Commerce, 1700–1760', unpublished Ph. D. thesis, University of Cambridge, 1973, pp. 133–6.

[25] M. Decker, *A Essay on the Causes of the Decline of the Foreign Trade ... of Great Britain* (London, 1744), pp. 10–13, 66, 69. On the authorship of this essay, see J. R. McCulloch (ed.), *A Select Collection of Scarce and Valuable Tracts on Commerce* (London, 1859), pp. viii–ix. Decker provided the most reasoned case for low duties and illustrated it with the example of the Dutch Republic.

specified time – usually within three years of import). Fortunately, this problem is not as serious as it might at first sight appear.

By the end of the seventeenth century, the method of claiming drawbacks had become so complicated, and the scope for making fraudulent claims correspondingly enlarged, that it became necessary to devise an alternative system. At its inception in 1700, the new system was applied only to Indian and Persian wrought silks, which formed the most valuable component of the re-export trade, but in 1709 it was extended to include pepper, in 1714 tobacco, and at later dates, rum, coffee and rice were covered.[26] That system was the so-called warehousing system by which imports were stored in warehouses under the joint locks of the crown and the merchant, and paid duty only when they were delivered out for home consumption. The drawback system therefore postulated the actual payment of duty, whereas the warehousing system postponed or waived payment of duty, or in some instances required only the payment of half duties. The temptation to re-land goods and make fraudulent drawback claims was much reduced, which pleased the Revenue Commissioners, and the system was simpler and more convenient, which suited both merchants and customs officers. But most interesting to the historian are two important long-term effects which influenced the course of the already well-established re-export trade, and which must have assumed a greater weight in proportion to progressive increases in the level of duties. They have been curiously overlooked by commercial historians. The first was the tendency of the new system to divert imported colonial and East Indian products away from home consumption and towards re-export markets; and the second was its discouragement of any form of processing prior to re-export. Goods simply went directly into the warehouses and out again. In the case of those goods purchased by brokers at public sales, they were frequently never even seen by the merchants on whose accounts they were re-exported. When the firm of London linen drapers Jasper Waters & Sons heard from their Amsterdam correspondent that two bales of chintz had been received in poor condition, they replied:

as to what you mention about the damage, we have no notion of it, they being sent in good condition out of our Company's warehouse; and if there be any damage upon them, it must have been received on board of Bredemos, and therefore he ought to be accountable for it, and we depend upon our being clear from any charge upon that account.[27]

[26] E. E. Hoon, *The Organisation of the English Customs System, 1696–1786* (New York, 1938), pp. 262–4.
[27] GAA, Archief Brants, 1344, Jasper Waters & Sons, London, to J. I. de Neufville, Amsterdam, 12 March 1730.

If the English fiscal system actually discouraged the growth of processing industries dependent upon imported goods, the Dutch system of low duties, low interest rates and cheap freight rates clearly had the reverse effect. The Dutch *verkeersindustrien* (literally 'traffic industries') overwhelmed the rest of the Republic's industrial sector, and England's commercial relations with Holland during the first half of the eighteenth century were conditioned as much by the capacities of these industries as by the declining importance of the Dutch entrepôt.[28] In some respects, the English economy in 1700 or even 1730 can still be viewed as a hinterland subservient to the finishing industries of Holland, which stood at the centre of a world re-export system. A sizeable proportion of English woollens exported to Holland were sent in a white state to be dyed and finished at Leiden, though mixtures were sent chiefly for the transit trade to Germany and the Empire. The bulk of the English grain export trade consisted of the malt required by the Dutch brewing and distilling industries; whilst coal exports likewise served the needs of those industries in Rotterdam and Schiedam, together with those of sugar bakers, smiths and others. And much of the English lead and tin exported entered into the largely Dutch-controlled international arms trade. On the import side, most of the Holland linens shipped to England had been manufactured in Germany prior to bleaching and finishing at Haarlem. Most significant, however, was the fact that Holland remained the initial destination for the bulk of English re-exports in the earlier decades of the century – from whence they were re-exported a second time by the Dutch, in some cases after processing. This is the real measure of the success of the Dutch re-export system in the late seventeenth and early eighteenth centuries. As late as 1773, Wyndham Beawes complained that 'our products and manufactures, Plantation and East-India goods furnish materials for a great part of their trade [i.e. of the Dutch] with other nations; by which they are so far from being sufferers, that, on the contrary, the more they take from us, the more they enlarge their universal traffic, and consequently increase their riches'.[29] By this time, such a view was anachronistic, but it illustrates the surprising persistence of anti-Dutch feelings in some quarters.

When, in fact, did the Dutch entrepôt begin to lose its importance as a market for English re-exports? Some indication is provided by the statistics of the re-export trade, which have been extracted from the

---

[28] See Ormrod, 'Anglo-Dutch Commerce', Chapter 1.
[29] W. Beawes, *Lex Mercatoria or The Merchant's Directory*, 6th edn (Dublin, 1773), p. 521.

Table 6.1. The re-export trade 1700–60, annual averages, £000 (official values)

	Total re-exports from England and Wales	Total re-exports to Holland	Re-exports to Holland as % of total	Re-exports to Holland of			
				Indian textiles	Groceries	Tobacco	Others
1700–05	1,822.4	781.9	42.9	234.6	165.2	157.5	224.6
1706–10	1,539.6	605.4	39.3	209.3	121.7	164.8	109.6
1711–15	2,072.3	938.2	45.3	387.1	251.7	116.9	182.5
1716–20	2,291.4	820.2	35.8	277.3	265.1	138.8	139.0
1721–25	2,278.2	941.6	34.5	413.5	294.0	118.4	115.7
1726–30	3,096.2	1,075.0	34.7	463.2	182.1	199.3	230.4
1731–35	3,058.4	981.6	32.1	548.9	137.7	148.8	146.2
1736–40	3,314.2	902.9	27.2	451.9	113.7	195.5	141.8
1741–45	3,722.0	1,059.4	28.5	448.3	242.4	250.8	117.9
1746–50	3,448.8	933.3	27.1	393.8	123.9	248.3	167.3
1751–55	3,448.8	843.8	24.5	376.1	142.7	240.8	84.2
1756–60	3,656.4	678.3	18.6	270.2	142.6	183.4	82.1

Sources: PRO Customs 3; Custom House, London: Customs Ledgers.

Customs Ledgers compiled by the Inspectors General of Imports and Exports and are shown in Table 6.1. Total re-exports from England and Wales are expressed in terms of the official values and converted into annual averages for five-year periods. Against these figures are shown the size and proportion of re-exports absorbed by the Dutch staplemarket (namely Dutch domestic consumption plus further re-export); and this is broken down into its component parts, distinguishing groceries, Indian textiles, tobacco and a miscellaneous category consisting mainly of 'drugs' (mostly dyestuffs), silk, diamonds, wood, foreign wool and linen. Fig. 6.1 attempts to show the same information graphically. It must be emphasized that, for reasons which will be explained below, these figures represent only an approximation to the real state of affairs which they purport to describe. But at least two major conclusions can safely be drawn from them. The first is the great importance of Holland as a market or initial destination for English re-exports during the War of the Spanish Succession; and during this period specifically, the figures underestimate this fact. After the war, and during the 1720s, the proportion of re-exports absorbed by the Dutch declines to just over one-third of the total, and by the early 1750s it has fallen to about one-quarter. But if we look at the absolute figures involved, and make some correction for the undervaluation of certain commodities during the first decade of the century, we can see that the trend is a fairly stable or stagnant one, rather than a case of decline. This is a state of affairs which is reflected in so many other areas of Dutch economic life, this 'relative economic decline', that it has become a commonplace amongst Dutch economic historians.[30] But another way of looking at this phenomenon may be suggested which makes some allowance for the historian's overdeveloped faculty of hindsight, and that is to emphasize the continuing subordination of the English entrepôt to the Dutch in the world re-export system of the early eighteenth century. Contemporaries, of course, were unaware of the subsequently diverging commercial and industrial paths of the two economies. As Hugh Dunthorne has pointed out:

Dutch economic decline, so much discussed today, did not prevent the Republic from being regarded in Walpole's Britain as a formidable trade competitor–particularly as the supposed decline seems to have been much less evident to outsiders than to the Dutch themselves. If a foreigner remarked on the Republic's economic difficulties at all, generally he either dismissed them as merely temporary, or else distinguished between the indebtedness of the Dutch state and

---

[30] The underlying argument of de Vries, *Economische achteruitgang*, e.g. pp. 30, 83.

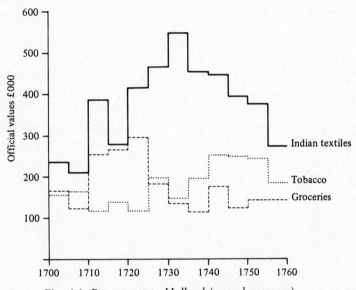

Fig. 6.1. Re-exports to Holland (annual averages)

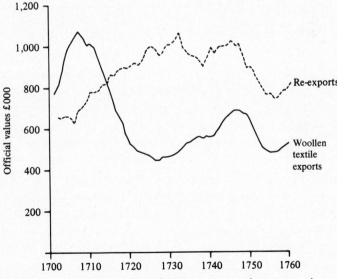

Fig. 6.2. Anglo-Dutch trade (nine-year moving averages)

99

the reputedly immense wealth of 'multitudes of their magistrates and merchants'.[31]

The second major conclusion to be drawn from these data is the overwhelming dominance of Indian textiles (which include calicoes) over other categories of re-export products. This is especially clear in Figs. 6.1 and 6.2, comparison of which shows that it was movements of Indian textiles which determined trends in the re-export trade to Holland as a whole. When we place the Inspector General's statistics alongside those of the East India Company's own figures for total imports of textiles from Asia into Britain, and make correction for the undervaluation of the latter so as to make the two sets of figures roughly comparable, it is evident that a very high proportion of the Indian textiles imported into Britain, usually around two-thirds or above, were re-exported to Holland up to the 1740s.[32] Those contemporaries who complained that the Dutch controlled the most lucrative part of the English re-export trade spoke with some truth. Davenant, as one of the early Inspectors General, was well aware of the direction in which the statistics pointed when he wrote, in 1711:

As the case now stands, Amsterdam and Rotterdam are in a manner the magazines for the wrought silk, Bengal stuffs mixed with silk, or herba of the manufacture of Persia, China, or East India, and of all callicoes painted, dyed, printed, or stained there, the use of which commodities being prohibited here, are chiefly sent to Holland ... Which goods being bought cheap in the Indies, and sold dear in Europe, ought to turn richly to the importers account; but it is to be feared our neighbours make a greater profit from them than England, which sends out its bullion, runs all the hazards of the sea and by-captures, and is at the expense of forts, castles and factories to support this traffic.[33]

Davenant's comments highlight two of the most significant and contentious questions arising from the trade in Indian textiles – the first concerning the effects of the prohibitions against their use in England, and the second concerning their official valuation and real value, with implications for the question of 'unequal exchange' between Europe and Asia, between 'core and periphery'. The valuation of Indian fabrics on re-exportation posed a difficult problem for the Inspectors General because of the enormous range of imported textiles which had to be

[31] H. Dunthorne, 'The Alliance of the Maritime Powers, 1721–1740', unpublished Ph.D thesis, University of London, 1978.
[32] Statistics of total imports of textiles from Asia by the English East India Company are provided in Appendix 5 of Chaudhuri, *Trading World of Asia*, pp. 547–8.
[33] C. Davenant, 'Second Report to the Honourable Commissioners for Stating the Public Accounts', Part II, 10 December 1711, printed in Davenant's *Political and Commercial Works*, ed. C. Whitworth (London, 1771), v, 430.

identified and the difficulty of estimating handling and shipping charges. The question of valuations continues to perplex historians and doubtless explains an evident reluctance to examine the re-export trade in any detail.[34] In fact there are two separate problems involved – that of changes in the official values, since there appear to have been adjustments during the first decade of the century, and that of the authenticity of the official values, that is, the extent to which they represented real selling prices. Table 6.2 attempts to throw some light on these questions by comparing the official values with real wholesale prices taken from merchants' correspondence. This indicates that a firm list of official values for Indian textiles emerged after the first decade of the century. It should be understood that, as in the case of tea, coffee and diamonds, Indian textiles were entered in the ledgers 'at value', that is to say, at the merchant's valuation. But in practice, a list of official values seems to have fossilized by 1711, certainly by 1716, in the case of all Asian textiles with the important exception of calicoes, which had always been valued at 12s per piece.[35] Tea, on the other hand, seems to have been entered at a variable valuation, presumably approaching its real value.[36] The practical implication of this is that the Inspector General's statistics can be used to give a fairly reliable indication of changes in the *volume* of re-exports of Indian textiles from about the middle of the second decade of the century, but that before this date the upward drift of valuations gives an exaggerated impression of the true rate of growth. A further point to emerge from Table 6.2 is that if the official statistics are considered in their approximation to real values, comparison of valuations with real wholesale prices taken from merchants' correspondence shows that the

---

[34] Prof. Davis in his article 'English Foreign Trade, 1660–1700' conducted a careful investigation of valuations in the 'Book of Tables' for London's trade in the 1660s, but not of the Customs Ledgers; and in his later article, 'English Foreign Trade, 1700–1774', he avoided the problem altogether by referring his readers, in a footnote, to T. S. Ashton's introduction to Mrs Schumpeter's *English Overseas Trade Statistics, 1697–1808* (Oxford, 1960). As far as re-exports were concerned, Ashton believed that 'the only substantial revaluation [of re-exports] was that of coffee, at the end of the [eighteenth] century' (*ibid.*, p. 4). Yet in his *Economic History of England: The Eighteenth Century* (London, 1955), Ashton wrote (p. 161) 'The statistics are too unreliable to make it possible to give even approximate estimates of the value (or 'volume') of re-exports... In official values, re-exports were generally about a third of total exports. Whether in terms of market prices they were above or below this, it is impossible to say.' And so he confined his remarks on re-exports to a single paragraph. Defoe had a similar difficulty: the value of re-exported groceries, he wrote, was 'hard to determine' though 'exceeding great' (*Plan of the English Commerce*). Perhaps, in the last analysis, this is all that can be said.

[35] G. N. Clark (ed.), *Guide to English Commercial Statistics, 1696–1782* (London, 1938), pp. 86–7.

[36] Tea was entered 'at value' in the Customs Ledgers (PRO Customs 3) as follows (per lb.), 1700, 3s 2d; 1706, 19s; 1711, 6s 2d; 1716, 11s; 1721, 12s 6d; 1731, 10s.

Table 6.2. *Official values of Indian textiles compared with real prices, 1727–49*

	Official values					Real wholesale prices				
	1700	1706	1711	1716	1721	1727	1728	1730	1731	1749
Cossacs	12s	12s	20s	55s	49s	54s6d–55s6d	17s8d–59s	31s–54s6d	52s6d–55s6d	37s6d–44s6d
Calicoes	12s5d	20s	12s	12s6d	12s					
Chintzes		20s	16s6d	26s6d	26s6d			17s9d–19s2d		
Chucklees	40s		45s	45s	45s	32s				
Chelloes		15s	17s	17s	17s		8s1d–12s4d–13s2d			
Ginghams	4s4d	20s	27s	27s	27s			10s8d–11s4d		
Humhums		10s					32s–34s	29s6d–32s6d		
Mulmulls	20s4d	20s	40s	25s	41s	49s	40s6d	32s6d–57s6d		63s6d
Nilleas	13s2d	15s	25s6d	25s	25s			13s2d–13s10d		
Photaes	22s2d	10s	10s	10s	10s	9s2d		9s2d	7s7d–8s5d	
Romalls	18s8d		21s6d	28s	28s	9s–10s	10s1d	9s3d		8s4d
Seersuckers	21s2d				24s6d	18s–19s 2d	14s8d–17s2d			
Soosaies	38s1d	40s	48s3d	52s	52s	29s–31s	31s6d–34s6d	41s		32s–34s
Tanjeebs	54s6d		101s1d		55s4d	33s–44s	17s8d	31s6d		
Tepoys	16s6d		36s	36s						

Sources: Official values, PRO Customs 3/4, 9, 14, 18, 23.
Real prices represent wholesale prices of textiles re-exported to Amsterdam by English merchants, and taken from Archief Brants 1344, J. Waters & Sons, London, January–December 1727 and May–June 1728; *ibid.*, C. Bosanquet, London, February and October 1749; and PRO C108/132, H. Gambier, London, November 1730 and October 1731.

later, post-1716, valuations probably overestimated the real value of Indian textile re-exports. The official values current at the start of the century were probably more authentic, and from the historian's point of view it is unfortunate that these were revised and increased. These qualifications must therefore be borne in mind when reading the official statistics of Table 6.1.

The valuations discussed so far refer to prices at the point of re-export, but how do these compare with values on import from Asia? In 1719, the Inspector General, Henry Martin, suggested that calicoes, 'which is much the greatest part of the whole value imported from the East Indies', were correctly valued on re-export at 12s, but overvalued 'clear on board from East India' (i.e. at import), by between 2s and 3s. The correct import valuation, he judged, was 5s rather than the East India Company's valuation of 7s 6d.[37] As far as other categories of East Indian textile are concerned, it seems that these were overvalued both on import *and* at re-export. It may be concluded, therefore, that goods were indeed bought cheap in Asia and if not exactly sold dear in Europe, for reasons which will be explained below, were sold at prices which could be described as only 'moderately expensive'. The correspondence of merchants engaged in the re-export trade suggests that profits were small, little more than five or six per cent. John Eccleston of London wrote, typically, to one of his Amsterdam correspondents in 1733 that the sale of his chintzes there had 'rendered a very poor produce, but as the balance is on the right side, tho' small, I must be content'.[38] Claude Bosanquet of London pressed the same Amsterdam house more urgently: 'The French have no muslin and calico of their own and taking ours, the Dutch and Germans must of necessity conform to give good prices so hope you'll sell ours advantageously; for 4 or 5 percent one may make that here without trouble or any risk.'[39] If large profits were made in the trade in Indian textiles, these must have accrued to the East India Company on import rather than to merchants in the re-export trade who sustained their business in the hope of an occasional speculative windfall.

As we have seen, Davenant was also concerned about the effects of the legislation prohibiting the use of printed Indian textiles in Britain on the course of overseas trade. The history of the campaign mounted by the woollen industry to protect itself against the rising tide of Indian textile

---

[37] Henry Martin, 'An Essay Towards Finding the Balance of our Whole Trade Annually from Christmas of 1698 to Christmas 1719', PRO CO 390/14, reprinted in Clark, (ed.), *English Commercial Statistics*, p. 86.

[38] GAA, Archief Brants, 1344, John Eccleston, London, to J. I. de Neufville, Amsterdam, 19 June 1733; also 7 December 1733.

[39] *Ibid.*, Claude Bosanquet, London, to J. I. de Neufville, Amsterdam, 2 March 1749.

imports is fairly well known. Defoe lent his support to the weavers' case, and contemporary descriptions of the weavers' riots which led to the passage of the Prohibition Acts of 1700 and 1720 are invariably quoted in standard accounts of the period.[40] The legislation, it is commonly accepted, was prompted by riots and unemployment in the weaving districts, and the general economic background both to the late 1690s and to the early 1720s was certainly one of commercial dislocation and financial crisis. But it is astonishing that interested contemporaries, especially within the woollen industry, paid such slight attention to the possible long-term commercial repercussions of the prohibition policy, and historians have likewise avoided the question. As Chaudhuri says, 'the significance of the re-export trade was generally forgotten in the fears that England was importing and consuming too many foreign goods'.[41] The repercussions of the prohibitions, in fact, must have been felt at two levels: first, that of diverting overseas Indian textiles which otherwise would have been consumed at home; and second, the enlarged flow of such textiles into Europe, especially Holland, must have reduced the overseas demand for English woollens, particularly as Holland remained the principal market for these goods also. The two categories of textile were not, of course, close substitutes, but the growing trend towards the production of lighter fabrics within the English woollen industry, especially mixtures such as the East Anglian 'stuffs mixed with silk', meant that there was a strong element of competition between them. It was one which was largely absent from the Dutch woollen industry, which, as Posthumus showed, shifted gradually towards the production of *laakens* (the heavier broadcloths) during the course of the seventeenth century at the expense of new drapery manufacture.[42] Before proceeding further with this argument, it is important to recapitulate the provisions of the two Prohibition Acts.[43]

The first act, passed in 1700 but taking effect from 29 September 1701, prohibited the wearing and household use of all wrought silks, Bengals (Bengal silks), stuffs mixed with silk (known as herba) from Persia, China or India, and all calicoes painted, dyed, printed or stained abroad; these goods were to be warehoused and accounted for by warehouse keepers; any unwarehoused goods were liable to seizure and their owners to fines; and no duties were to be paid on import, apart from the half

[40] See Chapter 14, 'Daniel Defoe and the Calico Madams', in A. Plummer, *The London Weavers' Company, 1600–1970* (London, 1972), pp. 292–311.
[41] Chaudhuri, *Trading World of Asia*, p. 12.
[42] See C. H. Wilson, 'Cloth Production and International Competition in the Seventeenth Century', *Economic History Review*, 2nd series 13 (1960).
[43] 11 and 12 Wm III c. 10 (1700); 7 Geo I c. 7 (1720).

subsidy. The import of white calicoes was, of course, permitted. The second act, passed in 1720 but taking effect from 25 December 1722, prohibited the wear and household use of painted, dyed, printed or stained calicoes, whether coloured at home or abroad, and established a £5 penalty to be paid by the wearer to the informer. Muslins, neckcloths, fustians and calicoes dyed blue were exempted from the provisions of the act. It will be seen at once that the 1720 act was a much more direct attempt to impose a piece of sumptuary legislation than that of 1700; the earlier act concentrated mainly on controlling and diverting the import trade, whilst the later act introduced a simple and practicable means of limiting the consumption of the offending textiles. It also attempted to restrain the developing textile-printing industry.

It is difficult to estimate the long-term effects of the prohibitions and the extent to which they fulfilled the expectations of those who had steered them through Parliament, two related but by no means identical questions. The Inspector General's commercial statistics provide some indication of the changing course of trade, but the growth of a smuggling trade in prohibited goods creates obvious problems for the historian. Contemporary comments may provide a guide, but, as noted above, most contemporaries were preoccupied with the domestic consumption of imported Indian textiles and the internal demand for woollens, rather than with the re-export trade in these fabrics and the extent to which this displaced English woollens in European markets. Davenant was an exception and considered the question in some detail. His remarks are worth quoting, although his role as a Tory polemicist in the early years of the century, together with his strong defence of the East India Company (which finally gave him a post in 1698), mean that he is not the most reliable of commentators.[44] Of all his writings, it has been suggested that Davenant's 'Memorial concerning the free trade now tolerated between France and Holland' is most sympathetic to the Dutch and relatively moderate.[45] It was written after a visit to Holland in 1705 and contains these comments:

I found the Dutch universally pleased with our Prohibition to wear East India and Persia wrought silks, Bengalls, dyed, printed or stained callicoes. And, whereas we expected it would advance our woollen manufactures, they affirm the

---

[44] The tone of Davenant's remarks is always deceptively uncommitted and informed, so it is important to remember that he was opposed to the protection of English textiles against Indian competition on the grounds that trade with India improved the overall balance of trade and that, as a leading Tory pamphleteer, he was at pains to point out that the Dutch were profiting at England's expense during the war, whenever possible.

[45] See D. Waddell, 'Charles Davenant (1656–1714): A Biographical Sketch', *Economic History Review*, 2nd series, 11 (1958), 286.

contrary, and that these Indian goods are worne by their own people, and sold by the Hollanders to other countries with whom they deale in the very room of our Woollen Manufactures which they dayly beat out abroad by being as well cheaper as finer to the eye.[46]

The official statistics tend to confirm this view. Some of the problems raised by the official valuations have already been mentioned, and allowance must be made when using this material for the smuggling trade in prohibited goods between Holland and the eastern ports of England.[47] Entirely reputable merchants engaged in occasional smuggling ventures at times when opportunities for profitable legal trade were few. Jones & Cross, for example, linen drapers of London, during the 1750s placed regular orders with de Neufvilles in Amsterdam for prohibited goods, French and Flemish lace and russells and Indian goods, although their main business was the import of linen through legal channels.[48] Another importer of linen, Ciprien Rondeau, suggested that 'one might have a case made pretty strong and a dubb bottom, the vacancy not to exceed three-quarters of an inch and the inside bottom to be thin and nailed also with paper as usual at the bottom of the case' for the handling of prohibited goods.[49] But ventures such as these would not have been worth the great trouble and expense involved for any but the most expensive silks and laces. When we turn to the commercial statistics, there seems to be little doubt that the prohibitions greatly reduced the consumption of Indian goods, though some illegal trade was carried on.

The figures assembled in Table 6.3, which show the extent to which Indian textiles were diverted from home consumption to the chief

[46] PRO CO 389/18, f. 523. In his 'Second Report to the Commissioners for Stating the Public Accounts' of 1711, however, Davenant reversed his argument that the prohibition had adversely affected the demand for English woollens abroad: 'Nor does it appear to me, from any observation I can make, that East India goods have hurt the general traffic of our woollen manufactures in foreign markets; these silks and stuffs seem rather a commodity calculated for the middle rank of people; they are too vulgar to be worn by the best sort, and too costly for the lowest rank, so that the use of them remains in the middle rank, who (the luxuries of the world still increasing) would wear European silks if they had not East India stuffs and painted calicoes, whereby the rest of our woollen goods abroad would certainly be lessened.' But this document has been described by D. C. Coleman as 'an anti-Dutch polemic' with 'a spurious air of impartiality' ('Politics and Economics in the Age of Anne: The Case of the Anglo-French Trade Treaty of 1713', in D. C. Coleman and A. H. John (eds.), *Trade, Government and Economy in Pre-Industrial England* (London, 1976), p. 190).
[47] Ormrod, 'Anglo-Dutch Commerce', Chapter 6.
[48] GAA, Archief Brants, 1344, Jones & Cross, London, to J. I. de Neufville, Amsterdam, 29 October 1756, 26 August 1757, 5 May 1758, 31 January 1759.
[49] *Ibid.*, C. Rondeau, London, to J. I. de Neufville, Amsterdam, 8 November 1745.

Table 6.3. Re-exports of Indian textiles to Holland following the Prohibition Acts
£000 (official values)

1697–8	63.6	1717	194.0
1699	123.0	1718	120.2
1700	243.7	1719	333.4
1701	228.8	1720	470.2
		1721	540.1
1702	181.3		
1703	255.4	1722	485.9
1704	210.5	1723	213.4
		1724	376.0

Source: PRO Customs 3.

re-export markets in Holland, are reasonably clear. Although the acts did not take effect until September 1701 and December 1722, the controversy and uncertainty surrounding their passage through Parliament might be expected to produce changes in the direction of trade at earlier moments – since the trade in these and indeed in all re-export commodities was highly speculative. The so-called calico controversy was especially acute during the period 1719–21, and the expected change in the course of trade can be identified with little difficulty. The longer-term effects of the second prohibition may well be reflected in the data of Fig. 6.1, although it is difficult to say what other influences were at work. As P. J. Thomas explained, contemporaries were by no means agreed even on the immediate effects of the prohibitions, although there was some acknowledgement that the second act was more effective than the first, if only because of its greater simplicity and the extent to which it allowed the woollen and silk weavers to take the law into their own hands – which indeed they did.[50] Norwich weavers instituted prosecutions on the 1720 act and inserted notices in the local press pointing out that the wearing of printed fabrics was illegal. At the same time, the use of calico was similarly prohibited in all parts of Europe except, significantly, Holland.[51]

Perhaps the most suggestive evidence lies in a comparison of trends in the re-export trade to Holland with the course of exports of woollen manufactures to that market shown in Fig. 6.2. It is fairly clear that there is an inverse correlation between the two. As re-exports of Indian textiles increased, it seems that exports of woollens declined, and vice versa.

[50] P. J. Thomas, *Mercantilism and the East India Trade* (London, 1926), pp. 118–21, 159–65.
[51] *Ibid.*, pp. 164, 86–7.

107

This is not to say that independent influences did not effect the course of the woollen trade such as conditions of wartime trading, clothing contracts for troops, and movements in the exchange rate;[52] but simply to suggest that in a period of stagnant population and overstocked markets (a favourite phrase bandied about by merchants in the 1720s and 1730s), there were certain limits to the demand for all types of textile taken together so that buoyancy in one area of the market was liable to produce depression in another.

This inverse relationship between movements of woollen manufactures and of Indian goods seems to hold until at least 1740. It is linked with an unmistakable tendency, which emerges from contemporary merchants' correspondence, for European markets to become saturated with re-exported products of all kinds, but particularly textiles, during the 1720s and early 1730s. This state of affairs was admirably summarized by an English merchant resident in Amsterdam in 1730, Diederick Smith: 'Nobody can imagine him the poor and miserable state of trade of all India goods; almost a man doth not know which way he shall turn himself and on what article he shall touch.'[53] Similarly, Jasper Waters & Sons, who exported chintzes, muslins and Bengals from London to Amsterdam, complained by 1734 that: 'you reap a certain profit by this correspondence, which is more than we do; this trade is indeed not worth our carrying on.'[54] Such instances and comments could be multiplied to show that individual merchants gradually abandoned the London–Amsterdam trade in these goods during the 1730s. Jasper Waters, for example, turned increasingly to the African trade which absorbed the cheapest Indian fabrics. In 1733 he wrote:

Our company have gone a great way in selling their Bengal goods. Last week they sold their seersuckers; there was but 26 bales of them of which we bought 18–16 of them in our own names, and two by brokers. We must own they are ordinary goods but much wanted for our Guinea trade. We have sold lately some bales of a former buying for a very great profit to those who trade for Africa, and an inferior sort will serve for them. We know they won't do for your market [Amsterdam], and indeed not one bale of this sale is bought for any market in the world besides Africa; all ours are designed for the same.[55]

In the case of tea, coffee and other groceries, it was clear that too many were participating in the Amsterdam trade – as Sir Jacob Senserf put it,

---

[52] Ormrod, 'Anglo-Dutch Commerce', pp. 156–68.
[53] PRO C103/131, bundle 5, Diederick Smith, Amsterdam, to Thomas Hall, London, 5 May 1780.
[54] GAA Archief Brants, 1344, J. Waters & Sons, London, to J. I. de Neufville, Amsterdam, 4 June 1734.
[55] Ibid., J. Waters & Sons, London, to J. I. de Neufville, Amsterdam, 30 October 1733.

business was 'overdone on all sides'.[56] The margin between selling prices in England and in Holland was too narrow to sustain trade at this level, and during the later 1730s the volume of re-exports sent to Holland contracted. It was during the 1720s that tea drinking reached enormous proportions in Europe. 'The consumption of tea', wrote one merchant in 1733, 'is become an epidemical distemper, and even the Northern People who used to drink brandy begin to drink tea.' 'We believe our common people [in Holland] would rather want bread than tea.'[57] Coffee drinking had likewise affected all levels of society: 'The world is so debauched here that all people from the highest to the lowest drink regularly their coffee in the morning and tea in the afternoon.' Yet by 1739 the same merchant wrote: 'What will become of these articles [tea and coffee] God knows, but it is impossible to consume them.'[58] A fairly high elasticity of demand for groceries, and the almost unlimited possibility of increasing supplies in Europe, had greatly extended their markets in the 1720s and 1730s; but by the later 1730s it seems that lower prices meant disappearing profits. The problem facing merchants was undoubtedly one of over-supply, particularly as the hitherto monopolistic market situation governing Asian products became an oligopolistic one in the second quarter of the century, chiefly as a result of the activities of the Ostend Company and its Danish and Swedish successors. Before the rise of the Ostend traders, it was the buying policies of the English and Dutch East India Companies which determined world prices for Asian goods. The English company, from the mid seventeenth century, auctioned its imports at quarterly sales held in London, though the September/October sale seems to have been the most notable. The prices obtained at these sales provided the Directors with the information they needed to determine buying policies in Asia, and both buyers and sellers kept a close watch on the level of prices reached in Amsterdam and Middelburg where the Dutch East India Company's sales were held.[59] India goods were increasingly auctioned at private sales, and with the passage of the Prohibition Acts and the rising level of import duties, sales of seizures and 'damaged goods' were held more frequently by the

---

[56] PRO C103/133, bundle 17, J. Senserf & Son, Rotterdam, to Thomas Hall, London, 23 September 1735: 'We seldom encourage our friends to engage in any commodity because we daily finde by experience how little there is to be depended upon, trade being overdone on all sides.'

[57] *Ibid.*, J. Senserf & Son, Rotterdam, to Thomas Hall, London, 2 October 1733, 2 February 1734.

[58] *Ibid.*, J. Senserf & Son, Rotterdam, to Thomas Hall, London, 8 November 1735, 15 September 1739.

[59] Chaudhuri, *Trading World of Asia*, pp. 131–5.

customs authorities. The circulation of printed lists and sale notices was common.[60]

But it was the progress of the Ostend Company which disturbed the entrenched positions of the English and Dutch companies more than anything else. In one respect, the formation of the Ostend Company was part of the Southern Netherlanders' protracted struggle to break the economic stranglehold established over them by England and Holland during the seventeenth century and confirmed in the Barrier Treaty of 1715. But it was more than this; it represented a wider offensive, attracting discontented merchants from all over north-western Europe, against the commercial chauvinism practised by the great monopoly India Companies of England and Holland. Amongst the Ostend traders were to be found not only Flemings but also Dutchmen, French, English, Scots and Irish.[61] Their impact on European commerce has not been fully recognized by English historians

From about 1715 to 1722, the Ostend Company's activities took the form of unorganized individual ventures which were licensed by the imperial authorities in Brussels. In 1722 it was formally established by imperial charter, and there followed five years of rapidly growing trade with Bengal and China, until its activities were suspended in 1727 before dissolution in 1731. The vigour of the Ostend tea sales during this period was attested by several merchants, such as Isaac & Willem Kops of Amsterdam, who wrote in 1719 that they were resorted to by great numbers of Dutch, French and English buyers, who would 'fetch their belly full at Ostend'.[62] By the early 1730s, Ostend had been eclipsed by the markets of Middelburg and Rotterdam, especially the former, where port charges were low and duties non-existent, which, as one merchant said, was 'a vast encouragement for them to resort thither and abandon Ostend as they have all done '.[63] But although the company's formal organization fell apart in 1731, the Ostenders found ways of continuing their trade – by sailing under Polish or Prussian colours, by using other ports, such as Hamburg or Cadiz, or by transferring their allegiance to other companies of a similar kind newly established in Sweden (1731),

---

[60] Hoon, *English Customs System*, pp. 281–6; GAA, Archief Brants, 1344, C. Bosanquet, London, to J. I. de Neufville, Amsterdam, sale notices of 26 September 1750, 10 December 1750.

[61] Dunthorne, 'Alliance of the Maritime Powers', p. 57.

[62] *Ibid.*, p. 58; PRO C108/132, I. & W. Kops, Amsterdam, to Henry Gambier, London, 8 August 1719.

[63] PRO C103/131, Charles Pike, Amsterdam, to Thomas Hall, London, 14 December 1731.

Denmark (1732), Spain (1733) and Prussia (1750).[64] In 1737, Sir Jacob Senserf of Rotterdam wrote: 'There is little prospect that tea will ever bear a high price; those Danish and Swedish ships knock down at speculation in these parts, because they furnish now what this country [Holland] used to do formerly.' And three years later: 'The article of tea is very bad and will hardly mend as long as so many European nations trade to China.'[65]

Various efforts were made by the English and the Dutch to put these companies out of business, either through conventional diplomatic channels, through bribery, or by commercial strategies such as flooding the market and depressing prices.[66] Their failure stemmed largely from the very limited degree of cooperation between the British and Dutch governments and the two East India Companies. Hugh Dunthorne suggests that 'The undoubted community of interest among ordinary British and Dutch merchants seems to have been rather less in evidence at the higher level of government ministers and East India directors.'[67] The British governmentt's half-hearted concern over the Ostend question no doubt stemmed from a mild suspicion of the East Indian interest, and possibly from a feeling that the Dutch were a greater threat than the Ostenders who were perhaps serving a useful function in undermining the Dutch East India Company.

There seems to be little doubt that these developments, which evidently lay outside the control of the British and Dutch governments and the two great India monopolies, go far in explaining the 'dullness' of the re-export trade in groceries during the 1720s and 1730s which is depicted in the data of Table 6.1 and Fig 6.1. As a result of the new trading ventures to Asia, European and particularly Dutch markets were swollen with additional supplies producing low prices and profits and sluggish returns. And it seems that conditions of overstocked markets produced a declining trend in re-exports of Indian textiles from about the mid 1730s. Up to this point, the effect of the prohibitions had been to encourage the growth of a re-export trade in these fabrics to the Dutch staplemarket which appears to have been competitive with exports of English woollen manufactures.

If the English re-export trade was characterized by poor returns and

---

[64] Dunthorne, 'Alliance of the Maritime Powers', p. 58.
[65] PRO C103/133, bundle 22, J. Senserf & Son, Rotterdam, to Thomas Hall, London, 20 December 1737, 22 July 1740. See also Chaudhuri, *Trading World of Asia*, pp. 391–2.
[66] Dunthorne, 'Alliance of the Maritime Powers', pp. 62–5.
[67] *Ibid.*, pp. 73–4.

considerable damaging side-effects, it must also be pointed out that such profits as it produced did not accrue wholly to English merchants, since a proportion of the trade (possibly a high proportion) was carried on Dutch accounts. Many of the buyers at the English East India Company's sales were either visiting or resident Dutch merchants, or agents and brokers acting for Dutch buyers. Henry Gambier, a London merchant and broker whose bankruptcy in the 1730s caused his papers to acquire the doubtful status of Chancery Masters' Exhibits, was one of the largest brokers attending the London sales, and his most substantial purchases were those for two Dutch houses established in London, John and Mattheus de Neufville and Francis and John van Hemert.[68] Mattheus established the London firm with his cousin John in 1722, and the correspondence ends ten years later, when Mattheus returned to live in Amsterdam, though no longer as a merchant; John de Neufville remained in London until at least 1743.[69] The van Hemerts appear to have been established in London for a longer period.[70] As well as making purchases on behalf of Dutch customers or resident Dutch merchants such as these, Gambier also purchased teas, chinaware and Indian textiles on his own account and seems to have developed two major outlets for these commodities: North America, mainly S. Carolina, supplied via wholesale merchants, and provincial grocers in places such as Newbury, Epsom, Wantage, Poole and Tonbridge.[71] Apart from illustrating the extent to which it was possible to combine trade on one's own account with commissions, Gambier's interests indicate the tendency of merchants engaged in the re-export trade to avoid specialization. Trade in tea, for example, generally led to trade in other groceries, and this was usually combined with dealings in Indian textiles, and sometimes chinaware, spices and dyestuffs. The prevailing impression is that the larger dealers and brokers were likely to be most successful in the highly speculative East India trade; the London linen drapers on the other hand, who imported Dutch and German linen on their own accounts from Amsterdam and exported Indian cottons and silks from time to time to

---

[68] PRO C108/132 (Gambier Papers), e.g. list of purchases, November 1730, 20 October 1731. On de Neufville, see I. H. van Eeghen's editorial introduction to *Inventaris van het familie-archief Brants* (Amsterdam, 1959), pp. 13–14, and J. W. Veluwenkamp, *Ondernemersgedrag op de Hollandse stapelmarkt.*

[69] Van Eeghen (ed.), *Invertaris van het familie-archief Brants*, p.13.

[70] GAA, Archief Brants, 1344, van Hemert correspondence.

[71] PRO C108/132, correspondence with David Compigne, S. Carolina (bundle 3); Edward Crisp, Epsom; J. Lipyeatt, Newbury; J. Rosfield, London and Poole; C. Weekes, Dorchester.

be sold on commission by Dutch houses, obtained low returns and consistently disappointing results.[72]

It is impossible to say what proportion of the re-export trade in Indian textiles was carried on the accounts of Dutch houses, but the impression given by the London merchant Claude Bosanquet was that it was considerable, when he wrote to an Amsterdam correspondent in 1751: 'Can it be worthwhile for so many of your Gentry and others to cross the seas to continue from sale to sale such a trade? Surely they must have ways of disposing of their goods at some what better prices than you do.'[73] Since the late 1740s, Bosanquet had been trading on joint account with de Neufville in East Indian goods, and he continued to do so until 1753 when the correspondence peters out. Certainly, Davenant indicated early in the century that there were 'two sorts of buyers at the candle of these [Indian] goods, viz. those who bid by commission from Holland, and our own linen drapers and other dealers in those commodities'. The former, he suggested, predominated; for, if the prohibition against Indian goods were lifted, 'the Dutch will not have it so much in their power to set their own price upon them and London, instead of Rotterdam and Amsterdam, will be the great magazine for East India wares, as heretofore it was'.[74] In terms of commercial organization, therefore, the re-export trade was characterized by strong tendencies towards quasi-monopolistic and monopolistically competitive practices both in terms of original supply and in terms of control of the London–Amsterdam trade by Dutch houses. It was precisely the undermining of the English and Dutch East India monopolies in the 1720s and 1730s by the Ostend traders which greatly destabilized the trade, but the benefits to consumers in the shape of lower prices must have been obvious enough.

Some general observations may now be offered on the question raised towards the beginning of this essay: what light does the history of re-exports throw on the relative progress of the two major commercial economies during a period of stagnation? Much capital and energy had gone into the establishment of the colonial and re-export trades in the 1670s and 1680s, when they have been seen as representing major dynamic elements in the economy and ushering in a phase of import-led

[72] GAA, Archief Brants, 1344, correspondence of J. Eccleston, J. Higden Jr, T. Smith & Son, R. Peckham, J. Waters & Sons.
[73] *Ibid.*, C. Bosanquet, London, to J. I. de Neufville, Amsterdam, 1 January 1751.
[74] Davenant, 'Second Report', p. 434.

growth.[75] Re-exports did little, however, to stimulate either commercial or industrial growth over the succeeding half-century; in a situation in which population grew only slowly and the European woollen industry became much more competitive, Indian textile imports and re-exports probably damaged the English woollen industry; and re-exports in general provided little stimulus to the development of processing industry on the Dutch pattern. In so far as low grain prices and a depression in agriculture may be thought to have released purchasing power amongst wage-earners, much of this gain was probably spent on retained imports (both legal and illegal) of groceries and Indian goods. A major share of the profits of re-exporting went to the Dutch, who controlled not only a part of this branch of English trade but also a large slice of the English woollen export trade. Wholesale cloth merchants in Amsterdam and Rotterdam were drawing supplies of woollens on their own accounts from the late seventeenth century onwards, and in the 1730s were corresponding directly with English manufacturers.[76] There was therefore an organizational connection between flows of English woollens and Anglo-Indian textiles to Holland, so that the phenomenon of 'compensatory movement' between the two is hardly surprising. A further significant connection is of course the importance of Dutch holdings of English East India stock at this time.[77] The Asian voyages themselves as well as the disposal of re-exports in Europe were partly financed by the Dutch.

It is precisely these interconnections between English and Dutch financial and commercial activity in the early eighteenth century which, as much as strategic considerations, explain the strong determination, particularly on the Dutch side, to maintain the Anglo-Dutch alliance through periods of difficulty in the 1720s and 1730s.[78] By the later 1730s, however, a change in British policy became evident. As nearby European markets became saturated with colonial and Indian goods in the late 1720s and early 1730s, English merchants sought after more profitable areas of trade, and in the first instance turned from the North Sea towards the Atlantic colonies, where a growing population promised expanding markets.[79] Reaction to the commercial depression therefore

[75] F. J. Fisher, 'London as an Engine of Growth', in J. S. Bromley and E. H. Kossman (eds.), *Britain and the Netherlands*, IV (London, 1972), p. 7.
[76] Ormrod, 'Anglo-Dutch Commerce', pp. 183–203.
[77] See A. M. C. Carter, 'The Dutch and the English Public Debt in 1777', *Economica*, new series, 20 (1953); *idem*, 'Dutch Foreign Investment, 1738–1800', *ibid*; A. M. C. Carter and C. H. Wilson, 'Dutch Investment in Eighteenth Century England: A Note on Yardsticks', *Economic History Review*, 2nd series 13 (1960).
[78] Dunthorne, 'Alliance of the Maritime Powers', pp. 183–203.
[79] Davis, 'English Foreign Trade, 1700–1774'.

produced a decisive shift in trading patterns in at least three directions: away from dependence on woollen exports, away from the markets of nearby Europe, and towards the emancipation of British economic interests from the tutelage of the Dutch Republic. These shifts were clearly reflected in the changing course of British foreign policy. In going to war with Spain in the West Indies in 1739, and later with France in North America, Britain was taking the first step in a policy which turned her attention away from continental affairs in order to concentrate on the pursuit of empire overseas.[80] At the same time, the Dutch slid into the quasi-neutrality of the 1740s, before opting for complete neutrality during the Seven Years' War. In 1737, Horatio Walpole spoke of 'our being so rich and the Dutch being much weaker in every respect than they formerly were, their Marine ... now reduced to so low a state that they can hardly be called a Maritime Power'.[81] Underneath this kind of boasting, however, lay the inescapable fact that price movements and politics were awkwardly intertwined, a fact which historians are more apt to forget than politicians.

[80] Dunthorne, 'Alliance of the Maritime Powers', p. 323.   [81] Quoted *ibid*.

7

'Little London': British merchants in Rotterdam during the seventeenth and eighteenth centuries

P. W. KLEIN

The economic relationship between Great Britain and the Netherlands during the seventeenth and eighteenth centuries has attracted some of the best minds of historical scholarship of both countries.[1] Their fascinating studies have demonstrated convincingly that the antagonism, bitter rivalry and open conflict dividing the two nations in the seventeenth century did not necessarily result from economic or commercial causes. Nor was the development of 'uneasy political neutrality' during the eighteenth century due to any change in their economic relations, even though these relations obviously did change. At the time Dutch capital exports to Britain were gaining in importance. Accordingly, the mutual financial alliance between the two nations may have been strengthened, but this implied 'no increased warmth'.[2]

As far as the Dutch side of the matter is concerned, the above views have been derived almost exclusively from sources relating to the main centre of Dutch commerce and finance, the city of Amsterdam. Such an approach to the matter is certainly to the point. That city, after all, to a very large extent controlled not only the country's economy but also its political affairs. On the other hand, this view tends to overlook the fact that commercial relations with Britain were far from centring on Amsterdam. It is indeed a moot point whether Rotterdam – on the whole second only to Amsterdam – was not in this particular case of greater importance. The town's nickname, 'Little London', was not unjustified.

This essay seeks to specify the position of Rotterdam as far as its

---

[1] Joh. E. Elias, *Het voorspel van de eerste Engelse oorlog*, I, II, (the Hague, 1920); Charles Wilson, *Profit and Power: A Study of England and the Dutch Wars* (The Hague and London, 1978)[2]; idem, *Anglo-Dutch Commerce and Finance in the Eighteenth Century* (Cambridge, 1941).

[2] Wilson, *Anglo-Dutch Commerce*, p. 201.

economic relations with Britain are concerned. As will become clear, these relations were of crucial importance to the town's welfare, as its economic life had become largely dependent on trade with England, Scotland and Ireland. But however strong these links may have been, they carried no weight whatsoever in the political understanding between the two nations. As I will try to show, however, Rotterdam still presented a quite different picture, in this respect, from Amsterdam. In the latter, trade and finance were under the very active control of Dutch merchants and capitalists, excluding foreign interests almost completely. This was a long way from the workings of the great trading centres of earlier times, where foreign control of commerce had been more or less usual. But it also stood in marked contrast to Rotterdam during the seventeenth and eighteenth centuries. Next to their Dutch-born counterparts, British merchants, continued to hold their own, even playing a rather decisive role in all sorts of enterprise.

It would seem that this state of affairs was conditioned mainly by the economics of geography giving shape to the peculiar triangular trading-pattern that had been a characteristic feature of the town's commerce since its rise in the Middle Ages. During the sixteenth and seventeenth centuries this pattern was smoothly integrated into the general framework of the multilateral Dutch entrepôt trade.[3] At that time Rotterdam had already emerged as a centre of mainly regional trade and shipping, connecting the hinterland of the rivers Rhine and Meuse to the north and west of France on the one hand and to the British Isles on the other. When, during the 1580s, the important herring fishery was lost to more northern towns with a better access to the consumer markets in the Baltic,[4] Rotterdam sought compensation. Obviously it could be found in those areas where the city enjoyed natural cost advantages. Consequently, its harbour facilities were enlarged and improved.[5] As these facilities served to exploit the advantages offered by the expansion of the town's traditional regional trade this investment proved to be a very lucky one.

In the early sixteenth century the town had numbered probably less than 5,000 inhabitants. In 1622 the population had increased to about 20,000 persons. The population growth seems to have continued until the end of the century, when some 51,000 people lived in the town. The first half of

---

[3] The rapid rise of Rotterdam after 1500, leaving its competitors in the same area such as Dordrecht and Middelburg far behind, even though they had previously been more important, has never been satisfactorily explained.
[4] The loss of consumer markets in the Southern Netherlands after Antwerp had fallen into Spanish hands (1585) was also a set-back to Rotterdam's herring fishery.
[5] R. Bijlsma, *Rotterdams welvaren 1550–1650* (The Hague, 1918).

the eighteenth century, however, saw a decrease to about 44,000 inhabitants. Nevertheless the population had risen again to almost 60,000 by the beginning.of the nineteenth century.[6] In line with Rotterdam's restricted function as a regional entrepôt and trading centre, the transshipment of goods was confined, in the main, to a somewhat limited and inconspicuous assortment of merchandise. From the hinterland in Germany and the Southern Netherlands came wine, coal, iron and other minerals, glassware and textiles, such as linen, worsted and serge. France supplied wine, brandy, salt, cereals and some semi-tropical products, and the British Isles produced coal, lead, tin, clay, finished and unfinished cloth, tobacco and some foodstuffs. The exports from Rotterdam consisted of fish, cheese, butter, madder, cloth and a large variety of commodities drawn from the general entrepôt of Amsterdam.[7] The statistics concerning the Rotterdam trade during the seventeenth and eighteenth centuries are unfortunately very scarce.[8] They are also inconsistent and do not appear to correlate with each other. At first sight, however, it would appear that a large assortment of products was marketed, comprising more than 200 different items and qualities. But the large majority of these carried little weight and were of no great significance. Imports from overseas, in particular, presented a very lopsided picture, as may be shown by the telling example of 1788 – by no means an exceptional year. Imports from overseas then consisted of 133 different sorts of commodity at the total value of 3.63 million guilders. However, the imports of only eight of these each amounted to more than 100,000 guilders. They alone, however, accounted together for no less than 70 per cent of the total value of imports.[9] The products in question were coal (546,000 guilders), tobacco leaf (497,000 guilders), woollen manufactures (455,000 guilders), unrefined sugar (451,000 guilders), cochineal (182,000 guilders),[10] coffee

---

[6] G. Mentink and A. M. van der Woude, *De demografische ontwikkeling te Rotterdam en Cool in de 17e en 18e eeuw* (Rotterdam, 1965), p. 33.

[7] Biilsma, *Rotterdams welvaren.*

[8] N. W. Posthumus, 'Statistiek van de in- en uitvoer van Rotterdam en Dordrect in het jaar 1680', *Bijdragen en Mededelingen van het Historisch Genootschap*, 34 (1913); P. J. Dobbelaar, 'Een statistiek van de in- en uitvoer van Rotterdam c.a. in 1753', *Economisch-Historisch Jaarboek*, 7 (The Hague, 1921); Joh. de Vries, 'De statistiek van in- en uitvoer van de Admiraliteit op de Maaze 1784–1793, I, II, *Economisch-Historisch Jaarboek*, 29, 30 (The Hague, 1963, 1965).

[9] Computed from data supplied by de Vries, 'De statistiek'. Imports actually concerned the district of the Admiraliteit op de Maaze. Rotterdam's share of the imports into the district used to be about 60 per cent. If anything, the figures would be even more biased if Rotterdam alone had been considered.

[10] This was accidental and exceptional. Cochineal usually accounted for small imports into the district.

beans (176,000 guilders), cotton (136,000 guilders) and French wine (131,000 guilders). Most of these commodities had to be supplied by or through Great Britain. These figures evidently show that Britain had remained of dominant importance to the trade of Rotterdam, even after the fourth and last of the Anglo-Dutch wars (1780–4), commonly believed to have had disastrous effects on Dutch trade generally. But as far as the position of Rotterdam was concerned, there had actually been very little change since the middle of the century. Although there had been a considerable decline in the volume of trade, Britain's relative share in the imports of the customs area of Rotterdam had remained more or less the same since 1753. At that time, total imports into the district had amounted to the value of 9.5 million guilders and almost half of it – 45 per cent – had come from Britain. Britain's share in the exports from Rotterdam, totalling 15.3 million guilders, had amounted to the lesser figure of 23 per cent, but even so Britain had come second only to Germany.[11] Rotterdam's industrial production also depended to a large extent on Great Britain. Its export industries, especially, would have been idle had there been no supplies from overseas. These so-called *trafieken*, specializing in working up raw materials from abroad, were annually employing 4,000 to 5,000 hands during the second half of the eighteenth century,[12] roughly 20 to 25 per cent of the working population. Most important was the domestic system operated by the tobacco industry, accounting for the employment of some 3,500 labourers. This industry depended completely on the importation of Virginian tobacco from London or Glasgow. Sugar- and salt-refineries, breweries, distilleries and white-lead works were also important *trafieken*, depending in one way or another on the steady supply of British coal for fuel and of essential raw materials such as lead or malt.

The ties between the city of Rotterdam and Britain seem to have grown closer especially during the first half of the seventeenth century, when the town succeeded in connecting its regional trading system to the general upsurge of the Dutch economy.[13] The bond was confirmed and invigorated in 1635 at the official establishment of the Court of the Merchant Adventurers in Rotterdam.[14] It may be true that the Merchant

---

[11] Dobbelaar, 'Een statistiek'. Note that imports in this case also include imports by land.

[12] C. Visser, *Verkeersindustrieën te Rotterdam in de tweede helft der achttiende eeuw* (Rotterdam, 1927), p. 155.

[13] Bijlsma, *Rotterdams welvaren*; Z. W. Sneller, *Geschiedenis van de steenkolenhandel van Rotterdam* (Groningen and Batavia, 1946), pp. 92–108.

[14] C. te Lintum, *De Merchant Adventurers in de Nederlanden* (The Hague, 1905), pp. 103–207. The author even maintained that Rotterdam only became a centre of wholesale trade at that time.

Adventurers at that time 'lacked wider support' as 'their interest ran counter to the prevailing notions of national economic policy' in England and that therefore 'their fortunes were waning'[15] but this verdict rests on the hindsight that is the historian's prerogative. At the time, as their conduct testifies, the city fathers of Rotterdam clearly thought otherwise. For about twenty-five years they had spared no amount of effort and expense in their continuous endeavours to persuade that venerable association to make its move from Middelburg in Zeeland to Rotterdam. They bought and bribed, they flattered and cajoled, they promised and pledged.

Whatever requirements the Merchant Adventurers might put forward, the city of Rotterdam was more than ready to meet them. In the end it was only the 'jealousy' of other towns in Holland, especially Amsterdam, that obliged Rotterdam to set a limit to its concessions. Exemption from taxes, the right of jurisdiction, the construction of an English quarter, exemption from military obligations, a new Bourse, a proper bank of exchange fashioned after the example of Amsterdam – it was all for the asking. And the good Calvinists running the municipality did not mind overmuch dismantling the Calvinist Walloon church in order to make room for an Anglican place of worship that the English seemed to want. And the English and Scottish Presbyterian church that had found refuge in the city in 1611 was temporarily actually driven out. To crown it all, Rotterdam even promised to grant an amount of 60,000 guilders if England would only put an effective stop to the evasion of the Merchant Adventurers' privileges! The smuggling continued of course, but even so the city actually paid half of the sum.[16]

There followed seven years when all seemed well. Apart from the usual bickering and haggling between a paying host and his spending guest, the city had little occasion to regret its deal. It seems likely that about one hundred Englishmen, some sixty belonging to the Merchant Adventurers, established their business in Rotterdam at that time.[17] Trade, employment and prosperity came in their wake. The Civil War in England, however, interfered most unfortunately. As ships were taken and cargoes were seized, trade suffered. Worse still, the English colony in Rotterdam split into Royalists and Parliamentarians, both actively supporting their party in England. In a somewhat blind and over-hasty

---

[15] Wilson, *Profit*, p. 56.
[16] Smuggling or 'interloping' was actually encouraged by Dutch towns competing with Rotterdam. And Rotterdam itself turned a blind eye to the 'interlopers', who continued their illegal activities in the city.
[17] Bijlsma, *Rotterdams welvaren*, p. 153.

access to a m
exploit. The
concerned se
them into cl
Breda had so
organization

At the begin
Rotterdam h
economic ma
Colchester, f
was not only
and missiona
writings of W
as Penn's host
emigration o
intellectual de
was an intima
stay in Holla
of Rotterdam,
to propagate

Yet it was p
most deeply,
rocked the D
began in June
from London,
founding an i
of the notorio
collapse. After
official hearing
less experience
more pliable an
week to estab
Discontering

gamble to join the winner, the city fathers of Rotterdam miscalculated badly. Probably under pressure from Stadtholder Fredrik Hendrik – whose son had just been married to Mary Stuart – the municipality allowed Queen Henrietta, who had come for help in the Netherlands in 1642, to borrow a very substantial sum from the town's Loan Bank.[18] English crown jewels served as security at a taxation value of more than 800,000 guilders. In the meantime, however, the Rotterdam Court of Merchant Adventurers had opted formally for Parliament, and King Charles retaliated by revoking their charter. Although Parliament reaffirmed it, the old days were never to return. During the first of the Anglo-Dutch wars (1652–4), affairs came practically to a standstill. Even though the attitude of the city fathers remained accommodating, and they did their very best to protect English inhabitants and their possessions when they were threatened by rioting, the majority of the English seem to have left the town. Although Rotterdam tried to renew the connection afterwards, it was unable to prevent the Merchant Adventurers' departure for Dordrecht in 1656. In their constant efforts to boost the town's economy, the city fathers now thought it worthwhile to compete for the Scottish staple in the Netherlands, which had been established in Veere in Zeeland ever since the middle of the fifteenth century.[19] They failed, however, the Scottish staple temporarily also settling in Dordrecht before definitely returning to Veere in 1675.

Rotterdam did not really suffer from these apparent set-backs. As medieval instruments for regulating trade, court and staple were becoming more and more obsolete in the face of free enterprise, which was rising to dominance in international commerce. Illegal free trade had prospered even in Rotterdam during the days of the Merchant Adventurers. At that same time the Scottish trade of Rotterdam had grown and developed as well. In 1643 the Scottish community in Rotterdam had grown to such an extent that it was allowed to establish its own independent church, the city even granting a subsidy.[20] Since the third quarter of the seventeenth century Rotterdam certainly attracted the main part of the Dutch trade with Scotland and Ireland, whatever the official requirements might have been.

During the second half of the seventeenth century, official English regulation of commerce and shipping may even have strengthened the

22 W. I. Hull, Benj
   on Quaker Hist
23 R. A. Mandersl
   unpublished doc
   Universiteit Rot
24 F. Ph. Groenev
   Slechte, 'Een no
   (The Hague, 19

18 F. C. Koch, 'De Engelse kroonjuwelen in de Rotterdamse bank van lening', Rotterdams Jaarboekje (Rotterdam, 1915). In the end the city lost a substantial sum on the deal.
19 M. P. Rooseboom, The Scottish Staple in the Netherlands (The Hague, 1910).
20 J. Verheul, De Schotse gemeente en haar oude kerkgebouw te Rotterdam (Rotterdam, 1939); Jean Morrison, Scots on the Dijk: The Story of the Scots Church of Rotterdam (1981).

guilders – twice as much as the stock of the largest company in the world, the Dutch East India Company.[25] At that moment the Dutch investors and capitalists had already been feverishly occupied for some time, plunging deeply into John Law's financial adventures in France as well as into the speculative undertakings of the South Sea Bubble in England. Now the United Provinces themselves became the field of a wild gamble. An uncontrolled speculation raged through the nation, fostered by scores of fantastic and most unlikely new companies spreading all over the country. Charles Wilson has rightly drawn attention to the role of the Dutch during the speculative mania in England from January till August.[26] On the other hand, one may note that the English were not slow to return the service at the time of the Dutch bubble a couple of months later. More than 10 per cent of the stock of the Rotterdam company was issued to shareholders in England – bankers, merchants, Members of Parliament and the like. To that select group belonged such prominent men as Sir Jean Lambert, managing director of the South Sea Company, the London banker H. Cairns, Sir Matthew Decker, director of the East India Company and John Mitford, who held the majority of shares in the Sun Insurance office and briefly acted as its head before he went bankrupt. These men all held shares in the Rotterdam stock to the maximally allowed amount of 50,000 guilders.

During the summer of 1720 scores of other Englishmen crossed the sea to the United Provinces in order to plunge into the gamble as it spread to a growing variety of funds. Few followed the wise example of the co-founder of the Rotterdam company, Edmund Hoyle, who returned to England as soon as he had reaped his profits. Hoyle of course was protected by a brilliant mathematical mind that turned him into a passionate but careful gambler. He spent the rest of his days in comfortable circumstances, perfecting the noble game of whist and teaching it to admiring aristocratic ladies. A less fortunate speculator was Thomas Lombe, dealer in secret and largely imaginary inventions and sometime sheriff of London. He was the half-brother of John Lombe, said to have smuggled the secret of water-powered silk-throwing from Italy into England. After John's death Thomas too was involved in the management of the first English silk mill. The wealthy David Clarkson, from Albany in America, also met with ill luck, even though he later turned into a worthy member of New York's Provincial Assembly.

---

[25] They company still flourishes as Stad Rotterdam n.v., being the only remaining one of about thirty companies established in 1720. The companies of Middelburg and Utrecht, although also weathering the storn of 1720, were liquidated at some later date.
[26] Wilson, *Anglo-Dutch Commerce*, pp. 103–9.

Both men had to depart from Holland hurriedly and under a cloud, leaving a host of dissatisfied creditors behind.

It almost goes without saying that many British inhabitants of Rotterdam also joined the big gamble. According to Slechte's penetrating research, some 500 people were concerned with dealing in the Rotterdam stock alone. A relatively small group of 38 dealers, however, each turning over at least 60 shares, accounted for more than 40 per cent of all sales.[27] This group of leading speculators included no less than fourteen British merchants or merchants' houses of Rotterdam.

It is difficult to assess the British share in the gambling in funds of other companies. A notorious speculator like Thomas Lombe certainly seems to have been active where he could. The Utrecht company, for instance, received his promise of a fixed rate of 300 per cent for its shares, if only it would buy his splendid dredging machinery. The Scot Robert Pantoune, who had moved from Veere to Rotterdam, was elected to the board of the Rotterdam company, just like Benjohan Furly – Benjamin's eldest son. The Irishman Patrick Harper of Rotterdam and the Scot George Gregory of Veere secured for themselves membership of the board of the companies of Delft and Middelburg respectively. And many other prominent members of the British colony in Rotterdam plunged into large-scale stock-jobbery in the shares of a number of different companies: Alexander Andrew, Benjamin Bradly, William Dundas, John Goddard, Archibald Hope, Robert Partridge, Robert Stirling, Walter Vane and Henry Wilkinson, to name only a few. The Dutch speculative bubble of 1720 differed in origin, though not in kind, from the earlier gamble in France and Britain. The latter had resulted from the abominable state of government finance in both countries, but Dutch credit left little to be desired. The outcome, however, was everywhere the same. And although actual losses might have been worse, it does not come as a great surprise that some of the British speculators were left in dire straits. Robert Pantoune, for one, had to take flight for England, where he went bankrupt. Although Alexander Andrew, William Dundas and Robert Partridge narrowly escaped, Benjamin Bradly, John Goddard and Henry Wilkinson also failed. However, the episode seems to have done them little permanent harm. Henry Wilkinson, for instance, remained a most active chartering agent, and continued to specialize almost exclusively in trade with Britain.[28] John Goddard was also soon

27 Slechte, *'Een noodlottig jaar'*, p. 110.
28 Data on Rotterdam ship-chartering in the eighteenth century were collected from a number of sources in the municipal archives of Rotterdam by Mr J. van Popering, formerly of the Department of Economic History, Erasmus Universiteit Rotterdam. I

busy again and became one of Rotterdam's most prominent and versatile British traders.[29] Having arrived as a young man from Cork in 1715, he tended to specialize in trade with England and Ireland, dealing in butter, meat, bacon, hides, tallow, feathers and cole-seed. During the 1720s and 1730s, however, he enlarged and extended his business to the Baltic and Russia, Scandinavia, France, Portugal, Spain, the Mediterranean and the West Indies. He also acted as shipowner and underwriter. Like his friend and business associate Benjohan Furly, he was one of the few British entrepreneurs who, in the 1720s, started to transport large numbers of German and Swiss emigrants to Pennsylvania and other American colonies.[30] Before the American War of Independence finally put an end to this the Rotterdam merchant houses of Hope, Clarkson, Trimble, Gibson, Manlove and Crawfurd had sent hundreds of vessels to Philadelphia and other American ports, annually transporting many hundreds and even thousands of emigrants.

If the official registration of British subjects as burghers or inhabitants of the town is anything to go by, their number stood at its highest during the first half of the eighteenth century. Between 1698 and 1811 about 15,000 people were registered as new burghers of Rotterdam. Their number included almost 1,000 men or women of British origin, over 6 per cent of the total. During the first three decades of the century the British share was considerably higher, more than half of them entering into the records before 1729. At that time one in eight of all new burghers originated from Great Britain. As appears from Table 7.1, however, these data do not quite correspond with the probably less reliable administrative data of aliens settling in the town. The registered number of British adults moving into the town actually remained very low until the 1720s, peaking subsequently between 1729 and 1768, as more than two-thirds of the total number of 923 adults was entered into the records.

Whatever the shortcomings of these statistics, the fact that the British colony in Rotterdam was at its liveliest during the first half of the eighteenth century does not rest merely upon its all-too-daring adventures into speculative finance. The share of British principals in the more

---

am grateful to him for allowing me to use his notes. Wilkinson had come from Lincoln to Rotterdam, where he married a Dutch wife.

[29] H. C. Hazewinkel, 'John Goddard, Engels koopman te Rotterdam 1690–1767', *Rotterdams Jaarboekje* (Rotterdam, 1948). Goddard – probably an Irishman – died a very rich man.

[30] C. te Lintum, *Emigreren over Rotterdam in de 18e eeuw* (De Gids IV, 1908); L. A. van der Valk, 'Landverhuizersvervoer via Rotterdam in de negentiende eeuw', *Economisch- en Sociaal-Historisch Jaarboek*, 39 (The Hague, 1976).

Table 7.1. *British burghers and inhabitants registered at Rotterdam*
1699–1811[31]

| | Burghers (*poorters*) | | Inhabitants (*admissies*) | | | |
| | | | Adults | | Children | Single adults |
Period	Number	%	Number	%	Number	Number
1699–1708	146	15.5	6	0.7	1	–
1709–1718	152	16.2	17	1.8	6	3
1719–1728	188	19.9	62	6.8	33	6
1729–1738	79	8.4	103	11.2	35	7
1739–1748	97	10.3	163	17.7	70	19
1749–1758	81	8.6	188	20.4	59	34
1759–1768	49	5.2	112	12.1	–	38
1769–1778	64	6.8	81	8.8	–	45
1779–1788	22	2.3	47	5.1	–	29
1789–1798	23	2.4	39	4.2	–	25
1799–1808	41	4.3	94	10.2	–	42
1809–1811	1	0.1	11	1.2	–	7
Totals						
British	943[a]	100	923[b]	100	204	255
All new burghers	14,984					

[a] The registration of 'burghers' was confined to one person at a time, irrespective of marital status or family size. Assuming that the proportions of children, married couples and single persons in the category 'inhabitants' for the period 1719–58 also held good for the registration of burghers, the latter must have referred to about 2,600–2,800 persons in all.

[b] Of this number 106 persons (14.1 per cent) were married to a person from outside Great Britain, 9 per cent having a Dutch wife or husband. The actual number of true-born Britons therefore was 817. During the 1750s the registration obviously began omitting children and maybe also married partners. Moreover, one should not overlook the fact that many people were living illegally in the town and were not registered at all.

[31] Gemeente Archief Rotterdam, Oud Archief nos. 903–4, Poorterboeken 1699–1811; *ibid.*, nos. 1015–19, Registers van finale admissies 1698–1812. The figures for burghers do not include 251 English and Scottish seamen, serving on Dutch men-of-war, who between 1707 and 1709 were given the status of Rotterdam burgher 'for reasons of state'. I am obliged to Mrs M. P. A. Boonk of the Department of Economic History, Erasmus Universiteit Rotterdam for her help in collecting the data concerned.

Table 7.2. *Destination of chartered ships from Rotterdam 1720–1740*

	Number	%
Great Britain	563	27
Norway	443	21
W. of France/Southern Netherlands	393	19
N. W. Spain/Portugal	200	10
Rest of Spain	146	7
Baltic/N. Germany	107	5
S. of France	93	4
Italy	76	4
Miscellaneous	63	3
Total	2,084	100

solid field of ship-chartering was also very impressive, as may be deduced from its registration by public notaries.[32] Between 1720 and 1740 as many as 2,084 charter parties were formally concluded before Rotterdam notaries.[33] Although the chartering was done by a group of more than 300 merchants, a relatively small number of only 40 principals accounted for almost half (990) of the charter parties, each of them concluding more than 10 contracts. That group included no less than 13 British freighters, together accounting for 390 charterings. In view of the position of Rotterdam in international commodity trade, it is not surprising that a very substantial number of charterings had a British port as destination (Table 7.2)

It is perhaps rather more surprising that the trade to the British Isles should by this time be almost completely under British control. The chartering to Great Britain itself was almost entirely in British hands as a matter of course. But nearly all ships were British also, having a British skipper in command. Even the relatively small number of Dutchmen who also busied themselves in Anglo-Dutch trade – like the merchant Willem Konink who accounted for almost 100 charterings most of them to British ports – usually employed British ships. On the other hand, not all British charterers confined themselves to the carrying trade to their native country. There were others besides John Goddard who repeatedly dispatched ships to the Mediterranean, France, Spain, Portugal, the

[32] See above, note 28.
[33] It is doubtful whether the figure represents ship-chartering accurately. Charter parties were not required by law and could also be concluded privately. Trafficking by shipowners themselves is, of course, also excluded.

Table 7.3. *Provenance of British settlers in Rotterdam 1699–1811*[34]

	Burghers		Inhabitants	
	Number	%	Number	%
London	210	22	167	21
Scotland	287	31	216	26
Ireland	86	9	73	9
Rest/unknown	360	38	361	44
Total	943	100	817	100

Baltic and other destinations. Even less prominent British charterers like John Archdeacon, Andrew Andrews, William Bingley or Robert Partridge, each accounting for less than 10 charterings, found occasion to employ vessels in the carrying trade to distant ports in the Levant or the Americas. It seems as if Rotterdam during those days offered almost limitless opportunities to British enterprise. Small wonder that the attraction of Rotterdam made itself felt throughout Great Britain.

People came to Rotterdam from all over the country. The fact that London and Scotland figured as important places of origin in the migration movement obviously correspondend with their leading position in Anglo-Dutch trade. The role of England's north-eastern counties, another relatively important area in this respect, is not adequately represented in the figures of Table 7.3. However, this region, like Scotland, was of special significance to Rotterdam in view of its exports of coal, shipped from Hull, Scarborough, Newcastle and Sunderland. Yet even during the first half of the eighteenth century, Rotterdam may already have lost some of its glamour and attractiveness to enterprising men of mature experience. As time passed, British migrants seemed to grow younger: the average age of male settlers from Britain fell from 37.6 years in 1699–1728 to 36.6 and 33.6 years in the two decades that followed. The corresponding figures for females were 35.7, 33.4 and 32.3 years respectively.[35] Perhaps one should not draw a pessimistic conclusion from this comparative rejuvenation. Anyway, after the 1750s fewer and fewer British settlers figure in the relevant records. Yet it is not very clear why this should have been so. At that time the town

[34] See above, note 31.   [35] See above, note 3.

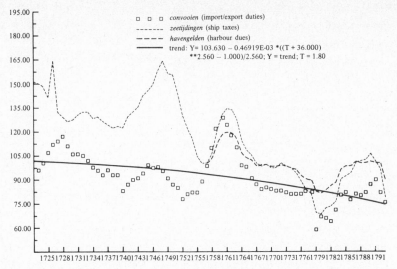

Fig. 7.1.   Indices of Rotterdam trade and shipping, 1720–1800 (five-year moving average: 1755–9 = 100)

had resumed its impressive population growth after some decline evident in the first half of the century. However, the available statistics of the town's international shipping and commodity trade present a somewhat different picture (Fig. 7.1).[36] The economic development indicated therein shows that the upswings – especially that after the war of 1780–4 – failed to hide the predominantly downward tendency. The decline may already have started some time before the 1750s but the phases of recovery at that time were still much more pronounced than later in the century. After commercial activities had reached a final high-water mark during the early sixties, decline was proceeding in an almost irresistible way. Whatever the cause of this adverse development, it can hardly have stimulated immigration from Britain. However, it seems unlikely that economic set-backs were alone in checking British settlements. The war of 1780–4 put an almost complete stop to the inflow. It never recovered fully, probably as a result of the ensuing turmoil, which disturbed the political and social life of the Dutch Republic and which in 1795 finally gave way to a period of French domination and renewed war against Great Britain. Tradition died hard, however. The number of new British citizens rose again almost to former levels as soon as the Treaty of Amiens, apparently promising

---

[36] Computed from data supplied by Joh. de Vries, *De economische achteruitgang der Republiek in de achttiende eeuw* (Amsterdam, 1959), Apps. I, II, III. *Convooien* were import and export duties; *zeetijdingen* and *havengelden* concerned ship taxes.

better times, was concluded. In 1802 and 1803, forty-five new British citizens were registered.

The surprising fact is not that British immigrants were keeping away during those troubled times, but that a still sizeable British colony actually survived.[37] During the turbulent decade 1781–90 scores of British citizens continued to live in Rotterdam and at least fifty-seven of them still conducted important business from the city. The majority of these merchants had only arrived after 1750, twenty-one having been born in Rotterdam itself where their fathers had already engaged in trade. The Anglo-Dutch war seems to have been of little consequence to these merchants. As far as could be ascertained, the war caused only one Anglo-Dutch firm any serious financial difficulties. The important merchant house of the widow A. Hamilton and Meynen had to apply for a licence. In 1790 the firm had still not cleared its debts.[38] It is noteworthy, however, that the war caused British shipowners in Rotterdam to sell their vessels as fast as they could to neutrals, trade under Dutch or British colours having become too dangerous.[39] It testifies to the ease and versatility with which these British merchants managed to ride out rough weather. As can be deduced from a number of testamentary dispositions, their wealth seems to have remained unaffected by the misfortunes of the day. Fourteen of the twenty-eight wills made by British merchants and their wives between 1781 and 1790 give details, for fiscal reasons, of the sums of money involved: they average the very substantial amount of 50,000 guilders per will.[40] The richest member of the British colony was probably George Crawfurd,[41] who

---

[37] M. Doortmont and R. Vroom, 'Engelse kooplieden gevestigd te Rotterdam in de 18e eeuw', unpublished doctoral thesis, Department of Social History, Erasmus Universitiet Rotterdam, 1982. At my request, Messrs Doortmont and Vroom instituted researches into a number of sources in the municipal archives of Rotterdam, relating to the periods 1781–90 and 1811–20. Unless indicated otherwise the following has been taken from their reports. I am very much obliged to them for allowing me to use the data they collected. My opinions do not necessarily coincide with theirs.

[38] Archibald Hamilton, probably the firm's founder, had arrived from Belfast in about 1720. The firm was active in trade with Surinam, where it owned large sugar plantations in the 1780s. It continued to function between 1811 and 1820, when it was run by Gerrit Cornelis Meynen, of Rotterdam patrician stock, who had married a Hamilton.

[39] During the war sixteen ships were sold by British shipowners in Rotterdam; during the rest of the decade only three were sold.

[40] Of the wills in question, five dealt with sums of 20,000 guilders, ten with sums of 50,000 guilders and three with as much as 100,000 guilders.

[41] James Crawfurd from Edinburgh became a burgher in 1736. His son Patrick carried the honorary title of Lord Conservator of the Scottish Privileges in the Netherlands – a title referring to the Scottish staple in Veere that by this time had become completely obsolete. He and his brothers James and George managed the firm in the 1780s together with George Gibson, also from Scotland and – like the Crawfurds – closely related to other British merchant families in Rotterdam.

left more than 1 million guilders at his death in 1819. Thomas Littledale must also have been a very rich man, dwelling in one of Rotterdam's most luxurious mansions, which had once been the home of the wealthiest man ever to have lived in the United Provinces.[42]

During the decade in question the British merchants in Rotterdam carried on not unlike their predecessors and forbears. Trading encompassed the same sorts of commodity as before, and was directed towards the same ports and areas. The group seems to have been very closely knit together in social respects. It is true that there was nothing like a special English quarter. If such a thing had ever really existed, it had long been dissolved. In Dutch society, wealth counting for more than birth or nationality, the houses of rich British merchants were mixed indiscriminately with those of their Dutch colleagues and were concentrated in the very fashionable area at the waterfront, which had the simultaneous advantage of offering easy access to the harbour facilities.

Business, however, was another matter. Anglo-Dutch trade associations were very rare indeed, the firm of Hamilton and Meynen being the exception rather than the rule. Moreover, when absent from town, British merchants usually entrusted their affairs to fellow-countrymen and not to any Dutch associate. The British kept together in private life too. In their wills they invariably named fellow-countrymen as executors. Those fifty-seven merchant families of British stock produced no less than twelve intermarriages. Others bent on marrying took the trouble of travelling to their native country in order to collect a bride or groom. Relatively few ventured into marrying a Dutch partner. Visiting the home country either for business and education or simply for a holiday was not at all unusual and sometimes even entire families crossed the sea. Some were never to return, either retiring or continuing their business in England. More than one family, staying on in Rotterdam, still held on to real property, estates or industrial possessions – ranging from a coal-mine to a malt-house[43] – in Great Britain.

---

[42] Littledale had been born in Whitehaven. He was admitted into Rotterdam in 1761, obtaining his burgher rights in 1767. His son-in-law John Dixon later became a partner in the firm. Littledale was related to the Brownes and Allans, also prominent merchant families in Rotterdam. The wealthy Dutchman referred to was the country's Treasurer Cornelis de Jonge van Ellemeet (1646–1721). See B. E. de Muinck, *Een regentenhuishouding omstreeks 1700: gegevens uit de privé-boekhouding van Mr. Cornelis de Jonge van Ellemeet* (The Hague, 1965).

[43] The Brownes in about 1800 still owned estates in Norfolk, where they had originated almost a century earlier. The Lloyds, coming from Bristol in about 1730, still ran a coal-mine in Scotland at the end of the century, and Robert Young – owner of four plantations in the West Indies – had inherited from his father a malting house in Northumberland.

The British colony in Rotterdam still existed a generation or so later, after the bad days of Napoleonic predominance had passed by. Some families, having moved into the town during the preceding century or maybe even earlier, still had descendants living there by the second decade of the nineteenth century. Family names still current about that time – Browne, Gibson, Lloyd, Martin, Smith, Turing, Twiss, Vether or Veder, Roche, Young, Maingay, Marchant, the last two originating from Guernsey – had a long-standing reputation in Rotterdam. It is very likely that there was a constant stream of newcomers, although this cannot be ascertained for sure. But the fashionable quarter in the harbour area still numbered quite a number of British dwellings. Harbour activities, however, had sadly diminished, and so had the business transactions of British merchants in Rotterdam. The relevant sources show that they had had to restrict their economic activities to pitifully small proportions. Apart from some occasional ship-chartering, they conducted a modest trade in the usual commodities of tobacco, coffee, sugar, rice, cotton, hides, madder and the like. Trading with Great Britain still came first. And for the rest they confined themselves to some dealings in real properties, stock-jobbing and other financial transactions.

The great days of the British merchant in Rotterdam had definitely passed. Small wonder, since the Dutch economy too had fallen into a deep, lasting depression from which no quick recovery seemed to be possible. But the British lingered on. As late as 1832 their Presbyterian community still counted proudly a membership of some 200 people.[44] In the meantime it seemed as if Rotterdam, like the whole of Dutch society, was living in a grey twilight of deadly silence, separating the shining activities of its past from its bright new future as a bustling industrial port. On 1 June 1816 the burgomasters of Rotterdam, for the very last time, followed their time-honoured, medieval custom of recognizing a new burgher – a honorary burgher as a matter of fact.[45] In view of the past it was maybe only fitting that the ceremony and the title were bestowed upon an Englishman. Yet it was a man of the future who was so honoured: William Wager, captain of the first steamer ever to moor in a Dutch port. The burgomasters were duly impressed, recording explicitly that they wanted to salute 'this useful invention of the Arts and Sciences'. The *ancien régime* thus dutifully paid its symbolic homage to the

[44] British church life in Rotterdam still flourishes.
[45] Gemeente Archief Rotterdam, Oud Archief, Poorterboeken, no. 934.

Industrial Revolution. Nevertheless, modern times had not yet arrived. It was another half-century before the Industrial Revolution really made itself felt in Rotterdam. The British mercantile community, gradually dwindling into oblivion, did not survive that long.

8

Prejudice and policy: Sir George Downing as parliamentary entrepreneur

HENRY ROSEVEARE

Three hundred years after his death, Sir George Downing's personal reputation shows little sign of recovery. He remains today the fawning turncoat and meddling braggart presented to us by Bishop Burnet and the Earl of Clarendon.[1] A steady trickle of calumny, fed from these fountain-heads of the Whig and Tory tradition, flowed unchecked through eighteenth- and nineteenth-century chronicles, officiously assisted by a handful of unfriendly memoirs such as Sir William Temple's, Lord Arlington's letters, or Governor Hutchinson's history of Massachusetts.[2] For Laurence E(a)chard, for White Kennet(t), for James Ralph, Sir George Downing was merely the betrayer of Barkstead, Corbet and Okey, and the insolent incendiary who started two Dutch wars.[3] For John Oldmixon he was something worse – 'an obscure New England fanatick' whose manners 'were as rude as those of an Iroquois, in whose neighbourhood he was bred'.[4] So much for Harvard and the class of '42.

With the publication of Pepys's *Diary* in the 1820s this habit of disparagement was enlivened by a richer flood of anecdote, and Downing emerged not merely treacherous but also mean – 'a niggardly fellow' as well as 'a perfidious rogue'.[5] The modern currency of Pepys's

---

[1] *The Life of Edward, Earl of Clarendon*, ed. T. H. Lister (1827), II, 289, 292–3; III, 4; G. Burnet, *History of My Own Time*, ed. O. Airy (1897), I, 356. (Place of publication is London unless otherwise stated.)

[2] Sir William Temple, *Memoirs*, ed. J. Swift (1692, 1709); *The Earl of Arlington's Letters*, ed. T. Bebington (1701), II, 250; T. Hutchinson, *The History of the Colony of Massachusetts Bay* (1764), I, 111.

[3] L. Echard, *The History of England . . .* (1718), III, 85, 121; [W. Kennet], *A Complete History of England* (1719), III, 271, 273, 309; J. Ralph, *The History of England . . .* (1744–6), I, 70, 196, 197, 200–1.

[4] J. Oldmixon, *The History of England . . .* (1730), pp. 454, 562.

[5] *The Diary of Samuel Pepys*, ed. R. C. Latham and W. Matthews (1970–83), I, 186; III, 45; VIII, 85 (28 June 1660, 12 March 1662, 27 February 1667).

account ensures that if Downing figures at all in the popular consciousness today it is as the grasping purveyor of bad faith and cold porridge,
the jerry-building 'Scoundrel Who Gave Us Downing Street'.[6] Yet in
fairness to Pepys it must be acknowledged that his natural loathing for
Downing struggled unsuccessfully with a grudging admiration for one of
his own kind, 'a man of the old ways, for taking pains', whose efficient
pursuit of the public welfare he recognized and respected. He was a man
who 'values himself upon having of things do well under his hand', and
'who labours very worthily to advance our own trade'.[7] These more
generous assessments of Downing may have helped to launch another,
more scholarly, tradition attentive to Downing's official and parliamentary career. It has a shorter history but can be traced back at least to
Sibley's sketches of Harvard graduates[8] and to C. H. Firth's article in the
Dictionary of National Biography, c. 1902. The materials had long been at
hand in Thurloe's *State Papers* (1742), Anchitel Grey's *Debates* (1763) and
Lister's *Life of Clarendon* (1837). Firth added the Clarke papers by 1901,
just as W. A. Shaw was working his tendentious way through the books
and papers of the Restoration Treasury. Shaw's fulsome assessment of
Downing's contribution to public finance and the foundations of the
Treasury[9] was closely followed by G. L. Beer's rehabilitation of 'the old
colonial system' in 1912. In this still-invaluable work Downing was
accorded full credit not merely for the Navigation Acts but for his
'marked intellectual consistency and great constructive ability'.[10] The
hint was quickly taken. By 1923 an historian of the East India Company
had found in Downing 'profound knowledge, rare versatility and
extraordinary insight'.[11] Clearly the time was ripe for a full-scale
investigation of this paragon and in 1925 a biography duly appeared.[12]

John Beresford's study belongs to a still-flourishing genre – the popular
biography romantically sensitive to local colour and quaint whimsy – but
it is a good deal better than most of its kind for it made thorough use of
both the English and the Dutch printed sources for Downing's career. It
did not aspire to analyse Downing's official career at the Exchequer,
Treasury or Customs,[13] nor did it make much use of the available

---

[6] *The Evening News*, 14 October 1955.
[7] Pepys, *Diary*, VIII, 238, 425 (27 May, 8 September 1667).
[8] J. L. Sibley, *Biographical Sketches of Graduates of Harvard University* (1873), I, 28–51.
[9] W. A. Shaw, 'The Beginnings of the National Debt', in *Historical Essays*, ed. T. F. Tout
and J. Tait (1902).
[10] G. L. Beer, *The Old Colonial System 1660–1754* (New York, 1912), pp. 9–11.
[11] S. A. Khan, *East India Trade in the XVIIth Century* (1923), p. 101.
[12] J. Beresford, *The Godfather of Downing Street: Sir George Downing 1623–1684* (1925).
[13] *Ibid.*, p. 219.

manuscript sources in the Public Record Office or the Bodleian, but it remains a useful point of departure for future work and certainly appears to have exhausted the sparse information about Downing's private life. After 1925 it was no longer necessary to introduce Downing as a total stranger for whose shortcomings of character some condescending apology had to be made. He could now stand on his own feet as one of the most formidable diplomats and administrative innovators of his age, and he appeared in this guise in works by Feiling, Harper, Jacobsen and Barbour.[14] By the 1950s, indeed, this new orthodoxy may have seemed sufficiently established and uncritical to require reappraisal. Stephen Baxter's suggestion that Downing's achievement at the Treasury was less original and creative than Shaw had claimed deserves some sympathy, if only because so much of Shaw's analysis was ill-founded.[15] It has been shown elsewhere that Baxter's strictures were largely unjustified, but it is some measure of Downing's standing that they needed to be made.[16] Clearly some balance had to be struck between the venomous mythology of the old view and the awe-struck generalizations of the new.

Happily the same year which saw Baxter's reassessment of Downing's administrative career also produced the best concise appraisal of his diplomatic and legislative achievement. In barely ten pages of his *Profit and Power* Charles Wilson encapsulated Downing's significance for Anglo-Dutch relations in particular and for England's economic destiny in general.[17] 'Downing's lasting contribution ... was that he brought to bear his observation of Dutch economic practice on English economic theory and policy.' With 'few equals in his age as an economic administrator and co-ordinator' Downing's name 'appears, after 1656, in connexion with every important Act affecting navigation and colonial trade for more than a quarter of a century'.[18]

The full force of this statement may not be immediately grasped: it may seem a pardonable exaggeration. But if one makes a pedantic analysis of Downing's parliamentary career its truth becomes strikingly apparent. Downing sat in both Cromwell's Parliaments and in all five of Charles

[14] K. Feiling, *British Foreign Policy 1660–1672* (1930), pp. 111–16; L. A. Harper, *The English Navigation Laws* (New York, 1939), pp. 57–9; G. A. Jacobsen, *William Blathwayt: A Late Seventeenth-Century Administrator* (1932), pp. 2, 112; V. Barbour, *Capitalism in Amsterdam in the Seventeenth Century* (Baltimore, 1951), pp. 35, 87–8, 139–40.
[15] S. Baxter, *The Development of the Treasury, 1660–1702* (1957), pp. 127, 168, 181, 217.
[16] H. Roseveare, *The Treasury 1660–1870: The Foundations of Control* (1973), pp. 19–45.
[17] C. Wilson, *Profit and Power: A Study of England and the Dutch Wars* (1957), pp. 94–103.
[18] *Ibid.*, pp. 95, 102–3.

II's. During these twenty-five years he was nominated to over four hundred committees, in several cases as the leading member. In the Restoration Parliaments alone he participated actively in framing nearly seventy public statutes as well as some fifty private bills, and if one makes allowance for his absence abroad for four whole sessions then his contribution amounts to 40 per cent of all public legislation in which he could possibly share. Of economic legislation alone his hand was on two-thirds, and in at least twenty-seven cases it is evident that his was the paramount influence in conducting measures through the House – chairing the committees, presenting the reports and often carrying the engrossed bill to the Lords. Over one hundred recorded speeches confirm and amplify the official record.[19] On this showing Downing emerges as one of the most remarkable legislative entrepreneurs of his times.

Certainly there were few contemporaries who could rival his record of committee-work,[20] and the scale of his activity makes it easier to understand why Downing was regarded as such a pertinacious and insufferable busybody. As a young Member in his first Parliament he had said, 'I do not love to talk out of Parliament. This is a place to speak one's conscience in', and it was a threat which he amply fulfilled. But if Downing was indeed 'a voluminous speaker, which naturally [the Commons] do not like' it seems evident that his initiatives were respected and supported by a generally deferential House. Some trace of this attitude can be found in correspondence from Sir William Coventry, a younger man whose deference was well worth having. Because Downing had to miss the unusually busy session of 1661–2, which dealt with a large number of economic issues, Coventry sought to keep Downing informed and to solicit his advice on matters of trade, revenue and the clothing industry in particular. Setting out his own, largely hostile, views on the Merchant Adventurers' monopoly, Coventry begged Downing 'if it bee erroneous pray rectify mee in your next' and concluded his account 'I heartily wish you heere upon these occasions.'[21] There is no reason to suspect him of flattery.

Yet one of the more valuable consequences of Downing's enforced

---

[19] I am greatly indebted to the History of Parliament Trust, and to Mr. J. P. Ferris in particular, for information enabling me to make this analysis.
[20] Downing's regular sparring partner was Col. John Birch (MP for Penryn) whose record of committee-work may well exceed Downing's, as may that of Sir Thomas Meres (Lincoln City), but neither is identified with a volume of legislation to equal Downing's. See *The Commons 1660–1690*, ed. B. D. Henning (1983). I am grateful to Mr Ferris for advice on this point.
[21] B[ritish] L[ibrary], Additional MS 22919, ff. 186–7.

absences is the surviving series of letters which he addressed to his immediate masters, the Secretaries of State, and to the effective head of the administration, Clarendon.[22] Dealing as he was with some of the major commercial disputes of the day, Downing had every excuse to expatiate generally on matters of trade, and he lost no opportunity to do so, proffering his forceful and unsolicited views on almost every aspect of the English and European economies. The result is to make his diplomatic correspondence an invaluable repository of comment, far more articulate and coherent than his recorded parliamentary speeches. A few of his disquisitions have been published[23] but only in a selective and abridged form upon which no complete assessment of his influence can be based. Indeed, the printed selection has probably done more to conceal than to reveal the full character of Downing's thinking, which was almost preposterously comprehensive in its geographical range. From Russia to Brazil, from Yarmouth to Macao, there were few focal points of world trade on which he did not venture an opinion. Downing's first-hand acquaintance with the areas he claimed to understand was only modest. His voyage from New England in 1645 had carried him to the West Indies and to Newfoundland; his first diplomatic mission in 1655 had taken him through France to Geneva. But at The Hague from January 1658 he was quickly absorbed in two major spheres of maritime conflict, between the Portuguese and the Dutch and between the Danes and the Swedes. Both disputes raised issues of profound importance for England's commercial interests, in the Baltic and the Atlantic, and months of intensive mediation by Downing seem to have educated him in some of the more vital intricacies of European trade. He was to draw on this experience for the rest of his life.

At the time, however, his letters to Thurloe were oddly constrained – mere factual reports, very different in character from the discursive, opinionated essays which followed the Restoration. It may well be that he was more in awe of Cromwell than he ever was of Charles II.

[22] Sir George Downing's official letters to Sir Edward Nicholas and Sir Henry Bennet (Lord Arlington) are in the P[ublic] R[ecord] O[ffice], State Papers Foreign (SP. 84/166–76); 37 letters to Nicholas are to be found in BL, Egerton MSS 2537, 2538; and 185 letters to the Earl of Clarendon are in the Bodleian Library, Clarendon State Papers, vols. 73–8, 80–2 and 104–8. The latter have been admirably calendared by F. J. Routledge (ed.), *Calendar of Clarendon State Papers*, v (Oxford, 1970).
[23] See 55 letters from the Clarendon collection in abridged versions in T. H. Lister, *Life and Administration of Edward, First Earl of Clarendon* (1837), III, *passim*. Selections from 42 letters are printed in N. Japikse, *De verwikkelingen tusschen de Republiek en Engeland van 1660–1665* (Leiden, 1900), Apps. IX and XII, pp. xxi–xxiv, xli–lv; 28 letters are abridged in *Bescheiden uit Vreemde Archieven omtrent de Groote Nederlandsche Zeeoorlogen, 1652–1676*, ed. H. T. Colenbrander (The Hague, 1919), pp. 126–287. In subsequent notes, where the printed version is satisfactory I have cited it in preference to the original.

Certainly it is only after Cromwell's death that one may glimpse
something of his suppressed passions in the asides which enliven two
letters, of January 1659 and March 1660.[24] In the latter he observed the
desperate need for parliamentary intervention in the English woollen
industry before it fell entirely into the hands of Silesia and the Dutch and
'England have nothing left but the groath of its wool'. Likewise in the
former he urged a vigorous parliamentary initiative which would
combine fiscal reform and financial regeneration with an active protection of England's merchant marine. Suggesting tariff reforms which
clearly foreshadow his work on the 1660 Book of Rates, Downing
stressed the crucial importance of healthy public revenues in European
power politics, 'for England's revenue though small yet held proportion
with the revenues of neighbouring Princes and States about them, and
that must be the rule now, or England is undone'.[25] In this combination
of commercial and financial policies, and the stress on parliamentary
action, one can discern the major themes which were to give coherence
to Downing's entire career. For the putative father of the mercantilist
system was the undoubted progenitor of a reformed Treasury, and his
diplomatic correspondence clearly shows that his work in Whitehall no
less than his work at Westminster was rooted in perceptions formed
years earlier during the frustrating exile at The Hague. To ignore this
coherence and to see in Downing merely the opinionated purveyor of
second-hand Dutch ideas is to miss the breadth and discrimination of his
observation.

A striking illustration of the way in which Downing marshalled
complex but coherent objectives is provided by the very long letter he
addressed to Clarendon in August 1661, soon after his return to The
Hague.[26] After a prelude which echoed the case he had made to Thurloe
in 1659 he 'humbly' offered his plan of fiscal innovation 'seeing your
Lo[rdshi]pp doth desire it'. It was an eleven-point programme, ranging
from the administrative reinforcement of existing taxes to the introduction of entirely new and highly controversial ones. Some of his
suggestions were unexceptionable, such as a salt tax (provided it spared
the fisheries), or taxes on legal documents and on hackney-coach
licences. A levy on gaming had moral as well as fiscal advantages, and

---

[24] *A Collection of the State Papers of John Thurloe*, ed. T. Birch (1742), vii, 847–9 (Downing to
the President of the Council, 16/26 March 1660); *Selections from the Papers of William
Clarke*, ed. C. H. Firth (Camden Society, 1891–1901), iii, 177–8 (Downing to ?, 28
January/7 February 1659).
[25] *Clarke Papers*, iii, 177–8.
[26] Bodleian, Clarendon MS 104, ff. 252–8 (16/26 August 1661, summarized in Routledge
(ed.), *Calendar*, v, 125–6.)

the erection of government pawn-shops or 'Lumbards' in country towns would be socially beneficial as well as profitable. But his tax on land-transfers would, he acknowledged, 'much stagger the Gentry', though grounded in ancient precedent. He noted that the gentry would be better pleased by his proposal for an alehouse-licensing tax, 'but whether it bee so equal to take all off from themselves and lay all upon this sort of people is a Question'. He left this implicit reproach hanging in the air, but the selfish and regressive character of the Restoration tax settlement, which had shifted burdens from the landed class to the general consumer,[27] was clearly in Downing's mind when he urged his most provocative proposal – a graduated tax on private brewing. This was a nettle which even later administrations were reluctant to grasp, but Downing strongly deplored the social inequity of the existing excise on retail brewing which meant, he wrote, that 'the poore pay who are not able to brew, and the rich, who are able to brew, pay not'. This should be redressed: all private brewing should be annually licensed with a tariff of fees related to social status.

This remarkably precocious essay in progressive taxation introduces a Downing rather different from the fawning turncoat we have been taught to imagine. The truth is, Sir George Downing in the 1660s and beyond was to prove a good deal bolder than the Mr Downing of the 1650s. Despite some sensitivity about his republican past he did not hesitate to make proposals and observations which might prove unpopular at the Restoration court. Thus, nothing could be less servile or more pointed than his warnings against the French in general and his denunciation of the sale of Dunkirk in particular. Initially, he rejected news of the sale as a malicious rumour: 'I will never beleeve it nor look upon it as other than a Rodamontado',[28] but as the unpleasant truth became clear his remarks acquired a deliberate cutting edge which must have made their recipients squirm.[29] As for French policies in general, he was quick to recognize in the 1660s the dangers which only obsessed his colleagues in the 1670s. As early as March 1662 he was warning the government against reliance on Louis XIV in terms which drew down

---

[27] See *Considerations Offered to the Corporations of England* (1681), reprinted in *Seventeenth Century Economic Documents*, ed. J. Thirsk and J. P. Cooper (Oxford, 1972), p. 408; but for a contrary view see C. D. Chandaman, *The English Public Revenue, 1660–1688* (1975), pp. 37–43. Something resembling Downing's proposed levy on home brewing was indeed put forward in 1661 – see *C[ommons] J[ournal]*, VIII, 301, 305 – but rejected, as it was in 1666 and 1671.

[28] BL, Egerton MS 2538, f. 29 (Downing to Nicholas, 21 February 1662).

[29] *Ibid.*, f. 33. 'This weeke it is strongly reported, and by persons who seem to know most, that his Ma[jes]ty is selling Dunkirke to the French, as if because the Duke of Lorraine hath sold his Countries others were of that mind also to do the like.'

sharp rebukes from Clarendon.[30] But he returned to the theme of France's commercial aggrandizement again and again, warning in November 1662 of the schemes of an emergent Colbert, 'who hath some understanding in business of trade, and makes it his business to make France considerable therein, and in shipping'.[31] Downing was later to make the French commercial threat a major object of public concern, and he was at the root of nearly all subsequent parliamentary action. The Staple Act of 1663, which he ushered through all its stages, began life as a measure to 'prevent encroachment by the Jews, French and other foreigners', but in 1666 action against France alone was set on foot by Downing's report from the Committee of Trade which culminated in the prohibition of French imports from 1 December that year.[32] Not satisfied with what might (and did) prove a temporary ban, the House selected Downing to chair a further committee against French manufactures on 22 January 1667, and he again led the committee when the issue was revived in November 1670.[33] But the major assault came in 1675, when it was Downing who reported the celebrated 'Scheme of Trade', exhibiting the unfavourable balance of Anglo-French trade, and it was Downing who chaired the subsequent committee for an Address against French manufacturers.[34] In 1677 and 1678, when parliamentary pressure against France reached a belated crescendo, it should be no surprise to find Downing serving on all the appropriate committees of trade and foreign affairs.[35] Though best known as an enemy to Dutch pretensions, he was a more far-sighted and consistent antagonist of French aggrandizement.

But Downing was no bigot, and the same precocious discrimination which alerted him to the French also obliged him to revise his position on another sensitive issue – religious toleration. At the outset of his diplomatic mission on Charles II's behalf he had dutifully drawn attention to the dangers posed by sectarian exiles resident in Holland,[36] and – as is too well known – he was to pursue some of the regicides to the death. But there is reason for believing that he regretted his early zeal,[37] and his preoccupation with English immigrants to the Netherlands soon

[30] Routledge (ed.), *Calendar*, v, 199; Lister, *Clarendon*, iii, 202.
[31] Lister, *Clarendon*, iii, 261; see also *ibid.*, pp. 221–2, 246, 348, 349.
[32] *CJ*, viii, 467–8, 632; *Tudor and Stuart Proclamations, 1485–1714*, ed. R. Steele (Oxford, 1910), i, 420 (10 November 1666).
[33] *CJ*, viii, 681, 687; ix, 174.
[34] *CJ*, ix, 359, 365; *The Somers Tracts*, viii, 32; PRO, CO 391/1, p. 84 (Downing's preliminary report to the Council of Trade, March 1675).
[35] *CJ*, ix, 394, 428, 447, 454, 472, 490, 507.
[36] Bodleian, Clarendon MS 104, ff. 136–9; Lister, *Clarendon*, iii, 144.
[37] *Memoirs of Edmund Ludlow*, ed. C. H. Firth (Oxford, 1894), ii, 428.

took on a social and economic, rather than a political, significance. He was increasingly disturbed by the number of skilled artisans among them – textile workers in the main, and craftsmen whom England badly needed.[38] He made piecemeal attempts to reverse the flow, persuading an Englishman skilled in the mysteries of Delft-ware to return to England and set up business with government support.[39] He sought out and induced several weavers and bleachers to follow the same route, and at the height of the Anglo-Dutch war he urged kindly treatment of Dutch prisoners to encourage them to remain.[40] But he saw that more was needed, and as early as June 1661 was arguing vigorously for an act of General Naturalization, 'for the making of all Protestants to be as natural borne subjects'.[41]

The proposal seems unexceptionable, and attempts to introduce such a measure were to recur throughout Restoration Parliaments. But the reception of the attempt in December 1667 clearly illustrates the objections which a largely Anglican House of Commons professed to see in such a step.[42] It was religious toleration by the back door, a veiled concession to nonconformity which was to be resisted to the bitter end. Warned by such rancour, Downing could not be blamed if he had kept his views to himself, particularly as Clarendon's attitude remained so ambiguous, but in fact Downing made quite clear his opinion of the persecuting measures emerging in the Cavalier Parliament between 1661 and 1664. The Act of Uniformity, much to Downing's disgust, was interpreted by the Dutch as a prelude to renewed civil war,[43] and it is ironic that he was to contribute unintentionally to its sequel, the Five Mile Act of 1665. But Downing's letters from The Hague had faithfully chronicled the movements of English dissidents in exile, and it was his reports as much as anything which justified two measures of the Oxford Parliament in October 1665. The first was the attainder of Dolman, Bampfield and Scott – leading republicans in exile. On this bill Downing chaired the committee. The other was the Five Mile Act itself, which was largely based on the premise of an active 'fifth column' of dissenting ministers working in collusion with the enemy Dutch.[44] These mea-

---

[38] BL, Egerton MS 2538, f. 97; Lister, *Clarendon*, III, 218; Routledge (ed.), *Calendar*, v, 246, 253.
[39] Bodleian, Clarendon MS 108, ff. 102, 108–9, 160, 162, 171, 255, 266.
[40] Lister, *Clarendon*, III, 361; Colenbrander (ed.), *Bescheiden*, p. 238; Routledge (ed.), *Calendar*, v, 468, 480, 485, 493, 496.
[41] Lister, *Clarendon*, III, 150.
[42] *The Diary of John Milward*, ed. C. Robbins (1938), pp. 152–3.
[43] Lister, *Clarendon*, III, 218; Routledge (ed.), *Calendar*, v, 253, 257, 263.
[44] *Lords Journal*, XI, 688, 699–700.

sures, together with Downing's better-known contributions to the Additional Aid of 1665, with its historic provisions for appropriation, borrowing and repayment-in-course, meant that he could claim responsibility for the session's most important achievements.

But he could have claimed the same for other sessions. Despite, or rather because of, his absence abroad in 1661–2, Downing was to be extremely active when he participated in the session of February–June 1663. Of the session's seventeen public acts, seven were bills in which he was involved at the committee stage and three more reflect proposals he had outlined to Clarendon in the preceding two years. Of the suggestions he had made in the long letter of August 1661 three of the least controversial were implemented by measures for the improved collection of the Excise and the Hearth Tax, though he was not on the committees for he was busy on thirty others. The Bill regulating the Herring and other Fisheries, which Downing reported and carried to the Lords, reflected objectives of which he had long been an advocate, as did the Act encouraging the manufacture of Linen cloth and Tapestry.[45] In August 1662 he had written one of his Cassandra-like prophecies of England's industrial eclipse: 'already Eng[land] is become but the poor mans clothier'. He went on: 'This business deserves a days debate in every week, otherwise I do see plainly Eng[land] will be brought to the old trade of sending out theire wooll unmanufactured the which is the losse of 2/3rds of the present profit, the working up of wooll being twice as valuable as the wool it selfe.' With Spanish wool entering the European market in larger quantities, he saw little chance of a full recovery for English exports, and the best remedy he could propose would be measures for import-substitution: 'setting up some other manufacture to Counterbalance the decay of those of wooll as for example that of making linnen, the which with a little care & encouragement might easily be brought to a great perfection'.[46] The act of 1663 went some way towards these objectives while at the same time encouraging immigration, and Downing – who had chaired the committee – could count this, together with Acts for the preservation of Timber and for the regulation of the fat-cattle trade, as work well done.[47]

To ascribe all these measures to Downing's sole initiative, particularly in the absence of corroborative diaries, is to push the evidence of the

[45] 15 Car. II c. 12; c. 13.
[46] Bodleian, Clarendon MS 71, ff. 171–2.
[47] 15 Car. II c. 2; c. 8. The text of the Linen and Tapestry Act is reprinted in Thirsk and Cooper (eds.), *Documents*, pp. 738–9.

Commons Journal too far, though it is worth observing that if it were not for Clarendon's jaundiced account and the happy accident of a Pepys's *Diary* we would know little of Downing's responsibility for the revolutionary provisos to the Additional Aid, when he was not even on the committee. But there has never been any doubt about his role in the most important measure of 1663, the 'Act for the Encouragement of Trade', or Staple Act, which completed the structure of the navigation code.[48] He chaired all three committees which shaped its evolution, presented their reports, and carried the completed bill to the Lords.[49] Back at The Hague in 1664 he could rejoice in Dutch discomfiture at its effects, for it broke their links with the English West Indies 'and hinders them of the sale of vast quantities of manufactures'.[50] On this measure alone, with its complex provisions for coal, corn, cattle, coinage, fish and tobacco – as well as for the plantations trade – Downing's reputation as a practical legislator should stand high enough.

Yet doubts will return at this picture of Downing as a parliamentary buccaneer, hacking his path single-handed to the statute book. Commonsense requires one to look around for the colleagues and collaborators, the pressure groups and interests, which deserve their share in the credit. Downing was only one figure on the large and influential Councils of Trade of 1660, 1668 and 1672, and on issues both commercial and financial it was possible to assemble impressive panels of independent experts. Such was the case with the notable House of Lords committee of 1669, on the fall of rents and decay of trade, to which Downing made no recorded contribution. Conversely, there were issues on which Downing performed an essentially subservient role. He was an obliging, and well-rewarded, spokesman for the East India Company,[51] both in Holland and in the House. As Secretary to the Treasury and as Commissioner of the Customs he was often acting as the agent of collective policy. Yet the search for Downing's parliamentary coadjutors runs into repeated difficulties and they fail to emerge. Without a large body of personal papers we can discover nothing like Shaftesbury's collaboration with Benjamin Worsley or John Locke, though it is clear that Downing worked with Sir John Shaw of the Customs both in 1660 and in 1671. On the latter occasion we are able to glimpse him as a harassed administrator, sending for the draft Plantation Act which was to

---

[48] 15 Car. II c. 7; Beer, *Old Colonial System*, pp. 10, fn. 1, 76–9; Harper, *Navigation Laws*, p. 59; BL, Additional MS 22920, ff. 11, 12.
[49] *CJ*, VIII, 447, 468, 480, 494, 502, 522.
[50] Lister, *Clarendon*, III, 308.
[51] Khan, *East India Trade*, p. 100, fn. 2.

bear his stamp: 'Tomorrow being holiday I shall have leisure to look it over.'[52] One would also expect collaboration with Sir William Coventry, whose deference has been observed. But Downing appears to have had few friends, and Coventry's sympathies for Downing may have been as divided as those of Pepys. Downing clashed openly with both Clifford and Coventry on the floor of the House, and as Lords of the Treasury they cordially resented his domineering ways.[53] Indeed, it must be said that if Downing was admired at all at the court of Charles II it was not as an economic adviser, let alone as father of the mercantilist system, but as a prodigiously vigorous voluptuary. Parliamentary gossip credited Downing with six concurrent mistresses,[54] and Charles himself, sighing for the favours of a fifteen-year-old French actress, had to concede that Downing was one of the two men most likely to enjoy them.[55] Clearly his energies were not confined to legislation.

Downing himself liked to applaud his own, unaided parliamentary achievements,[56] and while we need not take him at his own valuation, Pepys was willing to do so, not only on the Act for the Additional Aid but also for its important sequel in 1667, the Act 'assigning Orders in the Exchequer without Revocation'.[57] By facilitating the Treasury's creation of negotiable government securities the act was a corner-stone of the 'financial revolution', with incalculable long-term significance. A similar claim could be made for Downing's Coinage Act of 1666 which, by removing the premium or seigniorage on private bullion brought to the Mint, devised a measure which endured until 1925.[58]

And there is another measure which Downing made his own, which illustrates several of his characteristic preoccupations. It is the Act of 1673 'for the Incouragement of the Greenland and Eastland Trades, and for the better secureing of the Plantation Trade'.[59] One significant effect of this important amendment to the colonial system was the destruction of the Eastland Company's exclusive privileges, and the probability of Downing's responsibility for this has long been appreciated, for the company's

[52] *Calendar of Treasury Books, 1669–72*, ed. W. A. Shaw p. 679 (Downing to Sir John Shaw, 31 October 1670).
[53] *Milward's Diary*, p. 140; Anchitel Grey, *Debates of the House of Commons from the Year 1667 to the Year 1694* (1793), IV, 23; Pepys, *Diary*, VIII, 240 (28 May 1667).
[54] BL, Lansdowne MS 805, f. 86; Harleian MS 7020, f. 37.
[55] Historical Manuscripts Commission, *Marquis of Bath MSS*(1904–8), II, 161 (Henry Savile to the Earl of Rochester, 17 December 1677).
[56] Pepys, *Diary*, VIII, 520 (6 November 1667).
[57] *Ibid.*, VII, 122; VIII, 520 (12 May 1666, 6 November 1667).
[58] 18 and 19 Car. II c. 5; *Milward's Diary*, pp. 10, 40, 59; *CJ*, VIII, 640, 648, 665, 674; A. E. Feavearyear, *The Pound Sterling* (Oxford, 1931), pp. 88–9, 109; Sir John Craig, *The Mint* (Cambridge, 1953), pp. 168–70.
[59] 25 Car. II c. 7.

agent himself alluded to it.[60] Historians have plausibly attributed his backing to the Council of Trade and Plantations but have also noted Downing's talent for ruthlessness and 'crooked ways'.[61] Yet it must be said that there was nothing 'crooked' or 'unnaturally swift'[62] about Downing's attack. He had long since given fair notice to the Company's leaders of his rooted objections to their conduct. Their unforgivable offence, in his eyes, was their refusal to construct or even employ English shipping suitable for the Baltic. They were complacently content to hire unwieldy vessels ('rather tubs than ships') which were incapable of self-defence and totally unsuited to bulk commodities. Worse still, they obstinately refused to learn from the Dutch who, by securing Danish 'branding' of their purpose-built ships, greatly cheapened and speeded their passage through the Sound. Downing had set out his case in a memorable letter of 25 December 1663, parts of which are well known for a version was printed by Japikse and is eminently quotable.[63] But the passages which most pointedly accuse the Eastland Company are omitted from the printed version: 'And for my owne part I doe not know what shadow of reason can be given for the maintenance of the Eastland Comp. & debarring all other English from trading thither if England hath not at least this advantage thereby that they Employ English Shipping.' After contrasting their practice unfavourably with that of other companies, Downing added: 'And I did when I was at London tell some of that Comp. that unles they would thinke of serving themselves with English shipping I would be a meanes so to open the matter to his Majest. as that they might be roundly dealt withall about it, and truly so they ought to be.'[64] He returned to the matter in March 1664, having heard from Clarendon that the Eastland Company persisted in its reluctance to employ 'branded' shipping. He was not surprised, he said, 'they had rather goe on in the road they are in', but the damage was great and the remedy must come from the government. Let the Company know that unless it mended its ways the king would withdraw its charter. He concluded: 'to expect that the Merchants of themselves without being thus putt upon it will ever doe it is vaine'.[65] Clarendon

---

[60] *Records of the Merchant Adventurers of Newcastle-upon-Tyne*, ed. J. R. Boyle and F. W. Dendy (Surtees Society, vol. XCIII, 1894), II, 153; R. W. K. Hinton, *The Eastland Trade and the Common Weal in the Seventeenth Century* (Cambridge, 1959), p. 155.

[61] Hinton, *Eastland Trade*, p. 155, quoting M. Sellers.

[62] *Ibid.*

[63] Japikse, *De verwikkelingen tusschen*, pp. xlv-vi, taken from Downing to Bennet (PRO, SP. 84/168, f. 219) but cf. Downing to Clarendon (Bodleian, Clarendon MS 107, ff. 52–3).

[64] Bodleian, Clarendon MS 107, ff. 52–3.

[65] *Ibid.*, f. 112 verso.

was later to accuse Downing of believing that he was 'wiser in trade than any of the merchants', and it is one charge Downing might have been glad to accept. The view that merchants and trading companies – selfish, short-sighted and complacent – were not necessarily the best judges of national requirements is at the root of Downing's legislative vigour. He made these feelings very clear in a passionate attack on the idea of incorporating a Spanish Company, in November 1664.[66] 'It would be a most destructive and mischievous thing.' 'Members being in a Company, though they shall not trade with Joint Stock yet they will so understand one another as that they will ... keep the marketts hungry.' Next they would want a company for France and another for Italy, 'by all which the King would imediatly finde himselfe desperatly wounded in his Customes, & the people in their trade & all the out Ports made meer Country villages'. He was not abashed to learn that it was a Canary Islands Company that was being formed: the same arguments applied, and in 1667 he was to address the House of Lords at length on the iniquity of its foundation.[67]

His mordant distrust of merchants was flanked by another equally jaundiced belief. Despite the charming horticultural simile in which he once compared government intervention in trade to a gardener tending his herbs and trees, and notwithstanding his discreet avowal that a monarchy was as competent as a commonwealth,[68] it is clear that he had little faith in the reliability of Charles II or of his ministers. From The Hague his letters seethed with frustration; at home he was bitter and disillusioned.[69] Charles II's jaunty contempt for Downing's safety and his cynical gaoling in 1672 were symptomatic of a consistent disregard.

Against this background it is not to be expected that Downing's legislative career should owe much to the prejudices of merchants or the policies of government. Downing was his own man, and the character of Charles II's Parliaments fortunately left abundant room for independent initiative despite the increasing discipline exercised by an organized 'court party'. Downing was actually a part of that discipline, described in a contemporary libel as 'the House bell to call the courtiers to vote', and Shaftesbury had him marked down for 'thrice vile' as a government supporter.[70] But a man who could champion the Irish Cattle bills, so

---

[66] PRO, SP. 84/173, ff. 29–30, 67 (Downing to Bennet, 15 November, 2 December 1664).
[67] *Lords Journal*, XII, 64–5 (3 January 1667).
[68] PRO, SP 84/168, ff. 219–20; partially printed in Japikse, *De verwikkelingen tusschen*, pp. xlv–xlvi (Downing to Bennet, 25 December 1663).
[69] Pepys, *Diary*, VII, 380–1; VIII, 425–7 (23 November 1666, 8 September 1667).
[70] J. P. F[erris], 'Sir George Downing', in Henning (ed.), *The Commons 1660–1690*, p. 228.

offensive to the court, or return again and again to the charge with unpopular bills for General Naturalization, does not fit into the categories of court toady or party hack. Downing was not even at ease with his own adopted class as a wealthy landowner. On poor relief, on hawkers and pedlars, on the stamp duty or 'Law bill', as on the Excise, he championed policies uncomfortable for the country gentry and urban corporations alike. Politically he showed some independence. Downing was to oppose the exclusion of the Duke of York in 1678–9, though wills reveal his family to have been quite hysterically anti-Catholic.[71] But he took part in the committees investigating the Popish Plot, and the choice of Sir George to chair the committee on the disabandment of Forces in 1679, and to serve again in 1680,[72] suggests that he was not distrusted by an increasingly Whig House of Commons.

Although there is evidence to suggest that Downing was resting on his oars by 1681,[73] his legislative efforts had not relaxed with increasing age and it is hard to understand how anyone could write of 'his virtual retirement in 1673'.[74] The truth is that some of Downing's later sessions were among his most active. Between January and July 1678 he was nominated to sixty-six committees, four of which he chaired. The fruit of all this work was not great but he could claim credit for the act regulating Newcastle coal measures and, after a strenuous cycle of conferences with the Lords, for the act reinforcing the requirement for burial in woollen.[75] Since 1666, when he had secured this compulsion, it was one of those policies which Downing had made his own, a peculiar but useful contribution to England's major industry which was to remain in force until 1814.

The longevity of Downing's central achievements is some mark of their importance. The stamp he left on the Treasury was to last even longer than the mercantilist system he helped to contrive. But survival is not the only index of value, and one object of this sketch has been to draw attention to the less familiar and possibly ephemeral aspects of Downing's work. Like any conscientious Member he attended to the sectional interests of his constituency and of his family. As Member for

[71] A Will made by Sir George Downing, 2nd Bart. on 15 September 1688', in *Downing Muniments*, ed. W. L. Cuttle and K. W. S. Mackenzie (1936); Grey, *Debates*, VI, 244–5.
[72] *CJ*, IX, 516, 517, 519, 530, 536, 581, 684.
[73] PRO, CO 389/11, ff. 109–10 (Sir Richard Temple to the Council of Trade and Foreign Plantations, 28 March 1681).
[74] C. A. Edie, 'The Irish Cattle Bills: A Study in Restoration Politics', *Transactions of the American Philosophical Society*, New Series, vol. 60, part 2 (Philadelphia, 1970), p. 12, fn. 42.
[75] 30 Car. II c. 3; c. 8; *CJ*, IX, 440, 443, 444, 447, 451, 453, 455, 478, 486, 489, 495, 503, 512, 513, 514.

Morpeth and brother-in-law of the Earl of Carlisle he was consistently involved in legislation to curb the lawlessness of the Border. Early familiarity with Scotland shaped his firm views and active intervention on Anglo-Scottish trade.[76] His East Anglian origins may have coloured his solicitude for Yarmouth and the Colchester bays trade.[77] Partiality and prejudice certainly played their part in the policies he advocated and not all of them were to be favourably received. His preference for a tin over a copper coinage was discredited in his own day;[78] the policy on leather exports which he had helped to inaugurate was repudiated after 1675;[79] the prohibition of Irish cattle created more problems than it solved,[80] and Downing's eloquent pessimism about the English cloth industry has been reproved as 'rhetoric'.[81] Yet behind the exaggeration and the arrogance of Downing's advocacy lay a sober realism that prosperity 'was not to be had in a day, nor by one good Act, but to be pursued from Step to Step'. Few men were more farsighted in discerning what those steps should be, or more effective in giving them legislative shape. It was this constructive will which made Downing the most creative parliamentary entrepreneur of his day.

---

[76] Downing, who had served in Scotland 1650–2 and been Member for Edinburgh in 1654, appears to have dominated the commissioners negotiating an Anglo-Scottish trade treaty in 1668, who met at his house: E. Hughes, 'The Negotiations for a Commercial Union between England and Scotland in 1668', *Scottish Historical Review*, 24 (1927), 35; M. Lee, *The Cabal* (Urbana, 1965), pp. 45, 46, 48.

[77] Lister, *Clarendon*, III, 150–1; *CJ*, VIII, 143; IX, 33, 125, 410.

[78] Routledge (ed.), *Calendar*, V, 476; *Calendar of State Papers Domestic, 1676–77*, p. 123.

[79] L. A. Clarkson, 'English Economic Policy in the Sixteenth and Seventeenth Centuries: The Case of the Leather Industry', *Bulletin of the Institute of Historical Research*, 38 (1965), 156.

[80] Edie, 'Irish Cattle Bills', pp. 42–4.

[81] C. Wilson, 'Cloth Production and International Competition in the Seventeenth Century', *Economic History Review*, 2nd Series 13 (1960), 219.

9

The lawyer as businessman in eighteenth-century England

PETER MATHIAS

This is a very large topic to discuss: available research materials are vast in quantity because solicitors' records (principally the files of their clients), a high proportion dating from the eighteenth century, have survived by the ton in county record offices, if now no longer in the offices of the solicitors themselves. Yet most economic historians, where they have touched on the subject at all, have only nibbled at it from a point on the periphery, by investigating lawyers as bankers, or as stewards of landed estates, or in local capital markets, rather than tackling the subject head-on. More recently great interest has been shown in the connections between property rights, transaction costs and the incentive structure for economic development. But this has been at a singularly abstract conceptual level, seldom invoking lawyers as creatures of flesh, blood and ambition.[1] Other historians, concerned with lawyers as a professional group, have been principally interested in different aspects of the institutionalization of legal functions, particularly the growing professionalization of the practice of law, rather than exploring systematically the actual economic roles undertaken by lawyers.[2] As was written now a generation ago, 'The country attorney touched eighteenth-century economic life at many points and was undoubtedly a key man; a fruitful field of study awaits a patient historian.'[3] That systematic study is still awaited. This essay is only a brief survey of the field, based, for the most part, on extant secondary

[1] E.g. D. C. North, *Structure and Change in Economic History* (New York and London, 1981); *idem* (with R. P. Thomas), *The Rise of the Western World: A New Economic History* (Cambridge, 1973).
[2] H. Kirk, *Portrait of a Profession* (London, 1976); M. Birks, *Gentlemen of the Law* (London, 1960); W. Prest (ed.), *Lawyers in Early Modern Europe and America* (London, 1980).
[3] L. S. Pressnell, *Country Banking in the Industrial Revolution* (Oxford, 1956), p. 39.

151

scholarship. It is not concerned with the conceptual relationships between property rights and economic growth; nor with the more empirical analysis of the different ways in which legal processes aided the process of economic change and, in other ways, acted as a brake upon such change. Its subject is the lawyers themselves, in particular the attorneys of provincial England.

Relationships between the law and economic activity are deep-seated and widespread. Virtually all economic activities in eighteenth-century England were bounded by legal processes, as they had been, of course, long before the eighteenth century and as they have been ever since. Legal processes were also always likely to invade the day-to-day operations of a business and were certainly present at its birth, crisis and death. In addition, the lawyers would be involved at all points touching the ownership or the transfer of ownership (whether of individual family firm or partnership), when disputes broke out, whenever money had to be loaned or borrowed, when property was owned or occupied, where debts could not be paid or collected, when bankruptcy or dissolution intervened. The main business of lawyers handling the affairs of private clients was dominated by property, probate and debt – functions all thoroughly intertwined as well as producing business separately. These were equally the roots of the attorney's commitment to business because these same functions operated; it was just that the clients were businessmen. Kinship determined so much in the ownership and control of, the financial provision for and the succession to eighteenth-century business (even within partnership enterprises). Possession of land and property were instrumental to much economic enterprise – whether industrial activity (often also concerned with water rights, wayleaves and the like) or mining beneath the surface, where minerals were to be won, as well as farming. And debt, at least of significant size, was normally secured on property in the mortgage market, which required legally drawn documents, conveyances and the like. Most eighteenth-century business operated in relationships as direct and face-to-face as those of eighteenth-century politics, but both were cocooned by the law.

Undoubtedly the land had been the greatest source of business for lawyers, whether in litigation or not, since medieval times. 'Every sentence [in the Paston letters of the fifteenth century]', it has been said, 'refers to lawsuits and title-deeds, extortions and injuries received from others, forged processes affecting property, suits of one kind and another... and matters of like description.'[4] Blackstone wrote of the

---

[4] E. B. V. Christian, *Solicitors: An Outline of their History* (London, 1925), p. 29.

'long and voluminous train of descents and conveyances, settlements, entails and incumbrances' concerned with the affairs of 'gentlemen of independent estates and fortunes' which formed 'the most intricate and most extensive object of legal knowledge'.[5] Anyone who has bought, or tried to buy, an old house in England is still likely to glimpse such complications. But as the sources of wealth and the institutional forms embodying economic activity grew and diversified so the role of lawyers in the business life of the country diversified accordingly. This was particularly the case in relatively small-town provincial life, where so much of the business arising from industrial, commercial, agricultural, transport and mining development in the eighteenth century was conducted.

The handling of these functions touched the local lawyers, in financial as well as legal terms, in many ways. The relationships are structurally dependent upon the fundamental political organization of society: the role of the state in economic and social relationships, the nature of property rights, the degree of economic freedom given to the individual and to privately associated groups, the nature of the market and the degree of market freedom in the economy. Much has been written about the importance of legal processes and the changed role of the state in the British economy after the restoration of the Stuarts in 1660, complemented by the changes in the political system after 1688. As the role of the central apparatus of the state became more confined, following the withdrawal of public authority from the direct control of many aspects of economic activity, the ending of the monopoly powers enjoyed by many statutory authorities, nationally and locally, so the importance of the common law and 'judge-made' law increased, confirming and enhancing private property rights. The changes in the political regime following the Stuarts – with the post-1688 monarchy showing much greater respect for the judiciary – brought a great rise in the status and independence of judges and lawyers in the reign of George I and after. The law became, in Lord Chesterfield's words, 'the truly independent profession', and this enhancement of status and local independent initiative spilled over to the solicitors and attorneys, in the many roles they began to play.[6]

Much impetus for economic change came from this liberation of the market, the enhancement of private property rights and individual economic initiative. But at the same time the intricacies of the law, with

[5] Sir William Blackstone, *Commentaries on the Laws of England*, 4th edn (Oxford, 1770), I, 7.
[6] G. Holmes, *Augustan England: Professions, State and Society, 1680–1730* (London, 1982), p. 116.

the need to follow legal forms with great precision if challenges on technical grounds were to be fended off, could be used to challenge and delay economic initiatives for changing the status quo. The activities of the provincial attorneys of eighteenth-century England, in relation to critical processes of economic change in transport, land improvement, estate administration, urban investment and banking, are to be explained by the special context within which such economic change was developing in England. Central government in England (with its formal apparatus of state and public administration) withdrew from many economic activities in mining, land improvement, industrial activity and transport investment, compared with continental states. In France or Prussia, Sweden or Russia many of these activities would be directly administered through the apparatus of state, by a specially constituted authority or locally controlled by the prefects and agents of central government, within the public sector of the economy and the official sector of administration. Doubtless many of such civil servants would have been trained in the law, but they operated in these roles as public officials.

In England the frontiers of central administration and its apparatus consequently shrank – the special agencies of state and crown, the state bureaucracy (apart from the directly administered customs and excise and the armed forces). The formal organs of state had little to do with the organization of new corporate forms of economic activity in the eighteenth century. But at the same time many processes of change had to embody legal authority in order to establish particular local institutions and allow them to operate: the power to purchase land (and to buy out recalcitrant minority landowners seeking to block the venture), the right to levy rates or tolls, to raise capital from the public, to sue for debts under a common seal, to enjoy limitation of liability and the like. Hence the importance of local initiative – the private act of Parliament rather than the general statute proposed at government initiative, related to just a local scheme, with authority confined to the local scheme as defined in the private act. Privately sponsored parliamentary legislation, setting up enclosure commissions, turnpike acts, canal companies, commissions of sewers and drainage, improvement commissions, authorities to build and adminster bridges and a host of what would now be called 'public utilities' became the characteristic legal form for the promotion of new sorts of economic activity requiring corporate form. In addition came private equitable trusts, operating under a legal deed of trust, with a self-recruiting set of trustees, but not involving a private act of Parliament.

154

These ventures were not within the system of public administration; not run by civil servants, state bureaucrats of central or local government. They were local and provincial: local in initiative, local in scope, at the grass-roots of provincial economic life – which was the main source of economic change and industrial growth – locally based. They needed to be established by legal instruments and were always accountable in terms of those legal instruments and legal processes. Hence they virtually had to be run by local lawyers. In most cases this meant the local attornies rather than the barristers (the small elite of lawyers, mainly London-based, whose legal careers centred on pleading in the principal courts, whether in London or on the circuits of Assize), even if the more prestigious positions were sought by barristers.[7] The attorneys found themselves at the interface between such local initiatives and the legal forms needed to embody them. The intimate connections between legal and financial business were manifold, in an attorney's business with private clients no less than through his assumption of local offices. As Dr Miles remarked, 'The fields of law and finance were close together and a good attorney needed a sound knowledge of both.'[8]

Financial dealings had thus become by 1700 an important component of almost every provincial attorney's practice. They could balance the supply and demand for loans amongst their own clients, negotiate such deals with fellow-attorneys similarly placed (sometimes advertising in the local press), but almost always on a local basis, where their personal knowledge ran. For clients they knew well, bonds or notes of hand might suffice for smaller loans but larger borrowings (and loans to strangers) would be secured, if not always by a mortgage.[9] Trusteeship and executor work brought in most financial business to the attorneys, and this was integral to their legal roles, but some also set out deliberately to pursue financial transactions for their own sake, following in the footsteps of the old 'money-scriveners'. The accounts of John Eagle of Bradford show a steady stream of such transactions. Evidently attorneys acted as deposit banks for the small savings of less-wealthy clients. Isaac Greene offered 'something very like investment consultancy' for his wealthier clients.[10] To advance down any of these roads would

[7] *Ibid.*, pp. 139–42.

[8] M. Miles, 'The Money Market in the Early Industrial Revolution: The Evidence from West Riding Attornies *c.* 1750–1800', *Business History*, 23 (1981). The following dicussion draws heavily on this important article. See also B. L. Anderson, 'The Attorney and the Local Capital Market in Lancashire', in J. R. Harris (ed.), *Liverpool and Merseyside* (London, 1969), pp. 50–77.

[9] B. A. Holderness, 'Credit in a Rural Community, 1660–1800', *Midland History*, 3 (1970), 109.

[10] Holmes, *Augustan England*, p. 157.

lead the attorneys into more formal banking functions. In the absence of country banks in smaller English provincial towns before the closing decades of the eighteenth century the attorney occupied this ground informally: after the country banker had emerged to occupy his own place in the local business community the attorney became more his ally and associate than his rival. This was in a context where (in the absence of village and small-town usurers) 'nearly everyone with surplus cash appears to have let it out at interest on a private and personal basis'.[11]

Property provided the most intimate link between law and financial dealings, particularly through conveyancing and mortgage work. The attorney had taken over most conveyancing work from the scriveners, and, with mortgaging, this placed him, as the key intermediary, in the centre of informal, local long-term lending and borrowing. Personal knowledge as to the reliability of both parties to such transactions remained an important precondition for the attorney's role (if he was to retain the confidence of prospective lenders) which kept the mortgage market 'not only fundamentally local but distinctly personal'.[12] Often, moreover, involvement as an intermediary in the mortgage market provided the route for the attorney to become a landed proprietor himself.[13]

In a small-community setting specialization of function developed relatively slowly in response to rising need, so that the lawyers, already well represented and well placed in these communities before the eighteenth century, tended to accrete such business functions to themselves. The attorney's great advantage in the eighteenth century was that he was already there. The subsequent separate institutionalization of business and financial services during the nineteenth century with the evolution of specialized accountants, land agents, insurance company offices – even in certain ways, the larger joint-stock banks with national networks of branches – and, we might add, for the twentieth century, building societies, progressively confined the roles of the local solicitors. But anyone with experience of the profession in the late twentieth century will immediately recognize the lawyer standing behind the men of affairs in all these other professional services, even if not himself a principal in business. The links between the local solicitor and the local

[11] Holderness, 'Credit in a Rural Community', p. 108.
[12] *Ibid.*, p. 111.
[13] Holmes, *Augustan England*, pp. 164–5; Holderness, 'Credit in a Rural Community', pp. 109–10; Miles, 'Money Market', pp. 175–7.

representatives (if not the local principals) of these other specialized functions, remain of necessity very close.

Of the universality of attorneys and solicitors in towns, however small, across the length and breadth of Britain in the eighteenth century there is ample evidence, even if the exact numbers remain a matter of dispute. Gregory King, no mean judge of such numbers, thought the families of 'persons in the law' numbered 10,000 in 1688, and Joseph Massie assumed 12,000 in 1760.[14] Several other counts suggest that these assumptions may exaggerate the numbers of solicitors and attorneys.[15] Returns made to Parliament in 1729 counted 4,829 attorneys in all (with some double counting).[16] In March 1731, 6,000 names of attorneys and solicitors were returned to Parliament from the total of those sworn in various London and provincial courts (of whom 4,252 were attorneys).[17] There were said to be 'over 6,000' practising attorneys in England and Wales in 1759. A tax return of 1792 suggests between 4,000 and 5,000, and another estimate for 1800 gives 3,500 solicitors and attorneys in the provinces, with a further 1,800 in London.[18] Patrick Colquhoun assumed a total of 11,000 persons engaged in the law at all levels.[19].

The preliminary returns printed by act of Parliament in 1729 – a very incomplete list, being less than 20 per cent of the numbers counted under the same statute during the following year – do give the exact addresses of the attorneys and solicitors registering with the judges on this occasion. Using this as a sample, even if a skewed one, we can see how widely they were scattered, and in such tiny towns. London (with Middlesex) had just less than a quarter (198) of the total on this list, with the leading counties (in descending order of numbers registering) Devon (74), Yorkshire (59), Lancashire (42), Cornwall (33), Shropshire (29), Norfolk

---

[14] P. Mathias, 'The Social Structure of the Eighteenth Century; A Calculation by Joseph Massie', *Economic History Review*, 2nd Series, 10 (1957), 42; reprinted in *idem, The Transformation of England* (London, 1979), p. 186.

[15] G. S. Holmes, 'Gregory King and the Social Structure of Pre-Industrial England', *Transactions of the Royal Historical Society*, 5th Series, 27 (1977), 56; P. H. Lindert and G. J. Williamson, 'Revising England's Social Tables, 1688–1812', *Explorations in Economic History*, 19 (1982), 390.

[16] *Lists of Attornies and Solicitors Admitted in Pursuance of the Late Act ...* (London, 1729).

[17] *Additional Lists of Attornies and Solicitors ... Presented to the House of Commons ... 22 February 1730* (London, 1731).

[18] W. A. Robson, *The Attorney in Eighteenth-Century England* (Cambridge, 1959), pp. 166–7; Christian, *Solicitors*, pp. 111, 116–17, 140–1.

[19] P. Colquhoun, *A Treatise on Indigence* (London, 1806); *idem, A Treatise on the Wealth, Power and Resources of the British Empire* (London, 1815); Lindert and Williamson, 'Revising England's Social Tables', p. 400.

(29), Herefordshire (27), Worcestershire (26), Lincolnshire (23), Gloucestershire (22), Suffolk (22), Berkshire (21). Of the 42 registering in Lancashire such places as Warrington (2), Prescot (3) and Manchester (3), then a rather unimportant market town, boasted their attorneys. So it was in the smallest market towns across the face of Britain. More systematic counts, for example, reveal 10 attorneys in Brecon, 8 in Helston and 32 in Norwich in 1730.[20] This mattered a great deal in view of the very local organization and provincial location of business, the local basis of financing most forms of enterprise and the very strong premium placed upon personal knowledge of a man's or a family's status (what we should now call their 'credit rating'). There was virtually always an attorney on the spot, and it is no wonder that the adjective 'local' has customarily been appended to the title.

Attorneys and solicitors followed the regional and local specializations of their clients, as the 'serving' professions must always do. Their principal role in aiding economic activity was hidden, or at one stage removed, by virtue of these professional services rendered to other principals. Depending on the range of economic activities pursued in their localities the attorneys developed appropriate expertise. Only in the larger towns, particularly the ports, was the concentration of business and the number of attorneys large enough to encourage specialization, above all, of course, in London. In 1790 about 1,755 attorneys were registered in London, against 68 in Liverpool, 61 in Bristol, 40 in Manchester, 32 in Norwich, 29 each in Chester and Newcastle, 26 in Leeds. The surviving papers of attorneys reflect the gamut of economic activities their clients pursued. I shall take this contribution of the lawyers to the economy, through the advice rendered to their clients, whether or not it involved court work, for granted, and also not consider particular London specializations which brought attractive business to certain firms – such as patent registration and litigation, bankruptcy and court practice, particularly in Chancery and King's Bench. The local attorneys were, in certain respects, analogous to the family doctor, referring to more specialized professionals where the need arose.

What distinguished the attorneys and solicitors in their roles in eighteenth-century Britain, and set them apart from the professional lawyers in continental countries, was precisely the extent of their non-court activities and responsibilities. Professor Holmes explains the increase of provincial attorneys after 1680 largely in terms of 'the extraordinary range of functions performed ... and how little many of

---

[20] Holmes, *Augustan England*, pp. 155, 161.

them needed to come into direct contact with the King's courts' because of the 'massive inflation of non-litigious business'.[21] This essay concentrates also upon their own activities in economic roles, and upon the wider implications of the functions they developed. A hostile critic in 1785 begrudged Blackstone 'ingeniously connecting their Encrease and their Improvement with that of the Civilisation, of Arts, of Science and of Trade, out of which they regularly grew'.[22] Corporate forms, particularly the company and trust, through which many new economic roles were developed in eighteenth-century England, reinforced the central position of the attorney, because they demanded a combination of legal expertise with basic financial and business skills supported by a local position of probity. Hence attorneys flooded into positions as clerks and treasurers to enclosure commissions, bridge and turnpike trusts, canal companies, river navigation companies, drainage commissions in the Fens, commissioners of sewers, local improvement commissions, workhouses, boards of guardians of the poor, hospitals, schools, 'cost book' companies in mining areas and corporate bodies such as the Merchant Venturers of Bristol, although prestigious offices such as the latter often attracted barristers. Clauses in enclosure and canal acts often required that monies should be deposited with a 'banker or other suitable person' which usually meant, in practice, the attorney. Indeed, as a later section describes, the intricate merging of legal and financial functions created strong inducements for the attorney himself to become associated with banking.

A leading characteristic of the attorney in these business functions is that they were usually accommodated to his continuing formal role as an attorney – which serviced and legitimized these other activities. Thus, attorneys became clerks and treasurers to these various corporate bodies and trusts, clerks to justices, town clerks, partners in banks, stewards to estates, without ceasing to be attorneys. Pluralism flourished. Their contribution to economic change in England has principally to be assessed within their formal roles as attorneys. It is impossible to judge to what extent an informal training in an attorney's office (the principal form of apprenticeship to the profession) became a launching pad to a business career without the imprimatur of practising as an attorney. There are individual instances of this, but I do not envisage that an attorney's training alone provided an important contribution to the management and financial skills supporting economic growth in

---

[21] *Ibid.*, pp. 156–7.
[22] H. C. Jennings, *A Free Enquiry into the Enormous Increase of Attornies ...* (Chelmsford, 1785). p. 9.

eighteenth-century England. At the other end of the spectrum, the instance of the practising attorney who abandoned his professional legal role in the interests of a full-time commitment to a business career is also unrepresentative.

The most spectacular instance of the latter case is undoubtedly that of Thomas Williams, a successful, but originally humble, attorney of Anglesey, who entered the profession after a typical training with a local Welsh attorney firm of Caerwys in Flint.[23] He prospered with a clientele of leading Anglesey families and in the course of this business acted for a local family with modest estates who found themselves in a typical legal conflict with another, more powerful, landowner – the family of Lord Uxbridge – over the exploitation of mineral rights (recently discovered copper lodes) in a piece of land held jointly. The determining factor in the ensuing sequence was clearly Thomas Williams's unrestrained ambition to take over the mines. He found himself acting for an old lady with only a life interest in the estate. She leased her share to Thomas Williams, giving him power of attorney to act in trust for the heir, an innocuous country parson. This got Williams immediate possession. He then obtained an injunction which blocked the other family (essentially, Lord Uxbridge) from exploiting the mine, and while this legal action was pending over the summer recess of the courts he moved a large gang of miners of his own into action – a 'capital stroke' as a fellow-attorney noted. The Uxbridge family, acknowledging defeat at the hands of a master, thereupon leased their section of the property to Williams who, now also in partnership with the parson, set up the Parys Mines Company for joint exploitation, with himself as managing partner. Within twenty years he controlled the entire copper industry of Anglesey and Cornwall, with mines, smelting companies, rolling mills and other works in Swansea, Cornwall, Lancashire and Anglesey, as well as warehouses and offices in Birmingham, Liverpool and London and even a bank. His assets totalled more than £1 m. The Revd Edwards Hughes, the passive partner throughout this saga, pulled himself up to riches on Thomas Williams's coat-tails and died worth £350,000.

Needless to say, this was quite atypical, both in the scale of achievement and in the fact that Thomas Williams abandoned his practice as attorney in the process of becoming the 'copper king'. Much more representative was the local attorney who acquired a whole range of part-time business commitments supplementing his position as attorney. The potential extent of such supplementary activities acquired

[23] J. R. Harris, *The Copper King* (Liverpool, 1964).

by a central figure in a provincial town is astonishing and demonstrates the centrality of the lawyer's position in the economic life of the community. A few instances must suffice in illustration. Job Brough, attorney of Nottinghamshire, became clerk and treasurer to the local turnpike trust, clerk to the River Trent Navigation Company, Town Clerk of Newark, Clerk of the Peace to Nottinghamshire, clerk to the Commissioners of Sewers, steward to the Duke of Newcastle and to the copyhold courts of the manor of Newark.[24] All this lay apart from his economic influence in advising private individual clients. Philip Case of King's Lynn had been apprenticed to the town clerk at the age of 16 in 1733. He became Deputy Clerk, and then Clerk of the Peace for Norfolk in 1760, Comptroller of Customs at Lynn, Wisbech and Wells in 1754, and steward of 'many' manors. He was elected Mayor of Lynn in 1745, 1764 and 1786. Throughout he numbered the leading aristocratic families of Norfolk (led by the Walpoles and Townshends) amongst his clients. Clearly here was a major political figure, as well as business leader, for the locality, who died with extensive properties and a fortune in the Funds.[25]

Isaac Greene, described by Professor Holmes as 'the Liverpool comet', became Town Clerk of Liverpool, handling the Weaver Navigation Bill for the Corporation, was steward of half a dozen manorial courts and was said to have 'half the merchants of Liverpool and half the gentry families of South Lancashire' among his clients before he was forty.[26] Alexander Leigh, Town Clerk of Wigan, collected the stewardship of seventeen manorial courts. A legion of similar instances could be quoted. It will be more illuminating, however, to consider the functions of eighteenth-century attorneys in relation to two key roles: in agricultural improvement and in the development of banking.

Enclosure procedures deserve a preliminary word because they illustrate the interrelated functions which attorneys fulfilled in economic processes requiring private acts of Parliament as a precondition of their existence in such matters as transport, drainage and urban improvements. All these functions concerned changes in the ownership and control of property, enmeshed in complex legal formulae, to be negotiated individually with all those having a legal interest. All required residual legal authority to enforce compulsory purchase of land or other

---

[24] Pressnell, *Country Banking*, pp. 39–40.
[25] Robson, *The Attorney in Eighteenth-Century England*, pp. 73–4.
[26] R. Stewart-Brown, *Isaac Greene: A Lancashire Lawyer of the Eighteenth Century* (Liverpool, 1921); Holmes, *Augustan England*, pp. 157–62.

assets or if a protesting minority of proprietors sought to block such schemes or to hold their promoters to ransom. At the same time, 'start-up' finance was integral for preliminary procedures for meetings, hiring rooms, printing, conducting searches of title, making surveys of the area or the route (and gaining access to private properties for this where necessary), drawing plans, assembling pledges for financial contributions, levying a rate, issuing shares, mortgaging land owned by trustees in the case of turnpikes, pledging future tolls as securities for loans and finding legal expenses for the parliamentary bill (where legal documentation, submission procedures and fees were both complex and very specific). The bill might need to be solicited in parliamentary committee by the attorney. This is a long and complicated list of functions, some of them intricately dependent upon others, and all offering scope for blocking tactics if due legal procedures and etiquette had not been followed. Trustees, canal company proprietors and enclosure commissioners turned to their clerks and treasurers to arrange loans and to organize such initial expenses. Considerable sums then passed through the hands of the attorney as clerk or treasurer (or both) when the parliamentary act had authorized the undertaking. Apart from construction expenses, financial commitments were obviously on a continuing basis for turnpike trusts, canal companies, drainage and improvement commissions levying a rate etc., and facing regular wage, repair and maintenance expenses. Before considering the banking functions associated with attorneys, which such commitments encouraged, we should return to the land.

The most generalized contribution which the lawyers made to the British economy in the eighteenth and nineteenth centuries, apart from the dealings they had with individual clients, probably lay in their role as stewards, agents and auditors of landed estates. Only a few points may be made here about a very large subject. There were, of course, other routes to these functions, notably from being a tenant farmer or manager of a 'home farm', kept in hand on the estate. On the Leveson-Gower estates during the eighteenth century all the chief stewards were lawyers educated at the Inns of Court – save for two. One was a remarkable Yorkshire clergyman, George Plaxton (whose son, trained in the law, succeeded him), and the second was a substantial tenant farmer and small landowner.[27] The exact nature of the job, and the range of functions

---

[27] J. R. Wordie, *Estate Management in Eighteenth-Century England*, Royal Historical Society, Studies in History, 30 (London, 1982), pp. 25–6, 36, 41, 46, 54–6, 63. Dr Parker does not reveal the provenance of the stewards on the Coke (Leicester) estates in his study *Coke of Norfolk* (Oxford, 1975). See also R. Hainsworth (ed.), *The Correspondence of Sir John Lowther*, Records of Social and Economic History, British Academy, (London, 1983).

embraced, depended above all on the size of the estate with the consequent elaboration in the hierarchy and specialization of those employed to manage it. The main officials of large estates would usually be full-time employees, handsomely paid and commonly provided with better houses than the tenant farmers (which could be saying a lot). Christopher Haedy, for example, a solicitor, chief agent for the Bedfords' Bloomsbury estate and auditor of all the Bedford property, received £1,800 p.a. and a London house in the 1840s.[28] Larger, aristocratic estates tended towards barristers as their chief agents and auditors: these were often university-educated men whose social status and professional horizons were felt to be more in keeping with the family whose fortunes their attentions sustained than were those of an attorney or farmer. Doubtless this was encouraged where the estates were principally administered from a London base – because it seems that in the course of the eighteenth century the work of barristers (the circuits of Assize apart) became increasingly centred on London. James Loch, the famous (to some infamous) agent on the Sutherland and Ellesmere estates, is a prime example: educated in the law at Edinburgh University, he was a remarkably efficient administrator who transformed the standards of the profession.[29]

Stewards and bailiffs could be critical agents of improvements in local agriculture, whilst in the mining areas they became virtually departmental managers of large enterprises or supervisors of many concessions. For a landowner much depended on the effectiveness of his steward – above all in recommending able, honest tenants, in ensuring good husbandry to augment rents where possible and certainly to sustain the capital value of the properties, and, not least, in representing the proper interests of the tenants to the landlord. Mediation between tenant and landlord took various forms. It was most important for the landlord to know when honest, reasonably efficient tenants had reached the sticking-point – the limit of increased rents in good times – or even the point at which rents might have to be mitigated or foresworn and rebates accepted in bad times. On the whole the administration of English estates, particularly the larger estates perhaps – to make a crass generalization – proved an acceptable and profitable partnership for owner, tenant farmer and steward – save in the occasional times of falling prices, and in some

[28] David Spring, *The English Landed Estate in the Nineteenth Century* (Baltimore, 1963), p. 68; D. Duman, 'The English Bar in the Georgian Era', in Prest (ed.), *Lawyers in Early Modern Europe and America*, pp. 95–7.
[29] Wordie, *Estate Management*, pp. 63–74; F. C. Mather, *After the Canal Duke* (Oxford, 1970); E. Richards, *The Leviathan of Wealth* (London, 1973).

special local circumstances. The two best writers and advisers on agricultural improvement in eighteenth-century England, Nathaniel Kent and William Marshall, gained most of their experience as stewards.

It is impossible to know what proportion of agents and stewards of estates were attorneys in the eighteenth and early nineteenth centuries, but the pattern is clear: the full-time stewards had very commonly been recruited from the ranks of the attorneys and the solicitors, often consolidating a previous part-time commitment, while the part-time stewards were usually local attorneys – as the abuse heaped upon them by hostile critics made clear. This pattern changed with the progressive development and specialization of land agents and accountants during the nineteenth century, when the attorney/solicitor lost his prominence, but certainly not his presence, as part-time agent. The need arose, essentially, because estates, although consolidated as units of ownership, were commonly very scattered geographically. Full-time officials and a solicitor close to the main house or in London, handling the central affairs of the estate, thus had to be supplemented by local part-time stewards or agents keeping an eye on outlying properties. The essence of the day-to-day business lay in collecting rents, settling terms of tenancies, surveying property, renegotiating leases, recommending new tenants and handling debts and legal processes where necessary, often in the copyhold court. Hence the steward also became a natural election agent.

The standing grievance was that, although the attorney might be admirably suited for conveyancing and handling the money side of estate administration, and for coping with the legal niceties of a manorial court, he was usually short on technical knowledge and practical experience about farming. These accusations may be interpreted as premature claims for the burgeoning professional status of the future land agent. A handbook written in 1761 noted that 'it is requisite in a Steward that he has not only honesty and integrity to recommend him but likewise judgment and experience founded upon some skills and knowledge in the law (especially parish law), in agriculture, in trade, arithmetic, the mathematics, mechanics, etcetera'.[30] According to an earlier tract of 1727, the right combination of expertise for a steward was 'honest Arts of good Husbandry and good Accompts' which were most likely to be attained by farmers' sons rather than by attorneys. 'Noblemen and Gentlemen lie under great Evils and inconveniences', ran the accusation,

[30] J. Mordant, *The Complete Steward or the Duty of a Steward to his Lord* (London, 1761).

when they suffer themselves to be persuaded to employ Country Attorneys for their stewards because it seldom happens that they are qualified for that Trust .... A Steward's business is not such as may be done as it were *by the by*: 'tis his *whole* employment and a full one too. The Attorney, if he has any character, has business enough of his own, of the Law, and therefore should not undertake the office of Steward which, in most Parts of it, he does not understand; neither will his employment let him. But I would always have the Steward consult the Attorney in matters relating to the Law and to attend him at his Court-Keeping. I have known Instances where a country Attorney has been Steward to seven or eight Noblemen and others and yet has done nothing else but attend the Court-Keeping and collecting of rents, by which means the Tenants have taken the advantage of doing what they would with their Farms, quickly lessening the value of the Estate by *Overploughing* etc.[31]

There was doubtless truth in such complaints–the chorus is long and loud–but scattered properties could not sustain the overhead costs of permanent resident stewards, and the local attorney was the least unfavourable solution before land-agency firms became institutionalized to perform such functions in provincial towns as independent businesses in later years, and even then the local firm of solicitors would be invoked for conveyancing and other legal functions. Before then, one of the essential functions of the local attorney acting as part-time steward for local estates was the handling of money, which brings the discussion back to the last economic function of the attorneys to be considered in this essay: capital accumulation and banking.

As earlier topics have made clear, so much business and finance was enmeshed with legal expertise that, where the attorney found himself acting as a clerk or treasurer or steward, he would be handling financial matters as much as legal – and probably more so in his day-to-day affairs. Quite a lot of money would lie with him on occasion – as rent gatherer, tax receiver, recipient of annual rates (for drainage and improvement commissions) and tolls. Where these undertakings needed to borrow, they would look to their clerk or treasurer to make these arrangements so that, on occasion, major sums might flow the other way from the attorney to the undertaking. Much of this financial business involved transfers between different regions, or between the provinces and London. In addition, when acting for private clients, the attorney would be called on for financial advice and would often have the responsibility for disposing (or recommending the disposal) of monies concerned with probate or for the handling of estates (with powers of attorney) for

---

[31] E. Lawrence, *The Duty of a Steward to his Lord* (London, 1727), pp. 5–6, 16–17. See also N. Kent, *Hints to Gentlemen of Landed Property* (London, 1775).

absentee landlords, minors, widows and orphans. Where loans and debts were secured on property (as they were wherever possible), he was instrumental in drawing up the deeds for the purpose, quite apart from the large flow of conveyancing business arising from the normal operation of the property market, in probate or otherwise. From here the paths to further financial commitment led forward in several directions.

As Dr Anderson first determined for Lancashire and Dr Miles for the West Riding of Yorkshire – a story doubtless replicated over much of England and Wales – the attorney became the centre point of a flourishing informal, local, capital market.[32] His clients, and himself, had need of secure, profitable outlets for the monies deposited with him – either on a transient basis or more permanently. Even when this money was passing through his hands, on its way elsewhere, the balances at any one time could be considerable. He was well placed to know the local status of those seeking accommodation – the probity of their titles to property or inheritance – in local communities where personal knowledge and the personal bond of trust in a face-to-face society were the cement of business relationships. 'Money-scrivening' attorneys accepted monies on deposit, which they would then place securely, for a fee, using their expertise. This, Professor Pressnell stresses, was a principal route by which the attorney became an embryo banker, particularly before the beginnings of country banking in provincial towns during the second half of the century and with rapid growth only after 1780. As banking specialized out as a financial function in its own right, other options opened, although the attorney continued the informal role of acting as intermediary for lending even when it was no longer customary for attorneys to bid for deposits.

Not unnaturally, attorneys were known as principal customers of banks. Not a few were led to become bankers themselves, but typically by becoming a partner in a local bank without relinquishing their position as attorneys. Over 12 per cent of country banks listed in the *Universal British Directory* of the 1790s show identifiable attorneys as partners – and it is unlikely that the identification is complete.[33] The more business an attorney brought to a local bank, the greater the incentive for him to consolidate the connection with a partnership. He could share in the prosperity which his custom enhanced and keep a close eye on the security of the operation. By becoming a partner (and only by so doing) he had access to the books of the bank. Financial dealings by the banker,

---

[32] Anderson, 'The Attorney and the Local Capital Market'; Miles, 'Money Market'.
[33] *Universal British Directory*: 36 attorneys were partners in banks out of a total of 291 banks. See also Pressnell, *Country Banking*, p. 44.

particularly those concerning land, also produced legal business useful to the attorney: banking and conveyancing were closely associated. But perhaps the banker needed the attorney more than the attorney needed the banker. As partner the attorney was in the best position of anyone in the community to know the status of the clients having dealings with the bank. Banks found it attractive to have an attorney amongst their partners – and would often make a feature of this information when announcing the establishment of the bank.[34] Professor Pressnell has argued that this connection seems particularly fertile in country towns which were foci of transport undertakings, where the continuous legal and financial business provided by such undertakings based on land made the long-term connection very profitable. He cites the three treasurers of the Oxford Canal, at Oxford, Banbury and Coventry – all attorneys, one of whom went into banking in Banbury in 1784.

Capital accumulation was a critical process for enabling economic change to gather pace in eighteenth-century England, as was agricultural progress and transport improvement. The attorneys took a prominent part in these processes, by virtue of being already on the spot, established in virtually every nodal urban point in the land, however small, long before other professions had specialized out from amongst the wide range of financial and business expertise they had offered in association with their legal skills. The local scale and local horizons within which such activities were organized during the eighteenth century strengthened their positions. Increasingly as the nineteenth century advanced, with growing scale, greater specialization of functions within this bundle of technical and financial services with the emergence of other professions, the growth of national banking organizations, better links with London and more national co-ordination, their roles declined but have never disappeared. The attorneys were never so prominent, in general terms, in such roles in London in the eighteenth century for similar reasons, although specialized firms of solicitors in the City concentrated more and more upon company work during the nineteenth century. They form another legal interest group of equal fascination to the economic historian, taking initiatives in the promotion and financing of new enterprise occasionally reminiscent of German investment bankers. But this is another story, far removed in time and context, if not in motivation, from the eighteenth-century attorneys in small-town English provincial society and business.

[34] Pressnell, *Country Banking*, pp. 42–3.

PART III

Enterprise, finance and politics in the modern world

10

The Bank of Rome and commercial credit, 1880–1914

L. DE ROSA

I

From the time of its creation in 1880, the Bank of Rome has never operated solely in Italy itself. Its formal presence abroad began twenty-two years after its foundation when in 1902 an agency was opened in Paris. Despite this relatively late start, the next twelve years were to witness a considerable expansion in the number of the Bank's foreign agencies and branches. Following the branch in Paris came further agencies in Malta;[1] then at Cairo[2] and Alexandria[3] in Egypt; at Tripoli,[4] Benghazi[5] and Derna[6] in Libya; at Barcelona, Tarragona and Montblanch[7] in Spain; and at Constantinople[8] in the Ottoman Empire. There were also plans in 1910 to open a branch at Jerusalem,[9] but these were not realized until after the First World War and the division of the Turkish Empire.

Not all of these branches were engaged in investment operations, and the Bank's particular ties with the Roman Catholic Church meant that one of their principal functions was to safeguard the deposits and savings of local Catholic corporations (monasteries, churches, confraternities, etc.) and the Catholic communities that gravitated around them. The Malta agency was typical of this type.[10] But more often the links with the

---

[1] *Archivio del Banco di Roma* (hereafter *ABR*), Consiglio di Amministrazione (hereafter CA), Verbali, 7 May 1906.
[2] *Ibid.*, Feb. 1905.
[3] *Ibid.*, 17 Nov. and 11 Dec. 1908.
[4] *Ibid.*, 18 Feb. 1907.
[5] *Ibid.*, 24 May 1907.
[6] Cf. L. de Rosa, *Storia del Banco di Roma*, I (1880–1914) (Rome, 1982), 265.
[7] *ABR*, CA, Verbali, 3 Nov. 1909, 15 April and 5 Sept. 1910.
[8] *Ibid.*, 13 May 1911.
[9] *Ibid.*, 21 Jan. 1911.
[10] Cf. de Rosa, *Storia del Banco di Roma*, I, 196ff.

Church provided opportunities for investment as well as attracting savings, and the Bank's agencies provided long- and short-term loans. In Paris, for example, the agency began to attract an increasingly large share of the savings of French Catholics, taking over at least in part the function of Bontoux's Union Générale that had crashed in 1882.[11] But it also played a more dynamic role, making investments on its own account and also profiting from the international importance of the Paris foreign exchange and finance markets by handling currency transfers between Italy and various other foreign countries, including the United States, that normally routed their business through the French capital.[12]

The Catalan agencies also acted as both deposit and investment banks, at a time when the region was drawing heavily on English, American, German and French capital in order to expand its mining and textile industries.[13] The Catalan agencies also took an active interest in the trade in various agricultural products, especially olive oil.[14]

In North Africa and in the Ottoman Empire the Bank of Rome's agencies functioned on a rather different basis, although there are distinctions to be drawn between those in Libya and the others in Egypt and in the Ottoman Empire. In the case of Egypt, the main function of the Bank's agencies was investment:[15] Italy was at that time a major importer of Egyptian cotton for its own textile industry which was in full technological and organizational expansion, while an active local Italian community was also heavily involved in various Egyptian public works projects.[16] Apart from a small local savings bank run and managed by Italians, the Bank of Rome was to remain until the 1920s the only Italian bank operating in Egypt. Through its agencies in Cairo and Alexandria it was to take a leading part in the operations relating to the buying and selling of cotton, both running on its account large warehousing facilities and making large advances to producers and merchants prior to the harvest. But it also penetrated more directly to the heart of local economic life by investing in river transportation and in prospecting for phosphates along the shores of the Red Sea.[17] The Constantinople agency was also from the start meant to be an investment

---

[11] J. Bouvier, *Le Krack de l'Union Générale (1878–1885)* (Paris, 1960), pp. 172ff.
[12] *ABR*, CA, Verbali, 11 Jan. 1902.
[13] *Ibid.*, Presidenza, box 9 bis.
[14] *Ibid.*, Verbali, 26 Jan. 1910; cf. also de Rosa, *Storia del Banco di Roma*, I, 211–13.
[15] De Rosa, *Storia del Banco di Roma*, I, 173–4.
[16] Cf. *Ministero degli Affari Esteri*, Servizio Storico e Documentazione, Collana di testi diplomatici, no. 6 (Rome, 1977), pp. 69, 72, 73.
[17] Cf. de Rosa, *Storia del Banco di Roma*, II.

bank.[18] Again, German, French and English capital was at that time flooding into the Ottoman Empire, attracted by the high interest rates on offer, by the road and railway building programmes then in progress and by the ease with which mineral resources could be extracted.

On the other hand, the character of the Libyan agencies was from the beginning quite different. The Bank of Rome arrived in Libya in 1907 at the invitation of the Italian government in order to set in motion the process of peaceful penetration which would legitimate – should political opposition arise from the Ottoman Empire – an Italian occupation of the country on the basis of the agreements established with both France and Great Britain in 1902. As a result it was an area in which the Bank of Rome made major investments directly in the local economy, including for example the construction of a rolling-mill at Tripoli and plant for processing olive oil at Benghazi and Homs. The Bank was also responsible for the direct management of shipping lines along the Libyan coast (and, after 1910, along the Egyptian coast), as well as for investment in the fishing industry and the sponge trade, in land destined for new cultivation and in the building of new quays and warehousing facilities in Tripoli. Finally, the Bank also ran a network of commercial agencies not only along the Libyan coast but also in the oases and markets of the interior.[19]

While these foreign agencies were engaged in a wide range of major activities, they did not constitute the only medium through which the Bank of Rome was expanding its foreign operations. Within only a few months of its creation in 1880 the Bank had made an investment in the bitumen mines of Valona in Albania,[20] and a few years later it was to provide financial assistance for Filonardi's Compagnia Commerciale, thereby financing the first Italian settlement in Somalia.[21] Thereafter the Bank continued to make direct investments both within and outside Italy, including areas where it was not represented by its own agencies. A typical case of this type of investment was the Bank's interest in Bulgarian mining.[22]

---

[18] *Ibid.*, I, 220–2.
[19] On Italy's so-called 'peaceful penetration' of Libya see *ibid.*, pp. 239–304.
[20] *Ibid.*, pp. 42–7.
[21] On the Italian settlement in Somalia see C. Giglio, 'Primi contatti dell'Italia con Zanzibar e il Benadir', in *Ricerche storiche ed economiche in memoria di Corrado Barbagallo*, ed. L. de Rosa (Naples, 1970), III; see also G. Finazzo, *L'Italia nel Benadir: l'azione di Vincenzo Filonardi (1884–1894)* (Rome, 1966). On the relations between Filonardi and the Bank of Rome see de Rosa, *Storia del Banco di Roma*, I, 88ff.
[22] ABR, CA, Verbali, 2 March and 29 April 1911.

II

As well as extending its foreign operations, the Bank of Rome also considerably increased the network of Italian agencies between 1880 and 1914. The Bank had started as an essentially Roman enterprise, in response to the rapid expansion both of the city itself and of its population once it had been raised to the status of capital of the new Kingdom of Italy,[23] but by the end of the century its operations stretched well beyond the city walls.[24] In addition to Rome itself, the Bank had agencies operating in the province of Lazio (at Viterbo, Corneto Tarquinia, Tivoli, Frascati, Albano, Laziale and Frosinone) as well as in Tuscany at Siena. By 1904 the Bank had moved into two other regions: Piedmont (agencies at Turin, Pinerolo and Alba) and Liguria (agencies at Genoa and Sampierdarena). At the same time the number of agencies in Lazio had been increased, with new branches at Bracciano and Palestrina. By 1911 its presence in all these regions had been further strengthened by the addition of more agencies in Piedmont (at Canale, Canelli, Carrù, Centallo, Fossano and Mondovì), in Tuscany (at Arezzo, Florence, Lucca, Bagni a Montecatini, Orbetello and Viareggio), and in Lazio (Bracciano, Fara Sabina, Subiaco and Velletri), and it had also begun to penetrate other regions as well. The opening of a branch at Orvieto brought the Bank into Umbria; a new agency in the rich agricultural region of Avezzano took it into Abruzzo; and finally it stretched down into Campania with the establishment of a branch in Naples and in the nearby industrial centre of Torre Annunziata, some twenty kilometres outside Naples. This expansion was to continue in the years leading up to the outbreak of the First World War, with the opening of yet more agencies in Tuscany (at Castelnuovo di Garfagnana near Lucca) and in the hitherto untouched Adriatic province of the Marche, at Fabriano, Fermo and Porto San Giorgio. By the outbreak of the war, the Bank had at least one or more branches operating in some eight different regions of Italy – Campania, Lazio, Abruzzo, Umbria, Marche, Tuscany, Liguria and Piedmont.

In creating this network of agencies the Bank followed a very clear policy, which meant taking over whenever possible some local credit agency, either of reasonably small scale or else facing difficulties, rather

---

[23] In 1871 when Rome was annexed to the new Italian state it contained 244,484 inhabitants; the census return of 1901 registered 424,943, showing that the population had nearly doubled within thirty years. See Istituto Centrale di Statistica, *Comuni e loro popolazione ai censimenti dal 1861 al 1951* (Rome, 1960), p. 204.

[24] *ABR*, CA, Verbali, 30 August 1899.

[25] *Ibid.*, 29 Sept. 1901, 11 Jan 1902 and 1 Dec. 1903.

than creating a completely new institution. The same strategy was also followed when establishing foreign branches. In Paris, for example, the agency developed from the take-over of a small bank – the Caisse d'Entrepôt[25] – while the Catalan branches at Barcelona, Tarragona and Montblanch similarly grew out of the take-over of another small local credit bank – the Catalana General de Credito – which had traditionally provided finance for local commercial activities.[26]

In Italy itself, the first agencies in Lazio and Tuscany resulted from a similar strategy, and the Bank first moved outside the confines of Rome in 1899, when it took over the Banca Artistico-Operaia and its branches at Albano, Laziale, Corneto Tarquinia, Frascati, Frosinone, Tivoli and Viterbo in Lazio, as well as the Tuscan branch at Siena.[27] The Piedmontese agency at Fossano, opened in 1907, resulted from the acquisition of another small local bank, the Banca Popolare e di Risparmio;[28] and the Lucca branch arose from the purchase of the small local Banca Giorgio Gori.[29] The branches at Naples and Torre Annunziata had formerly belonged to a very old Neapolitan credit bank, the Società di Assicurazioni Diverse;[30] the Florence branch came with the take-over of the former Florentine Banca di Depositi e Credito and the Cassa di Sconto;[31] the agency at Fabriano was the fruit of a merger with the Banca Cattolica Cooperativa.[32]

This technique of absorbing local banks offered many advantages and made it easier for the Bank of Rome to penetrate local economic life in terms both of attracting savings and of finding investment outlets. It had the added advantage of not requiring any capital outlays, since the Bank of Rome purchased these local credit agencies with issues of its own shares – in other words, by increasing its own registered capital through the issue of new shares. The Bank followed the same strategy when taking over other credit institutions in areas where its own operations were already established. A typical example was the take-over in 1911 of the important Genoese Banco della Liguria, which had major holdings in the sugar refining industry: the Bank of Rome effected the purchase by issuing share capital of 10 million lire.[33]

---

[26] *Ibid.*, 3 Nov. 1909 and 15 April 1910. It should be added that the Cairo branch resulted from a take-over of the local agency of the Banque de Salonique–Cf. *ibid.*, 17 Nov. and 11 Dec. 1908.
[27] Cf. de Rosa, *Storia del Banco di Roma*, I, 139 ff.
[28] *ABR*, CA, Verbali, 22 April 1907.
[29] *Ibid.*, 6 Oct. 1908 and 12 August 1909.
[30] *Ibid.*, 9 and 14 June 1909.
[31] *Ibid.*, 21 July and 21 Dec. 1910.
[32] *Ibid.*, 15 March and 29 April 1913.
[33] *Ibid.*, 25 Sept and 7 Nov. 1911, 25 Jan 1912.

III

As a result of these share issues, the capital of the Bank of Rome, which had amounted to 6 million lire (only 3 million of which were paid-up) at the time of its foundation in 1880, had risen by 1914 to 200 million lire. But this expansion had not been continuous, and until 1891 there had been little change in either the Bank's nominal or paid-up capital. In 1892, however, the situation began to change, and although in that year nominal capital remained unchanged at 6 million lire, the paid-up capital rose to 4,200,000 lire. In 1893 there were further changes, and nominal capital fell to 5,928,500 lire, while paid-up capital rose again to 5,180,450 lire. The following year, 1894, was particularly bleak due to the impact of the economic crisis which had affected Italy since 1888 and which had been further aggravated by the world recession of 1892. Both nominal and paid-up capital fell back to 2,500,000 lire. It was on this base that the Bank was to operate until 1897, when the consolidation of Italy's economic revovery and the beginning of the country's industrial 'take-off' saw both nominal and paid-up capital start to grow again.[34] By 1898 both had risen to 3 million lire; in 1899 they stood at 6 million; in 1902 at 10 million; in 1905 at 30 million; in 1906 at 40 million; in 1908 at 50 million; in 1909 at 80 million; in 1910 at 100 million; in 1911 at 150 million; and in 1912 at 200 million. In the space of only fifteen years therefore, the nominal and paid-up capital of the Bank had risen from 2,500,000 (in 1897) to 200 million lire (in 1912) – an almost hundredfold increase. No other Italian credit institution experienced a comparable expansion. Among the other leading Italian banks of the period, if we leave aside the three banks of issue (Bank of Italy, Bank of Naples and Bank of Sicily)[35] none of the three major credit banks (the Banca Commerciale Italiana, the Credito Italiano and the Società Bancaria Italiana) could compete with the Bank of Rome in terms of capital assets. Even though the first two had been founded after the crisis of 1892 (the first in 1894, the second in 1895) and were the products of both German and Italian capital, while the third had been created in 1898, their capital was quickly outstripped by that of the Bank of Rome. By 1914 the comparative capital assets of the four banks were as follows: Bank of Rome, 200 million lire; Banca Commerciale Italiana, 156 million lire;

---

[34] Cf. de Rosa, *La Rivoluzione Industriale in Italia* (Bari, 1980), pp. 32 ff.
[35] A single bank of issue was created in Italy in 1926 by changing the status of the Bank of Italy.

Credito Italiano, 75 million lire; Società Bancaria Italiana, 50 million lire.[36]

Even though part of this capital had been raised through the issue of shares to purchase local banks in Italy and elsewhere, no less important was the capital raised by placing packages of Bank stock with the Administrative Commission for the Properties of the Holy See and with other religious institutions and corporations,[37] both in Italy and abroad.[38] Large amounts of the share capital of the Bank of Rome were in fact held in the leading Catholic countries of Europe (France, Spain, Malta, Hungary, Austria and Germany), as well as in non-European countries like Egypt. The acceptance of the Bank's stock by the Paris Stock Exchange in 1906 obviously greatly facilitated placement, and I have described elsewhere the long struggle that ensued to gain this recognition.[39] Once obtained there can be no doubt that this greatly increased the circulation of the Bank's stock, and a further success was chalked up when the stock was also accepted for quotation in Egypt on the Alexandria Stock Exchange.[40] But in comparison with the Banca Commerciale, the Bank of Rome's reserves were slightly lower, which gave the former an overall primacy. With its larger total assets the Banca

---

[36] The capital of the four leading commercial credit banks operating in Italy in this period is illustrated in the following table (millions of lire: current prices):

	1910	1911	1912	1913	1914
Banco di Roma	100	150	200	200	200
Banca Commerciale Italiana	105	130	130	130	156
Credito Italiano	75	75	75	75	75
Società Bancaria Italiana	40	50	50	50	50

Sources: R. Bachi, L'Italia economica nell'anno 1910 (Turin, 1910), p. 47; idem, L'Italia economica nell'anno 1911 (Turin, 1912), p. 46; idem, L'Italia economica nell'anno 1912 (Città di Castello, 1913), p. 56; idem, L'Italia economica nell'anno 1913 (Città di Castello, 1914), p. 60; idem, L'Italia economica nell'anno 1914 (Città di Castello, 1915), p. 72.

[37] On the relations between the Bank of Rome and the Vatican, which survived until Mussolini in 1924 succeeded in making the Bank a Fascist institution, see B. Lai, Finanze e finanzieri Vaticani fra 1'800 e il 900 : da Pio IX a Benedetto XV (Milan, 1979); idem, Finanze e finanzieri Vaticani fra 1'800 e il 900: da Pio IX a Benedetto XV, Atti e Documenti (Milan, 1979); the volume of memories and documents published by the Treasury Minister of the priod, Alberto de Stefani, Baraonda bancaria (Rome, 1960); and de Rosa, Storia del Banco di Roma.

[38] ABR, CA, Verbali, 29 Sept. 1901; E. Faye to Ministère des Affaires Etrangères Paris, 6 Dec. 1905, in Archives du Ministère des Affaires Etrangères, n.s, Italie, vol. 27.

[39] Cf. de Rosa, Storia del Banco di Roma, I, 186–92, 224–5.

[40] ABR, CA, Verbali, 8 March 1906.

Commerciale ranked as Italy's leading credit bank, followed closely by the Bank of Rome.[41]

Starting from the Administrative Commission for the Properties of the Holy See, nearly every ecclesiastical institution in Italy and other European countries deposited its funds with the Bank of Rome. It is difficult to say whether the particular nature of the ownership of the Bank and the particular clientele that it attracted meant that the deposits of its two main rivals (the Banca Commerciale and the Credito Italiano) were in fact greater. Both in absolute terms and in relation to its total capital asssets, including its large reserves, the deposits of the Banca Commerciale were certainly larger than those of the Bank of Rome. The Credito Italiano and the Società Bancaria Italiana were some distance behind.[42] At the same time, however, the fact that the Directors of the Bank of Rome could rely on a large block of Catholic shareholdings, as well as on considerable Catholic savings deposits, gave them many advantages over their competitors. Many of these funds were not, given their nature and origins, liable to sudden or unexpected withdrawal, but tended to be deposited over long periods, thereby enabling investments to be made without any great anxiety. Among the four leading ordinary

[41] The position was as follows (reserves in millions of lire: current prices):

	1910	1911	1912	1913	1914
Banco di Roma	6.41	6.71	7.29	8.06	8.71
Banca Commerciale Italiana	36.0	49.90	48.72	47.96	59.47
Credito Italiano	9.28	9.53	10.00	10.50	11.00
Società Bancaria Italiana	0.23	0.35	0.59	1.02	1.19

Sources: Bachi volumes cited in note 36 above.

[42] Deposits on current account as savings or interest-bearing securities for the four major commercial credit banks at 31 December each year were as follows (in millions of lire: current prices):

	1910	1911	1912	1913	1914
Banco di Roma	124.29	138.99	157.87	169.70	126.50
Banca Commerciale Italiana	183.55	207.17	218.66	232.84	166.68
Credito Italiano	148.94	167.35	175.49	182.26	146.90
Società Bancaria Italiana	42.38	45.03	59.07	66.12	51.61

Sources: Bachi volumes cited in note 36 above.

credit banks, there can be no doubt that the stock in hand, in relation to total assets, with which the Bank of Rome operated was very much lower than that of the other three.[43]

IV

The Bank of Rome's relative freedom in the employment of its funds did not lead to any marked increase in short-term loans. The volume of cash-credits, discounts and continuation accounts in relation to funds available was always much lower in the case of the Bank of Rome than for the other three credit banks. Only the Società Bancaria employed a lower proportion of its capital in discount and contango operations: the Banca Commerciale's operations in these fields were two and three times as great, those of the Credito Italiano at least twice as great, as those of the Bank of Rome.[44]

There are a number of explanations for this. Unlike the Bank of Rome, the other two leading credit banks were based in Milan (Banca Commerciale) and Genoa (Credito Italiano), operated mainly in northern Italy and were closely involved in the major industrial changes that were taking place there. The expansion of the Banca Commerciale was very closely tied to the massive development of the Italian hydro-electrical industry, which had begun in the final decade of the nineteenth century. As a result, it was also closely involved in the development of the electrical engineering industry which was born out of the former. From these bases, its operations fanned out more widely across all the principal industries which were growing up within the so-called industrial triangle between Milan, Turin and Genoa.[45] Both the other two major credit

[43] This had been the case from the start and remained so (cf. de Rosa, *Storia del Banco di Roma*) but the situation became even more pronounced in the years immediately prior to the First World War. Whereas the other leading credit banks held between a third and a half of their deposits as stock in hand, that of the Bank of Rome was barely a tenth of its total deposit funds. See the statistical sources cited in note 36 above.

[44] The discount and Stock Exchange continuation account operations of the four leading commercial credit banks at 31 December were as follows (millions of lire: current prices):

	1910	1911	1912	1913	1914
Banco di Roma	127.41	157.70	172.88	200.18	118.73
Banca Commerciale Italiana	389.00	439.38	509.14	556.96	508.78
Credito Italiano	237.68	274.33	293.02	323.41	301.82
Società Bancaria Italiana	80.80	78.11	95.18	82.39	81.69

Sources: Bachi volumes cited in note 36 above.

[45] Cf. A. Confalonieri, *Banca e industria in Italia 1894–1906*, 3 vols. (Milan, 1976); *idem*, *Banca e industria in Italia della crisi del 1907 all'agosto 1914*, 2 vols. (Milan, 1982).

banks, the Credito Italiano and the Società Bancaria Italiana, were also primarily involved in industrial investment in the same region – in fact, the Società Bancaria had come into being through the merger of a number of smaller local credit institutions and at the instigation of industrial interests in northern Italy from Piedmont to the Veneto.[46] And it is of course the direct links between these three major credit banks and expanding northern industries which explain why their short-term investments in cash-credits, discounting and continuation accounts on the Stock Exchange should have absorbed a much higher percentage of their assets and deposits than was the case for the Bank of Rome. These close ties with Italian industry also explain why it was that these three banks operated mainly in Italy alone, while the Bank of Rome was driven to seek not only deposits and funds but also rewarding investment opportunities abroad. It should also be mentioned that, among the leading credit banks, only the Bank of Rome was engaged in agrarian credit operations – through its agencies in Lazio, Tuscany, Umbria, Abruzzo and even, at times, Piedmont. The Bank's interest in this field arose from the fact that many of the institutions which it had acquired were situated in agricultural regions and were essentially agrarian credit banks.

This is not to say, of course, that the Bank of Rome made no attempt to increase its involvement in industrial investment. But it faced two important handicaps. The first lay in the fact that the Bank was based in Rome, a city which then, as now, was notoriously uninterested in any industrial development in the modern sense. The second lay in the fact that the Bank had come into being on the initiative of a group of aristocratic landowners who had close ties with the Vatican, but whose mentality was far removed from the new world of industrial development – although they were particularly open to the opportunities for profit provided by the expansion of the metropolis itself. Indeed, during the first decade and more of the life of the new Bank, its activities were directed primarily towards urban service industries. It held large investments in the Roman Società dei Mulini e Magazzini Generali and in the Società Tramways–Omnibus di Roma, as well as in the Società Sicula Tramways–Omnibus in the distant Sicilian capital of Palermo. The Bank also had extensive holdings in the food and victualling industries, in the new transport systems linking the major cities with their suburbs and outlying towns, and in enterprises engaged in constructing urban storage facilities, canals and aqueducts: the former

---

[46] Cf. F. Bonelli, *La crisi del 1907* (Turin, 1971), pp. 29ff.

may be illustrated by investment in the newly formed Societa Italiana per la Costruzione delle Ferrovie Complementari, the latter by the Bank's participation in the founding of the Società Italiana per le Condotte d'Acqua. But all of these were still essentially service industries, and investment in industrial ventures proper remained rare, the only exception of any importance being the Bank's investment in the Società per l'Industria dei Saponi ed Oli which owned factories in Tuscany and Campania – but this was again an industry that catered primarily for urban consumer demand.[47]

V

For the first ten years of its existence, the management of the Bank of Rome remained firmly in the hands of the landowning noblemen who had originally been responsible for its foundation. Some attempts were made to seek investment outlets outside Italy in places like Albania and Somalia, but there do not appear to have been any serious proposals that the Bank should take an active interest either in the development of the new hydro-electrical industry, which was promising greatly to improve Italy's balance of payments by renovating and expanding the country's whole energy supply structure, or even in Italy's textile industries (notably cotton, wool, silk and linen), which were experiencing rapid mechanization. Nor was any interest shown in the expanding chemical industry or in the secondary steel and engineering industries. The Bank of Rome continued to operate in a world dominated by the assumptions of an agrarian economy, and its activities were orientated primarily towards the opportunities generated by the expansion of the city of Rome itself, and towards building speculation in particular. Yet the Bank did succeed in extricating itself from many of the dangers inherent in this form of investment and was thereby able to escape the fate that befell many other leading credit banks in the crisis between 1888 and 1894, which engulfed even one leading bank of issue, the Banca Romana.[48]

Towards the turn of the century, however, the Bank of Rome began to change its investment strategy and gradually became less heavily dependent on financing service and infrastructural industries. This was, according to Gerschenkron, the period of Italy's 'industrial take-off',[49]

---

[47] For information on these investments see de Rosa, *Storia del Banco di Roma*.

[48] Cf. N. Quilici, *Fine di Secolo: La Banca Romana* (Milan, 1935); see also L. de Rosa, 'Il Banco di Napoli e la crisi economica del 1888–1894', in *Rassegna Economica* (1963–5).

[49] A. Gershenkron, 'Notes on the Rate of Industrial Growth in Italy 1881–1913', in *idem, Economic Backwardness in Historical Perspective* (Cambridge, Mass., 1962).

and as industrial expansion became more intense the Bank of Rome could hardly continue to ignore the emergence of new forms of industry which were to be of fundamental importance in the future economic life of the country. From 1894 onwards the Bank of Rome became more alert to opportunities for investment in industry, especially those provided by the introduction of new technologies and methods of production. By the turn of the century the Bank already had important holdings in the following ventures: the Società Italo-Tedesca per la Fabbricazione dello Zucchero da Barbietola (sugar-beet); the Società Romana per la Fabbricazione del Solfato di Rame e Concimi Chimici (copper-sulphates and chemical fertilizers); the Società Telefonica Nazionale; the Società degli Oli Minerali (mineral oils); the Società Romana di Costruzioni Metalliche.[50]

Yet, alongside this new opening towards industrial investment, the Bank retained its traditional interests in urban and suburban services, even though their proportional importance diminished. Although the Bank sold off the Società Sicula Tramways–Omnibus and reduced its share in the Società dei Mulini e Magazzini Generali, at the same time it played an important role in founding the Società dell 'Albergo Minerva, which ran what was then one of Rome's leading hotels, and in financing the building of the Messina aqueduct in Sicily.[51]

The scale of the Bank's participation in Italy's industrial expansion grew in the years leading up to the First World War, although these were years of increasing difficulty due to the recession of 1907/8, the Libyan invasion of 1911, the subsequent Balkan Wars of 1912/13 and the impact of international competition, which was particularly damaging for the Italian steel industry. As the situation became more serious there were fewer opportunities open to the Bank, yet in addition to maintaining its interest in those companies in which it already held significant investments, the Bank of Rome also helped found a number of new ventures including the Società Parmigiana di Prodotti Alimentari (the Parma Food Co.), the Società Automobili Roma, the Società Anonima Scamosceria Italiana di Torino (suede leather), and the Società Anonima per l'Esercizio delle Sorgenti Minerali dell'Aspio (Aspio Joint-Stock Mineral Water Co.). It also acquired share packages of varying sizes in established companies like the Società Petrolifera Italo-Rumena (Italo-Romanian Petrol Co.) and in the Società per i Concimi Organici (Organic Fertilizer Co.). But by far the most important of these was the Bank's investment in the leading cinematographical company of the day,

[50] See de Rosa, *Storia del Banco di Roma*, i, 134ff. [51] *Ibid.*, pp. 144ff.

Cines, which not only produced films that had a world-wide distribution but also had taken over one of the first synthetic fibre industries, thereafter known as Cines-seta, which was expanding very rapidly. The bulk of the Cines share package finished up in the hands of the Bank of Rome, and by 1914 the Bank had also acquired important holdings in the Società Conservazione del Legno (timber preservation), the Società Selva and the Società di Automobili 'Itala'.[52]

Apart from the holdings in the automobile industry (the Società Roma and Itala) and in the Società Romana di Costruzioni Metalliche, which quickly went into decline, by the outbreak of the First World War the Bank of Rome was still only marginally involved in the new key sectors of Italy's industrial economy, even though it had played a more important role in the country's modernization through its involvement in the expansion of the food industry, the agriculturally based chemical, petrol and mineral oil industries, and the service industries, including the new cinematographical industry. But much of the Bank's activity continued to be directed abroad, through the foreign agencies which had been established and also in partnership with foreign enterprises. Between 1905 and 1914 it contributed, albeit on a modest scale, capital funds to the Bank of Abyssinia,[53] the Bank of Morocco,[54] the Benadir Company[55] and the Belgian Banking Company.[56] It also held shares in the company that held the contract for the construction of the Asmara–Massawa railway[57] in Eritrea, and in the Italo-French Danube–Adriatic Railway Company[58] among others.

VI

The strategy which the Bank normally followed when investing in commercial companies was to act as partner in the formation of the company, thereby assuming a sufficient quota of shares to guarantee effective control. Once the company had been established on the market, the Bank would then sell off a large part of its shares, dividing them among its own clients, while retaining overall control and in particular

---

[52] *Ibid.*, p. 236.
[53] *Banco di Roma, Assemblea generale ordinaria degli azionisti del 28 marzo 1907*, Relazione del Consiglio Generale di Amministrazione e dei Sindaci (Rome, 1907), p. 11.
[54] Cf. the observations in S. Sonnino, *Diario* (Bari, 1972), i, 472; *ABR*, CA, Verbali, 26 June 1906.
[55] *Ibid.*, 7 Feb. and 2 March 1911.
[56] *Ibid.*, 14 June 1911.
[57] *Ibid.*, 26 Feb. 1906.
[58] *Ibid.*, 22 Dec. 1911.

reserving for itself all the company's banking transactions, in terms both of savings and deposit accounts and of the provision of short-term credit. The types of obligation that resulted meant that in moments of economic difficulty the Bank frequently found itself with heavy liabilities towards those companies in which it had formed partnerships, in some cases causing its capital to be immobilized. When one considers the territorial extent both in Italy and abroad of the Bank's operations and the political risks that necessarily accompanied them, together with the heterogeneity and often the novelty of many of the sectors in which it had invested – not to mention the military operations that were to involve both Libya and Constantinople,[59] and the damage caused by the cotton and financial crises in Egypt[60] – then it becomes easier to understand why it was that the Bank of Rome's short-term investments (in cash-credits, discounting and continuation accounts) never achieved the same importance in relation to its assets and deposit holdings as did those of the other two leading Italian credit banks, the Banca Commerciale Italiana and the Credito Italiano. It was certainly true that the Libyan war and the occupation of the country, far from bringing immediate advantage to the Bank of Rome, caused it massive losses. As well as the heavy material damage sustained during the war and as a result of Arab resistance, even after the war ended the guerrilla warfare continued to be particularly bloody in Cirenaica, which was precisely the region where the Bank had invested most heavily, and virtually brought local trade to a standstill so that any further investment was paralysed.[61] The losses suffered in Libya were aggravated by the damage inflicted on the Bank's interests in Egypt by the Arab boycott in protest against the Italian occupation of Libya, and also by the reprisals taken against the agency in Constantinople.[62]

As a result the Bank of Rome found itself in a very difficult position on the eve of the First World War, and rather than embark on new programmes of expansion it was obliged to scale down and liquidate some existing operations. The group of Directors who had, with the support of the Vatican, taken over the management of the Bank from the Roman patriciate who had founded it now in turn began to disintegrate. The leading figure had been Ernesto Pacelli, uncle of the future Pope Pius XII, and it was under the guidance of this group that the Bank had expanded its activities throughout Italy and into the western and eastern Mediterranean, as well as into East Africa. But very shortly, in 1916, they were in turn – and again with the approval of the Vatican – to hand

[59] Cf. de Rosa, *Storia del Banco di Roma*, II, 39ff.   [60] *Ibid*., I, 176 and II, 29ff.
[61] *Ibid*., II, 54ff.   [62] *Ibid*., pp. 32ff.

over the management of the Bank to another group of Catholic financiers who were of a decidedly more confessional stamp than their predecessors. The outgoing management had succeeded in employing the savings of the Catholic communities and corporations in Italy and beyond both to expand the Bank itself and to contribute to Italy's economic growth.[63]

[63] *Ibid.*

11

The scientific brewer:
founders and successors during the rise of the
modern brewing industry

KRISTOF GLAMANN

I

During the second half of the nineteenth century European breweries were experiencing a transitional phase from which the modern brewing industry emerged. It is true that large-scale brewing had existed in England since the eighteenth century, but even there decisive changes occurred during the course of the 1880s, especially in market conditions, which encouraged latent tendencies to concentration among the breweries and ushered in a new phase of their development.

On the European continent traditional markets were breaking up rapidly. The doctrines of economic liberalism and free trade were attracting support from more and more countries during the 1860s and 1870s. Whereas previously brewers had been hindered by the narrowness of the local market, resulting in part from the limited keeping qualities of the product, and had thus been unable to find outlets for their energies save within limited non-brewing fields of enterprise, the brewery itself now became the arena for their ingenuity and for the free play of forces. Although the national market was indubitably the mainstay of practically all the leading breweries of the day, the idea of beer as an article of export was a motivating factor in the establishment of many new firms.

Outside Europe, the American brewing industry entered upon a period of phenomenal growth after the Civil War, the most successful breweries being transformed by the 1880s from regional enterprises to firms spanning the entire continent, producing and bringing to the market standardized products under their own control, and also creating extensive purchasing organizations to ensure a continuous flow of raw materials into their new mass-producing facilities.[1]

[1] On the development of the brewing industry in Great Britain and the US, see John Vaizey, 'The Brewing Industry', Chapter 2, in *Effects of Mergers*, ed. P. Lesley Cook and

186

II

The breakthroughs achieved during this period of research into the brewing process were fundamental. For instance, Louis Pasteur's studies published in 1876 laid the foundations of modern techniques of sterilization and preservation. The Danish scientist Dr Emil Chr. Hansen's method for pure cultivation of yeast, in 1883 applied for the first time at the Carlsberg brewery in Copenhagen, became of similar importance not only for the brewing industry but also, later on, for the entire biotechnical industry. There were other milestones on the road towards large-scale production. Improved versions of the steam-boiling process, introduced experimentally about the middle of the century but received with scepticism at the time, gained ground during the 1860s and 1870s. At the Brewing Congress held in Vienna in 1873, the elite of Europe's brewers were shown three different kinds of cooling compressor. In 1875 Gabriel Sedlmayr the younger chose the compressor designed by Dr Carl Linde for his celebrated 'Zum Spaten' brewery in Munich, so launching the Linde system on its triumphal progress. In 1876 Anton Dreher introduced it in the Schwechat brewery in Vienna. A Linde machine was installed by J. C. Jacobsen at Carlsberg in Copenhagen in 1878, while two years later W. Feltmann, another of the pioneers of the modern European brewing industry, was responsible for bringing in the system at Heineken in Rotterdam. The industrial bottling of beer, either at the brewery or at special bottling plants, was a third technological field that opened up during this period, helping to revolutionize the distribution of beer and resulting in more direct marketing from the brewer to the consumer.[2]

Large-scale brewing implied not only more economical exploitation of the brewery's raw materials and energy sources but also more capital-intensive plants and equipment. New partners and interests were thus brought into the breweries, which had traditionally been a very closed and exclusive world everywhere in Europe. Just what this was to signify in terms of management I propose to consider in very broad outline, in what follows.

Whereas the era before 1850 had drawn heavily on British experience and the period after 1920 came increasingly to be influenced by American technology, the second half of the nineteenth century and the early

---

Ruth Cohen, Cambridge Studies in Industry (London, 1958) and John Vaizey, *The Brewing Industry* (London, 1960); see also Thomas C. Cochran, *The Pabst Brewing Company: The History of an American Business* (New York and London, 1948).
[2] A Fraenkel, *Gammel Carlsberg* (Copenhagen, 1897) and H. Holter and K. Max Møller (eds.), *The Carlsberg Laboratory 1876–1976* (Copenhagen, 1976).

decades of the twentieth century were the heyday of continental European, especially German-Austrian, technique and know-how.

These were the times when the lagers or bottom-fermented beers of the so-called Bavarian and Pilsen type hit the markets and were welcomed by the beer-drinking public at large. *Lager* is the German word for 'stored'; these beers were characterized by a slower method of fermentation and called for the installation at the brewery of large, cool cellars where the beer could be kept during the storage period. Lager brewing especially became a challenge to the innovative spirits of the entrepreneur-brewer. Financiers were attracted to the field. However, the founders of a number of Europe's most successful lager breweries were in fact descendants of local brewing dynasties with their pedigrees firmly rooted in the tradition of the guilds. They embarked upon the new trade on a family basis. But as they grew older and their firms increased in size they realized that the personally owned and managed firm was running into troubles that could only be solved by seeking new styles of management and by working out different types of organization.

III

Business literature often describes the change-over from family ownership to corporate management as a development from slightly amateurish management methods to the modern professionalism of salaried and well-educated managers. This picture has absolutely no validity as regards the founders of the modern European brewing industry. These people were not only trained empirically at various breweries but also often received additional theoretical education, especially in the natural sciences. Some of them were in this respect self-educated people: this, however, did not reduce their professional standard. Their hallmark was a dedication to the profession paired with a mind open to new methods and better insights. They were restless in their quest for knowledge. They travelled widely. They learned quickly. The leading brewers of the continent soon got acquainted with each other, many of them willingly sharing the know-how of their profession with their colleagues.

An outstanding example is provided by the careers of Gabriel Sedlmayr the elder and the younger, whose family had been brewers at Maisach near Munich since the end of the seventeenth century.[3] In 1807 Gabriel the elder acquired the Spaten brewery in Munich itself, at that

[3] Herald Thunaeus, *Märkliga Bryggare* (Stockholm, 1967), on 'Gabriel Sedlmayr, Far och Son' (pp. 85–94).

time one of the smallest of the city's fifty-two breweries. By the time of his death in 1838 it had advanced in size to fourth place in that city of brewing. As well as being skilled in the craft of brewing, Gabriel the elder was actively interested in technology. He enrolled in the Polytechnic Society for the Kingdom of Bavaria. He experimented with steam engines and steam-boiling. He was one of the first brewers in Germany to introduce the use of thermometers and even manufactured them as a hobby. His greatest contribution to the improvement of the quality of bottom-fermented beer, however, consisted in his installation in 1833 of ice-boxes for cooling the storage cellars. At the instance of his father, Gabriel the younger received private education in physics and chemistry, and after serving his apprenticeship in the brewers' guild he went off on numerous study tours. In 1832 he arrived in Vienna where he made the acquaintance of the young Austrian brewer Anton Dreher, who became his travelling companion and lifelong friend. From Austria Sedlmayr continued to Bohemia and Saxony. The following year his travels took him to the Rhineland, the Netherlands and Belgium. From there he went on to London, where he met Dreher and a couple of Bavarian brewers' sons.

The great London breweries astounded the young trainees, but in general the English were reluctant to introduce them to their methods of brewing. Only when Sedlmayr and his friends got to know David Booth, the English author on brewing technique, did they acquire any detailed knowledge of English brewing methods, including the use of the saccharometer. Booth supplied them with letters of introduction to a large number of breweries in England and Scotland. In his letters home to his father, Gabriel relates all the tricks they employed in order to penetrate the English art, from the secret measurement of temperatures to hollow walking-sticks with valves for taking samples of wort and beer without being observed. We would call this industrial espionage. Of one place where they were received with greater friendliness than usual Sedlmayr wrote: 'Die Brauerei stahlen wir aber doch so gut als möglich aus.' ('From this brewery we stole nearly everything.') From England the route homeward went via Paris and Strasburg, with visits to breweries in each of these cities.

Their English experiences were of crucial significance for the firms subsequently controlled by both Sedlmayr and Dreher, which grew until they ranked among the largest on the continent. As is well known, Anton Dreher created one of the first European brewing empires, with breweries in Vienna, Budapest, Trieste and Micholup in Czechoslovakia. It is true of both these brewers that they not only took but also gave.

They supplied information to David Booth for his book about breweries on the continent, and they took on foreign brewers as apprentices. The founder of the Carlsberg Breweries, J. C. Jacobsen, learned from Sedlmayr the art of brewing bottom-fermented beer after numerous vain attempts in Copenhagen. It was from Munich that he obtained the yeast which became the basic strain for his own brewery. There is a legendary account of how Jacobsen kept the yeast in a tin in his hatbox as he journeyed home to Denmark. Every time the stage-coach stopped he hurried to the nearest source of water in order to cool the tin. Jacobsen belonged to the second generation of a dynasty of brewers.[4] As an apprentice he attended the public lectures of H. C. Ørsted, whose discovery of electromagnetism had brought him international fame, at the Danish Polytechnical University. At the beginning of the century, Orsted had served on a government commission investigating ways and means to the improvement of the brewing profession in Denmark. He was also the founder and ardent promoter of the Danish Society for the Propagation of Science, of which both Jacobsens, father and son, became members. Having acquired the Bavarian know-how, J. C. Jacobsen in 1847 left his family brewery, located on the narrow premises of Brolæggerstræde inside Copenhagen, and moved to an open industrial site outside the city at Valby, where he built a modern brewery situated close to the first railway line connecting the metropolis with the provinces. He named this brewery after his son, Carl, whom he later pushed very hard professionally – obviously a Jacobsen family trait – sending him on a four-year training tour to leading breweries all over Europe.

Carl Jacobsen stayed at Erhardt's brewery in Strasburg, at Eugen Velten's in Marseilles, at Sedlmayr's 'Zum Spaten' brewery in Munich, and at Dreher's breweries in Vienna and Budapest; finally, in 1868, he ended up at William Younger's brewery in Edinburgh and at Everhed's in Burton-on-Trent where he got acquainted with the English making of pale ales and stout. Before that, Carl Jacobsen studied chemistry at the Royal Danish Agricultural University, as well as construction drawing at the Polytechnical University. His father was convinced that success in the trade was chiefly a matter of the brewer's command of chemistry and its auxiliary sciences. In 1855 J. C. Jacobsen wrote from abroad to his thirteen-year-old son that only by mastering theoretical insight and combining it with practical technical training would one qualify for a

---

[4] On the Jacobsen dynasty see articles in *Dansk Biografisk Leksikon*, 3rd edn, VII (Cophenhagen, 1981), by Birgit Nüchel Thomsen on J. C. Jacobsen, Torben Holck Colding on Carl Jacobsen and Fr. Sander on Vagn Jacobsen.

leading place in what he thought to be a very close race. The fourth generation of the Jacobsen family, Vagn Jacobsen, received his brewmaster's degree in 1904 from the Wahl–Henius Institute in Chicago and made further educational visits to breweries in Austria and Germany, finally obtaining a special certificate from the Versuchs- und Lehranstalt für Brauerei in Berlin.

In the continuing rivalry between the German brewing schools, Berlin had now won supremacy over Munich, and America had entered the scene as a country considered by the young and ambitious among professional brewers to be worthwhile visiting. In 1908 the Austrian brewery technologist, Dr Adolf Cluss, summarized his impressions of a study tour in the United States in the following words:

It may justly be stated that the Americans, not only as regards the size of their breweries but also as far as the scale of their technical equipment and technical management is concerned, are ahead of not only us Austrians, but also of the Germans. We might also become pupils of the American brewer as regards business methods. If we conduct our businesses on a large scale and with real foresight we can also learn from the Americans how to adapt ourselves better to existing circumstances, and more especially how to utilize space to better advantage.[5]

IV

It was not only the brewers who travelled. Their beers did also. After the English had led the way with the Great Exhibition of 1851, the first large-scale world exhibition, other exhibitions sprang up like mushrooms. At the international exposition of arts and industry held in Paris in 1867, Gabriel Sedlmayr was awarded the gold medal in competition with seventy other brewers in the class for bottom-fermented beer. Gerard A. Heineken, who had established the firm of Heineken & Co. in 1864, with the idea of making English types of beer for export, had found at an international exhibition held in Amsterdam in 1869 that the public flocked to the beer pavilion of Anton Dreher while his own pavilion was almost deserted. This clearly convinced him that the future belonged to the Bavarian type of beer, with the result that he changed his strategy. At the world exhibition in Vienna in 1873, J. C. Jacobsen presented his bottled beer, which created a sensation and for which he was rewarded. On the same occasion he reported on his new method of heating mash with steam in the brew-house. At the world exhibition held in Antwerp in 1885 Germany emerged as the leading brewing nation in the world.

[5] *American Brewer's Review*, 25 (Chicago and New York, 1911), 623.

The German brewing industry also led the way in other respects, such as the starting-up of professional journals and the establishment of vocational schools and research laboratories. The *Allgemeine Brauer- und Hopfen-Zeitung* (known today as *Brauwelt*) was founded in 1861 at Roth near Nuremberg. In 1866, Professor Carl Lindtner senior began publishing from Munich the first trade journal of Bavarian brewing, *Der Bayerische Bierbrauer*, whose title was changed in 1878 to *Zeitschrift für das gesamte Brauwesen*. In 1873, Lindtner collaborated with Reischauer to found the first institute of brewing science at Weihenstephan, near Munich. Largest of all these establishments was the Versuchs- und Lehranstalt für Brauerei, which was inaugurated in Berlin in 1883 and which shortly after its inception began publishing the *Wochenschrift für Brauerei* with Max Delbrück and M. Hayduck as editors. Congresses flourished as well. The meeting held in Vienna in 1873, at which the leading brewers in Europe assembled by mutual agreement, inaugurated a series of international congresses.

In Britain some brewers had founded laboratories for the control of brewing processes at their breweries from the 1850s, at first with German chemists, later with chemists from London University. This led, fairly directly, to the foundation of the Laboratory Club, which eventually became the Institute of Brewing (1894). Later, this produced the foundation of the Birmingham Brewing School (1900). Adrian J. Brown, an eminent chemist who formerly worked for Salt's brewery in Burton-on-Trent and had contributed notable papers on yeast propagation and fermentation, was invited to be the first professor. At the Watt Institution and School of Arts in Edinburgh the first training in brewing started in 1903 when Dr Emil Westergaard was appointed lecturer in brewing within the chemistry department to give a two-month intensive summer course. He combined his college duties with those required of him as brewer at Tennants brewery in Glasgow. By 1906 a department of technical mycology was in being and Dr Westergaard was appointed a full-time staff member, collaborating also with the Carlsberg brewery in Copenhagen.[6]

V

Dr Emil Chr. Hansen's case provides a graphic example of the speed with which a scientific discovery of immediate practical value was

---

[6] Mr Birger Breyen, Technical Vice-President, The United Breweries, Copenhagen, has very kindly assisted me in obtaining data on the European brewing schools. See also Anna M. Macleod, 'Brewing at Heriot-Watt University', *The Brewer* (January, 1972), pp. 7–13.

disseminated.[7] Dr Hansen had conceived the idea that the main reason for the frequent occurrence of aberrant brews resulting in unsaleable beer was not bacterial infection, as was generally assumed by Pasteur and others, but contamination by 'wild' yeasts. He devised a method for the isolation of a single yeast cell and its propagations into an absolutely pure culture. J. C. Jacobsen at first had his doubts about Hansen's theory but gave in when confronted with the results of the experiments: the new yeast was used for the first time in 1883 on a production scale at Carlsberg.

It was Dr Hansen's aim to provide the brewery with additional income through his inventions, and he therefore suggested that Jacobsen might establish a factory to produce pure strains to be sold all over the world. Jacobsen, however, turned down this proposal, a somewhat unusual gesture from an industrial entrepreneur. The brewery owner refused to take out a patent for the discovery of his science employee. On the contrary he offered free delivery of pure yeast to others. Jacobsen maintained that Hansen was the head, with full pay, of the physiology department at a basic research laboratory, the Carlsberg Laboratory. This had been established in 1875 and in 1876 formally turned over to the Carlsberg Foundation, another of J. C. Jacobsen's initiatives, sponsored by him but directed by a board of five scholars appointed by the Royal Danish Academy of Science and Letters from among its own ranks.[8]

Although the intimacy between the Carlsberg Laboratory (with its two departments of chemistry and physiology) and the brewery is illustrated by the fact that during the first years of its existence every newly appointed assistant had to undergo a three-month training course at the brewery before taking up his duties at the laboratory and in order to familiarize himself with the practical background of his future research work, Jacobsen maintained that the laboratory's primary object was basic research, not the diffusion of industrially useful knowledge and techniques. For purely technical problems at his breweries, special process-control laboratories had already been established in 1871. The research results from the Carlsberg Laboratory were to be published in a scientific journal of international circulation. Independent commercial

---

[7] On Emil Chr. Hansen, see Alb. Klöcker, in Holter and Møller (eds.), *The Carlsberg Laboratory*, pp. 168ff.; see also Mikuláš Teich, 'From "Enzyme" to "Cutoskeleton"', in M. Teich and R. Young (eds.), *Changing Perspectives in the History of Science: Essays in Honour of Joseph Needham* (London, 1973), p. 443. On Alfred Jørgensen, who was a close friend of Emil Chr. Hansen, see the biography by Robert Djurtoft (Albert Hansen) in *Dansk Biografisk Leksikon*, VII.
[8] Kristof Glamann, *Carlsbergfondet* (Copenhagen, 1976), on the history of the Carlsberg Foundation.

exploitation of Dr Hansen's discovery took place at the Alfred Jørgensen Laboratory (founded in 1881), which also functioned as a practical brewing school. Together with Dr Aa Kühle, Jacobsen's assistant manager, and a Copenhagen coppersmith, Mr Jensen, Dr Hansen also developed an apparatus for the propagation of pure yeast which was sold in great numbers all over the world.

Accordingly, and as early as 1882, Dr Hansen arranged his first course at the laboratory on his pure yeast cultivation thesis and method. His Copenhagen seminars were attended by people from many quarters. Thus Dr Elion and Dr Dupont of Heineken visited Hansen in the autumn of 1885 and, influenced by what they had seen, established their own laboratory immediately on their return to Rotterdam. In the following years Heineken established a substantial exportation of yeast. Dr Elion was put in charge of the propagation work at Rotterdam. After some discussion with Heineken's management, an agreement was reached which gave him a certain royalty on the yeast sales.[9] Hansen's book was not translated into English until 1896, but the open-minded Milwaukee brewers learned of his work very quickly. Pure yeast culture was introduced at the Pabst brewery in 1887, and a research chemist was added to the staff to supervise brewing operations.[10]

VI

The professional freemasonry of the continental founding fathers lasted for life. In 1884 J. C. Jacobsen made a last tour to meet his colleagues in Europe, visiting among others his old friend the brewer Johan Edlen von Götz in Okocim (Galicia).[11] The entire personnel assembled in the evening, accompanied by a brass band and attired in firemen's uniforms, to greet 'Altmeister' Jacobsen, who returned the compliment by praising the fine patriarchal relationship between the brewery owners and the workers. During the visit Jacobsen was in a mood of retrospection and, in the same year, at the Technical Institute in Copenhagen, he gave a survey of the progress of the brewing industry over the previous fifty years, taking in a broad vista of European development.[12]

[9] [H. A. Korthals], *Korte geschiednis der Heinekens Bierbrouwerij Maatschappij N. V. 1873–1948* (Utrecht, 1948), pp. 105ff.
[10] Cochran, *The Pabst Brewing Company*, p. 112.
[11] Franz Fasbender's obituary on J. C. Jacobsen in *Allgemeine Zeitschrift für Bierbrauerei und Malzfabrikation*, vol. 15, no. 20 (Vienna, 18 May 1887), p. 383.
[12] On Jacobsen's retrospect and the Danish brewing industry, see Kristof Glamann, *Bryggeriets historie i Danmark indtil slutningen af det 19. århundrede* (Copenhagen, 1962), p. 214, and *idem, Carlsbergfondet*, pp. 35ff.

There were three problems that worried him in the evening of his life. The first was the question of management. The growth of firms made it more and more difficult for the individual entrepreneur to overlook and manage the entire enterprise. However, he did see here some opportunity to train a cadre of technical managers in the brewing schools which were appearing in Bavaria, Austria and elsewhere. The second problem concerned how to continue the research into brewing processes without making concessions with a view to commercial gains. In this respect he had himself been a pioneer when he took the exceptional step of setting up a foundation and endowing it with his breweries on the explicit condition that after his death the Carlsberg Foundation should ensure that his policy of research and development continued. J. C. Jacobsen did not believe that his son Carl had sufficient strength of character to stick to this policy, and for this reason the rapidly growing and very modern brewery of New Carlsberg, which belonged to the son and had been started with the father's help, had become an irrelevancy in his eyes. This worry led to the third problem – the strong interest evinced by anonymous capital in the 1870s and 1880s in joint-stock company investment in the beer industry. 'Experience has shown', said Jacobsen, 'that shareholders merely seek the biggest possible immediate dividends and are very reluctant to commit themselves to expenditure on improvements which are of importance for the greater perfection of the product but which cannot instantly bring forth fruit in the form of money.'

Several of Jacobsen's fellow-founders had to nod in acknowledgement of this. One of these was G. A. Heineken, whose firm had been reorganized as a joint-stock company in 1873, at the time of a merger between the original brewery in Amsterdam and a Rotterdam brewery, the aim being to go over to Bavarian-type brewing.[13] Heineken himself, as chief shareholder, retained control over the newly established company, whose management he shared with W. Feltmann. Profits during the 1880s were large, a feature common to the brewing industry as a whole in those years, since it enjoyed very low raw material prices. In 1886 Heineken's board of directors wanted to declare a dividend of 19 per cent. Heineken would only give 10 per cent and had to replace his board of directors in order to accomplish this. His ground for sticking to this low distribution was not that 19 per cent was an irresponsible payment but that a very high dividend would attract investors to the brewing industry. The previous year Gabriel Sedlmayr had actually

---

[13] [Korthals], *Korte geschiednis der Heinekens Bierbrouwerij*, pp. 170ff.

reduced the price of his beer in a similar attempt to cool the ardour of outside investors.

VII

The joint-stock company form had long been a topic of controversy. The frequent bankruptcies among joint-stock companies in the nineteenth century, especially during the 1840s and the 1870s, nourished this mistrust. One of that century's wizards of free enterprise, the American Andrew Carnegie, once boasted that by working in a partnership he could outmanoeuvre slower corporations with their need for formal meetings and much-discussed decisions. In other words, incorporation produced bureaucratic red tape. Furthermore, the old-fashioned way of raising capital, possibly by merger, possibly by marriage, was well proven and still working.

On the other hand, incorporation offered clear advantages. There were capital gains to be made from share issues. There was an opportunity to find money on a scale adequate to finance considerable expansion and growth. Incorporation also meant a self-perpetuating organization that would not be disrupted by the death of a partner. In America, where the big companies did a large inter-state business and unknowingly could infringe state laws, there was greater personal protection for the owners in having responsibility assumed by legal entity. Here the corporate title possibly also added dignity and importance to a big concern in a business community where most production was still in the hands of small proprietors. To the case for the joint-stock company form can be added a further element culled from Danish brewing history: Tuborg had been established in 1873 as a stockholding company, and Tuborg's management believed that the joint-stock company was more popular than the family- or foundation-owned company, because the interest of shareholders in the firm would transmit itself to the population at large, to the benefit of products and sales.

Nearly all major breweries of the Western world went public during the 1870s and 1880s. The most important result of this wave of incorporation was undoubtedly the growth of salaried management. As Professor Jürgen Kocka has stated, the new salaried entrepreneur became the object of high expectations and remarkable fears. Some thought him less honest and less ambitious than the owner-entrepreneur; others regarded him as a sign of the bureaucratization of the capitalist economy and thus of its decline. In contrast, many expected the manager to be more socially enlightened and more sensitive to the public good than the owner and to be less strongly influenced by the hope of private profit. He was expected to resolve traditional class conflicts and to be an agent of moderate social reform. These expectations and fears were not realized. It is Professor Kocka's conclusion that, in terms of economic and social behaviour and political outlook, the distinction between owner-entrepreneurs and salaried entrepreneurs did not make much relevant difference in the late nineteenth century.[14] One may add that, with regard to philanthropy and patronage, where the owner-entrepreneur and especially the founder had displayed much activity and dedication, the salaried manager generally speaking felt little sense of obligation and regarded this task more as a corporate than as a personal duty.

German company law prescribed a dual company structure, namely a supervisory board (*Aufsichtsrat*) on the one hand and an executive board (*Vorstand*) on the other. The members of the supervisory board were elected by the shareholders or their representatives; they made the most basic decisions, particularly those about strategies, investments and top-level appointments. The supervisory board appointed the members of the executive board, who made the day-to-day decisions and actually ran the company. While the executive board members were salaried employees who worked full-time as directors, department heads and executives of the corporation, the members of the supervisory board met only a few times a year. Most of them also held positions in other firms. Before 1914, bank directors made up the largest single group among supervisory board members of German joint-stock companies and accounted for 20 per cent of all positions. It is in the heavy industries that the presence of the banks is particularly striking, reaching a peak around 1900. After that date the supervisory board lost ground, partly because the increasing complexity of technical and business matters tended to strengthen the position of the full-time working salaried managers.[15] However, we lack studies of the managerial structure of the German brewing industry, so that it is impossible to discover whether it follows this general trend.

In Britain, the issuing of shares, which started in 1886, when Guinness went public, meant that in most brewing companies the board of directors increased in size.[16] The input of outsiders consisted mainly of

---

[14] Jürgen Kocka, 'The Rise of Modern Industrial Enterprise in Germany', in Alfred D. Chandler Jr and Herman Daems (eds.), *Managerial Hierarchies: Comparative Perspectives on the Rise of the Modern Industrial Enterprise* (Cambridge, Mass., 1980), p. 93.
[15] *Ibid.*
[16] I am indebted to Mr Tom Corran for supplying me with information about Great Britain. Mr Corran is at present preparing a major work on the history of the British

bankers, lawyers and accountants. However, incorporation did little to alter the basic control of breweries exercised by the former partners. They tended to retain control of the business after 'going public' through the retention of blocks of shares. It can therefore be said that incorporation was a device for raising extra capital rather than for transferring control. The family interest hid behind the mask of the corporation. This lessened the prospects of promotion for specialist managers, especially technical managers who seldom became members of the boards of directors. There was a low degree of mobility within the company structure. In fact, the British brewing industry saw little cause to change its methods. Up to the early twentieth century when it was the largest block of companies on the Stock Exchange list, the brewing industry performed so well under traditional family control that the impetus to change barely existed.

brewing industry from 1830 onwards for the Brewers' Society under the supervision of Professor Peter Mathias.

12

Large firms in Belgium, 1892–1974: an analysis of their structure and growth[1]

HERMAN VAN DER WEE

The problem

The beginning of the Industrial Revolution in Belgium was closely connected with the development of the iron and coal industries in Wallonia, the southern part of the country. Gradually, modern industrialization extended to the glass industry and to several sub-sectors of metal-processing, linked in particular with the construction of railways and tramways. The Walloon as well as the Flemish textile industry was mechanized early. The mechanization of the Walloon textile industry in the area of Verviers contributed decisively towards the mechanization of heavy industry in the province of Liège. Nevertheless, during the first half of the nineteenth century, modern textiles did not develop into a leading sector. They became a dominant industry only in Flanders, and this occurred towards the end of the century, when modern industrialization in Flanders had become generally established.

The early success of the Belgian Industrial Revolution can be attributed to two principal factors. First, the Belgian entrepreneurs assimilated British technological 'know-how' very quickly and extended it further in a creative way. Second, Belgian bankers, by introducing the system of 'mixed banks', achieved remarkable progress in the field of financial organization. Imitation and innovation stimulated a rapid accumulation of capital in the leading sectors and facilitated the opening of the world market to Belgian industrial products and services. Thus the

[1] The preparation of this essay was made possible by a research grant from the National Fonds voor Wetenschappelijk Onderzoek (research project no. 2.0051.75; Theme: 'Financial Intermediation and Economic Growth: The Belgian Experience in the 19th and 20th Centuries'). The results were worked out during a stay at the Institute for Advanced Study in Princeton, New Jersey. Thanks are due to both institutions for their valuable support.

interplay of technological and organizational factors and the alliance which this provoked between the industrial and financial sectors gave a particular dynamism to the early growth of the Belgian economy.

In this essay I will try to integrate business history into the general story of the Belgian Industrial Revolution and the later economic development of the country. Four major problems demand consideration. To what extent did the specific pattern of technological and financial organization in Belgium induce a particular industrial structure? What was the effect of this pattern on economic development during the nineteenth century? Why did the structure of Belgian industry not change during the twentieth century, and how did this inertia, in its turn, affect the country's economy? By emphasizing the crucial role of business organization, this study draws upon the seminal research of A.D. Chandler Jr.[2] At the same time, it has very close links with the important research into Belgian business history recently carried out by H. Daems.[3]

The kinds of question asked and the reference to these authors imply an underlying assumption: that it was the large-scale enterprises that formed the framework from which modern industry developed. This assumption should be emphasized. For this reason, the analysis concentrates on the structure of big industrial enterprise in Belgium. Which firms ranked among the fifty biggest industrial enterprises in the country? How were they distributed over the different industrial sectors? What shifts happened within this group over time? What marked these shifts? What linkages can be ascertained between the structure of Belgian big business and economic development as a whole?

Source analysis and methodology

The most interesting source for constructing and analysing a sample of the biggest industrial enterprises of Belgium is undeniably the *Recueil financier*.[4] It provides an important series of annual data concerning all Belgian enterprises quoted on the Brussels Stock Exchange. Along with the publication of the balance sheets and income statements, data concerning the history and management of these enterprises are also available. It is certainly not a perfect source. Companies not having the status of a limited liability company, or not quoted on the Stock

---

[2] A. D. Chandler Jr, *Strategy and Structure* (Cambridge, Mass., 1972); *idem, The Visible Hand: The Managerial Revolution in American Business* (Cambridge, Mass., 1977).

[3] H. Daems, *The Holding Company and Corporate Control* (Leiden and Boston, Mass., 1978).

[4] *Le Recueil financier*, ed. E. Bruylant (Brussels, 1893–1975).

Exchange, are not mentioned in it. Thus some big enterprises, such as the family firm of Solvay, are missing. Fortunately, the gaps remain limited and rather exceptional. The vast majority of the large industrial firms do appear in the yearly publication.

Along with the industrial enterprises, the *Recueil financier* includes financial intermediaries such as insurance companies, banks, mortgage banks and others. This last group of enterprises has not been analysed. On the other hand, holding companies have been included in the sample in so far as they were mainly concerned with industrial investments. In the *Recueil financier* these holding companies were classified according to the dominant industrial sector in each portfolio. The same classification has been used in this analysis.

The more detailed information about each enterprise, as it appears in the *Recueil financier*, is also susceptible to criticism. The balance sheets, for example, were not always drafted on a uniform scheme. Sometimes, adjustment proved to be necessary. The biggest problem concerned depreciation: in some cases, it was charged on a particular depreciation account as a part of the liabilities. In periods of sharp inflation, the question of the revaluation of the assets, in particular the fixed assets, created further problems. In addition, qualitative information has been used when necessary to try to find a reasonable solution. A sample of companies with homogeneous balance sheets could then be used for a cross-sectional and time-series analysis.

For comparison over time, a ten-yearly analysis has been used as a guideline. In principle the decade years have been taken as the framework for analysis, though in two cases there has been a deviation from this. First, a proximate year for a decade was selected when the data concerning the decade year were not available. Second, when as a consequence of special circumstances (for example, a war) a bias seemed to exist in the data of the decade year, an adjoining normal year was taken; for example, 1938 was used instead of 1940. Finally, the last available year of the *Recueil financier*, namely 1974, was selected as the closing year.[5]

The applied statistical calculations were very simple and merely descriptive. They were used only as an aid to explore the characteristics of Belgian big business. On the basis of these characteristics it is intended to formulate some useful working hypotheses on the relationship between financial and technical organization, industrial structure and economic development.

[5] The following years were selected for analysis: 1892, 1900, 1910, 1920, 1930, 1938, 1950, 1960 and 1974.

201

The fifty biggest industrial enterprises

Tables 12.1 and 12.2 show the sectoral composition per decade of the fifty biggest enterprises in Belgium. Table 12.1 shows the number of enterprises per sector, while Table 12.2 (see p. 203) shows the proportions of the total balance-sheet values held by the different sectors in the fifty biggest enterprises.

The message of these tables is clear. In Table 12.1, which shows the sectoral composition in terms of the number of enterprises, the basic sectors of heavy industry are strongly represented. Until 1920, the transport sector was clearly dominant. The temporary diminution in the number of transport enterprises at the turn of the century was the consequence of merger movement in the railways. Meanwhile, the number of tramway and *metro* companies increased, though they were mainly still too small to be classified among the fifty biggest enterprises. This picture changed from about 1910 onwards. In particular the Belgian tramway companies, which were active abroad, for example in tsarist Russia, grew spectacularly at the beginning of the twentieth century. Some of these companies, however, had financial problems during the First World War. Many others failed during the Russian Revolution. In 1926 the railway and tramway systems in Belgium itself were national-ized. The world crisis of the thirties produced new failures among Belgian transport enterprises abroad. Table 12.1 shows very clearly the influence of these circumstances on the evolution of the number of

Table 12.1. *Sectoral composition of the fifty biggest enterprises in Belgium, 1892–1974 (number of enterprises)*

	1892	1900	1910	1920	1930	1938	1950	1960	1974
Transport	27	19	26	17	7	3	3	3	3
Metals and metal-processing	7	12	7	14	11	10	10	11	10
Non-ferrous metals	2	2	2	4	4	3	4	3	5
Electricity and gas	5	6	8	5	11	12	11	9	8
Coal	3	5	3	1	2	4	6	6	1
Miscellaneous	6	6	4	9	15	18[a]	16[a]	18[a]	23
Total	50	50	50	50	50	50	50	50	50

[a] In 1938, 1950 and 1960 exactly half of these enterprises were colonial companies.

transport companies among the fifty biggest industrial enterprises of Belgium.

The metals and metal-processing sector is also well represented in Table 12.1. This particularly underlines the important role which Walloon heavy industry continued to play in the Belgian economy during the whole period from 1892 until 1974. Initially, coal reinforced the position of heavy industry. But, as Table 12.1 clearly shows, the coal sector was in full decline from the beginning of the twentieth century onwards. The increase in the number of large mines after 1920 is attributable solely to the rise of the new coal industry of Limburg, which went through a short period of expansion between the two World Wars. Finally, from 1950 onwards, the coal industry as a whole no longer had any growth potential in Belgium.

The data with respect to the non-ferrous sector show the increasing links between Belgium and the Belgian Congo. The expansion of the electricity and gas sector illustrates the soaring consumption of energy in Belgian, and especially Flemish, industry during the inter-war years. The 'miscellaneous' category is not particularly strongly represented at the beginning of the period but improves its position considerably after the First World War. Until 1960, colonial companies accounted for the greatest part of this group. Again, this stresses, indirectly, the sustained

Table 12.2. *Sectoral composition of the fifty biggest enterprises in Belgium, 1892–1974 (percentage shares in total balance-sheet values)*

	1892	1900	1910	1920	1930	1938	1950	1960	1974
Transport	64.1	53.7	65.3	46.2	20.2	5.4	8.0	6.5	3.8
Metals and metal-processing	12.5	18.0	11.1	27.0	26.6	22.1	24.0	27.8	25.3
Non-ferrous metals	4.2	2.7	2.0	8.0	8.0	7.2	7.5	5.9	7.2
Electricity and gas	8.7	8.7	9.1	5.0	16.0	21.3	19.8	19.1	23.4
Coal	3.1	6.3	3.9	0.9	1.9	4.7	7.8	5.9	0.7
Miscellaneous	7.4	10.6	8.6	12.9	27.3	39.3[a]	32.9[a]	34.8[a]	39.6
Total	100.0	100.0	100.0	100.0	100.0	100.0	100.0	100.0	100.0

[a] For the years 1938 and 1950 respectively 18.6 per cent and 20.6 per cent can be assigned to the colonial sector, while the only five remaining colonial enterprises in 1960 represent 17.7 per cent of the balance total of that year.

importance of heavy industry in Belgium: the colonial companies involved were controlled by holding companies, which also favoured the large firms in heavy industry. In 1974, however, although the 'miscellaneous' category had gained in importance, colonial companies were no longer represented in it. The traditional sectors lost their previous pre-eminence; and other firms not linked with the traditional holding companies came to the fore. The entry of Belgium into the Common Market in 1958, and the definitive breakthrough of the welfare economy from the sixties onwards, ultimately favoured the growth of firms which specialized in consumer goods and in consumer durables.

Table 12.2, showing the proportions of the balance-sheet values held by the different sectors in the total, does not radically change these conclusions. It suggests that the statistics of the number of enterprises still underestimate the predominance of the transport sector among the fifty biggest enterprises until 1930. In contrast, the coal sector seems to be rather overestimated. Thus the deterioration of the coal sector is a phenomenon that, in origin, already existed at the end of the nineteenth century. What Table 12.2 clearly shows is the very late escape of the Belgian economy from the domination of the traditional sectors. It also partially explains the dramatic extent of the Belgian structural crisis during the 1970s and 1980s.

The problem of entry and exit

Until the 1970s, the list of the fifty biggest enterprises in Belgium was dominated by heavy industry. However, this characteristic does not mean that the same enterprises continuously formed part of the top group. On the contrary, quite a number of enterprises frequently left the top group, while others entered. The reasons were varied. Some sectors grew faster than others, which favoured the growth of the enterprises of the most expansive sectors. Within the same sector, some enterprises were more dynamic than others. The rapid growth of some enterprises could be the result of an appropriate and competent management, but it could also be due to a strategy of merging. The analysis reveals that mergers were, to a large extent responsible for the shifting composition of the list of the biggest enterprises.[6]

---

[6] See also in this connection some interesting studies concerning other countries: G. Stigler, 'The Statistics of Monopoly and Merger', *Journal of Political Economy*, 64 (1956), 35–7; S. Friedland, 'Turnover and Growth of the Largest Industrial Firms, 1906–1950', *Review of Economics and Statistics*, 39 (1957), 79–83; D. Weder, 'Die 200 groszten Deutschen Aktiengesellschaften, 1913–1962', Frankfurt (dissertation), 1968.

The analysis of entry and exit has covered not only the fifty biggest enterprises but also those enterprises ranked by size in the next, second-50 group. The purpose of this extension was to investigate in more detail the historical composition of the top-50 group as found in 1974. How many enterprises in the top-50 group in 1974 were already part of this same group in 1960? How many of them were in the second-50 category? How many did not belong to either of these two categories? These questions were extended to cover a comparison of the composition of the top-50 group in 1974 with that in 1950, 1938, 1930, 1920, 1910, 1900 and 1892. Fig. 12.1 shows the results of these computations. The three surfaces A, B and C show the relative import-ance of the three possible situations over time: the big enterprises of 1974 already belonging, during the preceding decades, to the top-50 group (A); those belonging to the second-50 group (B); and those belonging to neither of those two categories (C).

Fig. 12.1 suggests the following conclusions. First, during some periods the shifts in the top group of the fifty biggest enterprises were clearly more explicit than during others. Between 1920 and 1938 and between 1960 and 1974 the transformations were very striking. In the top-50 group of 1974, 62 per cent of the enterprises were newcomers in comparison with the preceding decade; in other words, only 38 per cent of the fifty biggest enterprises in 1974 belonged to the top-50 group of 1960. Thus, the EEC and the accelerating internationalization of world trade since the sixties stimulated the expansion of new sectors and of new enterprises in a very dynamic way. The same can be said of the inter-war years though the conclusions here must be qualified: the expansion of the 1920s stimulated the growth of sectors and enterprises in a differential way but the depression of the thirties also produced an analogous effect.

Second, no crucial part in the transition of small enterprises to big ones was played by the second-50 category. Obviously, it had some influence, which increased over time: a growing number of enterprises

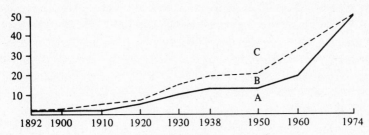

Fig. 12.1. Historical reconstruction of the list of the fifty biggest enterprises in Belgium, 1974

205

belonged first to the second-50 group and then, after one or two decades, pushed to the top-50 group. But moving up via the second-50 category was never a *necessary* precondition.

Third, the periods 1900–20 and 1938–60 can be considered as strikingly stable periods in regard to the composition of the top group of the 50 biggest enterprises. The economic expansion at the turn of the century thus appears not to have provoked important shifts in the composition of the top group. An investigation of the exit-history of the top group of 1892 confirms this completely.[7] This is a good illustration of the deficient innovating power of Belgian industry about 1900. On the other hand, as might be expected, the two World Wars appear to have blocked economic activity in Belgium, which meant that there were no important changes in the relative size of the enterprises.

The characteristics of the permanent core in the top group of the fifty biggest firms

To examine the rank-order of the enterprises that stayed in the top-50 group Spearman and Kendall rank-correlation coefficients were calculated. The rank-order of the enterprises which belonged to the permanent core shows a tendency to stabilize over time. Comparison between the balance-sheet totals of the permanent core and those of the entire top-50 group also generated some useful information (Table 12.3). Thus the balance-sheet totals of the permanent core were compared with the aggregate balance-sheet totals for each of two successive decades: what enterprises remained after a decade and what was the share of the balance-sheet totals of the permanent core in the aggregate balance-sheet totals during each of the two decades?

The share of the permanent core deteriorated steadily during the period 1892–1930. In contrast, it increased in a distinctive way between 1930 and 1974. Thus, before the crisis of 1930, the permanent core consisted of stagnating enterprises; or, more precisely, of those enterprises in the top-50 group which had the weakest growth. From 1930 onwards, the permanent core belonged to the most expansive and most rapidly growing sectors in the top-50 group. It is very significant that this watershed coincided with the time that the enterprises belonging to the 'miscellaneous' category took an ever-increasing share in the top-50 group. This illustrates once more how urgent it was to renovate the

[7] The results of these computations can be found in more detail in the report of the research project. This is available for consultation in NFWO, Egmontstraat 5, 1050 Brussels.

Table 12.3. *Percentage shares in the aggregate balance-sheet totals of the fifty biggest enterprises in Belgium, 1892–1974*

T_1	1892	1900	1910	1920	1930	1938	1950	1960	1900	1938
T_2	1900	1910	1920	1930	1938	1950	1960	1974	1938	1974
Outgoing members (T_1)	43.6	25.1	29.8	40.5	31.4	21.4	31.5	64.5	77.0	81.2
Joining members (T_2)	55.2	28.3	32.8	41.1	29.2	17.1	34.5	58.6	73.9	77.7
Average	49.4	26.7	31.3	40.8	30.3	19.3	33.0	61.6	75.5	79.5
Number of joining members (per cent)	56	40	48	60	34	28	36	62	82	78
Proportion	0.88	0.67	0.65	0.68	0.89	0.69	0.91	0.99	0.92	1.02
Permanent core (T_1)	56.4	74.9	70.2	59.5	68.5	78.6	68.5	35.5	23.0	18.8
Permanent core (T_2)	44.8	71.7	67.2	58.9	70.8	82.9	65.5	41.4	26.1	22.3
Average	50.6	73.3	68.7	59.2	69.7	80.7	67.0	38.4	24.5	20.5
Change of permanent core (per cent)	−20.6	−4.3	−4.3	−1.0	+3.2	+5.5	−4.4	+16.6	+13.5	+18.6

industrial structure in Belgium. A few indicators suggested the urgency from as early as 1892 onwards. In 1930, their number had increased so much that nobody could any longer doubt the necessity of a structural transformation in Belgian industry.

Size and growth in a sectoral perspective

The availability of balance-sheet totals allows a more precise investigation of the size of the big industries. On the basis of the balance-sheet totals, the average size by sector of enterprises in the top group (of the 100 largest firms) was analysed for each decade. The results are shown in Table 12.4. The computation concerned only the five sectors represented in the top group of the fifty biggest enterprises *during all the decades*: transport, metals and metal-processing, non-ferrous metals, electricity and gas, and coal. Inflation provoked no serious problems, although it did influence the balance-sheet totals over time. In fact, inflation has been assumed to influence all enterprises in the same way, giving no essential difficulties in the comparison of the data in Table 12.4.

The limitation of this comparative analysis to these five sectors does not mean that the other industrial sectors had no representation in the list of the fifty biggest enterprises. Enterprises of other sectors can be found

Table 12.4. *Rank-order by sector of the average size of enterprises in the hundred biggest firms in Belgium, 1892–1974*[a]

	1892	1900	1910	1920	1930	1938	1950	1960	1974
1	T	T	T	T	T	NF	T^e	M	EG
2	NF	M	M	NF	M	M^b	M^c	T^e	M
3	M	EG	C	M	NF	T	NF	EG^d	NF
4	EG	NF	EG	EG	EG	EG	EG	NF	T
5	C	C	NF	C	C	C	C	C	C

[a] T = transport; M = metals; NF = non-ferrous metals; EG = electricity and gas: C = coal

[b] The colonial enterprises, which were strongly represented in the top-100 category in 1938, had an average size similar to that of the enterprises in the metals sector.

[c] In 1950 the colonial enterprises came into the second rank. Moreover, textile and chemical enterprises had an average size that was greater than that in the coal sector.

[d] The colonial sector came into the third rank.

[e] In 1950 as well as in 1960, the transport sector was characterized by a high average balance-sheet total. However, in these two decades it was represented in the top-100 by only 4 enterprises.

in the lists from 1892 onwards. They increased in importance after 1920. The colonial companies formed a large part of this group between 1938 and 1960, but the chemical, glass, petroleum, textile, paper, coke and quarry sectors were also represented.

It would be wrong, however, to overestimate the importance of sectoral differences in the top group. In the analysis up to 1960, when colonial companies are removed from the group, no major sectors stand out; the 'miscellaneous' category then gives an impression of diffused unimportance. Even when colonial companies are left in that category, the balance-sheet total of the 'miscellaneous' category – for the decade years 1938, 1950 and 1960 – accounts for only one-third of the aggregate balance-sheet totals. In contrast, from 1974 onwards the sectoral differences in the 'miscellaneous' category have increased considerably. The balance-sheet total of the group accounted in 1974 for almost 40 per cent of the aggregate balance-sheet total (see Table 12.2), but the colonial companies have by then disappeared. Thus the progress of the 'miscellaneous' category was striking, but generally still weak when

Table 12.5. *Annual sectoral growth rates of average balance-sheet totals for the fifty biggest enterprises in Belgium, 1892–1974*

Sector	1892–1900	1900–10	1910–20	1920–30	1892–1930	1930–38	1938–50	1950–60	1960–74	1938–74
Transport	7.48	3.09	9.25	17.98	5.88	− 4.91	15.65[a]	5.03	4.44	7.25
Metals and metal-processing	2.91	4.88[a]	10.51	19.95	6.15[a]	− 0.18	12.59	8.93	8.71	8.72
Non-ferrous metals	− 0.23	1.47	16.26[a]	16.71	5.28	3.13	8.29	8.97	4.65	6.94
Electricity and gas	2.74	1.80	6.81	21.96[a]	4.93	4.52[a]	9.15	10.16[a]	9.86[a]	9.83[a]
Coal	7.90[a]	4.54	4.25	17.86	5.11	3.95	12.61	5.44	3.51	6.94
Average	4.16	3.16	9.42	18.89	5.47	1.30	11.65	7.71	6.23	7.94
Variation-coefficient	83.15	49.02	47.95	10.97	9.58	301.15	25.49	30.01	45.70	16.26

[a] Sector with the highest rate of growth

209

compared with the situation in other Western industrial countries. Table 12.4 illustrates once more the enormous preponderance of heavy industry and related enterprises in the Belgian economy of the nineteenth and twentieth centuries. The enterprises of the transport sector were, on average, the biggest in the country during six of the nine decades between 1892 and 1974. The metals and metal-processing sector followed in second place during six of the nine decades; once it even took first place. The non-ferrous sector and colonial companies, both having a close link with heavy industry, also came near the top.

Table 12.5 shows (per sector) the growth rates of the balance-sheet totals for average firms. The basic data are nominal, that is with no correction for inflation and deflation. Thus, for the diachronic overview, one has to take into account the inflation during the years 1914–30, 1938–50, 1960–74 and the deflation of the thirties. But the growth rates computed on the basis of the nominal data may clearly be used for sectoral comparisons.

Two of the five leading sectors show ever-increasing growth rates in the size of their firms between 1892 and 1930: metals and metal-processing and non-ferrous metals. The rate of growth in the size of firms in the transport sector was also impressive between 1892 and 1930, with the exception of the period 1900–10. Between 1930 and 1974 the situation was different. The transport sector clearly deteriorated in comparison with other sectors. The metals and metal-processing sector maintained a strong rate of growth, irrespective of the disappointing development during the thirties. Coal and electricity and gas, in particular, also showed impressive rates of growth after the Second World War, so far as the size of the average firm was concerned. For this evolution, the role of mergers was, of course, extremely important.

Conclusion

In Belgium, the merger movement was largely responsible for the shifts in the list of the fifty biggest enterprises between 1892 and 1974. It is therefore also reasonable to assume that both big industrial firms and holding companies followed a strategy of growth by means of absorption. Nevertheless, It would be wrong to ascribe all the shifts to mergers. Several other factors should also be taken into consideration. Armament production before and during each of the World Wars, for example, and Belgian reconstruction after those wars, were no doubt important, albeit accidental, factors. The distinctive interdependence of firms in heavy industry favoured special relationships between different enterprises: the sectors of coal, metals and transport were closely connected, for example, by much subcontracting. Government action was often involved herein. Colonial expansion also reinforced inter-dependence: the linkages between the basic industries in Belgium and the colonial companies were extremely strong. Finally, the actual opportunities for constructing railways and tramways all over the world were crucial factors in industrial growth in Belgium at the end of the nineteenth and beginning of the twentieth centuries. Co-operating with the mixed banks, Belgian industry took a chance, and by seizing the opportunities offered, grew in a spectacular way and at the same time created growth possibilities for the new transport enterprises.[8] Obviously, the shifts in the top-50 group reflect this basic interdependence. The disruption caused by the First World War was a negative influence on the development of Belgian transport enterprises abroad. Moreover, the nationalization of the Belgian railway and tramway systems in 1926 eliminated the possibility of new transport enterprises. And, finally, the world crisis of the thirties caused serious financial difficulties for many large-scale Belgian enterprises and, in particular, for those which were active abroad. All these circumstances affected the composition of the group of the fifty biggest enterprises very strongly. Government policy and the strategy of the holding companies and large firms kept most shifts within the framework of heavy industry and associated sectors. Despite this conservative policy, enterprises from the new, more dynamic and expansive sectors entered the top-50 group. The process of transformation, however, was slow and too sluggish to modernize the industrial structure of the country in a fundamental and definite manner. The crisis of the seventies consequently hit the Belgian economy very hard. The data of 1974 undoubtedly show how far Belgian industry was from complete structural renovation. It remains a difficult but very real question to decide whether the present world crisis will accelerate the transition to modernization, or whether it will inaugurate a period of industrial stagnation and backwardness in Belgium.

[8] H. Van der Wee, 'Investment Strategy of Belgian Industrial Enterprise between 1830 and 1980 and its Influence on the Economic Development of Europe', in G. Verbeke (ed.), *Belgium and Europe: Proceedings of the International Francqui-colloquium. Brussels – Ghent, 12–14 November 1980* (Brussels, 1981), pp. 81–4.

13

'No bloody revolutions but for obstinate reactions'? British coalowners in their context, 1919–20[1]

BARRY SUPPLE

Few groups of businessmen have received such a bad press in the twentieth century as the British coalowners.[2] Hysterically individualistic, obstinate to a socially destructive degree, inhumane in their dealings with wages and with working and living conditions, above all reactionary in their attitudes to economic systems and technical or organizational change – their stereotyped characteristics have lost them the historical argument as surely as they sapped their public authority in all the propaganda battles which culminated in their expropriation in 1946.

Even if it were possible to envisage an attempt to resuscitate the coalowners' moral, political or economic standing, this would not be the place for such a herculean task. Rather, the purpose of this essay is to examine the context and content of the views propounded by the coalowners' representatives in the years immediately following the First World War, and especially in 1919–20 – a brief period of particularly illuminating revelation, when, according to the Secretary of the Mining Association of Great Britain (henceforth MAGB or Mining Association) 'the whole country was in a state of nerves ... [and] there were very many people who thought we were on the brink of social revolution'.[3] For, even though historians are aware of the circumstances which shaped

---

[1] Research for this essay was greatly facilitated by support from the National Coal Board, which is sponsoring a history of the British coal industry by various authors. I am also particularly grateful to Sonia Supple, Stephanie Tailby and Nick Tiratsoo, who helped considerably with ideas as well as with the more detailed aspects of empirical research. I alone am responsible for the conclusions.
[2] 'Coalowners' is the customary term for the leading owners and managers of colliery enterprises. The landowner who owned the mineral (and therefore the right to charge a royalty for its exploitation) was known as the royalty owner.
[3] W. A. Lee, in evidence to the 1926 Royal Commission on the Coal Trade (the Samuel Commission), II, Q. 5952.

the coalowners' economic attitudes, there is still an understandable tendency to present them as a coherent, almost spontaneous, ideology – divorced from economic reality or culpably inconsistent with the goals of other groups in society. In fact, however, as is generally the case, policy and argument in the coal industry were shaped by 'external' economic and historical realities, by political pressures and concepts of self-respect and group antipathy, by the dynamics of organization and representation.

Three general characteristics of British coalowners form the ultimate themes of this essay. First, they acted in accord with their own vision of economic and political 'reality' and were most of all resistant to any 'external' attempt to single them out for extraordinary treatment or economic penalty. Second, they encompassed a variety of circumstances and interests, for they were involved in an industry with hundreds of enterprises, thousands of production units, scores of different products and markets, and a multitude of technical and geological conditions. In such a situation there is always a tension between the shared and the contrasting experiences. Finally, the institutional structures fashioned to encompass and represent their interests were neither monolithic nor unchanging. Rather they reflected the divisions between, as well as the unity of, their constituents; and they evolved together with the evolution of the problems with which coalowners had to deal, and with their perceptions of the meanings of those problems.

I

To the world at large, the coalowners were represented by the MAGB. Yet the national organization was shaped by its federal structure: it was, historically, merely an occasional mouthpiece of district associations, circumscribed constitutionally and by economic and political circumstance. In 1912 the MAGB annual report listed twenty-three district (mostly county) associations, although these included some with their own constituent county members. Of course, some were much more important than others: on the eve of the First World War, those in Durham, Northumberland, Derbyshire, Leicestershire, Nottinghamshire, Monmouthshire and South Wales, and the four districts of Scotland accounted for some 80 per cent of British coal output.[4]

---

[4] Apart from the printed volumes of their annual reports (which include some committee minutes) and fragments of the Central Committee minutes from the 1940s, the records of the Mining Association do not appear to have survived. The surviving records of the various district coalowners' associations are more abundant. Thus, those of the Leicester-

These district associations were fiercely jealous of their independence, in large part because their circumstances and therefore interests were often distinctive – and could clash with each other and with any attempt to impose a uniform national policy with respect to the economics of the industry. Indeed, for sixty years after its foundation in 1854 the MAGB was almost exclusively concerned with legislative matters. Except when legislation was needed to enunciate broad principles (as happened with maximum hours of work underground and minimum rates of pay, just before the First World War) the MAGB was specifically not concerned with wages, prices, employment conditions, industrial relations or business arrangements. These were considered to be matters for determination at the district level – or even within the firm.

During the First World War, however, the autonomy of the district associations could not be maintained in its pristine form, since the actual business of coalmining came to be considered a national affair, involving state control of prices, distribution, wages and investment. Consequently, some degree of national consultation and a national 'view' were necessary. This situation continued after the war because the government maintained its financial control of the industry until the spring of 1921. But although, in 1920, the MAGB's constitution was centralized and its authority increased, much of the turbulence in coal's industrial relations in the 1920s can be attributed to the attempts of the MAGB to extricate itself from a decisive national role and to return the question of wages to the districts. Certainly, the owners never admitted that the system of wage determination created in 1917–18 (which involved industry-wide additions to the district base rates) and the associated pooling of the industry's profits (which enabled the government to meet the costs of the poorer or less efficient companies from the proceeds of the more efficient or better-placed collieries) were anything other than regrettable and inefficient aberrations. Nevertheless, in 1919–20 the continuance of government control, the pressure for organizational change in the industry, and the new economic situation, meant that even the MAGB could not hope to return immediately to the institutional patterns and postures of the more buoyant and entrepreneurially confident days of 1913.

shire Coal Owners' Association (henceforth LCOA) are in the County Record Office; those of the Monmouthshire and South Wales Coal Owners' Association (MSWCOA) in the National Library of Wales; those of the Scottish Coal Owners' Association (SCOA) in the University of Glasgow's archives; those of the South Derbyshire Coal Owners' Association (SDCOA) in the Derbyshire Record Office; and those of the West Yorkshire Coal Owners' Association (WYCOA) in Leeds University Library. Other useful collections are in the Durham and the Northumberland Record Offices.

II

During the war itself there had been relatively little discussion of the likelihood of economic and business change in the industry.[5] And most systematic attention seems to have been given to questions of labour relations – not surprisingly, in view of the new authority and confidence of the labour force. Even here, however, the owners' wartime response was not particularly far-seeing, although the district associations generally welcomed the Whitley Report and, as the war ended, the trade journal, the *Colliery Guardian*, extended a platitudinous welcome to the possibility that popular and political opinion might tame 'the virus of passionate class hatred' and 'the stiff-necked reactionary battling for the employers'.[6] More concretely, although with relatively little publicity, since October 1916 the MAGB's Parliamentary Committee had been considering the post-war coal trade, and especially the question of labour relations and wage determination.[7] In February 1919, coinciding with the political crisis that led to the creation of the Sankey Commission, the association circulated a consultative document – *A Suggested Scheme for the Reconstruction of the Coal Mining Industry* – to the various district associations.[8] This document contained two types of proposal, for labour relations and for marketing, although only the former, and less radical, survived serious consideration by the MAGB's members. Industrial relations, it argued, 'will require to be regulated on different lines from those which have existed in the past'. It therefore advocated the creation of consultative committees which, by providing detailed information about the collieries to the work-force, might introduce a new 'spirit of harmony and co-operation'. Further, it proposed that wages should be determined in relation to the performance of the industry in each district, by a division of surplus proceeds (after the deduction of basic minimum wages, capital charges and non-wage costs) between wages and profits in proportions to be determined within each district by separate negotiations.

The proposals for consultation were in themselves innocuous, although the miners had never been attracted by the idea that psychological reassurance could be divorced from a share in actual

---

[5] See the reports of the Coal Conservation Committee and the Board of Trade's departmental committee on the position of Britain's post-war coal trade: *Parliamentary Papers* (henceforth *PP*), *1917–18*, xvii; *PP*, *1918*, vii and xiii.

[6] *Colliery Guardian* (henceforth *CG*), 10 January 1919, p. 87; *ibid.*, 17 January 1919, p. 144.

[7] W. A. Lee, 'History of Organisation', in Mining Association of Great Britain, *Historical Review of the Coal Mining Industry* (London, 1926), p. 35.

[8] Three consecutive editions of this document are in the Scottish Record Office: CB6/2. The first is dated 15 February 1919.

management – and the coalowners, throughout the period of private ownership, were to remain adamant that neither pit committees nor any other form of consultation should entail the sharing of management control with the miners.[9] The proposal for district- and performance-based wage determination, on the other hand, although enforced from 1921, when the government abandoned its financial control of the industry, was intensely disliked by the miners (in the main because it precluded the possibility of 'pooling' profits on a national basis and thereby supporting wages in the less profitable districts). It was, in the event, the principal stumbling-block to harmonious labour relations throughout the 1920s.

However, although these proposals seem cautious and 'unprogressive' in the light of subsequent events, it seems as if the MAGB itself imagined that they represented a fairly radical departure. Moreover, discussion of the document was launched just as the government, bending under pressure from the miners' union, was moving towards a major inquiry into the industry – a situation which, in the words of Sir Adam Nimmo (a leading Scottish coalowner who wrote the introduction to the MAGB's consultative document), marked 'a distinct turning point in the industry'. 'We stand to-day facing a new order of things', he argued, 'we cannot go back to the past, even if we would.' Consistent with this view, the MAGB pamphlet proposed an extremely radical change in the industry's organization: the creation of a single corporation to market the industry's entire output of coal on behalf of the collieries. Of course, among the coalowners the idea that the salvation of the industry lay in the restraint of competition had a long pedigree. But the opposition of important groups of owners, especially in the exporting districts, where there was scepticism about the possibility of market control, was sufficiency strong to stifle any realistic discussion of marketing regulation until the miseries of the later 1920s persuaded a majority to experiment with cartel arrangements. Nevertheless, hopeless as the suggestion proved in 1919, such a proposal then did at least reflect the beginning of a new mood, a feeling that 'extreme individualism may have its drawbacks, and that private enterprise alone is powerless to obviate certain evils arising from unrestricted world competition'.[10] On the

---

[9] SCOA, UGD/161/1/5, 13 March 1919 and 18 April 1919. For the strength of the opposition to nationalization and joint control, see below.

[10] CG, 29 November 1919, p. 1139. Nimmo continued to be a strong advocate of selling arrangements for Scotland, which involved him in sharp disagreements with Wallace Thorneycroft. In the later 1920s, however, these former adversaries were to join forces in a successful proposal to the Scottish association for a scheme to co-ordinate sales and maintain prices.

other hand, although MAGB's recommendations might, indeed, have reflected a 'deep-seated belief that radical changes in organisation are inevitable',[11] they were pitched at an entirely different level of radicalism from that which suffused the atmosphere in which they came to be launched.

In January 1919 the Miner's Federation of Great Britain (henceforth the MFGB) submitted a claim for a 30 per cent increase in basic earnings, a reduction in underground working hours from eight to six, and public ownership of coal and coal-mines. To the *Colliery Guardian* the claim seemed a 'thunderbolt' – a 'flouting of economic values ... a creed that ignores the virtues of productivity and ends by destroying it for a set purpose'.[12] Ironically, the MFGB might well have agreed with at least part of this verdict, since its claim was quite explicitly based, not on the pre-war principle of securing wages which the industry might 'afford' to pay, but on 'social' criteria – the desire to secure an enhancement of living standards commensurate with the union's interpretation of the character and social significance of the miners' work. Social decency rather than economic possibility was the basis of their demands.

The claim, and the government's apprehensive response (which was conditioned by the miners' new confidence and power and by the general air of social dislocation and political unease in the spring of 1919), tugged the discussion of the industry's future into uncharted and unexpected waters. Confronted with widespread labour unrest, the government was obliged to make concessions to the most powerful union of all. It therefore agreed to establish a Royal Commission of inquiry chaired by a distinguished judge, Sir John Sankey, and on which the miners – through three officials of the MFGB and three other nominees from political sympathizers – had a 50 per cent representation.[13] The Sankey Commission was created by act of Parliament on 25 February 1919, and, under the threat of direct action by the miner's union, was committed to

---

[11] *Ibid.*, 21 February 1919, p. 431. The MAGB proposals to bring wages into line with profits and to create a system of consultation with greater access to information for the miners were officially announced on 21 February 1919. See *The Times*, 22 February 1919.

[12] *CG*, 24 January 1919, pp. 199–200. The editorial was somewhat provocatively entitled 'The Miners' Next Step' – an echo of the pre-war radicalism of the South Wales Unofficial Reform Committee.

[13] The original membership of the Sankey Commission was: the Chairman; three officials of the MFGB (Robert Smillie, Frank Hodges, Herbert Smith); three radicals nominated by the union (Sir Leo Chiozza Money, R. H. Tawney, Sidney Webb); three officials of the MAGB (R. W. Cooper, J. T. Forgie, Evan Williams); and three other businessmen nominated by the government (Arthur Balfour, Sir Arthur Duckham, Thomas Royden). For the subsequent stage of the inquiry Forgie and Royden were replaced by Sir Adam Nimmo and Sir Allan M. Smith.

producing an interim report on wages and hours by 20 March. It set about its task with enormous vigour and dramatic publicity; and the heated exchanges of its daily sittings in the King's Robing Room of the House of Lords, together with the ruthless and penetrating questioning of coalowners by the miners' representatives, made, and continue to make, an enormous impact. To their horrified surprise, the owners found themselves having to defend an entire economic system. The Commission, wrote Beatrice Webb on 12 March, had become 'a revolutionary tribunal' and its business 'a state trial of the coal owners and royalty owners culminating in the question "why not nationalise the industry?" ... The official evidence against the coal owners' administration of the mines has been overwhelming.'[14] Lloyd George himself argued that the Commission's hearings were 'arousing the social conscience in a way that no inquiry of modern times had succeeded in doing'.[15] And it came as no surprise (indeed, for some members of the government it came as a welcome safety-valve against extreme reaction from an otherwise frustrated miners' union) that, in their interim report, the most 'independent' opinion on the Commission (the Chairman and the three non-mining businessmen) recommended not merely a substantial increase in wages and a reduction in underground working hours but also a strict limit on profits and, more significantly, went sufficiently beyond the remit of the first stage of the inquiry as to pronounce on the basic issue of industrial organization (which the coalowners, in their political innocence, had imagined would be postponed until the second stage). Sankey's report argued that 'Even on the evidence already given, the present system of ownership and working in the coal industry stands condemned, and some other system must be substitute for it, either nationalisation or a method of unification by national purchase and/or by joint control.'[16]

The government was obliged to accept the report 'in the spirit and the

---

[14] *The Diaries of Beatrice Webb*, ed. M.I. Cole (London, 1952), pp. 152–3 (12 March 1919).

[15] House of Lords Record Office (henceforth HLRO), F/23/4/37: Lloyd George to Thomas Jones, 17 March 1919.

[16] The Sankey Commission's three separate interim reports are in *PP, 1919*, xi. The words quoted, and the recommendation for a limitation on profits, occurred in the report signed by the Chairman and the three 'independent' businessmen. The MFGB officials and their allies advocated nationalization unconditionally. The three coalowners confined their report to the issue of wages and hours (on the grounds that that was the remit of the first stage of the inquiry). All three reports advocated an increase in wages and a reduction in hours. (The 'independent' group recommended an extra 2s per shift and a reduction to seven hours; the MFGB group recommended a 30 per cent increase in wages and a six-hour shift, and the owners recommended an increase of 1s 6d and a seven-hour shift.)

letter' (although it was subsequently claimed that this commitment applied only to the recommendations for wages, hours and profits). A pay award of 2s per day for adults and 1s for boys was backdated to 9 January, while discussions with a view to limiting profits to 1s 2d per ton began in the spring, and the necessary legislation to reduce hours of work was passed on 15 August. The Commission's second stage–a more detailed and systematic examination of the organization and ownership of the industry–occupied about two months from 24 March. But the die had been cast in the first stage: the coalowners were faced with a new and alarming context for the discussion of their post-war world. Almost overnight, as the result of pressure from a major trade union at a time of social and political unrest, the central issue had become public ownership of the coal mines. At the same time, however, the *Colliery Guardian* felt that the coal trade itself bore much of the blame:

By refusing to organise itself on the common advantage, it not only has played into the hands of the enemy, but, by sacrificing an excellent chance of redeeming its character on business lines, has invited the very dubious alternative of nationalisation. For there can be no hesitation in saying, that we cannot go back to the old order of things, and it is only too true that there would be no bloody revolutions but for obstinate reactions.[17]

In the event, of course, the terminology of 'bloody revolutions' turned out to be altogether too apocalyptic to describe the events of 1919 (although not far removed from the occasional fears of the Cabinet). Yet the fact was that the year's vigorous and sustained controversies were related to far more fundamental questions than had been raised by the owners in the initial proposals. As the inquiry unwound, the owners were stunned and temporarily demoralized not merely because of the 'scandalous' interpretation placed upon its terms of reference,[18] but because of the unprecedentedly ruthless way in which the MAGB witnesses were pilloried and humiliated by the robust questions of the miners and the barbed sophistication of 'their socio-political abettors'.[19] Indeed, the adamant obstinacy with which the owners took stock of their position in late March undoubtedly derived from outrage at the pre-emption of the most contentious issue by the Chairman's apparently premature condemnation of the existing system of ownership. To the

[17] *CG*, 28 February 1919, p. 487.
[18] *Ibid.*, 23 May 1919, p. 1219.
[19] *Ibid.*, 21 March 1919, p. 663. In retrospect, R. H. Tawney, with an unaccustomed lack of modesty, said that 'Our opponents, though formidable people, were not skilled advocates. In fact, as far as mere dialectic was concerned, one could go through them like butter.' Quoted in Ross Terrill, *R. H. Tawney and His Times: Socialism as Fellowship* (London, 1973), p. 56.

Prime Minister, concerned above all with the immediate political crisis and the need to cool the miners' dangerous wrath, the Commission's continuance promised a flow of 'healing testimony'.[20] But to the owners it promised more anguished effort, more public wounds, and more destructiveness.

III

Not surprisingly, then, in late February, within days of Sir John Sankey's chilling verdict on their trusteeship, the MAGB and its constituent associations were preparing for more systematic fray. In London, the MAGB began a counter-attack in the general propaganda battle and on the specific fronts of wage increases and profit limitations.[21] In the provinces, the district associations were informed that, as a consequence of the first stage of the Commission's inquiry, the MAGB had withdrawn its scheme for the reconstruction of the industry and proposed to draw up a new one. In fact, in early April it seemed as if the MAGB, having discussed twenty drafts, could not agree on any – to the exasperation of observers otherwise sympathetic to their position.[22] And the *Colliery Guardian* pointed out that the owners needed to put their house in order very urgently, and that it might already be too late to counter public suspicion. (Indeed, immediately after the publication of Sankey's report both the *Colliery Guardian* and *The Times* had expressed regret that the coalowners on the Commission had not signed the report, even though it included such an outright condemnation of the existing system: 'No enlightened employer can regard the present system ... as anything other than unsatisfactory.')[23] And in the event the MAGB's official submission to the second stage of the inquiry followed the lines of the association's original discussion document in that it advocated district-based wage assessments and an institutionalized pattern of consultation.[24]

[20] HLRO, F/23/4/37: Lloyd George to Thomas Jones, 17 March 1919.
[21] Mining Association of Great Britain, printed reports for 1919 (henceforth, *MAGB, 1919*), pp. 90ff. (1 May 1919).
[22] *The Times*, 10 April 1919, p. 13d. The paper argued that if the owners entered the second stage of the Sankey inquiry without formulating definite proposals of their own, they would once again be thrown on the defensive, and appear simply negative. And if they let the argument against nationalization go by default, they would forfeit public sympathy.
[23] *CG*, 21 March 1919, p. 663; *The Times*, 21 March 1919, p. 11a. The *Colliery Guardian* subsequently retracted this criticism on the grounds that the owners had not been shown the draft until a matter of hours before publication: *CG*, 2 May 1919, p. 1026.
[24] Royal Commission on the Coal Industry (Sankey Commission), II: *PP, 1919*, XII, evidence of Baron Gainford of Headlam, 20 May 1919.

More significantly, the district associations were all consulted on the issue of joint control and nationalization, albeit with some heavy overt guidance from the national body – for the evidence and conclusions of the Sankey Commissions had persuaded the owners' leaders that there was an even greater danger than expropriation, namely an enforced participation in management by men whose skills, motives and commitment they did not trust. And to this they were 'violently opposed'.[25] Taking their cue from the national leadership, therefore, the various districts rejected both nationalization and joint control, and offered instead some form of consultation. One after the other they argued that if, nevertheless, they were obliged to make a choice, then they were determined that 'they shall absolutely refuse to agree to any scheme of joint control' and would instead opt for nationalization by outright purchase of their assets. Indeed, in the private discussions there was an air of profound resignation about the possibility of national ownership (and not a few hints that opposition to it was desirable as a means of enhancing the owners' bargaining position in the determination of any compensation). Thus, addressing the Monmouthshire and South Wales Coal Owners' Association, the formidable Evan Williams (shortly to be elected to a virtual life-time tenure of the MAGB's Presidency) argued that some alteration in structure was 'inevitable' and that 'there are certain owners who think it would be advisable to accept Nationalisation. There is, to an extent, an amount of justification for this, but it must be remembered that it is not in the Nation's interests, as well as the Owners' interests, that this should be resorted to.'[26]

Two days later, the leaders of the Scottish Coal Owners' Association agreed with their Chairman's assertion:

the Owners should tell the Government that in their view the Industry should remain as at present, and that the Owners were willing to co-operate with the Workmen and give them the information they desire, and that wages should be based on the results of the Industry. Further, they are willing to establish Pit Committees as Advisory Committees to consider questions which might arise at the Collieries with machinery to carry these questions right up to the Conciliation Board if necessary. These Committees, however, would not have the power to decide how the Collieries would be worked. If the Government decided that this was not acceptable and the only alternative was joint control or Nationalisation, then the Owners would recommend that Nationalisation should be carried out.[27]

[25] Thomas Jones, *Whitehall Diary*, 2 vols., ed. R. K. Middlemas, I (London, 1969), 83–4.
[26] MSWCOA, MG 14, 29 March 1919.
[27] SCOA, UGD/161/1/5, 31 March 1919.

Stimulated by pressure from the national association, but vehemently confirmed by the opinion of the districts, the owners as an interest group were beginning to formulate a firm and definitive opinion in March, and by late spring the MAGB's Central Committee (itself an executive body created under the stress of the Sankey inquiry) had laid down a fundamental principle

that any dual control is unworkable, and prejudicial to the safe and efficient carrying on of the collieries, and also an unjust interference with private property; and rather than that any dual control should be imposed upon them, [the owners] feel they are reluctantly driven to the conclusion that the only practical alternative left is for the State to purchase the collieries at their fair selling value, and to undertake the responsibility of the carrying on of the coal industry in such manner as the State may deem best.[28]

As far as the official consideration was concerned, this principle was to be exactly embodied in the MAGB's submission to the second stage of the Sankey inquiry, enunciated by Lord Gainford and destined to become as notorious among the owners' critics as Sir John Sankey's original condemnation was among the owners themselves: 'I am authorised to say, on behalf of the Mining Association, that if owners are not to be left complete executive control, they will decline to accept the responsibility of carrying on the industry, and though they regard nationalisation as disastrous to the country, they feel they would, in such event, be driven to the only alternative – nationalisation on fair terms.'[29]

This statement, and the tone of the association's response to public criticism of the industry and proposals for its restructuring, are normally interpreted as the reactions of a crass and selfish obstinacy, flowing from a determination to avoid compromise and to secure the status quo by denying any possibility of change short of a huge measure of dislocation. Certainly, the owners were aware that it would be impossible to run the industry without the help of those already engaged in its administration. Hence, by offering only the most extreme exchange, they may have hoped to preclude *any* change. Yet, even while they might not have been averse to such brinkmanship, the posture they adopted had a more rational economic aspect. To the owners, the idea that the miners' representatives might share in the management of the mines was not merely intrinsically (or 'ideologically') abhorrent. It also carried with it a genuine threat. For very little in their personal experience led them to believe that the miners would employ their new-found authority for any other purpose than to maximize short-run gains – wages and leisure – and

[28] *MAGB, 1919*, p. 90 (1 May 1919).
[29] *PP, 1919*, xii, evidence of Baron Gainford of Headlam.

222

therefore to diminish investment, productivity and profitability. To the coalowners, as to any other group of businessmen, the industry they ran represented an asset; and the suggestion that, without compensation, they should share its disposition with another group who would not be concerned with capital values (including the potential future flow of output and income) embodied in the industry, but who, rather, seemed to them to be motivated largely by an 'aggregated individualism'[30] was tantamount to the suggestion that they should co-operate in the drastic diminution of the value of their own property. And that was a suggestion made to no other major industry at the time.

For all these reasons, then, the owners ruled out joint control on what seemed to them severely 'practical', rather than simply 'ideological', grounds. At the same time, however, they were by no means sure that even without joint control their assets were safe from erosion by the activity of their disaffected work-force aided, perhaps, by an unthinking government. Meeting in May 1919, the MAGB listened to its President sketching an uncomfortable scenario: by July the higher wages and shorter hours proposed by Sankey and accepted by the government might (in the absence of a price increase) have eliminated all profits, and 'If that goes on for some considerable time, and nationalisation comes afterwards, I am afraid that the value of our collieries will be next to nothing.' In other words, the owners' attitude towards industrial policy was naturally conditioned by their estimate of how the labour force would respond to post-war circumstances (in this respect the record of labour productivity in the post-war months was hardly encouraging)[31] and, even more important, of how the government would react to the enormous political pressures on it. As the Chairman of the Scottish Owners' Association put it, if nationalization was the only alternative to joint control, 'the Owners desired to have Nationalisation now, rather than five years hence when the Collieries have been reduced to a ruinous condition'.[32] Very nice judgement was therefore called for at a time when the consensus among many informed observers seemed to be that nationalization, or something like it, was inevitable. In the districts, as in the MAGB's Central Committee, those who felt that public ownership was very likely would naturally conclude that the sooner it came – with the industry still relatively healthy and its asset values and likely compensation not yet sapped by years of prolonged strife and economic

---

[30] *CG*, 17 January 1919, p. 144.
[31] *MAGB, 1919*, p. 92 (1 May 1919); Hansard, *Parliamentary Debates* (henceforth *Hansard*), 26 November 1919, col. 1029.
[32] SCOA, UGD/161/1/5, 31 March 1919.

and structural dislocation – the better. In the enfeebled West Yorkshire field, for example, there were apparently many who positively wanted nationalization, simply because any feasible alternative seemed worse.[33]

Given all this, it was not surprising that, as controversy mounted in 1919, the suspicion grew in some minds that the MAGB's public position reflected a bargaining ploy and that a significant number of the coalowners actually agreed with Sir John Sankey that 'the present system of ownership and working stands condemned', but were reluctant to state this publicly for fear of damaging their future case for compensation in any negotiations with the government.[34] It was this possibility which led *The Times* to criticize the owners early in April for not being more active in making counter-proposals or attacking nationalization – a neglect which might lead to the suspicion that 'they are prepared for nationalisation in the assurance that the present House of Commons will secure for them generous terms of compensation'.[35]

IV

Whatever the logic of, or even the economic justification for, their position, however, the owners' response to the arguments for radical change contained serious weaknesses – first, because there remained the important question of public opinion, and, second, because the issue of nationalization was of general rather than purely sectional significance. In late June, but which time the MAGB had indeed stirred itself to more vigorous action, the *Colliery Guardian*, in an editorial entitled 'Take the Gloves Off', argued that the debate was not simply about coal: the owners 'merely occupy the front trench' in a battle which might mean that 'England will change hands'.[36] Hence, for the sake of others as well as themselves, the owners had to take a general stand against nationalization – which they did, with some vehemence, in their evidence to the second stage of the Sankey Commission's inquiry, as well as in their much more widespread public-relations activity[37] and, of course, in

[33] WYCOA, 25 March 1919.
[34] HLRO, F/30/3/33: Lloyd George to Bonar Law, 20 March 1919 (also in Public Record Office (henceforth PRO), CAB 23/9/18).
[35] *The Times*, 10 April 1919, p. 13d.
[36] *CG*, 27 June 1919, p. 1554. The occasion of this outburst was the publication of Sankey's second report, advocating nationalization of the industry. The report, the *Colliery Guardian* argued, showed no sign of tranquil judgement, but rather demonstrated the 'same passion for facile extemporisation and the same panicky trepidation that has marked the Government's attitude towards labour in recent months'.
[37] Although as late as May, to judge from heated exchanges at the West Yorkshire Coal Owners' Association on 12 May, it was felt by some that the government had prejudiced

their representatives' contribution to the Commission's final report, in which they otherwise supported such 'radical' proposals as the nationalization of mining royalties, the extension to local authorities of the power to market coal, the establishment of a Mines Department and the creation of an extensive network of consultative committees.[38]

On the other hand, the rest of the Commission (with the exception of two of the non-coalowning businessmen, who signed the MAGB's representatives' report) were much more radical. Sir John Sankey advocated nationalization as the only way of avoiding industrial-relations strife; the miners and their associates also proposed outright public ownership; and Sir Arthur Duckham suggested a scheme of regional mergers and combinations, on the boards of which the local miners would have direct representation. A (bare) majority of the Commission therefore favoured nationalization.

Many historians have doubted whether Lloyd George and his Cabinet ever really intended to take the possibility of nationalizing the mines seriously (in which case the Sankey Commission was merely a means of postponing a refusal until dangerous emotions had subsided). Yet this was certainly not the view of the coalowners at the time;[39] and throughout the summer of 1919 they were keenly active in the discussion of public ownership. Morover, the Cabinet discussions appeared to be serious enough, even though, as the need for decision approached, it became clear that the government appreciated the flagging intensity of the campaign for public ownership, and, while remaining willing to entertain the possibility of some drastic structural experiment, was unwilling to go all the way to state purchase. On 7 August, for example, there was an extensive Cabinet discussion of the principal issues, from which it emerged that, while some members imagined that nationalization might ultimately prove inevitable, something short of that was to be the immediate policy. Interestingly, Lord Gainford, who had been such a determined spokesman for the MAGB's unyielding stance before the Sankey Commission, at this stage submitted a proposal (apparently in his personal capacity) for a form of voluntary reorganization, which in some ways resembled the Duckham scheme.[40] On 18 August Lloyd George

private enterprise by encouraging disruption – and some participants in the discussion wanted outright nationalization.

[38] Two of the three independent businessmen (Smith and Balfour) joined the coalowners in signing one report.

[39] *CG*, 4 July 1919, p. 33 – a reference to a rumour that the late Coal Controller had prepared a plan for nationalization. The *Colliery Guardian* argued that the government needed to be saved from itself, and 'by the good sense of the public, to be protected from an ill-starred alliance with the Bolshevist adventurers'.

[40] The Gainford proposals did, however, suggest that a Ministry of Mines should

announced the government's rejection of nationalization and proposed instead the reorganization of the industry along the lines recommended by Duckham (although without continuing government oversight), with effective representation of the miners on the management boards of regional companies, as well as the nationalization of mining royalties, and an extended welfare scheme (including the provision of pit-head baths) to be financed by a levy on coal.

This announcement effectively sterilized serious discussion of major structural change in the coal industry. For the reorganization of the industry was immediately spurned by the miners' representatives, whose expectations had been raised so high and dashed so drastically. As a result, the owners had no immediate need to respond to a proposal for enforced reorganization, which officially they would have been bound to oppose – although in August the trade journal argued that 'the unification issue must be faced in the future' and that many owners would accept the Duckham plan, albeit unenthusiastically, since most enlightened owners knew that co-ordination was inevitable.[41] In the event, although the controversy about nationalization dragged on until the spring of 1920, the new and favourable wages and conditions gained by the miners (and augmented by a 20 per cent increase in basic wages in March 1920) seemed to take much of the impetus out of the rank-and-file campaign. Probably from the summer of 1919, certainly from the following winter, bread-and-butter gains dulled their appetites for the more exotic fare of structural reform.

As so often happened in the twentieth-century history of the coal industry, the principal factor determining the immediate outcome of political and economic controversy was less the apparent merits of the rival arguments than the single-minded, unyielding, even obdurate postures adopted by the principal controversialists. To the MAGB in 1919, the fears excited by what they took to be the opportunism and cowardice of the Lloyd George Coalition Government combined with their resentment as well as anxiety at the treatment meted out to them by Sankey Commission's inquiries. The result was not merely a tactical concentration on the blocking of proposals for an organizational

demarcate the large districts within which colliery companies would be encouraged to amalgamate. Miners and consumers would be represented on the boards. Llewelly Smith pointed out to the Cabinet: 'A year ago such a scheme would have been considered to be a very great concession in the direction of associating labour representatives with colliery management.' HLRO, F/188/1/4 (5 August 1919). For the Cabinet discussion of nationalization, see PRO, CAB 23/15/174ff.

[41] *CG*, 1 August 1919, p. 302. The journal advocated an experiment in amalgamation in one district.

experiment but a fierce reluctance to contemplate any compromise for fear of what it might smuggle into the industry. (In any case, the compromises which they were offered all seemed to involve them in costs and risks far in excess of those which other industries were asked to bear.) On the other side, the miners' union made a perfectly reasonable, although in the event erroneous, assumption that circumstances were favourable for a determined attempt to scale the peak of outright nationalization. It is, no doubt, fruitless to attempt to guess at the outcome if either or both parties (or even the government) had adopted a different attitude; but it certainly seems that the words of public discussion and official opinion did not preclude really quite far-reaching changes in organization if only the two protagonists could have been brought simultaneously to co-operate in them.[42] In fact, for much of 1919 nearly every informed observer had imagined that, in the new circumstances of post-war society, some degree of very radical change in structure and probably ownership in the coal industry was inevitable. In retrospect, the weakness of the argument for nationalization was that it derived from a naive view (well exemplified in Justice Sankey's own report) that nationalization would end industrial strife. On the other side, the strength of the owners' political position lay in the fact that they were the first group to assume that it might be possible to hold on and come through their political crisis without any substantial structural change at all and without a social upheaval – an attitude which occasionally worried and even exasperated their supporters,[43] but which was justified by events in both the short and medium runs.

V

Although the troubles of 1919 did not enforce any major organizational changes, they did have significant consequences for the coalowners and for the arena within which future discussion of the industry was to be carried out. On the one hand, the singling-out of coal-mining and coal-miners for special treatment obliged the MAGB both to mobilize itself with more determination and aggression and to undertake major

---

[42] HLRO, F/23/4/35: Thomas Jones to Lloyd George, 18 March 1919. Jones reported that Bonar Law 'was not really himself very frightened' at the prospect of nationalization and that Baldwin thought that it was 'inevitable'. Also see Arthur Shadwell, *Coal Mines and Nationalization* (London, 1919), pp. 30–2.

[43] Other industrialists as well as politicians resented the unyielding attitude of the coalowners. For arguments by leading members of the iron and steel inustry, rejecting the owners' 'purely negative policy' and advocating compulsory amalgamation, see PRO, MUN 5/207/1870/5 (17 February 1920).

reforms in its own representative structures and attitudes. On the other hand, as the issue of nationalization was put to one side, in a debate in which structural alternatives were precluded by the attitudes of the participants, so the economic problems of the coal industry – and particularly its precarious ability to provide a living for those who worked in it – were exposed to the uncompromising blasts of the market.

The first task of the owners was to come to terms with the government's acceptance of Sankey's recommendations for substantial improvements in hours and wages (with both of which the owners on the Commission had broadly agreed) and of his proposal that mining profits be limited to 1s 2d per ton (in part in order to pay the new wages) – a proposal the exact meaning of which was not immediately apparent, but which would undoubtedly mean the restriction of profits to a level lower than that allowed in 1918–19 and, it was argued by the owners, lower than that of the pre-war years.

The Sankey wage award was confirmed by the government immediately it was published, and was backdated to 9 January. Immediately, in the districts and in London, the owners protested that they were in no position to pay the extra wages and that the government, having ordered the increase and controlling the industry's finances, should assume the responsibility for its payment.[44] In official discussions, Sir Adam Nimmo demonstrated a confidence which had been lacking in the owners who had appeared as witnesses in the first stage of the Sankey hearings:

[He] very emphatically laid down that we should not pay this back pay and the 2s a day to all the [adult] workmen which had been awarded by the Government. It would have to be found by the Government, and not by the colliery owners, so long as the agreement that we have with the Coal Controller is still in existence. Only by the firm way in which Sir Adam put it did he bring the Government to book and obtain a promise to pay the back pay which has already been paid in nearly every case .... It was the Government's gift, and it was the Government's responsibility; therefore they have to find the money.[45]

In the event, however, as some of the more pessimistic owners predicted,[46] although the Coal Control did, indeed, advance money, its effective subsidy to the industry was to be confined solely to the element of back-pay, and it ultimately recovered advances made with respect to

[44] SDCOA, N9/B4, 13 April 1919.
[45] *MAGB, 1919*, p. 90.
[46] *Ibid.*, pp. 94–7.

the period from April to July 1919. (From July, the extra wages were to be covered by a substantial price increase.)[47]

The Sankey proposals for a limitation of profits in the coal industry posed a much more serious threat to the coalowners. For the suggested basis – an aggregate (not individual) limit of 1s 2d per ton – would mean a reduction of some 40 per cent on the standard (guaranteed) profits then in force. Such a change necessitated a change in the legislation embodying the existing financial agreement. But, although the MAGB entered into discussion with the government immediately after the recommendation, they were careful to reassure their membership (particularly in view of a successful mustering of forces against any voluntary agreement) that they utterly declined to co-operate in any new arrangement – which would therefore have to be enacted by, and argued out in, Parliament. At an MAGB meeting on 1 May 1919 Sir Clifford Cory, a South Wales owner who was vehemently opposed to any co-operation with the government, urged that the MAGB 'fight it out in Parliament' where, he held, 'the owning classes are more largely represented than they were in the last Parliament'. And he successfully introduced a motion prohibiting negotiations.[48]

Faced with the refusal of the MAGB to accept a voluntary agreement, the Cabinet was obliged to introduce its own legislation to secure profit limitation.[49] This it did in November 1919, to the accompaniment of a storm of protests and telegrams (orchestrated by the MAGB) from the various district associations, which 'strongly and indignantly'[50] protested against what they took to be the punitive action of a weak and confused government, selecting their industry for severe profit restriction at a time of rapid inflation and falling money values – wholesale prices had doubled between 1913 and March 1919, and had risen by about 30 per cent between March and late November.[51] In fact, it was clear that the Cabinet was extremely embarrassed at having to legislate for this purpose – solely because of a commitment given earlier in the year, at a

[47] PRO, POWE 26/51: 'History of Financial Control', n.d.? 1920. The government's subsidy for the Sankey award for the period 9 January to 1 April 1919 was £7 million.
[48] *MAGB, 1919*, pp. 93–113. Sir Clifford Cory also described the meetings between leading owners and the President of the Board of Trade in the House of Commons: *Hansard*, 11 December 1919, col. 1675.
[49] PRO, POWE 26/22: Memorandum by Coal Controller, 7 May 1919, points 6 and 7.
[50] *MAGB, 1920*, pp. 19–20; SDCOA, N9/B4, 18 November 1919. See also LCOA, 19D 55/1, 17 November 1919; MSWCOA, MG14, 18 November 1919 and 26 January 1919; WYCOA, 17 November 1919.
[51] J. A. Dowie, '1919–20 is in Need of Attention', *Economic History Review*, 2nd series, 28 (1975), 429–50.

time of potential social upheaval, in order to secure 'peace in the coalfields'.[52] Indeed, in a meeting with the MAGB on 14 November, Lloyd George and Bonar Law, while insisting that they were unable, for political and moral reasons, to go back on their pledge to accept Sankey's proposal for profit limitation (the MAGB leaders referred to it as 'an illegitimate child of the first sitting of the Commission' and as part of concessions extorted by the MFGB 'at the point of a bayonet'), nevertheless went out of their way to indicate that they would attempt to protect the colliery enterprises from any very drastic consequences for their total profits.[53] At the same time, however, it does seem as if the indignation of the owners was genuine – and, indeed, in some part justified: for, as they pointed out, the commitment was extracted as the price of social peace, which benefited the nation as a whole, yet it was the coalowners alone who were being asked to pay for it in the form a reduction of their profits.

In the event, however, the owners' cause was well served by the miners, who opposed the profit-limitation bill on the grounds that it was not associated with any adequate proposals for the future regulation of the industry. A relieved Cabinet thereupon withdrew the bill. At the same time, it still had to revise the financial arrangements for the control of the industry, which allowed export collieries to earn huge profits but obliged inland collieries to sell at artificially low domestic prices and left the Treasury committed to covering their loses – or any losses which might emerge from the industry's precarious future.[54] However, now that the threats of both nationalization and a Sankey-type restriction on profits were lifted, there seemed no obstacle to amicable discussions between the coalowners and the government (indeed, these had already begun in the middle of November); and the MAGB's negotiating team, which had originally consisted only of representatives of the politically powerful export districts (Evan Williams, Lord Gainford and Sir Adam Nimmo) was augmented for the purpose by two influential representatives of the inland districts. Discussions took place in December – February 1919–20 and covered not merely a new financial scheme (which came to be embodied in the Coal Mines (Emergency) Act of March 1920) but also the reform of the official framework of the industry by the Mining Industry Act of August 1920, which created the

[52] *Hansard*, 11 December 1919, col. 1668. The bill was withdrawn when it became clear that the miners, who felt that a more systematic form of control should be introduced, would not support it.
[53] Hobert House (National Coal Board) Library, P622 : 388: 'Deputation of the Coal Owners' Association to the Prime Minister' (14 November 1919).
[54] *Hansard*, 22 December 1919, cols. 967–70.

long-promised Ministry of Mines (albeit downgraded to a sub-department of the Board of Trade – the MAGB having helped dissuade the Cabinet from creating a separate Ministry), a welfare scheme, and a network of consultative committees which was never used since it was boycotted first by the MFGB and then (in 1921) by the MAGB.

By the MAGB's annual meeting in 1920, then, the President was able to congratulate his members on two successes: 'putting nationalization to sleep' and 'avoiding the financial proposals of the [Sankey] Report'.[55] How far these were due to the MAGB's efforts is not very clear. But what is certain is that the experience of the threatening political atmosphere of the spring of 1919 produced an enduring transformation of institutions and outlook among the coalowners. This response to crisis involved two related developments: the unprecedented use of systematic publicity and propaganda to present the owners' case to the public and the politicians; and the reorganization of the representative institutions so as to formulate that case and to act with coherence and decision.

Taken aback by the effectiveness of the miners' publicity ('We did not thoroughly understand the game', said one leading MAGB officer in May, 'but we are now beginning to learn it'), the MAGB immediately created a Propaganda Committee, which met daily, and appointed a Director of Propaganda, Philip Gee (who floated the Coal Association in the third week of April). The activities of the Propaganda Committee were financed by an initial levy on members of £1 per 10,000 tons of output (in July 1919 there was a further levy of £11 5s per 50,000 tons, which, it was said, would not pass through the association's accounts). Clearly, the MAGB was stirred by resentment at its public treatment, by grudging admiration for the union's much more effective use of the press and publicity, and even more by a sense that it had become vital to present its case more systematically and more professionally. The association's new publicity machine went into high gear very quickly – especially on the question of nationalization. Local propaganda committees were stimulated into being and activity; newspaper articles and talks were arranged and disseminated; 1.5 million pamphlets were circulated; and, in a particularly effective move, the Propaganda Committee organized a memorial opposing nationalization and secured some 300 signatures from MPs. This was widely held to have had a significant effect on the Cabinet's deliberations in July. In November – when the threat of public ownership had receded, but the need to reorganize and strengthen the MAGB itself was apparent – it was decided to establish

[55] *MAGB, 1920*, p. 57.

the Propaganda Committee on a permanent basis and to affiliate to it five or six district propaganda committees.[56]

The second, and related, development was the restructuring of the association. This reorganization was very far-reaching, involving as it did the centralization and strengthening of the MAGB's decision- and policy-making functions. Again, the immediate stimulus was the shock of Sir John Sankey's report. On the next day (21 March) the MAGB appointed a Central Committee to oversee future proceedings in a manner impossible for the huge and unwieldy Executive Council, and in June, when it seemed unlikely that the Sankey Commission would go beyond its second stage, the Executive Council nevertheless unanimously decided to continue the Central Committee in existence 'to sweep up all the debris that has been caused, or would be caused, by the Commission'.[57] This new executive body was to become the core of the reformed permanent structure.

Although, superficially, the passage from the old, loosely federated form to the new, more centralized, even authoritarian structure was relatively smooth, there were signs that the conventional independence and distinctiveness of the various districts was resistant to all but the most extreme emergency (which the Sankey Commission and the government's subsequent legislative intentions were taken to be). Cohesion therefore depended in part upon persuasive appeals to solidarity.

That cohesion was, of course, more than a question of a new committee with new powers. On 6 November 1919 Evan Williams pointed out to the Executive Council that the MAGB's constitution had to be brought into line with the changes in the association's role which had been induced by the growth of government intervention since 1914. 'There could be no doubt at all', he argued, 'that some central organization was absolutely necessary in the coal trade of the country, and particularly necessary in the immediate future.' What he, and other MAGB officials, had in mind was the creation of a permanent London secretariat with a full-time staff (itself an innovation, since the MAGB had traditionally been run by part-time officials), and the amendment of the constitution to enable the association 'to deal with all questions arising in the industry which were of common interest to the industry'.

---

[56] *MAGB, 1919*, p. 115; *MAGB, 1920*, pp. 21–3, 58; Gainford Papers (Nuffield College, Oxford), Wallace Thorneycroft to Lord Gainford, 10 September 1919. Local responses to the need to establish propaganda committees are in SDCOA, N9/B4, 3 April 1919; WYCOA, 29 April 1919 and 2 July 1919.
[57] *MAGB, 1920*, p. 14.

A new constitution was formally adopted in April 1920. Henceforth, membership was to be confined to district associations (previously, individual coalowners could also be members). Extensive powers were assumed and the earlier limiting reference to a role in relation to parliamentary and government proceedings was dropped: the revised rules specified new areas of responsibility for the collection and dissemination of statistics and other information, for propaganda and for the encouragement of research and scientific work. Provision was made for a full-time staff and a range of elected officers. The Executive Council was to have four standing committees: a Central Committee, a Parliamentary Committee, a Finance Committee, and a Propaganda and Statistical Committee.[58] Confirming the new needs and responsibilities, the Presidency became (albeit informally) a more important and powerful office: Evan Williams was re-elected after his first two-year term of office in 1921, and his *de facto* full-time status was recognized by a generous honorarium of £5,000 (to be repeated in later years). Moreover, Williams, whose dominating presence was felt in the politics of the coal industry throughout the inter-war years, was regularly re-elected until his retirement in 1944.

What had happened, therefore, was that, under the stress of economic change and government intervention during the war and the immediate post-war period, the coalowners had felt the need for a closer and more powerful form of association. Although, for the MAGB, the crucial task had been to deal with wages on a national level, the incentive to close ranks and strengthen defences was also felt in the districts. In Scotland, for example, the united district association (there were four county-based associations which combined for many purposes) formed its own committee to consider the industry's future, established a statistical committee and department, and made sufficient use of its President to award him, too, a regular honorarium.[59] Comparable developments took place in other districts. Indeed, the trend towards association and the presentation of a public face was exemplified throughout the economy – not merely in other industries, but also among employers as a whole: the Federation of British Industries was formed in 1917, the National Confederation of Employers' Organizations in 1919. (A similar trend was at work among the unions: in 1918 the MFGB decided to

---

[58] *MAGB, 1920*, pp. 52–5 (20 June and 6 November 1919). The new constitution is in *MAGB, 1921*, pp. 140–50. It specifically precluded the MAGB from dealing with questions relating to local wages or conditions of employment unless requested by the relevant district association.
[59] SCOA, 161/1/4, 11 December 1917, 16 December 1918, 22 December 1919; SCOA, 161/1/5, 24 April and 19 May 1920.

introduce a greater degree of centralization and permanence into its affairs and therefore established a permanent London headquarters and decided that its two senior officials – the President and the Secretary – should henceforth be full-time officials.)

VI

The abandonment of the campaign for nationalization, the new laws providing for government control, and the creation in the spring of 1920 of a more coherent, unified and confident national trade association of coalowners marked the end of the initial post-war crisis of political economy in the coal industry. But even though the issues which had been largely responsible for the reform of the MAGB's structure – the likelihood of nationalization, the extension of government intervention in matters of prices and profits, the national determination of wages levels – were to abate in the years that followed, the association, from the viewpoint of its members, was not the less necessary. For, as the government, denied (or unwilling to choose) the option of major structural reform of the coal industry, with a substantial degree of public ownership, moved towards the only alternative it could envisage (decontrol of the industry), those involved in the production of coal were obliged to confront the basic economic conditions of the industry and the issues that had been submerged in the drama of 1919: productivity, costs, the sources of wages and profits, the allocation of the proceeds of coal production.

It is, of course, customary to point to the callous obstinacy of the owners, especially in 1921 and 1926, in the face of very low wages and of the fruitless humanitarian appeals of others. Certainly, there is a case to answer. Yet as far as the level and system of wages were concerned it is as well to remember two points. First, in spite of its greater strengthening, the MAGB still had only a tenuous role in relation to wage bargaining (and there is no doubt that its members would not have co-operated if it had tried to exercise any more positive policy). It was, in this respect, utterly dependent, in practice as well as constitutionally, on the willingness of the districts to allow it to deal on their behalf. And although the notorious refusal of the MAGB to continue discussions with the government at a critical stage in negotiations in September 1926 (on the grounds that its members had withdrawn from it the right to negotiate on wages) was in fact stage-managed for the purpose, it also undoubtedly reflected an important political reality. Second, and perhaps more important, the MAGB's strength had been designed to protect the interests of all its members. But those interests were, at some levels, quite diverse. Coalowners were united – as the miners were united – as much by what they collectively opposed as by what they collectively wished to bring about. What they were understandably unhappy about was the prospect of having their interests merged if that merger involved them, or some of them, in paying for other people's policies. And the fact was that both the solution of the government's crisis and the proposed national pooling of profits in order to meet the social needs of the miners and to satisfy the moral aspirations of the nation at large, were to be paid for by the owners – just as, in 1919, it was they on the whole who were expected to pay for the joint control which was to solve the industry's social and political problems.

Of course, much of this argument is contentious. But it is certainly true that in the wages crises of the 1920s, as in the nationalization crisis of 1919, the owners were called upon to give up resources, or claims to future resources, to an extent and in a manner not expected of any other industry. Yet, whatever satisfaction they may have derived while concentrating their attention on the immediate issue of wages, their attitude towards the possible alternatives to low wages or longer hours was much more questionable. Here, indeed, they do seem to have shown a substantial lack of imagination. But even if, in the longer run, it took the force of economic and political circumstances to oblige the coalowners to accept alternative strategies (selling organizations to maintain prices and amalgamations to secure the economies of scale), in the years immediately after the First World War their assessment of the industry's prospects and of their own economic position was not obviously irrational. The line they took on the social aspects of industrial policy, or on the prospects for structural change which served the reasonable purpose of defending their economic position against what they took to be arbitrary depredations, no doubt eroded their political and moral capital in ways which were ultimately to prove costly. And the aggravation of industrial relations was clearly a factor leading to ultimate nationalization. But in the circumstances of 1919–20 it was not easy to see what other options were open to them. Even from broader viewpoints than their own rather sectional one, there were very few realistic alternative scenarios. Nearly every public proposal involved the coalowners paying a substantial voluntary or obligatory tax to purchase industrial harmony by arrangements which subsequent events have shown to have had little chance of success. In defending themselves against moral and political pressure, they undoubtedly made a poor, even distasteful, impression. But their response was by no means ill-conceived in terms of economic reality or even of equity of treatment in comparison with other tax-paying groups. And it was certainly as much a pragmatic as a dogmatically obstinate reaction to unprecedented events and political pressures.

14

French oil policy, 1917–30: the interaction between state and private interests*

R. W. FERRIER

Introduction

The role of oil in the contemporary international economy is no less prominent – and perhaps even more decisive – than that formerly played by spices, salt, silk, wool, cotton, fats, coal or minerals. The commercial exploits of Venice and Genoa, the Iberian states and the Dutch, English and French companies round the world manifested many motives of personal enterprise and government opportunism. Changing balances of power, technical innovation and the accelerating pace of communications have affected business methods, and new social attitudes have altered political relations, but the incentive of profit and the responsibilities of governments remain essential aspects of human activity. The interaction of these elements and the increasing exploitation of natural resources present individuals and states with challenging opportunities for self-advancement and national prosperity as well as with difficult problems of reconciling divergent interests. Such issues have also been raised by the emergence of the oil industry in the late nineteenth century, and French experience provides a pertinent example. Diplomacy was no more immune from economic realities than business was exempt from the impact of political activities.

The commercial discovery of oil in 1859 has transformed the modes of transportation and added a new factor to the energy equation. Moreover, as a result of the introduction of mechanized warfare in the First World War, oil acquired strategic implications of no less importance in the

* In the compilation of this essay I am grateful to the archivists of the French Foreign Ministry and Finance Ministry, the Keeper and staff of the Public Record Office, Mr Hans Gabriëls of Royal Dutch-Shell and my colleagues, Julian Bowden and Pamela Tansey.

237

sphere of international relations. French business, although possessing a small and technically competent shale oil industry in Alsace, was relatively slow to appreciate the potential of oil, though its industrialists early recognized the importance of the automobile.[1] Whilst American, German, English and Dutch oil interests established a series of port installations and inland depots in Europe, French supplies, sheltering behind tariff barriers, were distributed by an association of some twenty refining distributors.

By 1900 most French oil imports were of crude oil from the United States requiring the simplest process of refining in France. Within a few years almost all imports, brought in mainly by Standard Oil (NJ) through Marseilles or up the Seine, were of finished products masquerading as crude oil on a dubious specification formula to take advantage of the lower tariffs levied on crude oil, supposedly to protect the local refining industry.[2] By 1903 much comment condemned a small number of industrialists, who had created 'un véritable monopole' from which they were able to make considerable fortunes.[3] The idea of 'un monopole de l'Etat' was raised, but it was not possible to find an acceptable balance between the profits which the state might be expected to make and the costs which it would incur. Unlike the state tobacco and match monopolies, which conferred a considerable advantage on the government because of the low costs of raw materials and manufacturing in relation to the sales price, comparable profits could not be expected from a state oil monopoly. Besides, the government of the time had neither the expertise not the personnel to take charge of importing, refining, distributing and selling. It was not thought reasonable for it to negotiate for supplies with American companies and thus involve itself in a constant clash of conflicting interests.[4]

Nevertheless, although concern remained and there were more debates in the National Assembly in 1904 and 1906, the political climate was not favourable to such adventurous initiatives. Raymond Poincaré, Minister of Finance, declared on 12 July 1906 that 'l'Etat est moins bon industriel et moins bon commerçant que les particuliers, les frais généraux sont

---

[1] On the early French oil industry see Pierre M. Edmond Schmitz, *L'Epopée du pétrole* (Paris, 1947), and on the automobile industry see James M. Laux, *In First Gear: The French Automobile Industry to 1919* (Liverpool, 1976) and P. Fridenson, *Histoire des usines Renault* (Paris, 1972).

[2] See Schmitz, *L'Epopée du pétrole*.

[3] Ministère des Finances (MF) B 34034 (formerly F³⁰ 4091), 'Note sur un project de monopolisation du pétrole au profit de l'état', 3 January 1903.

[4] *Ibid.*, 'Note concernant la monopolisation du raffinage des pétroles', July 1906; *ibid.*, Marty to Poincaré, 26 July 1906.

proportionellement plus élevés que ceux de l'industrie privée, son personnel d'employés et d'ouvriers lui coûte plus cher sans fournir la même somme de travail; enfin les règles d'administration et de comptabilité auxquelles il est soumis entravent ses opérations et arrêtent l'initiative de ses agents'.[5] Because oil was the lighting of the poor, the government would have had difficulty in raising prices, and there was the danger that a permanent budgetary deficit would be created. Furthermore, as a result of some competitive pressure and of increasing consumption, which doubled between 1901 and 1905, prices fell, so a state monopoly was not considered to be justified.[6] Liberal rather than socialist principles prevailed and the trade associations were too strong. Private enterprise was the motor of progress. Civilisation rested on freedom and individual initiative. 'The essence of socialism', wrote Paul Leroy-Beaulieu, protagonist of the market economy, in 1891, 'consists in despoiling the individual of part of the functions which naturally belong to him in order to confer them upon the state.'[7]

Yet in Romania, for example, Vintila Bratianu, Liberal politician, proclaimed his nationalization policy in 1907 to protect national interests against foreign encroachments. In collaboration with Constantin Halaceanu, he published in 1911 *Politica de stat în industria petrolului,* the first study of economic nationalism in relation to the development of oil resources.[8] In Germany too, in 1908 and later, proposals were floated for a state monopoly to eliminate the predominant influence which Standard Oil (NJ) exerted on the German petroleum market, but in this case Royal Dutch-Shell could be detected stirring the troubled waters for its own advantage.[9] In France, although 85 per cent of supplies came from the United States, the impulse for monopoly was political rather than national. In 1914 the issue was raised again by M. de Monzie, who

---

[5] *Ibid.*, 'Monopole des petroles', n.d.
[6] See reminiscences of the French oil industry, by M. Léon Martin, 'Origines de l'industrie du pétrole en France et son développement' (18 April 1942) and M. Henri Bavière, 'Les Etapes du développement de l'industrie du pétrole en France 1860–1940' (6 March, 1943), published by the Association Française des Techniciens du Pétrole. I am grateful to the Association for making these papers available to me.
[7] Paul Leroy-Beaulieu, *The Modern State in Relation to Society and the Individual* (London, 1891), p. 158, quoted in Richard F. Kuisel, *Capitalism and the State in Modern France* (Cambridge, 1981), p. 7.
[8] Maurice Pearton, *Oil and the Romanian State* (Oxford, 1971), pp. 62–8.
[9] F. C. Gerretson, *History of the Royal Dutch,* 4 vols. (Leiden, 1958), III, 64–6; Ralph W. Hidy and Muriel E. Hidy, *History of the Standard Oil Company (New Jersey): Pioneering in Big Business 1882–1911* (New York, 1955), pp. 563–71, 578–9, and George Sweet Gibb and Evelyn H. Knowlton, *History of the Standard Oil Company (New Jersey): The Resurgent Years, 1911–1927* (New York, 1956), pp. 203–20. MF B 34034 (F^{30} 4091), Lefaivre to Pichon, 28 February 1908.

proposed a modified form of state monopoly related to imports of crude oil and to refinery activities.[10] More relevant economically, this scheme was no more. acceptable politically. France, therefore, entered the war with a vulnerable oil industry unduly dependent on American sources. In comparison with its major enemy it was technically inefficient in refining operations and possessed inadequate distribution facilities.

The impact of the First World War

On the outbreak of war, oil consumption was some 400,000 tonnes annually and stocks were 77,500 tonnes. The government immediately requisitioned all petroleum supplies, but on 6 September it relaxed its controls.[11] For a couple of years these arrangements seemed satisfactory, for hostilities were distinguished by immobility rather than by activity. Yet the growing use of aviation and of motorized transport, as well as the increasing success of the German submarine offensive in reducing supplies, led early in 1917 to the first signs of a crisis. Henry Bérenger, rapporteur of the Senate Army Committee and an advocate of fuel oil for the French navy, remarked in March on a deteriorating situation. On 4 May he warned of a transportation crisis, of the deficiencies of the distribution facilities, of the desirability of improved research into petroleum products and of the need for better departmental co-ordination in petroleum affairs.[12]

Appropriately on 14 July the government constituted a Comité Général du Pétrole, appointed Bérenger as its Chairman and agreed to inter-allied conferences to coordinate supply and shipping arrangements. His terms of reference were extensive, advisory rather than executive.[13] Some improvement was made by rationing and by instituting the registration of vehicles. On 7 November Bérenger informed Paul Painlevé, Prime Minister and Minister of War, that petroleum requirements had reached 45,000 tonnes of motor spirit and 30,000 tonnes of kerosene per month and an estimated 10,000 tonnes of aviation spirit.[14]

---

[10] MF B 34034 (F^{30} 4091), on the Proposition de loi No. 3382 of M. de Monzie, 9 February 1914.

[11] Ministère des Affaires Etrangères (AE) Y International, vol. 193, de Valleuil, Inspector of Finance, Note, 15 February 1919. Also contains information on the working of the Petroleum Consortium.

[12] AE Y International, vol. 192, Bérenger, 'Note au sujet de l'organisation du ravitaillement de l'essence en France', 4 May 1917.

[13] Ibid., Senate, 'Rapport fait à la Commission de l'Armée sur le ravitaillement de la France en pétrole, essence, huiles lourdes et huiles à graisser', by Bérenger, 11 December 1917, p. 11.

[14] Ibid., Bérenger to Painlevé, 7 November 1917.

By the end of the month the Chambre Syndicale de l'Industrie du Pétrole admitted dramatically that within three months stocks would no longer exist.[15]

At the instigation of Georges Clemenceau, who had become Prime Minister and Minister of War on 16 November, Bérenger was empowered to devise the appropriate measures through his committee. On 11 December he reported on the impending paralysis of the army. France, he declared, was dependent on its allies for petroleum products and transportation. He advocated the formation of an organization similar to the British Petroleum Executive. Bérenger proposed a central purchasing agency. Critical of the deplorable state of the French petroleum industry, he had no scruples about being interventionist in oil affairs. He proposed a scientifically based refining industry and called upon the government to take the appropriate action.[16]

Clemenceau attended a meeting of the committee three days later and pledged his complete support for further restrictions on oil consumption and for energetic measures for obtaining more tanker tonnage, the crux of the crisis. Bérenger drafted the note in which Clemenceau requested from President Wilson the immediate despatch of 100,000 tonnes of petroleum supplies, writing ominously: 'Si les Alliés ne veulent pas perdre la guerre, il faut que la France combattante, à l'heure du suprême choc germanique, possède l'essence aussi nécessaire que le sang dans les batailles de demain.'[17] The appeal was rapidly and effectively answered. The events of 1917 made a return to the pre-war situation unlikely. Indeed Calouste Gulbenkian remarked in January 1918 that they provided the pretext for direct government action in the direction of a monopoly.[18] Initially this was exercised through the formation of a Consortium Pétrolier Français, an organization similar to others created during the war for imported materials. Hardly radical in intent, for distribution was unaffected, its creation was, nevertheless, bitterly resisted by members of the French oil industry until final agreement was reached on 29 March 1918.[19] The following companies were involved: Fenaille et Despeaux

[15] MF B 32410 (F[30] 1506), Chambre Syndicale de l'Industrie du Pétrole to Minister of Supply, 5 December 1917, in Senate Report of 11 December 1917.

[16] *Ibid.*, Senate, 'Rapport fait à la Commission de l'Armée sur le ravitaillement de la France en pétrole, essence, huiles lourdes et huiles à graisser', by Bérenger, 11 December 1917.

[17] *Ibid.*, Senate, 'Rapport fait à la Commission de l'Armée sur le ravitaillement de la France en pétrole et essence', by Bérenger, 11 January 1918.

[18] 'Ce consortium n'est qu'un acheminement vers le Monopole et à la première occasion le Gouvernement fera main basse sous la forme d'une régie', Gulbenkian to Deterding, 27 January 1918; quoted in F. C. Gerretson, *Geschiedenis der 'Koninklijke'* (Baarn, 1973), 5 vols., v, 48.

[19] MF B 32410 (F[30] 1506); *ibid.*, 'Contrat relatif à la création d'un consortium pétrolier Français', 29 March 1918, and 'Accord de liquidation', 30 April 1921.

(15.75 per cent), Desmarais Frères (15.75 per cent), Les Fils de A. Deutsch (15.75 per cent), Cie Industrielle des Pétroles (12.87 per cent), Raffinerie du Midi (11.68 per cent), Ste. Lille, Bonnières et Colombes (8.42 per cent), Paix et Compagnie (7.46 per cent), G. Lesieur et ses Fils (4.28 per cent), Cie Générale des Pétroles (4.76 per cent) and Raffinerie de Pétrole du Nord (3.28 per cent).

La politique française du pétrole

(a) The proposals of Henri Bérenger

The petroleum crisis of the war deeply disturbed Bérenger. It was evident, he reported to Clemenceau, that France could not live without oil, any more than without coal. He affirmed 'la nécessité d'une politique pétrolifère française'.[20] After attending a highly euphoric meeting of the Inter-Allied Petroleum Conference in London, 16–23 November 1918, Bérenger was more than ever convinced of the appropriateness of his policy. What, then, was its practical basis? Bérenger had two principal objectives. Firstly he informed Walter Long, the First Lord of the Admiralty, who was in charge of petroleum affairs, that he wished to prolong Anglo-French wartime co-operation and to concentrate on 'l'exploitation en commun de diverses sources de production pétrolifère'.[21] This was the ambitious, if not ambivalent, programme which culminated in the Treaty of San Remo.

The second objective was less comprehensive, but curiously flawed. He recognized that the nature of the international petroleum industry, with its competitive groups and struggles for market ascendancy, could not be ignored, but he reached a short-sighted conclusion. Given the weak position of France, he argued for relying on Royal Dutch-Shell to take advantage of its industrial experience, financial strength, technical capacity and commercial knowledge.[22] Aware of the vital American petroleum assistance which France received in the decisive last phase of the war, he must have realized that this discrimination would antagonize American interests, if not incur their enmity. It even seemed to

---

[20] AE Y International, vol. 192, Bérenger, 'Rapport secret sur la politique française du pétrole et la paix', 5 November 1918.

[21] Ibid., 'Note sur la politique française du pétrole et la paix', Bérenger to Clemenceau, 29 November 1918; see also PRO FO 368/2095, Report of a meeting of the Inter-Allied Petroleum Conference, Paris, 17 December 1918, enclosed in Cadman to Foreign Office, 6 January 1919; for meetings of the Inter-Allied Petroleum Conference see PRO POWE 33/8.

[22] AE Y International, vol. 192, 'Note sur la politique française du pétrole et la paix', Bérenger to Clemenceau, 29 November 1918.

contradict his professions of an independent oil policy. Bérenger's enthusiasm may have distracted him from his inconsistency in placing so much reliance on an association with Royal Dutch-Shell. Henri Deterding, Managing Director of Royal Dutch-Shell, welcomed the idea and, desirous of French support in the Middle East and Asia, was ready to assist in 'la réalisation de notre politique pétrolifère'. Deterding was prepared to participate in a French company which would be responsible for the different interests allocated to France in the various oil-producing regions.[23] For Deterding it was more than an insurance policy against his rival competitors and the ambiguities of his relations with the British government; rather it provided the opportunity for an ambitious commercial coup.

Bérenger was naive, perhaps easily convinced by the persuasive advice of his friend, Calouste Gulbenkian, the Royal Dutch-Shell representative in Paris. Gulbenkian asserted that 'what I had at heart was to render a great service to France in the matter of creating a sound oil policy and economics'. He was scathing about the French oil industry, which he described as 'a monopolistic association of grocers'. He believed that he was 'rendering practical services to the French State and at the same time I was pushing ahead the interests of the Companies I was representing'. These apparently contradictory tendencies could be reconciled by providing the French with 'a direct source of supply'.[24] Bérenger wanted more than marketing arrangements; he desired French control over the sources of supply. It is in this context that the German shareholding in the Turkish Petroleum Company became the trump card in the French oil hand.

(b) The road to San Remo

Bérenger, in agreement with Clémenceau and Pichon, the Foreign Minister, communicated his proposals on 6 December to Paul Cambon, French Ambassador in London. The most significant suggestion concerned the shareholding of the Deutsche Bank in the Turkish Petroleum Company, which was to be reassigned to Royal Dutch-Shell, who would make it available to France. Joint construction of pipelines was envisaged.[25] Pichon himself eleven days later commended the proposals to the ambassador, acknowledging that:

---

[23] *Ibid.*
[24] Mémoires of Calouste Sarkis Gulbenkian (typescript), pp. 17, 19 and 20.
[25] AE Y International, vol. 192, 'Note relative à la politique française du pétrole et la paix', Bérenger to Cambon, 6 December 1918.

une entente de ce genre entre la France et l'Angleterre relèverait du système d'arrangements internationaux qui prévaudra après cette guerre pour régir plus ou moins directement la répartition dans le monde des grands produits naturels nécessaires à la vie économique de chaque nation. Elle serait en tout cas dès maintenant une des meilleures applications de la politique d'entraide et de collaboration interalliées.[26]

This was a very optimistic declaration. Other French officials expressed pessimism that the British would not only supplant the French in the Middle East but also deprive them of access to oil in the area.[27] In accordance with his instructions, M. A. de Fleuriau, chargé d'affaires. proposed to Arthur Balfour, the Foreign Secretary, on 6 January 1919, that the two governments should agree an oil policy together. France was determined not merely to receive supplies of petroleum products but to control the sources of oil.[28] The British government was unable to respond positively, but a Foreign Office official dismissed the French claim that they should be given the whole share of the Deutsche Bank in the Turkish Petroleum Company as being 'of course quite intenable'.[29] Just as in France there were different views between the diplomats and the oil protagonists, so was it in the United Kingdom.

Moreover the Harcourt Committee, set up in May 1918 by the British government and composed of officials of different departments and others, was then trying to formulate a government oil policy, concentrating at first on associating Royal Dutch-Shell more closely with British objectives.[30] Deterding was reluctant to see his political independence compromised except on terms which would guarantee his commercial freedom. He was therefore manoeuvring for the removal of the government shareholding in the Anglo-Persian Oil Company, against which he had long objected. The deliberations of the Harcourt Committee went on in a despairing, protracted and ineffectual fashion until the end of December. In principle there was agreement that the Royal Dutch-Shell shareholding could be increased by the allocation to it of the sequestered Deutsche Bank shareholding 'provided they made themselves permanently British'.

It seems that Sir John Cadman, Director of the Petroleum Executive, was the first, doubtless as a result of his earlier conversations with

---

[26] *Ibid.*, Pichon to Cambon, 17 December 1918.
[27] *Ibid.*, for example Note of Jean Gout, 26 December 1918.
[28] *Ibid.*, de Fleuriau to Balfour, 6 January 1919.
[29] PRO FO 368/2095, Kidston minute, 6 January 1919, supported by Lord Curzon, Foreign Secretary. The British government, apart from the Petroleum Executive, was generally unprepared for the French initiative.
[30] On the Harcourt Committee see R. W. Ferrier, *The History of The British Petroleum Company*, vol. I, *The Developing Years 1901–1932* (Cambridge, 1982), pp. 248–60.

Bérenger in November and December, to suggest to the committee that it might be in the interests of the Anglo-Persian Oil Company and Royal Dutch-Shell to have the French associated with them in the Turkish Petroleum Company. It seems likely that he was privy to the confidential discussions between Clemenceau and Lloyd George in London on 1 December, when the bargain was struck by which French claims on Mosul were relinquished in return for a guaranteed share of Mesopotamian oil if discovered and support for the French position over Syria.

In mid January 1919 Deterding was ready to 'discuss with the Government what are the practical steps so as to ensure such British control, as long as this is not a Government control'. The members of the Harcourt Committee, after considerable wrangling over offering a shareholding in the Turkish Petroleum Company to the French, agreed, subject to the Anglo-Persian Oil Company and Royal Dutch-Shell having equal interests in the company. The British government, apprehensive of American intervention, accepted the recommendations of the Harcourt Committee in early January, in order 'to get the French on our side and so prevent the oil question coming up before the Peace Conference at all'.[31] Though Clemenceau declared at the end of January that oil affairs would be 'une des questions économiques les plus importantes de la Conférence de la Paix',[32] they did not appear on the agenda. The two governments pursued their own tortuous negotiations, although Standard Oil (NJ) dominated the European oil supply situation.

Clemenceau, worried about the state of the French oil industry, appointed Bérenger on 25 January to take charge of all petroleum matters.[33] Arriving in London on 2 March, Bérenger had intensive friendly discussions with Cadman and Long and conversations with Deterding, whom he invested with the Légion d'honneur. General agreement was reached on petroleum co-operation, and in particular on French participation in the Turkish Petroleum Company, as well as on settling British and French joint representation in a company to be established for petroleum activities in Romania.[34] The preliminary

---

[31] See also PRO FO 368/2095, Curzon to Balfour, 20 February 1919, giving the divergent views of the Petroleum Executive and the Foreign Office; and AE Y International, vol. 192, reports of French representative of Bérenger in London to Bérenger, 16 and 21 January 1919.

[32] AE Y International, vol. 193, 'Rapport sur les pétroles', Bérenger to Clemenceau, 6 May 1919; Letter of Clemenceau to Bérenger, 30 January 1919.

[33] *Ibid.*, Letter of Clemenceau to Bérenger, 30 January 1919.

[34] *Ibid.*, Bérenger conversations with Cadman and Long, 3, 4 and 6 March and with Cambon, 7 March 1919; see also PRO FO 371/4209, Mallet to Curzon, 17 March 1919; *ibid.*, Curzon to Balfour, 2 April 1919 and *ibid.*, Memorandum of agreement between Bérenger and Long. Opposition to the agreement came from the Indian government,

agreement of 6 March was signed in Paris by Long and Bérenger on 8 April. Bérenger, delighted with his success, assured Long on 6 March that it was inconceivable that it would offend American interests. Cambon, a day later, was less easily convinced. Bérenger's vision was of Anglo-French co-operation in all areas where there were possibilities of petroleum exploitation. Bérenger's energy and conviction were remarkable, his realism less reliable and his optimism somewhat suspect.

Unfortunately the petroleum engagement hardly survived the quarrel on 21 May between Lloyd George and Clemenceau over the status of Syria, 'a complete bombshell to the Foreign Office'.[35] Bérenger was mystified.[36] The Foreign Ministry was relieved, and Pichon declared that Mosul reverted to the French sphere of influence, that the petroleum agreement was no longer applicable and that he looked forward to the reinstatement of the Sykes-Picot agreement of 1916.[37] Yet, in spite of the apparent impasse, the oil issue was too important to be submerged by diplomatic differences.[38] In December, after a new understanding between Clemenceau and Lloyd George had cleared the air, Philippe Berthelot, Secretary General of the Foreign Ministry, resumed negotiations with the British government representatives, Sir Hamar Greenwood and Cadman. Another agreement was signed on 21 December on similar terms designed to give France an independent oil policy in loyal association with the United Kingdom. Bérenger clashed with opposing officials in the Foreign Ministry, who claimed that the possession of territorial rights without oil rights 'c'est avoir les deux écailles de l'huître sans ni la perle ni l'huître'.[39]

Shortly afterwards Lloyd George, muddling matters again, challenged

PRO FO 371/4209, Minutes of inter-departmental conference at India Office, 8 April 1919, which only showed that other departments had failed to appreciate that the negotiations with the French and the recommendations of the Harcourt Committee were linked, 'the whole object of which is to give the Royal Dutch-Shell Group a share in the Turkish Petroleum Company in return for British control of this hitherto Dutch controlled group. This is the crux of the entire arrangement', PRO FO 608/231, Tufton minute, 9 April 1919. In fact Royal Dutch-Shell had two suitors.

[35] AE Y International, vol. 194, Pichon to de Fleuriau, 3 July and ibid., Foreign Ministry note, 1 August 1919; see also PRO FO 368/85781, Lloyd George to Clemenceau, 21 May 1919; PRO FO 368/2095, Villiers minute, 11 June 1919.
[36] AE Y International, vol. 194, Bérenger to Pichon, 25 June 1919.
[37] Ibid., Pichon to de Fleuriau, 23 June 1919.
[38] Ibid., de Fleuriau to Clemenceau, 18 December 1919, and PRO FO 368/2095, Long note, Oil Supplies, Memorandum for the Cabinet by the First Lord of the Admiralty, 4 November 1919, 'overwhelming fact that oil is becoming every day more vital to our national life', sentiments similar to Bérenger's.
[39] AE Y International, vol. 194, 'L'Accord franco-britannique sur le pétrole', Bérenger to Clemenceau, 12 January 1920, and PRO POWE 33/89. On Berthelot, see Richard A. Challener, 'The French Foreign Office: The Era of Philippe Berthelot', in Gordon A. Craig and Felix Gilbert (eds.), The Diplomats 1919–1939 (Princeton, 1953), pp. 49–85.

the right of private oil companies to be associated with the Mesopotamian oil concession and championed the idea of a public company to exploit it.[40] Coming in the wake of the electoral defeat of Clemenceau in January 1920, this put joint oil policy into further jeopardy. Berthelot was back in London again in March 1920, insisting unsuccessfully on absolute equality in Mesopotamian oil affairs. He alleged further that France was entitled to 'une entente pour une politique pétrolifère commune dans le monde entier sur la base économique des intérêts respectifs des deux pays'.

Agreement was finally concluded at San Remo on 20 April 1920 by Berthelot and Cadman on the basis of the status quo ante, with the definite commitment to France of a 25 per cent participation in the Turkish Petroleum Company, joint co-operation in Romania and professions of mutual co-operation in other oil spheres.[41] France recognized that, whatever the diplomatic attractions of political influence in the Levant, British assistance in oil affairs was essential. Access to the oil potential of Mesopotamia had become a determinant in French oil strategy; it was to remain a decisive factor in French diplomacy.

The San Remo agreement, almost unchanged since the earlier settlements, nevertheless provoked a very hostile reaction from American interests. With the diplomatic support of the State Department, a vociferous campaign was mounted to uphold the principles of the 'Open Door'.[42] This had a profound impact on the constitution and composition of the Turkish Petroleum Company and affected the relationship of American oil companies with the French government.

(c) Bérenger and the international oil companies

Bérenger's policy of a close alliance with Royal Dutch-Shell, probably first seriously mentioned officially in a despatch to Cambon of 17 December 1918, was sealed in London on 5 March 1919 during an

[40] AE Y International, vol. 194, Bérenger to Clemenceau, 15 March 1920 and CAB 23/20, 23 January 1920.

[41] *Ibid.*, Conversations of Berthelot in London, 3 and 11 March 1920; AE Asie 1918–1929 Mesopotamie, vol. 32, Berthelot letter, 11 March 1920. For French views on the San Remo agreement, see AE Y International, vol. 197, 'Note pour le Président du Conseil', 20 May 1922. See also André Nouschi, 'La Francia il petrolio e il Vicino Oriente', *Studii Storici*, 7 (1966), 97–127, and in a diplomatic context, Christopher M. Andrew and A. S. Kanya-Forstner, *France Overseas: The Great War and the Climax of French Imperial Expansion* (London, 1981). For an overall view of oil developments in the Middle East see S. H. Longrigg, *Oil in the Middle East* (Oxford, 1966). For a British view see V. H. Rothwell, 'Mesopotamia in British War Aims, 1914–1918', *Historical Journal*, 13, 2 (1970) and Marian Kent, *Oil and Empire: British Policy and Mesopotamian Oil 1900–1920* (London, 1976).

[42] See, for example, J. A. DeNovo, *American Interests and Policies in the Middle East, 1900–1939* (Minneapolis, 1963), pp. 169–84.

interval in his first discussions with Long and Cadman. Deterding pledged his total support for the French government. A more formal statement of his intentions was contained in a letter of 25 March from Gulbenkian to Bérenger.[43] This recalled the wartime co-operation between the group and the French government, pledged continuing collaboration and offered all its resources. The method of implementation was through a specially constituted company, the Société pour l'Exploitation des Pétroles, formed on 25 August in agreement with the French government, and with the assistance of the Banque de l'Union Parisienne, in order to capitalize the 25 per cent French shareholding in the Turkish Petroleum Company. Royal Dutch-Shell held 60 per cent of the shares, French interests 40 per cent. It was not to be a passive association confined to Mesopotamia but was concerned rather to accelerate the implementation of a French oil policy.[44] Gulbenkian also promised his support in the obtaining of a concession for France in northern Persia, but that remained a tantalizing mirage.[45]

Bérenger and Deterding had two other common objectives in mind. Firstly, the new company was to serve as a basis 'd'une large politique européenne de pétrole de manière à assurer à la France des moyens de se ravitailler en collaboration et non sous la dependance des groupements étrangers amis et en dehors de la seule source de l'Amérique du Nord'.[46] France needed to diversify her petroleum supplies and to reduce her dependence on American sources, but this could only mean increasing supplies from Royal Dutch-Shell at the expenses of Standard Oil (NJ). Secondly, the only way in which French interests could counterbalance the preponderant British shareholding in the Turkish Petroleum Company was by a close association with Royal Dutch-Shell which would strengthen Royal Dutch-Shell and prevent it from falling under British control.[47]

The alliance was a compact of much potential importance, which

---

[43] AE Y International, vol. 193, Gulbenkian to Bérenger, 25 March 1919. At the same time a detailed report was completed in the French embassy in The Hague on Royal Dutch and Company; see ibid., 26 March 1919. The earliest written mention of this idea appears to have been a letter of 4 November 1918 from Gulbenkian in Paris to Deterding in London. I am indebted to Mr Hans Gabriëls of Royal Dutch-Shell in The Hague for finding out this information for me from the company's archives.

[44] AE Y International, vol. 193, 'Rapport sur les pétroles', Bérenger to Clemenceau, 6 May 1919; MF B 32310 (F^{30} 1404), Deutsche de la Meurthe to Minister of Finance, 20 January 1921.

[45] AE Asie 1918–1929 Perse, vol. 49, Gulbenkian to Paleologue, 24 September 1920.

[46] MF B 32308 (F^{30} 1402), 'Note concernant la Société pour l'Exploitation des Pétroles et la part française dans l'exploitation des pétroles en Mésopotamie', enclosed in de la Meurthe to Minister of Finance, 17 October 1921.

[47] AE Y International, vol. 195, 'Pétroles', 7 June 1920.

might significantly have tilted the balance of commercial power in favour of Royal Dutch-Shell to the detriment of Standard Oil (NJ) and the Anglo-Persian Oil Company. Bérenger justified this aspect of his strategy, which seemed incompatible with his objective of an independent national oil policy, by claiming to be establishing a competitive balance between the great producing companies.[48]

The immediate post-war response of Standard Oil (NJ) to the petroleum situation of France was complacent, if not apathetic, satisfied with its dominant market position and reluctant to take any measures to alleviate French hardships in respect of product prices or freight rates. As the dollar increased in value and the franc depreciated, and as inflation rose, the French import position became desperate. Bérenger had met F. D. Asche, a Vice-President of Standard Oil (NJ), in November 1918, but had not been impressed by his apparent lack of concern for French interests, an indifference, as Bérenger pointed out to him, which was not shared by other companies, such as Royal Dutch-Shell.[49] On 10 and 13 May 1919, at the request of M. Etienne Clementel, Minister of Commerce and Industry, Bérenger met in Paris A. C. Bedford, Chairman of the Board of Standard Oil (NJ) and President of the American Petroleum Board during the war.[50] Bérenger was confident, was uncompromising in his justification of 'une politique nationale du pétrole' and was determined to impose controls on petroleum products. Bedford, insufficiently briefed, was horrified by these revelations and protested that the Americans preferred the market economy to monopoly control. Bérenger replied brusquely that it was an internal political matter for each nation to decide. He informed Bedford that France would give its preference to those companies supplying most cheaply.

If, as claimed by Gulbenkian, Bedford appeared 'dictatorial', Bérenger remained unintimidated by Bedford's demeanour. He argued that an import monopoly would be introduced sooner or later and that it was to the advantage of the importers to protect their interests by adapting their activities to government requirements. He did not anticipate distribution controls, which might only succeed in perpetuating the inefficient practices of the past. On the contrary, he wanted to stimulate competition in order to force the adoption of more modern technical methods and facilities, including better refining processes. The techno-

---

[48] *Ibid.*, vol. 193, 'Rapport sur les pétroles', Bérenger to Clemenceau, 6 May 1919.
[49] *Ibid.* On the reaction of Standard Oil (NJ) to the post-war oil situation in France and Europe see Gibb and Knowlton, *Standard Oil: The Resurgent Years*, pp. 259–75.
[50] AE Y International, vol. 199, Meetings of Bérenger and Bedford, 10 and 14 May 1919.

crats were emerging, stirring new forces in French industry. The changing direction of French petroleum policy was confirmed a month later when, on 17 June, M. Klotz, Minister of Finance, introduced a bill into the National Assembly to prolong the wartime regulations on the importation of petroleum products and the activities of the Petroleum Consortium.[51] M. Klotz also proposed the establishment of a permanent Petroleum Office, to be attached to the Ministry of Finance, and recommended state participation in the profits of sales and refining.

M. Klotz was also one of the first to advocate an energy policy: he sought to 'préparer dans notre pays une politique complète du combustible en coordination avec celle du charbon et d'électricité'. He was prepared to retain 'la liberté du commerce' for distribution. A compromise was reached and the existence of the Petroleum Consortium was extended for a further six months.

The reaction of Standard Oil (NJ) was to be uncooperative, refusing to accept bonds in place of cash settlements. Bérenger was firm but conciliatory, writing to Bedford in August that he would welcome frequent visits from the Standard Oil (NJ) representatives and hoping that the lifting of import restrictions on fuel oil would be mutually beneficial.[52] American resentment, however, was growing both over exclusion from possible oil-bearing regions of the Middle East and over threatened import discrimination. The American embassy in Paris and a member of the American Peace Commission, Bernard Baruch, complained of French oil policy in September. Bérenger was irritated at the American failure to understand the situation and informed Clementel that they were still supplying nearly 85 per cent of French petroleum requirements, 914,000 tonnes against 144,000 tonnes from other sources. Writing to Pichon, he disputed the right of the American ambassador to object to French legislation. American behaviour convinced him even more of the need for an independent French oil policy.[53]

Such American complaints played into the hands of Royal Dutch-Shell, who increased their supplies and were accommodating over credit arrangements, which reached some £5,000,000 at the end of 1919. The fall of Clemenceau's government in January 1920 marked the end of Bérenger's oil mandate. He had played a dominant role in the evolution of French oil policy, though his hopes of becoming the head of a strong

---

[51] *Ibid.*, vol. 194, 'Projet de loi instituant le monopole d'achat et d'importation des huiles raffinées et des essences de pétrole', 17 June 1919.
[52] *Ibid.*, vol. 199, Bérenger to Bedford, 9 August 1919.
[53] *Ibid.*, Baruch to Clementel, 12 June 1919; *ibid.*, Bérenger to Clementel, 17 June 1919; *ibid.*, Bérenger to Pichon, 30 September 1919.

250

petroleum department were disappointed. Strategically far-sighted, his immediate tactical moves of a petroleum alliance with the United Kingdom and an association with Royal Dutch-Shell were eventually unsuccessful, but the stimulus he brought to French oil affairs was decisive.

'La liberté du commerce'

M. Alexandre Millerand took office as Prime Minister on 21 January 1920, and a member of the Finance Ministry took charge of petroleum affairs on a temporary basis. On 13 March petroleum stocks dropped dramatically below the minimum level of 75,000 tonnes. The Petroleum Consortium expired on 21 April. The Commissariat Général aux Pétroles et Combustibles was terminated. The Finance Ministry permitted the issuing of new licences to re-establish the stock position, but the appointment on 28 April of a new oil commissioner, M. Laurent Eynac, who revoked them, plunged the French oil market into more uncertainty at the end of April, further antagonizing American companies.[54] These developments coincided with the signing of the San Remo agreement on 20 April, the news of which, although officially withheld, nevertheless percolated through diplomatic channels to the attention of American officials. A barrage of propaganda opened on the theme of the 'Open Door'. On 17 May Hugh Wallace, American ambassador to France, presented a list of American grievances. At the meeting of the International Chamber of Commerce held in Paris on 29 June, Thomas A. O'Donnell, President of the American Petroleum Institute, called for 'all Government restrictions to be removed'.[55] Sundry accusations followed: of the victimization of France by British duplicity, of Dutch complicity, and of discrimination against American oil interests. Royal Dutch-Shell failed to provide adequate alternative sources of supply, and with the subsequent liberalizing of oil regulations, some French petroleum companies, which had little capital to provide for their own transportation and distribution facilities, turned to the major foreign oil companies (Standard Oil (NJ), Royal Dutch-Shell and the Anglo-Persain Oil Company) for closer association. This resulted in

[54] MF B32410 (F^{30} 1506), 'Le Monopole d'importation en France pendant la guerre et sa liquidation en 1921', n.d.? 1930. A survey of the effects on customs revenues is given in B 34034 (F^{30} 4091), P. de Moüy, 11 May 1945.

[55] Quoted in Francis Delaisi, *Oil: Its Influence in Politics*, translated by C. Leonard Leese (London, 1922), p. 43. See also Pierre l'Espagnol de la Tramerye, *The World Struggle for Oil*, translated by C. Leonard Leese (London, 1924).

the formation of newly constituted French companies as subsidiaries of the larger foreign firms.

Thus whilst the French government prevaricated, the oil industry acted. Sir Basil Zaharoff succeeded in promoting the association of the Anglo-Persian Oil Company with a number of French companies, such as the Société Georges Lesieur et ses Fils, the Maison Paix et Cie and Le Groupe Société Navale de l'Ouest–Banque de la Seine. Together they formed on 27 October 1920 the Société Générale des Huiles de Pétrole. The French interests provided 55 per cent of the original capital of 100 million francs. It was only on 5 August that Zaharoff had first informed Berthelot of his intention to supply all the oil needed by France, especially fuel oil.[56] Standard Oil (NJ) also increased its affiliation with French companies through the assistance of the Banque de Paris et des Pays-Bas. In March 1920 it formed L'Economique, Société Anonyme de Distribution de Pétrole et Essence. In April it made an association with the Pétroléenne Société Anonyme (Fenaille et Despeaux) and in 1923 it increased its share in this company to 48 per cent. In 1921 it acquired a majority interest in the Compagnie Générale des Pétroles.[57] Royal Dutch-Shell also strengthened its representation amongst French oil interests by acquiring shares in the Société des Pétroles Jupiter.

As the major oil companies jockeyed for position, the politicians procrastinated. The Commissionaire Général aux Essences, M. Eynac, argued for the continuation of the government monopoly, but on 30 November 1920 the government decided in favour of 'un régime de liberté contrôlée'. The Foreign Ministry stressing the importance of the international dimension, demanded freedom of supplies so that France did not become dependent on any single foreign group. This did not bode well for the association with Royal Dutch-Shell. There was reluctance to sanction a government monopoly of imports, which, however theoretically attractive, was actually liable to corruption and exposed to constant threats of foreign government interference over financial or supply arrangements, with adverse effects on diplomatic relations. The Foreign Ministry preferred an inclusive to an exclusive policy, but accepted the need for the imposition upon importing companies of certain obligations, for instance to engage in exploration activities in French territories, to observe the provisions of French social legislation and to purchase a certain proportion of supplies from French

---

[56] AE Y International, vol. 195, Zaharoff to Berthelot, 5 August 1920.
[57] Gibb and Knowlton, *Standard Oil: The Resurgent Years*, pp. 507–19, particularly pp. 507–11.

sources. Oil issues were not to be allowed to rock the diplomatic boat.[58]

Many of these considerations were included in the bill presented to the National Assembly on 14 December 1920 by the Millerand government which professed 'la liberté du commerce' and believed that competition had moved from production to consumption. The national interest would be compromised if French petroleum supplies were restricted to a single foreign source. It was emphasized that: 'Le problème du pétrole n'est pas seulement commercial, c'est avant tout un problème d'activité nationale et de politique étrangère.' The government was ready to prevent any recurrence of an 'impérialisme du pétrole'. This was recognized by 'nos industriels du pétrole, hostiles à tout principe étatiste'. The long-term objective was to promote French enterprise but in the meantime to encourage political and geographical diversity.

A few months later, on 12 April 1921, another bill was introduced by the Millerand government, similar in its 'esprit de libéralisme commercial' but less restrictive towards market forces. Certain obligations were essential to encourage French petroleum interests but only in so far as they were compatible with 'l'exercice normal de ce commerce'.[59] Responsibility for petroleum administration was to be transferred from the Ministry of Public Works to the Ministry of Commerce and Industry. In general there was approval within the industry for the measures proposed, but political opposition existed in the National Assembly in favour of 'un monopole d'importation du pétrole'. This, however, was criticized because it would not be able to ensure deliveries of supplies from unwilling sellers or to guarantee reasonable prices to customers. Reliance on importation measures would not improve the security of national requirements. Opinion was swinging back from the immediate need for the import of oil products to the long-term strategic priority of controlled production, a feature of Bérenger's earlier proposals. Little progress was made in a confused political situation, which was characterized by procrastination rather than by resolve. On 23 May 1922 a supplementary series of parliamentary objections and amendments was tabled including yet again the proposed establishment of 'un Office National du Pétrole'.[60]

---

[58] AE Y International, vol. 195, 'Note d'information au sujet de la politique française en matière de pétroles', 1 December 1920; MF B 32309 (F^{30} 1403), Minister of Foreign Affairs to Président du Conseil, 'Politique française du pétrole', 24 January 1928, a useful survey from 1919 to 1927 from the viewpoint of the Ministy of Foreign Affairs.

[59] AE Y International, vol. 195, 'Projet de loi relatif au régime intérieur du pétrole', 14 December 1920.

[60] MF B 32308 (F^{30} 1402), enclosure in Minister of Commerce and Industry to Minister of Foreign Affairs, 28 September 1921.

The principal casualty of Bérenger's policy was the relationship between the French government and Royal Dutch-Shell, which attempted unsuccessfully to preserve its privileged position. In August 1921 the Foreign Ministry began to be apprehensive about the character of the Société pour l'Exploitation des Pétroles, wondering whether it sufficiently represented French policy.[61] The Ministry of Commerce and Industry, which, under the direction of M. Lucien Pineau, was responsible for petroleum affairs, shared these worries.[62] The Finance Ministry, however, had no such anxieties. The company, alarmed by these reservations, offered early in October to reconstitute its shareholding, in order to ensure a majority French shareholding of 51 per cent with wider representation, and stressed the importance of its world-wide connections.[63] The Foreign Ministry remained unimpressed, doubtful about conferring upon just one group the representation of French interests comprised in the San Remo agreement. The Foreign Minister, Pichon, informed the Ministry of Commerce and Industry that apart from Romanian affairs, which were being handled by the Banque de Paris, other concessionary activities should be considered separately in the most practical manner after departmental agreement.[64] Such matters could be co-ordinated by the proposed Petroleum Office.

The Minister of Finance, Paul Doumer, inquired on behalf of the Société about the state of the negotiations over French representation in the Turkish Petroleum Company, a matter which was also becoming the object of increasing American interest. Pichon replied that no action was contemplated and that no commitment had been made with any oil company.[65] Doumer in January 1922 was unsatisfied and reminded Pichon that the original arrangements with the Société had complete departmental approval.[66] He stressed the fundamental importance of the association with Royal Dutch-Shell, he mentioned the modification of the Articles of Association and he suggested that a decision on the acquisition of French rights in the Turkish Petroleum Company was imperative.

Doubtless Deterding knew that Cadman, who after resigning from

[61] *Ibid.*, Minister of Foreign Affairs to Minister of Commerce and Industry, 19 August 1921.
[62] *Ibid.*, Minister of Commerce and Industry to Minister of Foreign Affairs, 28 September 1921.
[63] *Ibid.*, de la Meurthe to Minister of Finance, 17 October 1921.
[64] *Ibid.*, Minister of Foreign Affairs to Minister of Commerce and Industry, 28 October 1921.
[65] *Ibid.*, Minister of Foreign Affairs to Minister of Finance, 29 October 1921.
[66] *Ibid.*, Minister of Finance to Minister of Foreign Affairs, 12 January 1921.

government service had joined the Anglo-Persian Oil Company, was negotiating in December 1921 with Standard Oil (NJ) on a joint interest in a concession in northern Persia and on other forms of co-operation, including participation in the Turkish Petroleum Company. Such developments disturbed Deterding, who wanted to reduce the influence of the Anglo-Persian Oil Company. In December he visited Paris and met Pineau, emphasizing that his group was Dutch and independent. He was ready to pursue his activities in a direction favourable to France. In so far as the Turkish Petroleum Company was concerned, he stressed the need for France and his group to balance the shareholding of the Anglo-Persian Oil Company, and he advised the French to take appropriate action to acquire their shareholding in the company.[67] The initiative was passing to the Foreign Ministry and the Ministry of Commerce and Industry, which requested in January 1922 that negotiations be commenced with the British government on the Turkish Petroleum Company issue. M. Dior, in the new government of Poincaré which took office on 22 January 1922, was concerned not just with importation but also with direct control over production.[68] Doumer pleaded that Royal Dutch-Shell be retained as an intermediary and, more importantly, to offset the British presence in the Turkish Petroleum Company.[69]

Doumer deplored the changed attitude of the Foreign Ministry and accused it of attempting to dictate French oil policy. He bitterly complained that the finance section of the Foreign Ministry, whose competence and indeed existence were both questionable, was planning the composition of a French petroleum group. He regarded it as an intolerable affront that for the previous two years his Ministry had been deliberately kept in the dark over petroleum affairs. To political pique was added administrative anger. Poincaré intervened to re-establish departmental collaboration. He requested proposals for the formation of a French petroleum group,[70] believing that Société pour l'Exploitation des Pétroles was inadequately constituted to safeguard French interests. Poincaré decided on a company 'entièrement française'. A last-minute warning by M. Sergent, Chairman of the Banque de l' Union Parisienne, that France would merely escape from Royal Dutch-Shell to fall into the clutches of Standard Oil (NJ) failed to reverse Poincaré's decision.[71]

[67] *Ibid.*, Minister of Commerce and Industry to Minister of Foreign Affairs, 12 December 1921, with enclosures concerning visit of Deterding to Pineau, 6 December 1921.
[68] *Ibid.*, Minister of Commerce and Industry to Poincaré, 28 January 1922.
[69] *Ibid.*, 'Note pour le Ministre', 1 February 1922.
[70] *Ibid.*, Poincaré to Minister of Finance, 23 March 1922.
[71] *Ibid.*, Ministry of Commerce and Industry, Note for Poincaré, 23 October 1922.

La Compagnie Française des Pétroles

Poincaré's decision was politically acceptable but commercially difficult. M. Seydoux at the Foreign Ministry admitted that 'Les intérêts privés sont tellement puissants et tellement complexes dans les affaires de pétroles.'[72] He suggested a holding company with state participation which would operate separate companies for different geographical areas. On 8 June 1922 Dior at a Cabinet meeting referred to the urgent need for a national oil policy and submitted a report prepared by Pineau who also proposed a form of holding company responsible for different operational areas.[73] Pineau proposed a private capital structure with a broad spread of investment from French industrialists and bankers, so that the state would not be responsible in any way.

A year followed of protracted deliberations but little decision. On 14 May 1923 Pineau submitted a more comprehensive survey of the issue.[74] He argued in favour of the control of production. France lacked capital, expertise, stocks, tankers and refinery capacity. He again advocated the creation 'd'une Société de portefeuille'. Pineau's presentation was crucial. Pineau, like Bérenger, was interventionist. There was general ministerial agreement, but the Ministry of Finance advised minimum government involvement, the encouragement of private initiative and the rejection of subsidies for tanker construction, though the latter was subsequently ignored.[75]

On 20 September 1923 Poincaré appointed M. Ernest Mercier to form 'un groupe national de pétrole'. Mercier accepted provided that his efforts were confirmed by the French oil companies. The new company was to supplement the existing French oil industry, not to supress it. The instructions which Mercier received were explicit – 'créer un outil capable de réaliser une politique nationale de pétrole', an independent organization with participation from all the industrial companies and banks to engage in production, transportation, refining and distribution. Its administration would include two government Directors nominated by the Ministers of Commerce and Finance respectively.[76] Mercier acted

---

[72] *Ibid.*, Seydoux, Ministry of Foreign Affairs Note for Poincaré, October 1922.
[73] *Ibid.*, Minister of Commerce and Industry to Minister of Finance, Pétroles, 8 June 1922.
[74] MF B 32313 (F^{30} 1408), Pineau, 'Rapport au sujet de la politique du pétrole en France', 24 May 1923.
[75] *Ibid.*, Minister of Finance to Poincaré, 7 July 1923.
[76] *Ibid.*, 'Projet de lettre à addresser par M. le Ministre du Commerce à M. Mercier', n.d.; *ibid.*, Poincaré to Mercier, 20 September 1923. For further details see *ibid.*, Poincaré to Minister of Foreign Affairs and Commerce, 19 November 1923. On Mercier see Richard F. Kuisel, *Ernest Mercier, French Technocrat* (Berkeley, 1967).

energetically to set up a Study Group composed of most members of the French oil industry. This first met on 12 October and had compiled a draft Articles of Association by 7 November.[77] Government relations, the distribution of the shareholdings and the position of the French subsidiaries of foreign oil companies were the most difficult details.

The main problem was the degree of autonomy which the new company was to enjoy, for the existing members of the oil industry and their bankers were determined not to finance a government noose around their own necks or to prejudice 'la liberté du commerce de pétrole'. The banks insisted on the shareholders of the company not having any exclusive privileges, not being obliged to increase their shareholdings proportionately and not being restricted in their activities in other petroleum spheres.[78]

Most members of the Chambre de l'Industrie du Pétrole on 2 December were adamant that the new company, known as the Compagnie Française des Pétroles (CFP), should abstain from distribution because it would constitute 'une superfétation, une concurrence officielle à un commerce libre et privé'. The government, though not under any illusion about such views from within the industry, refused, according to Dior in February, to be restricted in its objectives and reserved the right to construct one or more refineries whose products would be made available to shareholders with distribution facilities or for the requirements of national defence.[79]

Most of the French oil industry reluctantly concluded that participating in CFP rather than refusing to do so was the lesser of two evils. The later stages of the negotiations were dominated by a changing political situation as the Poincaré government stumbled from crisis to crisis and finally succumbed to an electoral defeat at the hands of the Cartel des Gauches. In order to anticipate a possible legislative *fait accompli* and to reach a reasonable settlement, Mercier, virtually on his own, negotiated with M. Loucheur, Minister of Commerce and Industry. For this he was subsequently criticized by his colleagues, particularly on the question of overriding supply rights to the government which he later had to retract when the Board of CFP threatened to repudiate the convention with the

[77] MF B 32308 (F³⁰ 1402), Draft constitution for a Syndicat Français d'Etudes Pétrolières; *ibid.*, Note, 10 October 1923; *ibid.*, Compagnie Nationale des Pétroles, 'Procès-verbal', 12 October 1923.
[78] *Ibid.*, Compagnie Nationale des Pétroles, 'Procès-verbal', 26 October 1923, concerning Banque de Paris to Mercier, 10 October 1923; *ibid.*, projected letter to Poincaré from Mercier, n.d.; see also comments of M. Loucheur.
[79] *Ibid.*, Minister of Commerce to Poincaré, 7 March 1923.

government unless it agreed to certain modifications incorporated in letters of 26 June.[80]

The creation of CFP was in itself a compromise between the demands of the public sector and the defence of private interests. It was occasioned by the need to constitute a French company to acquire the shares of the French government in the Turkish Petroleum Company, but certain members of the Poincaré government, with the exceptionally capable support of Pineau, saw in it an opportunity to promote an active interventionist strategy towards the petroleum industry. In fact, with the formation of CFP on 24 March 1924, the Radicals had sold the political pass. The incoming *gauchiste* government of Edouard Herriot inherited an instrument for its own more monopolistic national policy. On 4 June the transfer of the French shareholding in the Turkish Petroleum Company, which by then also included the participation of American companies, earlier rejected, later welcomed by the French government, was finally concluded. La Compagnie Française des Pétroles was actually in business.

Un système du monopole

The creation of CFP did not eliminate either the multiple tensions which existed between its participants or those between the company and the government. It did not terminate the controversy over the relative merits of 'la liberté du commerce' and 'le système du monopole', but it sharpened the focus of attention. Nevertheless, irrespective of the priority of petroleum affairs in the political debate, discussions were largely theoretical until France possessed its own production source. A share in a concession was no substitute for the possession of oil. CFP had to pay for its chips before it could throw the industrial dice. On 3 August 1926, 4 May 1927 and 2 April 1928 CFP had to increase its capital from 25 million francs to 50 million, 75 million and 150 million francs respectively. Keeping up its financial obligations towards the Turkish Petroleum Company and supporting its own modest concessionary activities was not easy. The discovery of oil at Baba Gurgur on 15 October 1927 brought greater opportunities but more expenses and required decisions not hypotheses. To a confident Mercier, nevertheless,

[80] *Ibid.*, Report to Ministry of Finance, 21 May 1924; *ibid.*, Mercier to Minister of Commerce and Industry and Posts and Telegraphs, 12 June 1924; *ibid.*, Mercier to Minister of Commerce and Industry, 26 June 1924. See also Jean Rondot, *La Compagnie Française des Pétroles* (Paris, 1962) pp. 31–8. Loucheur himself in 1922, as a banker, had not been impressed with the idea of such a French oil company (MF B 32308 (F[30] 1402), Memorandum, 8 June 1922), but as a Minister he was enthusiastic.

it seemed propitious to envisage 'avec une entière confiance le développement ultérieur de ses opérations, aussi bien sur le plan industriel que sur le plan financier', in the report which he made to the Prime Minister.[81]

He realized, nevertheless, that he had to preserve his good relations with the major oil companies because of being a partner with them in the shareholdings of the Turkish Petroleum Company, and because of the importance which they attached to their French markets. Mercier, therefore, was not contemplating competing in marketing, even if this were possible; nor was he planning to form a tanker company. Refining, however, was a different proposition. It had been an element in Bérenger's policy. It had become the keystone of Pineau's petroleum strategy, already publicly proclaimed on 5 July 1927 at the celebrations for the reconstruction of the Douai refinery of the Société Générale des Huiles de Pétrole. A French source of production made feasible such a strategy, for which political pressure had been mounting appreciably since 1925, not least because of other comparable national oil developments in Italy and South America and criticism of the foreign oil companies.[82]

Pineau, who had become Director of the Office National des Combustibles Liquides, in 1924 had come to dominate French oil policy. He persuaded the government to present two bills, on 16 and 30 March 1928, which effectively regulated the French petroleum industry for nearly fifty years.[83] These were the culmination of parliamentary pressure and government studies and commissions which dated back to 10 January 1925 and which had proposed a supervised form of 'liberté contrôlée' of oil importation.[84] The first bill modified customs duties on

---

[81] MF B 32311 (F[30] 1406), Mercier, 'Note au sujet du développement financier de la Compagnie Française des Pétroles', 7 January 1928. See also André Nouschi, 'Les Investissements pétroliers français dans l'entre-deux-guerres', in Maurice Lévy-Leboyer (ed.), *La Position internationale de la France* (Paris, 1977), pp. 377–85. Further light on the growth of CFP in the context of the French oil industry will be found in the forthcoming work of André Nouschi, *The History of the French Oil Industry* (Paris, 1984).

[82] See Edgar Faure, *Le Pétrole dans la paix et dans la guerre* (Paris, 1939). Ministerial comments in MF B 34034 (F[30] 4091), 'Note rappelant les divers projects et propositions de loi concernant le monopole des pétroles', n.d., and *ibid.*, 'Historique de la question des pétroles', 4 December 1930. For developments elsewhere, see for example Carl E. S. Solberg, *Oil and Nationalism in Argentina: A History* (Stanford, 1979), especially pp. 51–155; *idem*, 'Entrepreneurship in Public Enterprise: General Enrique Mosconi and the Argentine Petroleum Industry', *Business History Review*, 56, 3 (Autumn, 1982), 380–99; Franklin Tugwell, *The Politics of Oil in Venezuela* (Stanford, 1975).

[83] For a full consideration see Pineau, 'Rapport général, organisation du monopole d'importation du pétrole', in Commission des Pétroles, *Journal Officiel de la République Française*, 11 July 1934, in MF B 32314 (F[30] 1409).

[84] MF B 34034 (F[30] 4091). See note for the Président du Conseil by Director-General of Customs, 27 June 1927, with enclosure, 'Note au Ministère', 11 May 1925, and 'Note historique de la question des pétroles', 4 December 1930.

petroleum products in order to encourage imports of crude oil and to stimulate a French refining industry. The second bill proposed the direct state control of petroleum imports through the licensing of quotas, the imposition of certain regulations on contracts and stocks, technical assistance, fiscal changes, price control, tanker control and refining obligations. It embraced a comprehensive monopoly. In many respects the wheel of French oil policy had come full circle since the proposals of M. Klotz in 1919. According to Senator Roy, the state was the only authority capable of containing the power of the foreign oil companies which were criticized for damaging the French economy. It has also to be observed that from 1925 there were increasing imports of oil products from Russia, thus further diversifying French supplies.[85]

France now possessed and administered a directly interventionist state oil policy which controlled the operations of the French oil industry. Mercier found himself in a quandary, for he advocated CFP operating its own refineries, but most of his colleagues opposed him. According to Mercier, the company lacked a common financial interest and had little incentive to spend large sums on refineries, but this was essential, otherwise the company merely sold its crude oil allocation in the Turkish Petroleum Company to its partners without any appreciable profit or guarantee of sales. Moreover, only refining enabled returns to be realized on the whole range of products from crude oil and ensured the eventual success of the company. He offered to abstain from distribution activities if the other participants would market 25 per cent of their supplies from the company and accept the creation of a refining subsidiary. Mercier was opposed by most of his Board apart from M. Cayrol of Desmarais Frères and offered his resignation to Poincaré.[86] In most respects his analysis was correct. In the climate of overproduction and of measures to curtail production and concert distribution, as revealed in the Achnacarry agreement signed by Royal Dutch-Shell, Standard Oil (NJ) and the Anglo-Persian Oil Company in September 1928, there was little enthusiasm for an expansionist policy. International economic affairs were entering the doldrums and prices were falling. French banks were not favourably disposed to make any more loans available.

Poincaré in January 1929 once again decisively intervened, rejected

---

[85] AE Y International, vol. 198, Ministry of Foreign Affairs, a historical survey, 'Importance du pétrole pour la France', 24 January 1928; also in MF B 32309 (F^{30} 1403): 'le Gouvernement Française ne pouvait pas négliger plus longtemps le pétrole russe'.

[86] MF B 32311 (F^{30} 1406), 'Rapport sur la Compagnie Française des Pétroles', Mercier to Poincaré, 18 December 1928; *ibid.*, 'Note, Compagnie Française des Pétroles', by the Banque de Paris et des Pays-Bas, 19 December 1928; *ibid.*, Note on Compagnie Française des Pétroles and refining, 20 December 1928; *ibid.*, Minister of Finance to Poincaré, 21 December 1928.

Mercier's resignation and, reversing earlier decisions, agreed to sanction a 25 per cent state shareholding in CFP and to provide a quarter of the Board representation. A refining company, Compagnie Française de Raffinage, was authorized, in which CFP held 55 per cent of the shares and the government 10 per cent, and from which distributors were obliged to purchase 25 per cent of their requirements. This virtual diktat, resented and reluctantly accepted by the majority of the shareholders as their last concession, was signed on 19 March 1929.[87] It was not the end of the affair. Political controversy continued for almost two years after the agreement was presented for ratification in the National Assembly. The legal basis of the company was questioned by Leon Blum. Mercier was pilloried for his association with the conservative Redressment Français as a 'mortal enemy of the working class and the public interest'.[88] By the time a final agreement was reached on 4 March 1931 between the Board of CFP and the French government under Pierre Laval, and passed by the National Assembly on 30 July, the constitution of CFP had been modified, the convention with the state changed to incorporate a 40 per cent shareholding and its right to 80 per cent of the company's production reinstated.[89] The private French oil industry had been taken for a ride on the parliamentary machine.

It was ironical that in April 1929 Paul Claudel, French ambassador in Washington, was engaged in confidential discussions with Walter Teagle, President of Standard Oil (NJ) on a special petroleum supply agreement. At the same time Berthelot was informing Claudel that support from Standard Oil (NJ) was necessary in order to counter opposition from Royal Dutch-Shell and the Anglo-Persian Oil Company. The French government was grateful and was prepared to offer preferential treatment provided that Standard Oil (NJ) continued to support French policy; otherwise there would be unfavourable repercussions.[90] The effect of French policy, however, had been to

---

[87] *Ibid.*, 'Note au sujet de la question préalable posée par M. Blum', 18 June 1930; see also Henri de Chambon, 'La Question du pétrole devant les Chambres', *Revue Parlementaire*, 12 (1–15 June 1930).

[88] MF B 32311 (F[30] 1406), Poincaré to Minister of Commerce and Industry, 11 March 1929.

[89] MF B 34034 (F[30] 4091). An agreement on a new convention had been reached on 25 June 1930, signed by M. Paul Reynard, Minister of Finance, and M. Pierre Etienne Flandin, Minister of Commerce and Industry. On the parliamentary controversy over these agreements, see MF B 34034 (F[30] 4091), Ministère des Finances, 'Historique de la question des pétroles', n.d., 1930, and précis of parliamentary debates, February 1931. A useful survey of the French oil industry at this time is in Sir Robert Cahill, 'Economic Conditions in France', *Department of Overseas Trade*, No. 581, HMSO (London, 1934) pp. 152–76.

[90] AE Y International, vol. 198, Berthelot to Claudel, 8 and 16 April 1929; *ibid.*, Claudel to Berthelot, 19 April 1929.

reduce reliance on American supplies, which fell to 40.8 per cent in 1930, 31.6 per cent in 1931 and 27 per cent in 1932. Cadman, Chairman of the Anglo-Persian Oil Company, was then experiencing difficulties with Pineau over the unfair quotas he believed he had been allocated. The ebb and flow of French relations with the major foreign oil companies persisted throughout this period. The diversification of supplies, the revival of the refining industry, the formulation of a state oil policy and the creation of a national oil company were formidable political and economic achievements in just over a decade, in which politicians, officials and businessmen played their respective parts and had their particular differences.

Government policies seldom progress in predictable stages along a preconceived linear programme of decisions. As well as being multinational they are multidimensional, subject to a wide variety of influences, impressions and interpretations. Below the public political posturing is the quiet practical level which operates by results no less than by principle. Private enterprise, widely varying in its composition, ability and appeal, is not immune from political, economic or social pressures. The interaction of the state and the private sector over the centuries reveals an infinity of human combinations, part of the fascinating pursuit of economic history.

15

Reflections on the Dutch economic interests in the East Indies

H. BAUDET

It is about twenty years ago that, on several occasions, Charles Wilson and I discussed the consequences which the post-war political developments in the world would have for those Western business enterprises which of old had their main business in the colonies. Wilson had just written his second survey of the history of Unilever (*Unilever 1945–1965: Challenge and Response in the Post-War Industrial Revolution*) and I had adapted that publication for the Netherlands edition (*Unilever in de tweede Industriële Revolutie 1945–1965*). However, I was at the same time deeply involved in a study of post-war developments in the former Netherlands East Indies and of the radical changes following the transfer of sovereignty over that territory. In the early sixties the Netherlands had already experienced the loss of its empire and the relations between the Dutch and the Indonesians had fallen to their lowest point. The Dutch government's policy, pursued in the East Indies during the first period of revolt between 1945 and 1949, and the additional efforts after 1949 to maintain close and workable relations with independent Indonesia, had within thirteen years failed completely.

During those years the Netherlands experienced a very difficult time. It started immediately after the ending of the disastrous Japanese occupation of the East Indies, when the Dutch were not immediately allowed to re-establish their rightful administrative and military positions. From that early beginning the process of decolonization was certainly far from straightforward.

The first agreement on the principal issues outstanding between the Dutch and the Indonesians was only signed in mid 1947, after it had been laboriously negotiated in Linggadjati. Both sides accepted it, but without any enthusiasm, and subsequent squabbling over interpretations soon caused it to fail. Later negotiations, most of them undertaken with the good offices of a United Nations Commission of three members, were interrupted by large-scale military operations in July 1947 and December 1948. They were militarily more or less successful, but proved a miserable failure politically. Nevertheless the partners concerned returned each time to the joint conference table and under heavy pressure from the United Nations as well as from the USA in 1949 they came finally to a mutually acceptable understanding, which on 27 December resulted in the unconditional and irrevocable transfer of sovereignty over Indonesia to the new republic. At the same time the statute of a Netherlands Indonesian Union was signed, linking both independent nations in a rather loose union under the crown of the Netherlands. In addition agreement was reached on a variety of issues of an economic and financial, transitional or subsidiary nature, such as the protection of Dutch economic rights, withdrawal of armed forces, settlement of debts, rights of citizenship and so forth. One subject, however, remained unsettled for the time being – the future of Western New Guinea. Its position was to be determined later by direct negotiations.

This overall result of the conference promised certain expectations for the coming period and seemed to offer a reasonable prospect. The formal arrangements comprised principles for future collaboration, which were, notwithstanding the experiences of the troublesome post-war years, not necessarily doomed to fail. The 'special relationship', however, as embodied in the ample and detailed financial and economic agreement, as well as the elaborate establishment of the Netherlands Indonesian Union, both quickly proved to be too strained constructions for a long and lasting relationship. Differences of interpretation arose in the financial and economic field and, only a short time after its formation, the union lapsed into inactivity and was formally abolished.

The optimistic expectations which prevailed at the end of 1949 diminished rapidly. The reason for this decline was primarily to be found in the failure of the two parties to come to terms over the transfer of sovereignty over Western New Guinea. The settling of this matter, which had been set apart for a direct conference between the two nations, proved to be more difficult and complicated than had been foreseen and was to remain unsolved for years to come. Perhaps a breakthrough could have been reached if the realistic liberal minister Dirk Stikker had stayed on as head of the Dutch foreign affairs department at The Hague. In 1949 Stikker had been instrumental in bringing about the successful round-table conference, and in the following difficult years he could have been a great help in resolving the harmful dispute over Western New Guinea's sovereignty. Before this could be realized a change of Cabinet took place in Holland in mid-1952 and Stikker stepped down. The ministerial responsibility for handling Indonesian and New Guinea affairs was taken over by Joseph Luns, a new representative of the Catholic People's Party, whose political views were quite different. In consequence it was to be expected that the Dutch standpoint would harden considerably and become less subtle.

Such a change in policy was also fostered by the fact that the Indonesians became less and less willing to discuss differences, even if they were merely of minor importance. The result was that relations between the two nations gradually became more and more strained and a special conference on these issues, held at The Hague and later in Geneva in 1955/6 did not resolve them. Shortly afterwards Indonesia severed diplomatic relations and in 1957 even announced a complete boycott. This situation lasted till 1962 when, with the good offices of the American envoy Bunker, the United Nations succeeded in convening a new series of talks which ended in a Dutch promise to terminate its sovereignty over Western New Guinea. It is quite understandable that this political development greatly influenced the position of Dutch economic activities in Indonesia. In the early post-war years private enterprise had managed to maintain its position quite well. Later on it lost its hold as relations between the two nations deteriorated, and with the total eclipse of the Dutch position at the end of the 1950s private enterprise also perished.

In the last stages of this downfall a group of Dutch entrepreneurs showed some spectacular activity by trying to organize intervention designed to bring the two conflicting parties to an accommodation and to prevent a catastrophe. In the Netherlands these efforts only attracted general public disapproval. Condemnation of such moves came even from political groups which normally opposed the inflexible policy of the Dutch Cabinet. Their standpoint was based on the principle that private enterprise had to refrain from interfering with national foreign policy. Because of these conflicting opinions over New Guinea policy the general problem of the relationship between the two spheres of government and private enterprise came into sharp focus, sharper even than it had been in the earlier phase during the upheavals in the Dutch East Indies after 1945 when it was also constantly invoked. And perhaps this was already the case even before the Second World War.

Even if government and private enterprise had to be considered in principle as different and separate spheres of activity, much more

265

remained to be said about the relationship between them. In the first place, the government of the Indies itself had traditionally acted as an entrepreneur by dint of possessing substantial business interests. It is therefore worth asking if there were perhaps other lines of communication between private enterprise and government. It is true that very little light has been thrown upon such links, and public opinion has shown neither interest in nor awareness of such matters. Nevertheless a number of fairly general convictions linked in the public mind absolute relations between business and empire, of which three may be seen as particularly relevant:

– the Indies had usually been considered as the main source of Dutch prosperity, even by the large majority of the people who had no knowledge whatsoever of the fact that in pre-war years the East Indies had, in fact, contributed nearly 14 per cent of Dutch national income (according to calculations by Tinbergen and Derksen).

– in the second place, opinion in Holland had no doubt that this contribution from the Indies presupposed that Dutch colonial authority was a precondition for the prosperity of Dutch industry overseas: a sort of duality of 'trade and flag', even if the term itself was not used.

– in the third place, at the time of the Indonesian struggle for independence, there was a widespread consensus of opinion in the Netherlands – independent of national political differences and convictions – that the loss of the East Indies would turn out to be a serious disadvantage for the Dutch economy, and an extremely difficult disadvantage to overcome. For several years the Dutch expression was heard 'Indie verloren, rampspoed geboren', that is 'The Indies gone, prosperity doomed'. But this pessimistic slogan was to be denied by the facts and figures of the development of the Netherlands domestic economy in the 1950s and 1960s.

It is true that Dutch enterprise in Indonesia adapted with difficulty to the course of political events after 1945. Entrepreneurs entered a long dark period of uncertainty, trial and error, confidence and disappointment, that lasted until 1957/8. The milestone of 1949 – the transfer of sovereignty to the former colony – seemed less decisive from the entrepreneur's point of view than from the politician's. The future of entrepreneurial activities in the new republic looked reasonably secure and had been guaranteed by the agreements of 1949. Continuity appeared to be assured and hardly any entrepreneur, big or small, considered the situation threatening or realized how delicate the situation actually was. Almost nobody foresaw the risk of the general nationalization of Dutch enterprise in Indonesia which occurred in 1957/8. Many firms had, over several years, diversified their activities and interests around the world, which allowed them to reorient their commitments and limit their financial losses to an acceptable extent. Numerous others had, for various reasons, stuck to Indonesia as their exclusive field of activity and were left with no way out. They succumbed.

The Dutch government in The Hague also had to face the new political circumstances brought about by Indonesian independence. To a certain extent the government encountered the same problem as Dutch business and the internal discussions and varying viewpoints developed along similar lines. To decide on the nature of Dutch relations with the new republic was, however, not a matter of short-term solutions. On the one hand, the Netherlands Indonesian Union suggested very special trade preferences between the countries and implied something like a partly common future. On the other hand, realists in Dutch government circles soon appeared to be correct in their bleak estimate that the new-born Union would not last very long and that Indonesia then had to be considered in the same way as any other foreign country. This controversy lay at the root of long-standing endemic conflicts between different ministries as well as within the separate ministries involved – the former Colonial Ministry (since 1950 called the Ministry of Union and Overseas Affairs) and the Ministries of Finance, Foreign Affairs and Economic Affairs.

In January 1983 Meindert Fennema (University of Amsterdam) and I published a book dealing with the relations between the two spheres of private enterprise and government in the Indies and with the possible consequences of these relations for political and economic decision making from 1945 to 1962, covering a first period of five years' formal decolonization, and, subsequently, 12 years of evolving political and economic change and reorientation, both in the public and in the private sector. The special approach of the book is the study of the mutual influence and interaction of government and enterprise in the Netherlands. This contribution to the 'Liber Amicorum Charles Wilson' deals , with the arguments and main conclusions of this study: *Het Nederlands belang bij Indie*.[1]

The supposed existence of a network of interlocking functions

---

[1] *The Dutch Economic Interests in the East Indies* (Utrecht, 1983).

through which government and enterprise were possibly linked, through boards of directors, through official administrative bodies or by other means, formed the subject of a substantial part of our investigations. The outcome of our extensive research was twofold: (a) There actually existed links of various kinds and of differing degrees of importance between the two spheres. They were less numerous, however, than has often been supposed. Moreover, such links diminished considerably in number in the 1950s. Some of the most outstanding individuals concerned had a highly beneficial influence on the course of affairs. (b) Politics and economics developed to a considerable extent in fairly separate circuits and along lines which were different in many essential aspects. It was remarkable, however, that their paths met and interacted in fruitful co-operation in the process of industrialization in the Netherlands in the 1950s and 1960s. The audacious initiator of this new national development was van den Brink, Minister of Economic Affairs from 1948 until 1952, who had presented this bold innovating programme in a crucial official paper which now, rightly, bears his name.

Another noteworthy conclusion of our study is that the links between government and enterprise in the years covered by our research diverged widely because of differences in character and vision amongst protagonists and in the opportunities faced by the different groups. Private enterprise has, of course, a great interest in the maintenance not only of a favourable industrial climate but also of a favourable political context. However, it does not control the means to create this last condition. Some of the entrepreneurs who worked in the Indies became aware in the early post-war years that a *Présence néerlandaise* in the archipelago was neither a prerequisite for nor a guarantee of the necessary conditions for positive work and investment. Certainly in the first two years after Japan's capitulation this presence had been considered a necessity. But a real change in vision and analysis came about after 1947, when the troubles over the Linggadjati agreement commenced and the subsequent military action failed to bring about any improvement.

These developments evoked considerable animosity and controversy between business interests and government, and also between the entrepreneurs themselves. At the same time, however, a new basis was laid for industrial activities in Indonesia, whereby new starting-points were formulated which perhaps could have resisted the pressures of post-revolutionary Indonesian nationalism if a different Dutch governmental policy had prevailed. Since this last condition was not fulfilled, business lost its opportunity and declined, though entrepreneurs argued insistently that the best support for their work was that peaceful conditions should be maintained in the territory where they operated and this matter weighed for them more heavily than the national flag. The entrepreneurs were certainly willing to influence government policy decisions if they had a chance to do so, but the Dutch government seldom offered such an opportunity and virtually never by making official steps or inviting the entrepreneurs for a discussion at departmental level. Hence enterprise entrenched itself in its own isolation and merely launched demands and reproaches at the government.

The perspectives of enterprise and government were fundamentally too different to allow proper links to be established between them. The result of our research over those years therefore demonstrates an odd image, that might be called 'geometrical anti-parallelism'. The first period was characterized by a progressive government policy as far as this was politically possible while business interests in substance still thought and acted in pre-war terms. The second period, beginning around 1947, showed a less flexible Dutch official policy towards the republic, whilst from the side of the entrepreneurs came a growing tendency to accept the new facts and conceive a new business interest, which was opposed to the second Dutch military action. Then there developed a third period of reasonable harmony between the two groups: the time had arrived to come to terms with Indonesia at the round-table conference and to reach a financial and economic agreement. This improvement in atmosphere owed much to the activities of Mr Stikker, the Minister of Foreign Affairs.

Finally came the fourth period, in the 1950s, when Stikker left this ministry in 1952 and Joseph Luns became the minister responsible for handling Indonesian affairs. In that period all Dutch business interests in Indonesia were sacrificed to the prevailing policy conceptions. Even a child could have foreseen the serious risks involved. Yet the business interest that for so long had been concentrating on the Indies shifted that orientation only with great reluctance. Neither the ransacking and destroying of estates and factories during the Japanese occupation and the following revolutionary years, nor the damage suffered during the two large-scale military actions in 1947 and 1948, nor the subsequent period of high risk and uncertainty had persuaded the majority of private concerns that it was preferable to seek their salvation elsewhere – by returning to the Netherlands or by moving elsewhere in the world. Business had a preference for the East Indies, even when the region had become an independent republic. This predilection originated partly from tradition, reinforced by comparisons made with alternative markets, and, of course, partly from the fact that Indonesia remained a well-known market of 80–100 million people.

The agricultural interests had always had the strongest links with Indonesia; for industry and trade the ties were considerably less. The strength of the connections was, to some extent, inversely proportional to the mobility of the capital deployed. In contrast to Great Britain and France the Netherlands was practically a mono-colonial power. This fact limited the scope for everyone who wanted to operate with minimal risks and in any case made such operations more problematic. But at the same time it argued for active rehabilitation. The conviction that one had to try making something of the situation was, therefore, fairly general. And, finally, it was also believed that firms, when it came to the point, were very well able to look after their own business.

Since 1945 relations between the government and business had always been very formal. And this condition changed for the worse over the period before transfer of sovereignty. There was talk about the watertight partition that separated the two parties. In these circumstances, business considered it wise to go its own way and to pursue its own policy: whether or not to relocate elsewhere, to change traditional fields of operations or to spread risks by diversification. However, abandoning the Indies remained the exceptional course of action. The large majority of firms, even those who at the same time actually went elsewhere in the world to search for new fields of enterprise in other countries, never believed that they could be confronted with the nationalization of their businesses in Indonesia, or that at a certain moment Indonesia would expel them completely. When governmental archives become fully available, and for instance the files on the indemnity claims by private enterprise (which the Foreign Affairs Department at The Hague still holds behind closed doors) can finally be checked and analysed, they will undoubtedly disclose massive confirmation of so much unwarranted trust in Indonesia.

Our research showed that when important decisions on redeployment had been taken up to 1957 they had emanated from the head offices in Indonesia itself. Local estate managers considered their specialized know-how to be a powerful and almost inviolable asset. They were also of the opinion that Indonesia needed private enterprise for the reconstruction of the country. Entrepreneurs always consider themselves as realists, often with justice. Nevertheless, they showed little realism after the situation changed in 1954, and the term 'redeployment' or any equivalent could not be traced in an annual report before 1957.

Private firms had made almost no investigations into alternative possibilities. Much superficial improvisation occurred, particularly in the case of the agricultural estates. Certainly that accounted for the many failures. In addition it may also be reported that in many, perhaps in most, cases the important decisions depended on one man, the recognized 'boss' of the company. Although many firms had started in life as family businesses, often this family structure had already been abandoned many years before, although the spirit of the old family company with one decision taker at its head had been maintained. The majority of these leaders appear as rather conservative persons, who concentrated more on *ad hoc* tactics than on major strategy with long-term objectives, save of course for the goal of keeping the business in being.

Our research has offered no proof of the existence of any systematic influencing of the governments in The Hague or Batavia (Jakarta) by the entrepreneurs. Considering the prevailing formal relations between the two parties, such a fact should astonish nobody. At the time that business was involved in the process of reorientation, some ministerial departments at The Hague were also confronted with their own problems of adaptation and reorientation. This took place within the same context, but the two processes remained isolated from each other. Interconnections were exceptional. Research on the functional networks and structures of decision making on the side of both entrepreneurs and political policy planners, as well as our investigations into possible links between these two networks, led to the conclusion that the two sides remained isolated.

We have seen that many companies, which went on working in Indonesia because they were so highly specialized in that field (agricultural estates, transport firms, mining, etc.), perished in the end. Other firms, which were less totally committed to Indonesia, escaped complete collapse by partially or completely transferring their business elsewhere, although some burned their fingers badly before redeploying successfully. In many cases such firms played an important role in the reconstruction of war-stricken Holland or in the new industrialization of the Netherlands. Such a development was exactly in line with the ideas of the Ministries of Economic and Foreign Affairs, which preferred to look upon Indonesia as a foreign country and on a par with all other foreign nations. The Ministry of Overseas Territories, on the other hand, had different ideas on this matter. This Ministry identified more closely with those entrepreneurs in Indonesia who were unable or unwilling to reorient themselves: in the changing circumstances, however, it was soon abolished.

The research undertaken also pays attention to the question of the accumulation of functions amongst the senior personnel involved in these relationships. We limited the inquiry to five sample years (1946, 1950, 1954, 1958 and 1962) and the facts we traced indicate that accumulation over the total period decreased greatly. It is theoretically possible that in the intervening years the trend was different, but this is unlikely. Over the period as a whole the average number of different roles played by individuals in these functions diminished sharply, although a significant number did still accumulate roles, particularly on the entrepreneurs' side. As the total number of such 'top' business leaders diminished, however, more of them became at the same time active in two or more companies. We came ultimately to the conclusion that during the 1950s there were fewer civil servants with very many links than in some years earlier, but that more people on the list had only two or three links.

Our research did not disclose much about double-functions in which top leaders from government circles worked in conjunction with top leaders from enterprise. Roughly speaking we trace two sorts of double-function between government and private enterprise: the synchronic (where government leaders were appointed to the boards of partly government-owned companies such as KLM (Royal Dutch Airlines) and Hoogovens Blast Furnaces) and the asynchronic (career patterns which included transfers from government to enterprise or vice versa). Both types figure in our analyses (some ministers and secretaries of state were included), but as far as we observed such overlapping remained exceptional. But there were a few instances, and particularly at the most senior level, although this was not specifically encountered amongst those concerned with Indonesian interests. The ministers Stikker and van den Brink belonged to this most senior group as policy makers in government and decision takers in business. It may be stated that in our analyses only 'top leaders' in government circles were involved. No conclusions are therefore justified about civil servants in lower positions. At the top level, however, it became clear that no strong connections existed.

Our investigation about possible lobby activities, through which government and enterprise clearly could have been linked, showed only meagre results on both sides – certainly at the top level, although some scores of top leaders were to be found at this senior level of co-ordinators and approximately fifteen were 'very big' co-ordinators – i.e. persons who in one year combined eight or more double-functions (as executive managers or members of a board of directors). Next to that we found about forty other persons who were 'top co-ordinators' between government and enterprise. Our research in departmental papers clearly revealed the official process of decision making – officially printed 'white' and 'orange' papers, minutes of conferences and correspondence in which top-level civil servants were involved who were mentioned by function and name. Papers also existed in the records in which internal controversies and personal differences came under discussion. All these papers were systematically registered in the archives.

No such situation existed on the side of business. Perhaps such papers had never existed in most companies. Several firms often operated (and recorded in minutes or annual reports) without specifying the names of senior people responsible. The critical co-ordinators therefore remained in many cases anonymous. The results of our research in this area thus had their limitations because of the difficulties we encountered in obtaining precise data about the individuals concerned in negotiations and co-ordinations. We gained different perspectives on the process of co-ordination on the side of government and on that of business because of such differences in the evidence available. However, the analysis convinced us that the two spheres interrelated in a limited way, but the distance between the two was great and remained so, even when in some situations and for certain periods the links proved to be relatively close. Our research indicated that, already in 1947, business and certain governmental offices had become convinced that the promotion of Dutch interests in the Indies was not best served by the hard-line policy, which was championed by the representative ministers of the prominent Catholic People's Party, who occupied several key positions in the Dutch Cabinet for handling Indonesian affairs. At the Ministry of Overseas Territories this policy found widespread approval, even though considerable internal opposition existed.

The opinion that the Netherlands should definitely break with its colonial past, which had gained ground in 1948, had its most prominent exponent in Stikker, Minister of Foreign Affairs. He and some of his top-level advisers recognized quite clearly that Indonesia's self-consciousness had become an important factor in the development of that country's foreign relations. The same Dutch group also noted the growing consensus of opinion among the major entrepreneurs that demands for stipulating so many safeguards for the Dutch side were

273

threatening the wording of several articles in the drafting of the round-table agreements, and had become detrimental to the interest of the entrepreneurs. They were not particularly keen on insisting that a special long-term joint Board be set up between the Netherlands and Indonesia. They simply sought an agreement and regulations that might shape a workable business environment.

When in November 1949, on the threshold of signing the round-table agreements, the Dutch Minister of Economic Affairs, van den Brink, one of the prominent ministers representing the Catholic People's Party in Cabinet, offered Parliament the White paper on a new industrialization plan for the Netherlands, this programme made clear unequivocally that Indonesia during the fifties was not to be considered as a special factor in the Dutch economy. The paper mentioned co-ordination in the Benelux context, internationally regulated investment policy, extension of international trade agreements, multilateral trade with as few import restrictions as possible and the promotion of foreign investment in Dutch enterprises by Belgium, Luxemburg and the USA. It also recommended a policy of close collaboration with countries of Western Europe and with the USA and the promulgation of a world policy towards the underdeveloped countries as an off-setting factor in the process of re-orientation of the Dutch economy. But nowhere in the White paper was Indonesia mentioned. That country was written off as a special factor for the Dutch economy in the 1950s. According to the new official view, Dutch–Indonesian relationships were now to feature as part of the wider nexus with underdeveloped countries as a whole. In its new commitments with European partners in the Benelux, other Western European countries and the North Atlantic Treaty Organization the Netherlands could properly function without a special relationship with its former colony in south east Asia.

The publication of this White paper showed clearly that within the prominent Dutch Catholic People's Party a new force had gathered strength and now exerted an emphatic and positive influence on the political scene. However, this did not yet mean that the power of the old guard in the rather conservative Catholic political party had disappeared. Before long it would become clear that this power still went unbroken. Meanwhile the Minister of Economic Affairs could bring his wide-ranging new views into the open and at the Ministry of Foreign Affairs the pragmatic liberal minister Stikker fully shared the same ideas. In 1950 Stikker wrote in a ministerial memorandum: 'The transfer of sovereignty to Indonesia has opened the way for the Netherlands to resume the traditional position in the International economy.' That was a polite way of claiming that the Netherlands could regain her earlier role more easily in the absence of Indonesia. Thus, rupture and continuity became essentially identical.

According to Stikker's vision the fate of colonial capital, in fact, had already been sealed in 1949. The financial and economic agreement at that time contained the maximum attainable guarantees for the survival of Dutch enterprise in Indonesia. Stikker had provided important contributions for the realization of this agreement, albeit not without scepticism. Thereafter it became the duty of the High Commissioner's Office in Jakarta to aid Dutch entrepreneurs in a discreet manner to make the most of that agreement in their actual business. Stikker himself hoped, most of all, for a change of mentality amongst the Dutch entrepreneurs, because that would greatly help in shaping their future.

The role of Indonesia as a traditional source of foreign exchange seemed finished, at least for the near future, especially because the lasting disorder in the country had hindered the reconstruction of Dutch activities. This also explained the fact that the influence of 'colonial capital' had gradually declined.. In Holland itself, strikingly high expectations prevailed: a start had been made in the new industrialization programme and the outlook seemed promising. This prospect was reinforced by the presence of American aid resulting from the Marshall Plan for Western Europe, credits from which had just begun to arrive.

Meanwhile the Dutch entrepreneurs in Indonesia were busy trying to restart their activities under the changed conditions. They were more or less optimistic that they had secured their interests under the financial and economic agreement signed by the governments, because this dealt with such problems as the restoration of former business rights, concessions and licences, made arrangements for keeping taxes within reasonable limits, promised freedom to select labour and so on. Without going into details, it soon became clear that the prospects were not as good as many hoped. From both sides came complaints and claims, distrust and suspicion. There was endless quarrelling about the interpretation of articles in the agreement or about the additional provisions which had been added; there were also troubles about how prominent a part the Dutch could play in product marketing and Indonesian foreign trade. The Indonesians had grudges about the fact that they had to fulfil so many debt obligations from the former Indies to the Netherlands. Moreover, the Indonesian attitude became increasingly stubborn following the refusal of the Dutch to reach an accommodation over the issue of Western Guinea's sovereignty. The Indonesians put growing pressure on the Dutch to transfer sovereignty to them, and they showed openly that they would not hesitate to take military action in order to achieve their objective.

The Dutch entrepreneurs, who in later years declared that they had never envisaged what lay in store for them between 1949 and 1957 (the year in which expropriation without indemnity took place) might nevertheless have foreseen a few things if they had kept a realistic view. It seems difficult to believe that this was not the case, but the facts support it. In the mid 1950s troubles over the ambiguous character of the financial and economic arrangements had reached the point where both partners wanted to call off the agreement. Two facts prevented an amicable settlement: the worsening political relations had poisoned the atmosphere, and too much bickering about eventual alternatives prevented the parties from coming to terms.

Broadly speaking the agreement may be seen as an example of the bankruptcy of Dutch policy towards Indonesia. The Netherlands had tried to preserve its pre-war profitable position by means of precisely detailed agreements, but within ten years of the transfer of sovereignty the exact opposite result had been attained. This result was partly explained by the exaggerated trust which the Dutch placed in the rules of international law, whilst the Indonesians showed under all circumstances that for them the national interest came first Like many other newly independent states Indonesia considered that the existing levels of international law were based on centuries-old rules and regulations which Western countries had formulated and codified. Treaties were therefore less sacred to the Indonesians, particularly in this case because they were convinced that the financial and economic agreement had been concluded under pressure from their former colonial rulers. Moreover, the Netherlands missed the opportunity to specify sanctions against eventual Indonesian violations of the treaty. Since the Netherlands were powerless politically, in the final analysis, over the long run in Indonesia the Dutch had no financial and economic power either, however beautiful all the guarantees might look in print.

In 1949 the Dutch had certainly understood perfectly well that 'at some time' the day would come when they had to leave Indonesia. It was un-avoidable that eventually Indonesia would deem it unacceptable that she possessed an economy which was 90 per cent in Dutch or other foreign hands. But nobody then had any idea about how much time was left. Both the government and the entrepreneurs thought that their agreements with Indonesia had prolonged their stay for many years to come. At the time it was also impossible to foresee that in 1957 the final blow would bring a breakdown in all relations with the expropriation of the Dutch firms without indemnity. But that happened, and the economy of the Netherlands demonstrated that it was able to absorb the shock. The Indies were not so indispensable for maintaining an acceptable living standard in Holland as had traditionally been assumed. In spite of all set-backs during 1957 and 1958 national income and national prosperity in the Netherlands advanced in harmony late into the 1960s. Continued industrialization, varied activities in new markets within and beyond Europe, the growth of international services, the diverse gains from membership of the EEC, obviously compensated for the earlier quite substantial contributions derived from Dutch interests in the East Indies.

The Netherlands had found the path to a comfortable subsistence without the traditional flow of profits from the Indies. The post-war agreements establishing a special financial and economic relationship with Indonesia had lacked a sense of reality. It would have been impossible for the Netherlands, so soon after its own disastrous wartime experience, to raise the necessary financial means to sponsor the enormous extent of aid – in whatever form – required by Indonesia in order to realize a minimal acceptable rate of economic development. At the same time the industrialization of the Netherlands in the 1950s and 1960s led the development of the home country in a direction which was contradictory to the realization of any special relationship with other countries, Indonesia included. The era of a special Dutch interest in the East Indies had finally ended.

Bibliography of Charles Wilson's published works

Books and pamphlets

Anglo-Dutch Commerce and Finance in the Eighteenth Century (Cambridge, 1941; reprinted Cambridge, 1966, New York, 1977).

Holland and Britain (London, 1945).

The History of Unilever, 3 vols. (London, I and II, 1954; III, 1968; paperback, 1970; simultaneously published in Dutch translation, The Hague).

Profit and Power: A Study of England and the Dutch Wars (London, 1957; Dutch translation, The Hague, 1977).

(with William Reader), *Men and Machines: A History of D. Napier and Sons Ltd, Engineers, 1809–1958* (London, 1958).

Mercantilism (Historical Association, London, 1958).

A Man and his Times: A Memoir of Sir Ellis Hunter (London, 1962).

History in Special and in General, being the Inaugural Lecture as Professor of Modern History in the University of Cambridge, 12 March 1964 (Cambridge, 1964).

England's Apprenticeship, 1603–1763 (London, 1965; paperback, 1971).

The Dutch Republic and the Civilization of the Seventeenth Century (London, 1968; also published simultaneously in translation in France, Germany, Italy, Japan, Netherlands, Spain, Sweden).

Economic History and the Historian: Collected Essays (London, 1969).

Queen Elizabeth and the Revolt of the Netherlands (The Ford Lectures in the University of Oxford, Oxford, 1970; Dutch translation, 1979).

Parliament, Peoples and Mass Media (Inter-Parliamentary Union, London, 1970).

(with others), *Economic Issues in Immigration* (Institute of Economic Affairs, London, 1970).

On the Condition of the Human Sciences (Brussels, 1974).

The Transformation of Europe, 1558–1648 (London, 1976).

(with N. G. Parker), *An Introduction to the Sources of European Economic History* (London, 1978).

Contributions to collective works

'The Growth of Overseas Commerce and European Manufacture', in *New Cambridge Modern History*, vol. VII (Cambridge, 1957).

'Economic Conditions', in *New Cambridge Modern History*, vol. xi (Cambridge, 1962).

'Trade, Society and the State', in *The Cambridge Economic History of Europe*, vol. iv, ed. E. E. Rich and Charles Wilson (Cambridge, 1967).

'The Revolt of the Netherlands', in *The Twilight of Princes*, ed. Christopher Hibbert (London, 1970).

'Thomas Sackville: An Elizabethan Poet as Citizen', in *Ten Studies in Anglo-Dutch Relations*, presented to Prof. A. G. H. Bachrach, ed. J. van Dorsten (Leiden, 1974).

'The Multinational in Historical Perspective', in *Strategy and Structure in Big Business*, ed. K. Nakagawa (Tokyo, 1974).

'The Economic Role and Mainsprings of Imperialism', in *Colonialism in Africa 1870–1960*, vol. iv, ed. P. Duignan and L. H. Gann (Cambridge, 1975).

'Keynes and Economic History', in *Essays on John Maynard Keynes*, ed. Milo Keynes (Cambridge, 1975).

'Multinationals, Management and World Markets: A Historical View', in *The Evolution of International Management Structures,* ed. Harold F. Williamson (Delaware, 1975).

'The Anglo-Dutch Establishment in Eighteenth Century England', in *The Anglo-Dutch Contribution to the Civilization of Early Modern Society* (British Academy, London, 1976).

'Mountains of Gold and Iron: A Note on War and Economic History in the Seventeenth Century', in *Studi Dedicate a Franco Borlandi* (Bologna, 1976).

'Management and Policy in Large Scale Enterprises: Lever Bros and Unilever', in *Essays in British Business History*, ed. Barry Supple (Oxford, 1977).

'The Historical Study of Economic Growth and Decline in Early Modern History', in *The Cambridge Economic History of Europe*, vol. v, ed. E. E. Rich and Charles Wilson (Cambridge, 1977).

'The Historical Role of the Netherlands Delta in the North Sea Theatre of Trade', in *The Rhine–Meuse–Scheldt Delta: Historical Perspectives, Present Situations and Future Prospects*, ed. P. Klein and J. H. P. Paelinck (Rotterdam, 1978).

'Gerónimo de Uztariz, un Fundamento Intelectual para el Renacimiento Económico Español del Siglo XVIII', in *Dinero y Crédito (Siglos XVI al XIX)* (Madrid, 1978).

'A Measure of Humanity? Clio and Philanthropy', *Studi in Memoria di Federigo Melis* (Florence, 1978).

'Quantification: Past and Present', in *Festschrift für Hermann Kellenbenz*, ed. Jürgen Schneider (Stuttgart, 1978).

'Dutch Investment in Britain in the Seventeenth to Nineteenth Centuries', in *La Dette publique au XVIII et XIX siècles*, ed. H. van der Wee (Brussels, 1980).

'Poverty and Philanthropy in Early Modern England', in *Aspects of Poverty in Early Modern Europe*, ed. T. Riis (Florence, 1981).

Articles

'The Economic Decline of the Netherlands', *Economic History Review* (1939).

'Treasure and Trade Balances', *Econ. Hist. Rev.* (1949).

'Treasure and Trade Balances: Further Evidence', *Econ. Hist. Rev.* (1951).

Bibliography of Charles Wilson's works

'Canon Demant's Economic History', *Cambridge Journal* (1953).
'The Entrepreneur in the Industrial Revolution in Britain', *History* (1957).
'Mercantilism: Some Vicissitudes of an Idea', *Econ. Hist. Rev.* (1957).
'Who Captured New Amsterdam', *English Historical Review* (1957).
'The Other Face of Mercantilism', *Transactions of the Royal Historical Society* (1959).
'Cloth Production and International Competition in the Seventeenth Century', *Econ. Hist. Rev.* (1960).
'Dutch Investment in Eighteenth Century England: A Note on Yardsticks', *Econ. Hist. Rev.* (1960).
(with Peter Bauer), 'The Stages of Growth', *Economica* (1962).
'International Payments: An Interim Comment', *Econ. Hist. Rev.* (1962).
'Economics and Politics in the Seventeenth Century', *Historical Journal* (1962).
'Taxation and the Decline of Empires: An Unfashionable Theme', *Bijdragen en Mededelingen van het Historisch Genootschap* (1963).
'Government Policy and Private Interest in Modern English History', *Historical Studies* (1968).
'Europa im Spiegel russischer Geschichte – wie Alexander Gerschenkron es sieht', *Kölner Vorträge zur Sozial- und Wirtschaftsgeschichte* (1971).
'Twenty Years After: Some Reflections on Having Written a Business History', *Journal of European Economic History* (1972).
'Transport as a Factor in the History of Economic Development', *Jour. Eur. Econ. Hist.* (1973).
'The Relevance of History', *Mededelingen* (1975).
'The Anglo-Dutch Wars and the Power Struggle in Seventeenth Century Europe', *Mededelingen van het Koninklijke Instituut voor Marine* (1977).
'A Letter to Professor McCloskey', *Jour. Eur. Econ. Hist.* (1979).
'Land Carriage in the Seventeen Century', *Econ. Hist. Rev.* (1980).

Review articles

'Velvet Revolution', a review of Simon Schama's *Patriots and Liberators: Revolution in the Netherlands 1780–1813*, *New York Review of Books* (9 June 1977).
'Arbiter of the Republic', a review of Herbert H. Rowen's *John de Witt, Grand Pensionary of Holland, 1625–1672*, *Times Literary Supplement* (29 September 1978).

Editorial

Editorial Prefaces to the following volumes in the World Economic History series:
Ralph Davis, *The Rise of the Atlantic Economies* (1973).
D. K. Fieldhouse, *Economics and Empire, 1880–1914* (1973).
Georges Duby, *The Early Growth of the European Economy* (1974).
Hermann Kellenbenz, *The Rise of the European Economy, 1500–1750* (1976).
J. A. van Houtte, *An Economic History of the Low Countries* (1977).
Introduction to new edition of W. Cunningham, *Alien Immigrants to England* (1897, new edition London, 1969).

Index

Achnacarry agreement (1928), 260
acts of Parliament, private, 154, 161
Addison, Joseph, 37
Additional Aid Act (1665), 144, 145, 146
administrative co-ordination ('visible hand'), 14–15, 18, 19–20
administrative structure of large industrial corporations, 11–20; centralized ('unitary' or 'U' form), 11, 12, 14; decentralized ('multidivisional' or 'M' form), 13, 14, 15
African trade in 17th and 18th centuries, 86, 87, 108
agricultural depression, 18th-century, 92, 114
agricultural improvement, role of English attorneys in, 155, 161–5
Alba, Duke of, 79, 80, 81
Albert and Isabella, Archdukes, 73, 74
Alexandria: Bank of Rome agency at, 171, 172; Stock Exchange, 177
Alford, B. W. E., 6
Alfred Jørgensen Laboratory, Denmark, 194
Allgemeine Brauer- und Hopfen-Zeitung, 192
Alsace, shale oil industry of, 238
American Can Company, 43
American Tobacco Company, 18
American War of Independence, 74, 126
Amiens, Treaty of, 130
Amsterdam, 71, 116, 117, 118, 120; English re-export trade to, 90, 91, 100, 108, 109, 114; international exhibition (1869), 191
Andalusian 'nation', Bruges, 77
Anderson, Dr B. L., 166
Andrew, Alexander, 125
Andrews, Andrew, 129
Anglo-Dutch coalition, 74
Anglo-Dutch trade, 75, 89–115, 116–34

Anglo-Dutch Wars, 135, 143; first (1652–4), 121; fourth (1780–4), 87, 119, 131
Anglo-Persian Oil Company, 244, 245, 249, 251, 252, 255, 260, 261, 262
Antwerp, 71, 75–6, 81–2, 83, 85, 87, 91, 191; Hanse merchants in, 76, 78; Merchant Adventurers and, 79, 80, 82; navigation to, 73, 80, 88
Arando, Diego de, 84
Archdeacon, John, 129
Arlington, Henry Bennet, Earl of, 135
Armentières, France, 83
Armour and Swift, 18
Arnemuiden, Netherlands, 72
Asche, F. D., 249
Ashton, T. S., 101n; *The Industrial Revolution*, 57, 63
Asia, development of European trade with, 92
Astor, John Jacob, 5
attorneys, provincial, in 18th-century England, 151–67; numbers and distribution of, 157–8; range of functions, 158–61; role in agricultural improvement, 161–5; role in development of banking, 156, 159, 162, 165–7; *see also* barristers
Austin, Herbert, 30
Austria, Austrians, 74, 75
Austrian Netherlands, 87, 88

Baba Gurgur, Turkey, discovery of oil at, 258
Balfour, Arthur, 244
Baltic trade, 77, 92, 117, 139, 147
Banca Artistico-Operaia, 175
Banca Commerciale Italiana, 176, 177, 178, 179–80, 184

281

Index

266-77; Dutch relations with, 263-5,
267, 269, 271, 274, 276, 277; Japanese
occupation of, 263, 268, 269
industrial corporations, 6-7; Belgian,
199-211; comparative study of, 10-26;
see also administrative co-ordination;
administrative structure
Industrial Revolution, 34, 38, 55, 56, 57,
66-8, 134; in Belgium, 199-200; *see also*
civil disorder
industries, comparison of, 16-25
Ingram, Sir Arthur, 30-1, 34
Institute of Brewing, 192
institutional historians, 7-8, 9-10, 26
Inter-Allied Petroleum Conference,
London (1918), 242
investment, manufacturing and
non-manufacturing, 24-5
Irish Cattle bills, 148, 150
Italy, 259; industrial development, 176,
179-80, 181-3; *see also* Bank of Rome

Jacobsen, Carl, 190, 195
Jacobsen, G. A., 137
Jacobsen, J. C., 187, 190, 191, 193, 194-5
Jacobsen, Vagn, 191
James, Duke of York, later King James II,
149
Japan, Japanese: business studies, 6;
invasion of East Indies, 263, 268, 269;
manufacturing firms, 20, 21, 22, 24
Jensen, Copenhagen coppersmith, 194
Jersey Standard (Exxon), 14
Johnson, Samuel, 38, 44
Jones, Sir Alfred, 35
Jones & Cross, London linen drapers, 106
Jong-Keesing, E. E. de, 89
Joseph II, Emperor, 75

Kearton, Frank, 34
Kennet (t), White, 135
Kent, Nathaniel, 164
Keynesian macro-economic analysis, 8
King, Gregory, 157
Klein, P. W., 89-90
Klotz, Louis-Lucien, 250, 260
Kluckholm, Clyde, 8
Kocka, Professor Jürgen, 196-7
Konink, Willem, 128
Kooy, T. P. van der, 89
Kops, Isaac & Willem, Amsterdam, 110
Kühle, Dr Aa, 194

labourism, 61, 63
lager, bottom-fermented beer, 188, 189,
190, 191
Lambert, Sir Jean, 124

Larson, Henrietta, 5
Latham, T. P., 33
Laval, Pierre, 261
Law, Andrew Bonar, 227n, 230
Law, John, 87, 124
law and economic activity, relationship
between, 152-6
lawyers, *see* attorneys
Lazio, Bank of Rome agency in, 174, 175,
180
leather exports, English policy on, 150
Leiden cloth industry, 79, 96
Leigh, Alexander, 161
Lenin, 59
Leroy-Beaulieu, Paul, 239
Lesieur (Georges) et ses Fils, oil company,
242, 252
Lever, W. H., 1st Viscount Leverhulme,
28, 29, 32, 39, 44-5, 47, 48, 50
Lever Brothers, 28, 49
Leveson-Gower estates, stewards on, 162
Libya: Bank of Rome agencies in, 171, 172,
173; Italian invasion of (1911), 182, 184
Lille, Bonnières et Colombes, oil company,
242
Lille, France, 82, 83, 85
Lillo, George, *The London Merchant*, 37
Linde, Dr Carl, 187
Lindtner, Professor Carl, 192
Linen and Tapestry Act, (1663), 144
Linggadjati agreement (1947), 263, 268
Lister, T. H., *Life of Clarendon,* 136
Littledale, Thomas, 132
Lloyd George, David, 218, 220, 225, 226,
230, 245, 246
Lloyd merchant family, Rotterdam, 132n,
133
Loch, James, 163
Locke, John, 123
Lombe, John, 124
Lombe, Thomas, 124, 125
Long, Walter, 242, 245, 246, 248
Lootyns, Guillermo, 85
Loucheur, Louis, 257
Louis XIV, King of France, 141
Lübeck, Germany, 77, 78
Lucca: Bank of Rome agency in, 174, 175;
'consulate' in Bruges, 76
Luddism, 60, 66
Luns, Joseph, 265, 269

Maatschappij voor Assurantie,
Discontering en Beleening, Rotterdam,
123-5
McGowan, Harry, later Lord McGowan,
30, 46
McKendrick, Neil, 38

286